# HISTORY

## of the
## MAYFLOWER PLANTERS
## and
## First Comers
## to
## Ye Olde Colonie

By

*Leon Clark Hills*

Two Volumes in One

CLEARFIELD

Originally published
Washington, D.C.
1936, 1941

Reprinted
Two Volumes in One
Genealogical Publishing Co., Inc.
Baltimore, Maryland
1975, 1977, 1981

Reprinted for
Clearfield Company, Inc. by
Genealogical Publishing Co., Inc.
Baltimore, Maryland
1990, 1996, 2002

**Library of Congress Cataloging in Publication Data**
Hills, Leon Clark, 1877-1968.
    History and genealogy of the Mayflower planters and first comers to
ye olde colonie.
    Reprint of the 1936-1941 ed. published by Hills Pub. Co., Washington,
which was issued as v. 1-2 of Cape Cod series.
    1. Pilgrim Fathers.  2. Cape Cod—Genealogy.  3. Cape Cod—History.
4. Hopkins Family.  5. Mayflower (Ship)  6. Massachusetts—History—
New Plymouth, 1620-1691.  I. Title: History and genealogy of the Mayflower planters . . . II. Series: Cape Cod series, v. 1-2.
F68.H649                          974.4′92′01                       72-10914
ISBN 0-8063-0775-7

*Made in the United States of America*

# CAPE COD

## SERIES

### Vol. I

HISTORY AND GENEALOGY

OF THE

## MAYFLOWER PLANTERS

AND

## FIRST COMERS

TO

## YE OLDE COLONIE

By
LEON CLARK HILLS

Dedicated to the Memory of

MY MOTHER

A sterling character and worthy
Descendant of

STEPHEN HOPKINS AND THOMAS ROGERS

Mayflower Passengers

PLANTERS OF

NEW PLYMOUTH, MASSACHUSETTS

1620

"A great posterity will look back upon
us as the beginning of a mighty nation."

Gov. WILLIAM BRADFORD,
Plymouth, Mass., 1650.

# FOREWORD

The author of this series has spent many happy hours during the past thirty years or more in the study of colonial history, especially that pertaining to the New England States, and, particularly, the characteristics and genealogy of the people from the earliest times. He has found the subject a vast and fascinating one in numerous directions.

From a genealogist's point of view, Plymouth County and Barnstable County (Cape Cod) may rightfully be considered the most important cradle of New England genealogy and history, or, at least, the most interesting one.

Within the confines of these two counties for several generations, the ancestors of many thousands of individuals now scattered around the United States, and, in fact, the world, struggled to obtain food, shelter and clothing under the most trying conditions of climate and circumstance.

However, a people capable of framing and subscribing to a document such as the immortal "MAYFLOWER COMPACT" must ultimately succeed.

In the midst of untold difficulties, town and county governments were formed, churches and schools were organized. Stern discipline was established. Respect for law and order was demanded and insisted upon. Slackers were not tolerated.

The early church, town and court records of Plymouth Plantation might well be read with profit by present day "voters" and "government" officeholders, as well as citizens in general.

The problems which our fathers faced 300 years ago, resemble our difficulties of today, but were dealt with in a more direct manner. There were no frills. The public servant was paid little or nothing for services. Economy was a habit. The tax-payer and the thrifty ran the communities in "ye olden tyme". Today, the order of command appears reversed.

Throughout his study and investigation during these many years, the author has been made conscious of the confusion and scattered condition of the records as they bear upon these two counties, especially pertaining to genealogical matters. Much time was consumed in locating authorities which might have been saved through the availability of a book of ready reference having suitable maps of Barnstable and Plymouth counties, and a list of resources commonly referred to.

In an attempt to provide a reference of general usefulness for all those interested in tracing Cape Cod lineages, it has been decided to base this work substantially on the genealogy of the London Mayflower Planter Stephen Hopkins, including both male and female lines through a number of generations. Descendants of four of his children intermarried with descendants of most of the "first comers" to Plymouth and the Cape.

It will be noted that the scope of the work, so arranged, is considerably more than a Hopkins genealogy. There are, in fact, a number of genealogies involving important and far reaching Cape Cod family groups, such as the families of Snow, Cole, Ring, the Cookes—Francis and Josiah, Paine, Walker, Rogers, Smith, Mayo, Merrick, Williams, Cushman, Holmes, Rickard, Doty, Bartlett, Morton, Standish, Thomson, Sturdevant and many others.

Detailed stories and genealogies will be found in this work of the Mayflower Planters including those from whom descent is positively proved, or whose lines have been approved by competent authority, such as the Mayflower Society.

The author has found that the first few generations from Stephen Hopkins may be divided into two general groups. Andrew Ring and Jacob Cooke with their wives Deborah and Damaris Hopkins remained in Plymouth or vicinity, while Giles Hopkins and Nicholas Snow, with his wife Constance settled in Eastham on the opposite side of Cape Cod in Barnstable County.

It will be observed that the maps in this work, with their legends, cover a large field of some interest.

These maps together with several hundred group records, involving many old Cape Cod families and the citation of numerous references, cannot help but be of great aid to any investigator in this field.

The author, through force of circumstance, and other reasons, being compiler, editor, and publisher, assumes full responsibility for all errors of commission or omission in this work. There were many conflicting references, and a work of this kind can never be complete or free from errors. However, if brought to his attention they can be corrected in future publications, which it is hoped will follow this, within frequent intervals, dealing especially in later generations of the families mentioned in this work, and many other Cape Codders.

LEON CLARK HILLS.

Washington, D. C.
October 27, 1936.

# WHY THE MAYFLOWER PLANTERS AND OTHER PILGRIMS CAME TO AMERICA

We may define, roughly, the "Pilgrim" Planters as those who came to New Plymouth in the Mayflower 1620, Fortune 1621, Anne and Little James 1623, and the Mayflower 1629. There were a few, closely related to this group, who came over in the Handmaid, and other ships, in 1630 or soon thereafter.

The principal actors in Bradford's history of "Plimouth Plantation" are those with whom, as a young man, he made the famous voyage in 1620. Bradford, himself, was not in evidence as a leader until after the landing, and the very unfortunate deaths of most of the influential "Merchant Adventurers" during the first winter, 1620-21, of sickness.

Apparently, Bradford was not well informed regarding the preliminary negotiations leading up to the departure of the Mayflower from England, or the early history of many of his fellow voyagers, some of whom were influential, and all of whom, with the exception of Brewster and Carver, came from sections of England far removed from his beloved Yorkshire, famous for its ruins of old Castles and Monasteries, and although they were, no doubt, "Separatists", had never resided in Holland. His wonderful work, therefore, is unhappy and incomplete in the treatment of these matters.

The hardy voyagers sailed from England for "Southern Virginia" under the Pierce Patent. For some reason they were landed in "Northern Virginia" or New England. Before landing, however, a "Compact" was drawn including the phrase "a voyage to plant a colony in the 'Northern part of Virginia' ". Some historians claim that the Dutch were responsible for this change of plans. They were powerful at that time, and desired to keep the Manhattan area for their own use.

Fortunately, the Mayflower Pilgrims were not to be discouraged by petty politicians or greedy merchants. Landing unexpectedly upon bleak and uninviting shores was but another challenge, the like of which they and their ancestors had been accepting for hundreds of years. This little band had visions of founding a nation. Trifles did not count. The Mayflower "Compact" and Bradford's History prove that they were conscious of the mission.

The dramatic story of the Pilgrims is really, in part, the history of Separatism in England, which had its inception in the Reformation.

However, the great struggle for religious freedom occurred centuries before, even about the year 700, when the King of Northumbria, Eegfrith, near Austerfield, and the bishops of the realm, defied the edict of the Pope, deposed Saint Wilfred, Bishop of

York, and declared the independence of England of the control of the Bishop of Rome.

Unfortunately, during the next few hundred years, Rome struggled to gain a political foothold in England, with some success. In fact had accumulated vast domains, becoming rich, powerful and aggressive, especially in England.

After the Norman Invasion in 1066, and the compiling of the Domesday Book in 1085-86, the Church of Rome continued its aggressiveness in various objectionable ways. The sixteenth and seventeenth centuries were particularly rife with religious-political turmoil.

Owing to these conditions Henry VIII, 1509-47, although, personally, far from being religious, declared himself supreme as head of the Church and Clergy, as well as temporal Ruler of England. In 1534 Parliament passed an act confirming the King's title as Supreme Head of the Church. In 1535 an act was passed requiring the Priests to swear allegiance to the King ''in derogation of the Pope's authority''.

The Priests who refused to take the oath were beheaded without delay. Therefore ''From persecutors they sunk to men trembling for their lives''.

The English Church was now called ''Protestant''. In 1548, the ''First Book of Common Prayer'' was adopted for the English Church.

Henry VIII died in 1547, and his son, a boy nine years old, reigned as Edward VI, and as a Protestant, for six years, dying at the age of sixteen in 1553. During this period, however, Parliament passed a second act of uniformity, also an act removing the ban on marriage of Priests.

Mary, 1553-59, daughter of Henry VIII and wife Katherine, succeeded him. Like her mother Katherine of Aragon, Mary was a Catholic, and through her the Church of Rome again became master of the political and religious life of England.

The Priests who had married ''were driven from their Churches, the new Prayer Book was set aside and Mass restored''.

In addition to these severe blows to the cause of Protestantism in England, Queen Mary married her Cousin, Philip, of Catholic Spain.

Then followed a period of cruel and bloody persecution of Protestants. A Priest from Spain brought the horrors of the Inquisition into England. This condition brought about the burning at the stake in London of the Rev. John Rogers, in 1558 (see Fam. No. 7, Thomas Rogers).

However, an end came to this state of affairs. Mary died in 1559.

Elizabeth (''Good Queen Bess''), 1559-1603, daughter of Henry VIII, and Anne Boleyn, succeeded Mary as Queen of England. She was a Protestant. Catholicism was again dethroned, and Elizabeth became the Supreme Head of the Church in England.

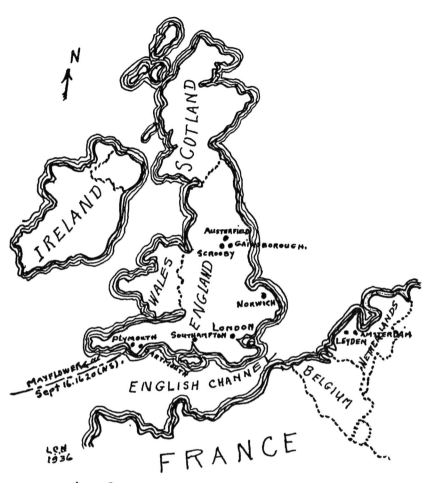

N

SCOTLAND

IRELAND

Austerfield
Gainsborough.
Scrooby

WALES

ENGLAND

Norwich

London
Southampton

Plymouth
DARTMOUTH

MAYFLOWER
Sept 16. 1620 (N.S.)

ENGLISH CHANNEL

AMSTERDAM
LEYDEN

NETHERLANDS

DOVER

BELGIUM

L.G.H
1936

FRANCE

## PILGRIM WANDERINGS IN EUROPE

LONDON – REV. JOHN ROGERS BURNED AT STAKE   1558.

LONDON – SECRET MEETINGS – PLUMBER HALL   1567.

LONDON – SECRET MEETINGS – WHITECHAPEL –   1571

NORWICH – REV. ROBERT BROWNE 1ST PREACHED HERE – 1580

NORWICH – REV. JOHN. ROBINSON – PREACHED HERE – 1600–1604.

GAINSBOROUGH – REV. ROBINSON PREACHED HERE – 1604–1609

AMSTERDAM – SEPARATISTS FLED HERE   1606

SCROOBY – SEPARATISTS UNDER BREWSTER – 1603–1609

LEYDEN – BODY UNDER REV. ROBINSON   1609–1620

PLYMOUTH – MAYFLOWER FROM HERE SEPT. 16. 1620 (N.S.)
       SIGHTED CAPE COD. NOV. 19. 1620 (N.S.)

Some changes were made in the "Book of Common Prayer". In 1559 acts were passed by Parliament such as the one requiring "Every one must go to Church on Sunday, and bide prayer and preaching".

As the years passed "dissenters" appeared in the English Church. It was claimed by some that the ceremonies were still too formal, and similar to those of the Church of Rome. Many turned from the Old to the New Testament. The name "PURITAN" was given to the reformers within the Church. These were hard, rigid, and stern individuals. The discussions were on form of worship, service and government, not the fundamentals.

Queen Elizabeth died in 1603.

James I, 1603-25, of Scotland succeeded her. There were then four different religious classes in England:

1. Catholic.
2. Members of English Church.
3. Members of English Church, but opposed to service and certain formal ceremonies. PURITANS.
4. Brownists (Separatists). These were the PILGRIMS. They proposed to organize a separate Church. They wished to break away entirely from any semblance to the Roman Church or State.

The first English Clergyman to preach this entire separation doctrine openly was Robert Browne. He appeared in Norwich about 1580, and taught that the "State had no right to regulate the religion of the subject". It had taken centuries of bloody effort to free the English Church and State from Rome, and many thought the job should be completed by a separation of State and Church in the mother country.

As the law then stood, the authorities could not condone such teachings, and Rev. Mr. Browne, with his followers, fled or removed to other places, where independent Churches were established. However, it was soon apparent that the English would have to lose their identity if they remained in places like Holland and after a while Browne decided to return to England and resume the old service. He served the English Church faithfully for forty years thereafter, and for this reason has been called the "Benedict Arnold of ecclesiastical history" by some writers. Apparently, he deserted the cause of "Separatism" under fire.

However, congregations of Separatists had sprung up in Scrooby, Gainsborough, London and other places.

About 1600-02 the Rev. John Robinson came to Norwich, and preached for four years. He became a Separatist, and died in Holland in 1625. He taught and preached the doctrine as early as 1604 at Gainsborough, and became the pastor of the Leyden congregation, thirty-five of whom were on the Mayflower.

It appears that the Separatist movement flourished in the north of England, forming the districts of Nottinghamshire, Lincolnshire and Yorkshire, called the North Country in those days, and infested with robbers.

Elder William Brewster lived at Scrooby, where he was born about 1566/7. This is a small hamlet in Nottinghamshire. In 1575/6 William Brewster, Sr., his father, had been appointed "receiver of Scrooby and all its liberties" in Nottinghamshire, also bailiff of the Manor House, to hold both offices for life.

Thus it became logical for young William Brewster, in 1589/90 to receive the appointment to the Post at Scrooby Manor, an important office at that time, and much sought after.

Young Brewster, on that eventful day in 1589/90, must have felt quite elated, for he was ambitious and enterprising. Of course, he had no way of knowing the great importance of an event which was taking place, during the same year, in the little village of Austerfield about three miles from Scrooby on the Yorkshire side. The Domesday Book calls it "Austrefeld", where about 900 years before the King Eegfrith defied the Pope and Rome.

In the year 1589/90, a boy, William Bradford, was born in Austerfield. He was a likely youngster, bright-eyed, strong and healthy, and on March 19, 1589 (O.S.), he was baptized in the ancient church of the Parish. This boy was destined to become a Governor of New Plymouth in America, and, above all, the author of one of the classics of the English language, "The History of the Plimoth Plantation", 1620-1647 (1650).

As early as 1603, Elder William Brewster, though a member of the established Church, and filling the official position as manager of the Post at Scrooby, was having the Separatists meet in secret at the Manor House, which is located near "Sherwood Forest" where Robin Hood and his merry archers roamed about, robbing the rich to give to the poor and needy, in the days of Richard the Lion Heart.

And what a place to meet in! Hundreds of years old, Scrooby Manor fairly reeks with hosts of ghostly tragedies, and romances. They flutter in and out of the massive entering gates, the stone-paved inner and outer courts ring with the clatter of the hoofbeats of knightly-ridden steeds, and the martial tread of the sturdy yeomenry.

The Great Hall is alive with the ghosts of fair ladies, Queens, Kings, Cardinals, Ladies in Waiting, Knights and all the grandeur of "ye olden tymes".

Scrooby Manor, even before William the Conqueror's time, was in possession of the Archbishop of York, and was a frequent place of sojourn, for high and low.

Mary Stuart, Queen of Scotland, daughter of Henry VII, one of the most romantic figures of all history, a widowed Queen of France while still a young girl, thrust suddenly as Queen among the feudal Scots. She of the famous love affair with Bothwell, the ruthless Baron, and center of the most bitter period of the struggle between Protestant and Catholic, slept in Scrooby Manor on her way to Scotland.

Here Cardinal Woolsey passed weeks ministering deeds of charity, and planted a mulberry tree.

Henry VIII, 1509-47, with a company of gay companions lodged here on his way north in 1541.

About 1606 the congregation of Separatists at Gainsborough divided into two "distinct" bodies. One under John Smyth fled to Amsterdam and organized an independent Church there.

The Rev. Richard Clifton became pastor of the other body which met at Scrooby. To this congregation belonged Rev. John Robinson, Elder William Brewster, and young William Bradford, a lad of about eighteen years, but showing marked promise of leadership even at that time.

Bradford, in his youth, was an apt pupil of Elder William Brewster, and held him in high regard.

Almost fifty years later, in 1650, when Bradford's part in the great drama was about finished, and he was to leave the stage forever, he wrote of Brewster,

> "They ordinarily mett at his house on ye Lords day (which was a manor of ye bishop) and with great love he entertained them when they came, making provision for them to his great charge."

Rev. John Robinson, Brewster and Bradford worked diligently among the families of the Parish to make converts to the Separatist Church.

The Scrooby congregation grew, and the authorities were forced to take action. Brewster found it necessary to give up the Post.

About one hundred in the Parish were finally prevailed upon by Rev. John Robinson to remove to Holland. Under the circumstances they found some difficulty in leaving England, but after several attempts they established themselves in Leyden in 1609.

This step was taken only after the most careful consideration. There seemed no other way, at the time, to accomplish the establishment of an independent Church, and, in this decision Robinson, Brewster and Bradford were backed up by friends of the cause, such as John Carver, Robert Cushman, Isaac Allerton and other men of means and influence, some of whom joined the congregation later in Leyden.

From the first, the leaders were doubtful about being able to establish homes in Holland satisfactorily. Others had attempted it and failed, and their fears were fully justified as events proved.

A number of unhappy years were passed in Leyden. There were many reasons for this condition of affairs, among them may be stated the following:

1. Foreign language and customs.
2. Feared absorption by Dutch in time.
3. Impending war between Holland and Spain.

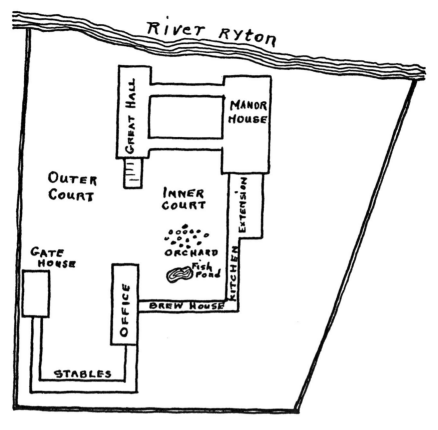

# SCROOBY MANOR
## Nottinghamshire England
Mecca of Pilgrim Descendants
### ELDER WILLIAM BREWSTER
"his house"
1603 - 1609

WRITING ABOUT ELDER BREWSTER IN 1650
BRADFORD STATES.

"They ordinarily mett at his house on ye Lords day (which was a manor of ye bishops) and with great love he entertained them when they came making provision for them to his great charge."

L.C.H.
1935.

4. Being forced to change occupations, and learn some uncongenial trade. Some of them were yeomen, or farmers in Old England. Many were small merchants.
5. Losing hold on children as they grow up.
6. Games, "White Lights", of the city life were affecting character of children adversely.
7. Boys joining Dutch Army and Navy.
8. Intermarrying with Dutch.
9. Discords in Church.
10. Danger of scattering.
11. Lack of full freedom of action.
12. Starving condition of Europe at the time.
13. High rents for land and the like.
14. Land being held by a few Lords.

After many conferences, it was decided to emigrate to one of the English Colonies, provided a liberal patent could be obtained respecting the establishing of a Church. At that time an expedition could not sail from England without a patent.

The ways and means of this proposition was not so simple. They were a people of small means and transportation was expensive.

However, emigration to the English American Colonies was increasing. Many encouraging reports were being circulated by promoting interests, such as the Merchant Adventurers, in London, the London Co. (Virginia Co.), Plymouth Co. and the like.

On April 10, 1606, King James I granted letters patent for settlement in America to two Companies:

1. To Sir Thomas Gates (London Co.), for Virginia.
2. To Sir George Popham (Plymouth Co.).

The Plymouth Co. did not succeed in planting a colony, and abandoned its grant.

In December, 1607, the Sarah Constant, Discovery, and Goodspeed, sailed down the Thames from Blackhall with parties of Planters for Virginia. They were sent out by the London Co. (Virginia Co.).

In June, 1607, the Mary & John, and Gift of God, sailed from Falmouth Harbor, Cornwall, for Maine. They were sent out by the Plymouth Co.

The above five boats may be said to have been the beginning of our Merchant Marine service. The Virginia Colony succeeded, while the Maine Colony failed.

The first permanent English settlement in America was, therefore, established at Jamestown, Va., in 1607, by colonists sent out by the London Co., commonly called the Virginia Co.

Many colonists followed, and by 1620 the (Southern) Virginia Colonies were well established.

This was the situation which confronted the Leyden congregation, and after due deliberation before a council composed of such

[ 14 ]

men as Robinson, Brewster, Bradford, Carver, Cushman, and Allerton, it was decided to try for a patent to Virginia.

In 1617 John Carver and Robert Cushman were sent as agents to London for the patent. They obtained the patent, but had to make some concessions regarding a separate Church, which far from pleased them. However, there was no other way to obtain the desired permission to plant a colony under the English flag.

In order to provide for the voyage, they made an agreement with Mr. Thomas Weston, of the Merchant Adventurers, substantially as follows:

The Merchant Adventurers to furnish money for shipping, supplies, and subsistence after arriving in the New World. The Planters to have their meat, drink, apparel, provisions, and, in fact, entire living out of common stock. At the end of seven years all profits made from all sources to be divided equally between the Adventurers and the Planters, this division to include land and all property.

The patent to Virginia territory was granted and apparently agreed to on July 1, 1620, by Robinson and Brewster, but only after they had been forced to "give a good degree of satisfaction" to Sir Edwin Sandys, Treasurer of the London Company, and showed a willingness to take the oath of "supremacie".

As agreed, Thomas Weston and other merchants put up the money, and supplies were purchased, including five cannon, guns and ammunition, which were requested by Capt. Miles Standish, the newly appointed military leader of the Pilgrims.

Nathaniel Morton, Secretary of the Plymouth Colony from 1647 to 1685, in his "New England Memorial" published 1669, writes:

> "a small ship was bought and fitted out in Holland, of about 60 tons, called the Speedwell, as to serve to transport some of them over, so also to stay in the country, and attend upon fishing and such other affairs as might be for the good and benefit of the colony when they came thither. Another ship was hired at London, of burthen, about nine score, called the Mayflower, and all other things got in readiness, so, being proposed to depart, they had a solemn day of humiliation, the pastor teaching a part of the day very profitably, and suitably to the present ocasion."

It must be stated that the Pilgrims were highly credulous or willing gamblers with the forces of nature to imagine they could have crossed the Atlantic Ocean, successfully, in that little sixty-ton boat. However, events proved they were a determined group, and no doubt the dangers were carefully discussed before the purchase of the boat.

All arrangements were now completed for departure to the New World. We can imagine a little, keeping historical facts in mind.

It was a typical mid-summer day in the year 1620. Through the London fog great activity could be observed on the good ship Mayflower, Capt. Christopher Jones commanding, as it rolled at anchor in the Thames. In boots and hat he looked every inch the powerful, grizzled old seadog that he was. He had sailed the seas, as master of ships for fourteen years, and was one-quarter owner of the Mayflower. The wide open sea was his workshop and playground. His boat had been chartered by a group of "Separatists" in Holland, and a full passenger quota guaranteed by the London Company and the Merchant Adventurers, for a voyage to Virginia.

It was just another voyage to Captain Jones, and all in the day's work to get his boat in shipshape for departure. Mates Clark and Coppin were aboard, and actively engaged in directing a score or more of tough looking sailors as they scrubbed down the decks, and loosened up the sails. The Captain had been forced to take on some hardboiled seamen this trip in order to obtain reliable men of experience, and they were already grumbling and cursing about nothing in particular.

Weaklings did not ship "before the mast". The old tars had no respect for a Captain or Mates who could not show prowess with fists. The day was young, but Captain Jones had already floored one for calling him a vile name, and the Mates were attending to certain situations in a like manner so that perfect obedience could be expected within a day or so.

Mate Clark steps to the Captain's side. "Sir, there are three score or more passengers—men, women and children on the starboard side in small boats waiting to come aboard."

"Yes, Tom Weston said he would have them here on time today," replied the Captain, "I told him to take decent pains in choosing passengers this trip because they would have to mix more or less with those religious people from Leyden, Holland, that we are to pick up and convoy at Southampton in their little ship Speedwell."

"Crazy bunch to attempt the trip in that boat, Sir," sneered Mate Clark.

"Well," said the Captain, "my understanding is they intend to transfer most of those Leyden people from the Speedwell to the Mayflower at Southampton, only a few will remain aboard. Their main object in purchasing the boat is to get it across to the colonies where they could make use of it in fishing and the like."

"Sir, ladder is lowered, passengers about to board ship," reported the Mate.

"You and Coppin, with some of your most reliable men stand by and extend every aid in getting passengers safely aboard," ordered Captain Jones, "Do not allow any of the women or children to trip on that ladder and fall in the river, and be sure to get all the baggage. There are some substantial passengers with families in the group."

"Apparently, there are some single men, and several unattached children in the group, Sir," reported Mate Clark.

"Check up carefully on the single men," ordered the Captain. "For the last two or three trips, since 1617, these unattached chil-

[ 16 ]

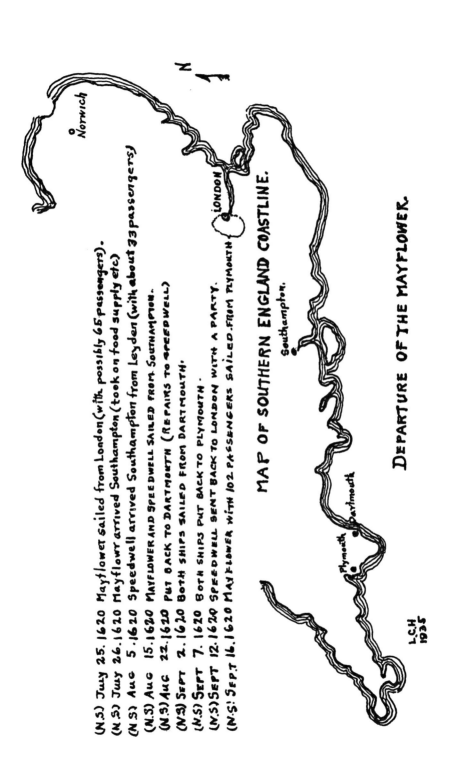

(N.S.) July 25.1620 Mayflower sailed from London (with possibly 65 passengers).
(N.S.) July 26.1620 Mayflower arrived Southampton (took on food supply etc)
(N.S) Aug 5.1620 Speedwell arrived Southampton from Leyden (with about 33 passengers)
(N.S) Aug 15.1620 Mayflower and Speedwell sailed from Southampton.
(N.S) Aug 22.1620 Put back to Dartmouth (repairs to Speedwell)
(N.S) Sept 2.1620 Both ships sailed from Dartmouth.
(N.S) Sept 7.1620 Both ships put back to Plymouth.
(N.S) Sept 12.1620 Speedwell sent back to London with a party.
(N.S) Sept 16.1620 Mayflower with 102 passengers sailed from Plymouth

MAP OF SOUTHERN ENGLAND COASTLINE.

DEPARTURE OF THE MAYFLOWER.

L.C.H
1935

dreñ have given me a lot of trouble. They are really forced on me by Weston, and the Company who contract with Parishes for shipping the children to the colonies.''

''Pardon me for suggesting it, Sir, but why not refuse to take on some of these passengers, including those children. Who will care for them on the way over? I am no nurse,'' said Mate Clark.

''We have to arrange for them, perhaps, PUT them to some of the other passengers,'' replied the Captain. ''It is the law since 1617, when the Lord Mayor and Aldermen of London passed the banishing edict, fearing lest the over-flowing multitude of inhabitants should, like too much blood, infect the whole city with plague and poverty.''

''Sir, that passenger over there,'' said Mate Clark, pointing to a stocky squareshouldered man in a flowing cape, high hat with broad brim, and shoes faced with huge silver buckles, ''is ordering my men around as if he owned the ship.''

The Captain smiled grimly, ''O, that is Master Stephen Hopkins. Mr. Weston prevailed upon him to go along with us. He is a sort of leader of the London crowd, and has made trips before to Virginia and other places. He has his family with him this time, and is evidently going to settle down in the Colonies.''

Quickly glancing over his passengers who were now assembled on deck, busily looking after their baggage, he turns to Mate Clark, and remarks, ''Yes, there are, also, Capt. Myles Standish; Master Richard Warren, Merchant; Master William Mullins, Merchant; and that dignified gentleman over there is Master Christopher Martin, who has been appointed Governor of The Mayflower on this trip. I must speak with him.''

''Sir, all aboard,'' replied Mate Clark.

''Get under weigh, immediately,'' ordered the Captain.

The short trip down the Thames and through the English Channel was uneventful, and soon the Mayflower was lazily swinging at anchor off Southampton.

While waiting for the Speedwell from Leyden, supplies were to be taken aboard, and a cooper hired.

After some search, a cooper, named John Alden, a likely young chap, was hired in Southampton by Captain Jones. Before accepting the job, he desired to make a personal inspection of the ship, and had hardly planted foot on deck, when he observed a dainty little Miss watching him with eyes entirely hidden beneath the rim of a big bonnet. That settled it. He lost no time in reporting to Captain Jones, and it didn't take John Alden long to find out that the eyes beneath the bonnet belonged to Precilla Mullins.

While the Mayflower was waiting so peacefully off Southampton, events were moving quite rapidly in the quaint old University City of Leyden, Holland.

The Pilgrim Colony in Leyden numbered two hundred ninety-eight persons, while the English Colony there numbered six hundred twenty-six persons. However, only thirty-five were prevailed

[ 18 ]

upon to cross the Atlantic in the Mayflower, three or four were passengers in the Fortune, and twenty-four in the Anne and Little James. The venture, therefore, did not appear to appeal to the large proportion of the Leyden group, most of whom were getting along in years.

Pastor Robinson, Brewster, and young Bradford had influenced thirty-three to make the immediate trip in the Speedwell. William Brewster with wife and two children, Love and Wrestling, were to join them at Southampton. Bradford says:

> "And the time being come that they must departe, they were accompanied with some of their brethren out of the citie, into a towne a few miles of called Delfes-Haven, wher the ship lay ready to receive them. So they lefte the goodly and pleasante citie, which had been their resting place near .12. years; but they knew they were PILGRIMS, and looked not much on those things, but lift up their eyes to the heavens, their dearest countrie, and quieted their spirits."

About August 1, 1620, a typical group of Church people were slowly emerging from the Dutch Reformed Church at Delfes-Haven, Holland, built in 1416. Their faces were grave, for farewell services had just been held for about thirty-three "Pilgrims" who were to depart for the New World. Intimate friendships of twelve years standing or more were about to be broken. Some among them were even leaving, temporarily, it was hoped, wives and children behind, knowing well that they could not hope to meet again for several years, and perhaps never more.

The Speedwell was moored at the edge of the Canal within a stone's throw of the old Church, and the good people, relatives and friends alike, stood in awed silence as the little band boarded the ship, which immediately got under weigh, and slowly passed from view in the direction of Southampton, England.

Winslow states in Mourt's Relation, 1622:

> "We only going aboard the ship lying to the key (quay) and ready to sail, the wind being fair, we gave them (their friends) a volley of small shot (musketry) and three pieces of ordinance and so lifting up our hands to each other and our hearts for each other to the Lord our God, we departed."

Several days were passed off Southampton adjusting matters and passengers between the two ships. The peaceloving and comparatively poor Leyden Pilgrims had, of course, been the original promoters of this enterprise, and had left all arrangements to Carver and Cushman. These two men, had, no doubt, done their best, but they were pitted against one of the shrewdest dealers of the times, Thomas Weston of the Merchant Adventurers.

On checking up, the Leyden group found themselves greatly outnumbered by the "Londoners" whom they classed as "strangers", and in some cases "undesirables", probably in a religious sense mostly. Apparently the "Londoners" had the same reasons for classing those from Leyden as "strangers".

The Speedwell could only carry twenty passengers, so that some were shifted to the Mayflower, and on August 15, 1620 (N.S.), the two ships sailed out of Southampton for the New World. However, the Speedwell proved unseaworthy and they had to put back, dropping anchor off Dartmouth. An attempt was made to repair the Speedwell. On September 2, 1620, the ships sailed out of Dartmouth, but after they were 100 leagues from Lands End they put back and anchored off Plymouth, because of the extremely poor condition of the Speedwell.

After much discussion it was decided to drop the Speedwell, and send her back to London with a small number of persons who had changed their minds about going to the New World.

Everything being in readiness, on September 16, 1620 (N.S.), the Mayflower, with 102 passengers (two more were born on the ship), and about forty-five crew members, weighed anchor, and departed out of old Plymouth, England, on, perhaps, the most famous voyage of history.

Mourt's Relations (1622) states:

> "Wednesday the sixt (O.S.) of September the wind comming East North East, a fine small gale, we loosed from Plimouth, having beene kindly entertained curteously, and fed by divers friends there dwelling, and after many difficulties in boysterous storms, at length by Gods providence upon the ninth (O.S.) of November following, by breake of the day we espied land which we deemed to be Cape Cod, and so afterward it proved."

### Passengers on Mayflower
### (probably from London or vicinity)

1. Mr. Stephen Hopkins, A Leader of London Party (see Fam. No. 1).
2.     Mrs. Elizabeth Hopkins.
3.     Giles Hopkins (see Fam. No. 3).
4.     Constance Hopkins (see Fam. No. 2).
5.     Damaris Hopkins d. soon after 1627.
6.     Oceanus Hopkins b. on Mayflower. d. young.
7.     Edward Doty Servant (see Fam. No. 39).
8.     Edward Leister Servant, removed to Va.
9. Mr. Christopher Martin d. Jan 18. 1621.
10.    Mrs. Martin d. 1st yr.
11.    Solomon Prower Servant d. 1st yr.
12.    John Langemore Servant d. 1st yr.
13. Mr. William Mullins d. Mar 3. 1621.
14.    Mrs. Mullins d. 1st yr.
15.    Joseph Mullins d. 1st yr.
16.    Precilla Mullins m. John Alden (see Fam. No. 1094).
17.    Robert Cartier Servant d. 1st yr.

18. Mr. Richard Warren (see Fam. No. 1007). *# 2004*
19. Capt. Myles Standish (see Fam. No. 183). *3517*
20.          Mrs. Rose Standish d. Feb. 8. 1621.
21. John Billington (see Fam. No. 860).
22.          Mrs. Elen Billington.
23.          John Billington d. bet. June 1, 1627 and Sept. 1630.
24.          Francis Billington (see Fam. No. 860).
25. Edward Tilly d. 1st yr.
26.          Mrs. Ann Tilly d. 1st yr.
27.          Henry Samson Kinsman (see Fam. No. 187).
28.          Humility Cooper Kinswoman, returned to Eng.
29. John Tilly d. 1st yr. *10204*
30.          Mrs. Tilly d. 1st yr. *10205*
31.          Elizabeth Tilly m. John Howland (see Fam. No. 220). *10203*
32. John Rigdale d. 1st yr.
33.          Mrs. Rigdale d. 1st yr.
34. James Chilton d. Dec. 8, 1620 (see Fam. No. 183). *3597*
35.          Mrs. Chilton d. 1st yr. *3598*
36.          Mary Chilton m. John Winslow (see Fam. No. 183).
37. Edward Fuller d. 1st yr. (see Fam. No. 186).
38.          Mrs. Fuller d. 1st year.
39.          Samuel Fuller (see Fam. No. 186).
40. Francis Eaton (see Fam. No. 1105).
41.          Mrs. Sarah Eaton d. 1st yr.
42.          Samuel Eaton (see Fam. No. 1105).
43. John Howland (see Fam. No. 220). *10202*
44. Roger Wilder d. 1st yr.
45. William Latham, returned to Eng, then to Bahama Islands.
46. George Soule (see Fam. No. 1140). *10026*
47. Elias Story d. 1st yr.
48. John Hooke d. 1st yr.
49. William Button d. 1st yr.
50. Jasper More d. 1st yr.
51. Ellen More d. 1st yr.
52. Richard More (see Fam. No. 928).
53. (          ) More d. 1st yr.
54. Desire Minter, returned to friends in Eng.
55. A "maidservant", not identified.
56. Edmond Margeson d. 1st yr.
57. Peter Browne (see Fam. No. 196).
58. Richard Britterage d. Dec. 31, 1620 (1st death at Ply).
59. Richarde Clarke d. 1st yr.
60. Richard Gardiner, returned to Eng.
61. Gilbert Winslow (see Fam. No. 183).
62. John Alden (see Fam. No. 1094). *# 3250*
63. William Trevore, returned to Eng.  Hired man.
64. "Ely", returned to Eng.  Hired man.
65. William Holbeck d. 1st yr.
66. Edward Thomson d. 1st yr.
Total 66 from London on Mayflower.

[ 21 ]

## Probable Mayflower Passengers
### (from Leyden, Holland)

3970    1. Mr. Isaac Allerton (see Fam. No. 43).
3971    2.      Mrs. Mary Allerton.
         3.      Bartholomew Allerton, returned to Eng.
         4.      Remember Allerton m. Moses Maverick (see Fam. No. 43).
3957    5.      Mary Allerton m. Thomas Cushman (see Fam. No. 43).
         6. Mr. William Bradford (see Fam. No. 926).
         7.      Mrs. Dorothy Bradford d. 1st yr.
3461    8. Mr. William Brewster (see Fam. No. 11).
3462    9.      Mrs. Mary Brewster.
3466   10.      Love Brewster (see Fam. No. 11).
3468   11.      Wrestling Brewster d. unmarried.
        12. Mr. John Carver d. 1st yr.
        13.      Mrs. Catherine Carver d. 1st yr.
        14. John Crackston d. 1st yr.
        15.      John Crackston, Jr., d. 1st yr.
        16. Thomas Rogers (see Fam. No. 2).
        17.      Joseph Rogers (see Fam. No. 2).
        18. Thomas Tinker d. 1st yr.
        19.      Mrs. Thomas Tinker d. 1st yr.
        20      (son) Tinker d. 1st yr.
        21. John Turner d. 1st yr.
        22.      (son) Turner d. 1st yr.
        23.      (son) Turner d. 1st yr.
        24. Mr. William White d. 1st yr. (see Fam. No. 336).
        25.      Mrs. Sussana White m. 2d w. of Edward Winslow.
        26.      Resolved White (see Fam. No. 336).
        27.      Perigrene White (see Fam. No. 336).
        28. Mr. Edward Winslow (see Fam. No. 183).
        29.      Mrs. Elizabeth Winslow d. 1st yr.
        30. Dr. Samuel Fuller (see Fam. No. 186).
        31. Thomas English d. 1st yr.
        32. John Allerton d. 1st yr.
3748   33. Francis Cooke (see Fam. No. 8).
        34.      John Cooke (see Fam. No. 8).
        35. Moses Fletcher d. 1st yr.
        36. John Goodman d. 1st yr.
        37. Degory Priest d. Jan. 11, 1620 (see Fam. No. 950).
        38. Thomas Williams d. 1st yr.
Total 38 from Leyden on the Mayflower.

Refs. Nos. 1, 2, 3, 4, 5, 6, 13, 15, 17, 26, 32, 38, 41, 43, 52, 53, 56, 65, 84, 85, 86, 87, 88, 97, 98, 99, 100, 103, 104, 105, 106, 107, 108, 109, 111, 113, 114, 115, 116, 117, 118, 119.

# THE MAYFLOWER SHIP AND CREW

Several years had passed since the granting of the first Virginia Charter on April 10, 1606, and the merchant fleet was steadily growing through the activities of the London Co. and other interested parties.

To accommodate the increasing trade, and increase the transportation facilities to the colonies, especially Virginia, many ships were being built by private parties, and chartered, when required, to the London Co. or otherwise.

Sometime previous to 1609, a ship named Mayflower was built and put into commission. She was owned by Christopher Jones, Robert Child, Thomas Short and Christopher Nichols, each having a quarter interest.

Her Master was that grizzled old veteran of many a sea battle, Christopher Jones, owner of a quarter interest, and mighty proud of his ship. He followed a man's vocation, commanding many tough and dangerous characters among the sailors "before the mast". It was a hard life, and the seamy side of it clearly showed in his strong features, bronzed to a copper color from the suns of many seas, and beset with a labyrinth of finely-chiseled wrinkles and "crowsfeet" due to much squinting at the heavens, moon and stars.

She was about sixty-four feet along the keel, twenty-six feet width of beam, depth eleven feet from beam to top of keel, and the length was about ninety feet.

The ship was of the "pot-bellied" type of merchantman, common at that period, and had a capacity of one hundred and eighty tons. She was being used, ordinarily, for handling cargoes of wines out of Mediterranean ports.

Christopher Jones had been Master of his own ship for fourteen years previous to 1620. When at home he resided at Rotherhith, Surrey Co., England, with a wife and children.

It was in the month of May, 1620, that the Mayflower, after a long voyage through the blue waters and under the bluer skies of the Mediterranean, found its way through the London fog into the Thames and slowly crept to her anchorage in the old "Home Port", probably off Blackhall or Wapping.

Master Jones was pleased, the wine cargoes had been profitable. He would put up for a time, overhaul, paint and scrape the accumulation of barnacles from the hull of his ship.

Mate Clark and other officers of the ship looked forward to a visit with friends and relatives.

The thirty, more or less, sailors before the mast were paid off, and discharged. They were a fierce-looking bunch, with bandanas, sashes, long mustachios, boots with wide tops, all set off with splashes of red, green and brown.

[ 23 ]

However, Master Jones and his good ship Mayflower were not to be allowed to rest for long, in fact hardly long enough to complete the overhauling.

Early in July, 1620, Thomas Weston, of the Merchant Adventurers, called on Master Jones and presented a proposition for a voyage to the colonies, for the purpose of transporting a group of English Planters and their families, some of whom were closely affiliated with the Adventurers, in fact, members of that organization, and, at the same time pick up on the way out at Southampton a small ship Speedwell, from Holland, having on board a company of "Separatists" seeking new homes in the Virginia Colony, and consort with it on the voyage to America, where the Speedwell was to remain in the capacity of a fishing smack for the use of the Planters.

It was hoped that the fishing business would develop into a paying proposition, both for the profit of the Planters and the Merchant Adventurers of London, sponsoring their transportation.

Captain Jones and Thomas Weston were old friends, and the ship was chartered to undertake what turned out to be one of the most historic voyages of history.

Repairs to the Mayflower were hurried, and a crew assembled, consisting of Capt. Christopher Jones, Master Mates John Clarke, Robert Coppin, Andrew Williamson and John Parker, Surgeon Doctor Giles Heale, four quartermasters, a carpenter, cook, boatswain and gunners.

About thirty-six sailors were hired to make the voyage. They were a hardboiled lot, but mollycoddles did not ship before the mast for a transatlantic voyage in those days. There are records to show that they cursed, threatened and grumbled during the trip.

On Saturday, July 15, 1620 (O.S.), the good ship Mayflower, with probably sixty-five Planters aboard, and lying off, very likely, Blackhall or Wapping, London, weighed anchor, and started on the memorable voyage, which was to last, for the ship and crew, until May 6, 1621, before they were back in the home port of London.

At Southampton, while waiting for the Speedwell from Holland, a young cooper, named John Alden, was hired by Captain Jones as a member of his crew.

When the Speedwell arrived with the Leyden group, there was some switching around of passengers, and finally the two ships started out together, as narrated in other portions of this work, but owing to alleged unseaworthiness, the Speedwell, after repeated attempts to proceed, was sent back to London with some of the passengers and crew, and the Mayflower then departed alone from Plymouth, England, on September 6, 1620 (O.S.), with 102 passengers, and about forty crew members including officers.

During the following eight months, including the New England winter of sickness and death, the good ship Mayflower, its captain and crew, performed wonderfully well. Perhaps they have not been given due credit.

[ 24 ]

During the voyage there were but two deaths. However, these sad events were balanced by two births, a pretty good record for any ship to make, and the crew during the crossing seems to have behaved very well, especially in view of the crowded condition of the ship, and the fact that it took about sixty-five days to cross the ocean. The Mayflower made the return voyage in about thirty days. It is not clear why Captain Jones took so many days in reaching the New England shores.

While the Mayflower lay in Cape Cod Harbor, and Plymouth Harbor, Captain Jones and crew did everything possible to make the Planters comfortable, especially the women and children. They took part in the "explorations" and other activities.

The ship was used as a place of refuge until March, 1621, while the men were preparing shelter on shore for their families. If the Mayflower had returned to England in December, as expected by the Merchant Adventurers, the story of that first winter would have been still more distressing.

The crew suffered severely in sickness and death. Approximately half their number including the cook, quartermaster, boatswain and gunman died during the winter, and lie buried on the shores of Cape Cod Bay. Perhaps, in many cases due to their self-sacrificing acts of kindness.

It appears conclusive that Master Jones was not only a brave, capable navigator. He must have been to have guided the ship safely across the ocean in those days of real sailing vessels, but he was also a shrewd business man, for he had sailed his ship for many years at a profit to himself and backers.

Captain Jones took a great deal of interest in the thirty-four young people under twenty years of age on the Mayflower, and for the very good reason that he had a wife and two children of his own.

Owing to much sickness and death among the crew during the winter months, and for other reasons, the Mayflower sailed from New Plymouth in April, 1621, without a cargo.

As a matter of fact, the ship's cook having died, the Captain offered a free return passage to England to any women who would undertake the task of cooking for the crew. Not a single woman of the colony accepted the offer.

On reaching England in May, 1621, after an uneventful voyage of about thirty days, Captain Jones left the good ship Mayflower, never to return. He retired to his home in Rotherhith, Surrey County, England, a broken and sick man due to the many hardships and responsibilities of 1620-21.

The Mayflower made numerous trips in later years to New Plymouth and other places, but for Captain Jones the great historic voyage was his last. He died March 5, 1622, leaving a wife and two little children. He was a true hero and a leading actor in the drama.

Refs. Nos. 20, 21, 22, 23, 24, 25, 27, 47.

## THE MAYFLOWER PASSENGERS AND PLANTERS

The "Virginia" of 1620 was, indeed, a vast territory. By the first charter, granted in 1606, it consisted of a strip of land, one hundred miles in width, lying on the Atlantic coast of North America from the thirty-fourth to forty-fifth degree of N. Latitude, and was divided in two parts.

The "Southerly" reached from the thirty-fourth to forty-first degree and was given to the First Colony, composed of "Knights, Gentlemen, Merchants and other adventurers of London and elsewhere".

The "Northerly" extended from the forty-first to the forty-fifth degree, and was given to the Second Colony made up of Adventurers from the cities of Bristol, Exeter, Plymouth and elsewhere. The territory afterwards known as New England, therefore, fell in the Second Colony, and the persons named in this grant were Thomas Hanham, Raleigh Gilbert, William Parker and George Popham.

In 1607, the "Popham" Planters were sent out to colonize the "Second Colony" on the Kennebec River. This was purely a commercial venture begun by Chief Justice John Popham, brother of George. It failed miserably.

Meanwhile the "Southerly" or "First Colony", at Jamestown and vicinity had succeeded, and the London or "Virginia Co." was flourishing.

No interest in the "Northerly" Colony could be revived until Capt. John Smith made one of his famous voyages in 1614, and Sir Ferdinando Gorges became the ruling spirit.

In 1617, when Robert Cushman and John Carver started negotiations for transporting our Pilgrim forefathers to America they were confronted with the above situation. The "Northerly" Company (Popham) was still inactive, although Captain Smith and Gorges were trying to revive it. They had to sail, if they departed at all, under some patent, and the only one they could obtain was through the Virginia or London Co.

The Mayflower Planters finally sailed under the John Peirce patent, which was sealed by the Virginia Co., 1619, and applied only to the "Southerly" or "First Colony". The landing of our Pilgrims in New England, therefore, caused much confusion and bitterness in London. The patent being voided, the Mayflower Planters framed and subscribed to a "Compact" of their own.

In considering the type of Planter who embarked on the Mayflower from Leyden and London in 1620, the reader should have in mind a number of circumstances which made the voyage possible.

The Virginia (or more properly, the London) Company for fourteen years had been struggling to obtain money and Adventurers for the purpose of turning the charter or patent into a profitable enterprise.

"Broadsides" had been issued giving the conditions of a voyage, and describing the kind of emigrant desired. The central idea of the Company was to develop a tenant class who would prove a source of profit, and provide a means for carrying on the plantations. Attacks had been made upon the Company because of its methods of close dealing with the colonists.

In order to better conditions, it was hoped, for all concerned, a Company was formed in London called the Merchant Adventurers. This Company was composed of a group of substantial merchants, who proposed to furnish capital and transportation to the colonies for certain considerations according to agreement. Thomas Weston was the active agent of this group.

About the year 1613 a series of nine tracts were printed, setting forth in glowing terms the wonderful opportunities in the Virginia Plantations. Among these were Whitaker's "Good News from Virginia", 1613, and Hamor's "True Discourse of the Present Estate of Virginia", 1615.

Thomas Weston was careful in selecting emigrants for "transportation", either with means or without. The terms of the agreement made it essential to choose young, strong and healthy emigrants. Concessions were offered to heads of families, especially those able to purchase stock in the Company. The transportation of family groups was encouraged.

The "Adventurers" who were interested in the Mayflower Planters, and the New Plymouth Colony, were so well described by Capt. John Smith in 1624-25, that his description is quoted, in part, as follows (Generall Historie 1626) p. 247:

> "The adventurers which raised the Stocke to begin and supply this Plantation were about 70. Some Gentlemen, some Merchants, some handicraftsmen, some adventuring great Summes, some small, as their estates and affection served. . . . These dwell most about London, they are not a corporation but knit together by a voluntary combination in a Society without constraint or penalty, aiming to doe good and to plant Religion; they have a President and Treasurer, every yeeere newly chosen by the most voices, who ordereth the affaires of their Courts meetings."

It seems quite clear from all the evidence that the Merchant Adventurers of London who sponsored and financed the voyage of the Mayflower were very friendly toward the "Separatist Movement". Thomas Weston, their agent, was a frequent visitor to Leyden, and it is more than likely that Carver, Cushman, Allerton, Rogers and others of London and Leyden were members of the Adventurers. Thomas Rogers was a "Camlet" merchant in Leyden, and had resided near Christopher Martin, Governor of the Mayflower and Treasurer of the Adventurers, in London.

The "Londoners" on board the Mayflower far outnumbered those from Leyden, and many of them were "Adventurers", such as Martin, Mullins, and probably Hopkins, Warren and others. They were also, no doubt, Separatists, and in fact Pilgrims in the true sense, many of them having sacrificed their homes and fortunes in the cause.

Meanwhile the Separatists in Leyden, Holland, were making careful plans for removal to some distant colony where they could at least be governed by magistrates of their own selection. Bradford says:

> "Experience haveing taught them many things those prudent governours with sundrie of the sagest members begane both deeply to apprehend their present dangers, and wisely to foresee the future; and think of timly remedy. In the agitation of their thoughts, and much discours of things hear aboute, at length they began to incline to this conclusion, of removall to some other place. Not out of any new fanglednes or other shuch like giddie humor, by which men are often times transported to their great hurt, and danger" also "all great, and honorable actions are accompanied with great difficulties."

At first they talked rather hopefully of "Guiana", a country that Sir Walter Raleigh wrote so beautifully about in 1596, and that was then being promoted.

Where to go was a problem, as Bradford so naively points out:

> "on the other hand, for Virginia, it was objected; that if they lived among the English which wear ther planted, or so near them as to be under their government; they should be in a great danger to be troubled, and persecuted for the cause of religion, as if they lived in England, and it might be worse."

After much discussion, probably in the Church meetings comprising about 298 Separatists, it was finally decided, as Bradford says:

> "to live as a distinct body by themselves, under the generale Government of Virginia and by their friends to sue to his majestie that he would be pleased to grant them freedom of Religion; and that this might be obtained, they weer putt in good hope (by some great person, of good ranke and qualitie) that were made their friends."

Among these "friends" were, no doubt, the Adventurers of London.

> "Whereupon.2.were chosen and sent in to England (at the charge of the rest) to Sollicite this matter."

The messengers appointed were Robert Cushman of Kent Co. and John Carver. They appear to have started negotiations in 1617, and may have been "Adventurers" themselves.

# YE OLDE ENGLAND
## 1620

LF.N
1936

## ENGLISH HOMES OF MAYFLOWER PLANTERS

**YORK** : Bradford, Carver, Masterson,
**NOTTS** : Brewster.
**NORFOLK** : Fuller.
**ESSEX** : Martin, Crakston, Prower, Eaton, Brown.
**LONDON** : Story, Wilder, Hooke, Rogers, Allerton, Howland, Warren,
Hopkins, Standish, Billington, Cartier, Doty, Litster,
Langmore, Latham, Button, Britterage, Clarke, Gardiner,
Trevore, Ely, Holbeek, Thomson, White, Turner, Tinker,
English, Priest, Goodman, Fletcher, Williams, Alderton.

**KENT.** : Cushman, Rigsdale, chilton, Minter, Cooke?
**SURREY** : Mullins.
**SALOP** : More, Tillie, Samson, Cooper.
**WORCESTER** : Winslow.
**HANTS** : Alden.

Of course, the Virginia Co. was glad to encourage the enterprise, but the messengers found it difficult to obtain from the King a "liberty in Religion" patent.

Gradually complications developed and the Leyden Company were in fear lest the whole proposal with the Virginia Co. would be dropped owing to misunderstandings concerning the "hiring and buying of shipping". Bradford says:

> "Mr. Thomas Weston, a marchant of London came to Leyden, and confered with Robinson and others. He represented the Merchant Adventurers of London, and advised them not to medle with the Dutch, or too much to depend on the Virginia Co., for if that failed; if they came to resolution, he and shuch marchants as were his friends (together with their owne means) would sett them forth; they should make ready, and neither feare wante of shipping nor money; for what they wanted should be provided."

Weston stated he did not ask for an agreement himself, but had to obtain one in order to satisfy some of his friends whom he hoped to "procure to adventure in this business".

An agreement was framed in Leyden, and carried to England by Mr. Carver, who together with Robert Cushman,

> "were to receive the moneys and make provisione both for shiping and other things for the vioage."

Bradford says:

> "aboute this time also they had heard, both from Mr Weston and others, that sundrie Honourable Lords had obtained a large grant from the king, for the more northerly parts of that countrie, derived out of the Virginia patents, and wholy secluded from their Governmente, and to be called by another name, viz. New-England."

Capt. John Smith was now reviving interest in the "Northerly" Colony.

> "But as in all businesses the acting part is most difficulte . . .; for some of that should have gone in England fell of and would not goe; other marchants and friends that had offered to adventure their moneys withdrew, and pretended many excuses. Some disliking they went not to Guiana; others againe would adventure nothing except the wente to Virginia. Some againe (and those that were most relied on) fell in utter dislike with Virginia, and would doe nothing if they wente thither. In the midds of these distractions they of Leyden, who had put of their estates and laid out their moneys, were brought into a greate streight."

While all of these matters were in confusion Weston came forth with a changed agreement, over the one made in Leyden. Cushman in London had agreed to the paper, because

"they which had put of their estates and paid in their money were in hazard to be undon."

Copy of Agreement

Anno 1620 July 1

1. The Adventurers and Planters doe agree, that every person that goeth being aged .16. years and upward, be rated at .10li. and ten pounds to be accounted a single share.
2. That he that goeth in person, and furnisheth him selfe out with .10li. either in money or other provisions, be accounted as having .20li. in stock, and in the divission shall receive a doble share.
3. The persons transported and adventurers shall continue their joynt stock and partnership together, the space of .7. years (excepte some unexpected impedimente doe cause the whole company to agree otherwise) during which time, all profits and benefits that were gotte by trade, traffick, trucking, working, fishing, or any other means of any person or persons, remaine still in the commone stock until the division.
4. That at their comming ther, they chose out shuch a number of fitt persons, as may furnish their ships and boats for fishing upon the sea; imploying the rest in their several faculties upon the land; as building houses, tilling, and planting the ground, and makeing shuch commodities as shall be most usefull for the collonie.
5. That at the end of the .7. years, the capital and profits viz. the houses, lands, goods and chatles, be equally divided betwixte the Adventurers and Planters; which done, every man shall be free from other of them of any debt or detrimente concerning this adventure.
6. Whosoever cometh to the colonie hereafter, or putteth any into the stock, shall at the ende of the .7. years be alowed proportionably to the time of his so doing.
7. He that shall carie his wife and children, or servants, shall be alowed for everie person now aged .16. years and upwards, a single share in the division, or if he provid them necessaries, a doble share, or if they be between .10. year olde and .16. then .2. of them to be reconed for a person, both in transportation and division.
8. That shuch children as now goe, and are under the age of ten years, have no other share in the division, but .50. acers of unmannured land.
9. That shuch persons as die before the .7. years be expired, their executors to have their parte or share at the devission, proportionably to the time of their life in the collonie.

[ 31 ]

10. That all such persons as are of this collonie, are to have their meate, drink, apparell, and all provisions out of the common stock and goods of the said collonie.

Although the above agreement was the approved one used by the Merchant Adventurers themselves, whenever any of them removed to the colonies, and there were several on the Mayflower, including Gov. Christopher Martin, William Mullins, and very likely Stephen Hopkins and others. In fact, it would appear that the whole group of sixty-five, more or less, "Londoners" accepted the proposition in the usual manner.

Also, in spite of the fact that the Merchant Adventurers (a body of seventy or more) many of whom were secretly in sympathy with the Separatists, were making it possible for them to leave the country, and, although their agent Robert Cushman had approved the matter, the Leyden leaders, due probably to the influence of Robinson, refused to sign the paper.

The Leyden Pilgrims apparently were holding out for better terms, something along these lines:

(a) "houses, improved lands, especially gardens and home lots should remaine undivided wholly to the planters at the 7 yrs end."

(b) "Two days a week for their own private employment, and their families."

It is unfortunate that Bradford, in his remarkable history, should have dwelt so lightly with the important matter of the relationship between the Adventurers and the Leyden Company.

However, it must be remembered that Bradford was only thirty years old at the time, and had nothing to do with the negotiations leading up to the embarkation. They were left to Robert Cushman, John Carver, Rev. John Robinson, Elder William Brewster and others.

It is a sad fact that such outstanding leaders of the expedition, as Gov. Christopher Martin, William Mullins, Gov. John Carver, and others including Robert Cushman, disappeared from the scene, by death or otherwise so soon after landing.

It is feared that Bradford's expressed opinion of Thomas Weston, Christopher Martin, and Robert Cushman is a little prejudiced from lack of understanding of the true situation. Of course he wrote from the Leyden point of view only, and that, many years after the events. In other words he painted a picture of events from the debtor angle only, giving little or no credit to those who made the voyage possible.

There is a great deal of evidence to show that Thomas Weston, representing the Adventurers, was a staunch friend of the Leyden Company, and, in fact, decidedly sympathetic, along with other Adventurers, of the whole Separatists movement, many of whom had sacrificed much in the cause, and some of whom were passengers on the Mayflower along with the Leyden contingent.

[ 32 ]

The Leyden leaders had not signed the agreement before leaving Holland in the Speedwell, although it had been approved tentatively by their agent Robert Cushman, and Weston was naturally worried. He went down from London to Southampton to meet the Speedwell, and there argued for a signature to the agreement again, stating, in effect, that the Adventurers were standing to lose, anyway, and that they could not change the agreement, and that many of his own personal friends among the passengers had approved of it.

However, the Leyden leaders on the Speedwell again refused to sign, stating they would not do so without placing the matter before those they left behind in Holland. This caused Weston to lose his temper, and he returned to London, after telling his old friends that they would have to stand on their own legs in the future, which created a very serious problem at the last moment for the Leyden Pilgrims.

Owing to the long delays the money they had raised in Holland and handed over to Cushman had all been spent, and in order to clear from the Southampton port they were forced to sell some of their provisions.

As narrated in other portions of this work, after much difficulty and delay owing to the alleged "leaky" Speedwell, the Mayflower alone departed from Plymouth with 102 Planters aboard, young and old, about sixty-five "Londoners" and thirty-seven from Leyden. Two boys were born on the ship.

It appears that the Adventurers and Thomas Weston had decided to permit the Leyden Company to make the voyage in the Mayflower, apparently without signing the contract, surely a friendly act. It is possible that Weston assumed the whole responsibility for this act, and other acts of generosity toward the Leyden people, especially, relating to the "Patent" under which the Mayflower Planters were supposed to be operating.

Weston, evidently, found it difficult to explain to his friends, the Adventurers, and others in England, the attitude of the Planters in landing in New England, and keeping the Mayflower there for many months, and then returning to England without a cargo, also the refusal of the Leyden group to sign the agreement.

In this connection it is recollected that the London Co. (Virginia Co.) had given a patent to one John Peirce, and associates, which was sealed by the Company February 2, 1619-20 (O.S.). This could only apply to the "Southerly" Colony. Under it the Mayflower Planters sailed for Virginia. Obviously landing in New England rendered it "void and useless". It became necessary to take steps for a new patent, and from the Company having control over New England. Of course, the Virginia Co. would have to recall the Peirce patent, unless the Planters still intended to begin a plantation within the limits of the Southern Colony. All of which left Weston in a rather delicate position.

It seems clear that the situation caused friction among the Adventurers in London who were standing to lose the money they had put up in fitting out the expedition.

The Mayflower having returned to London on May 6, 1621, without any cargo, and all the other complications regarding the patent having been placed in the lap of Weston, he wrote in despair to his friend, John Carver of New Plymouth, under date of July 6, 1621, in part as follows:

"I durst never acquainte the Adventurers with the alteration of the conditions first agreed on betweene us. . . . That you sent no loding in the shipis . . . distasted. I know your weakness was the cause of it. . . . A quarter of the time you spente in discoursing, argueing, and consulting would have done much . . . ; but that is past. . . . If you mean . . . to perform conditions agreed upon, doe us the favor to copy them out faire, and subscribe them with the principle of your names. . . . And then I shall be able to give them sum satisfaction whom I am now forced with good words to shift of. And consider that the life of the business depends on the loding of the ship (Fortune), which, if you doe to any good purpose that I may be freed from the great sumes I have disbursed for the former, and must doe for the later, I promise you I will never quit the business, though all the other Adventurers should. . . .

For anything that is els worth writing Mr Cushman can inform you. I pray write instantly for Mr Robinson to come to you. And so praying God to blesse you with all graces necessary both for this life and that to come, I rest

Your very loving frend,
Tho Weston"

This letter was despatched on the ship Fortune which arrived in New Plymouth on November 9, 1621. It also brought Robert Cushman of Kent, who was appointed by Weston to see that the conditions were carried out, and to return with the ship to England. This is the same Robert Cushman, who, together with John Carver had been appointed by the Leyden Company to negotiate for them before the London Co., and the Adventurers. Apparently, after returning to London on the Speedwell, Cushman had joined the staff of the Adventurers.

On arrival Cushman found that Carver, Martin, Mullins, the Tillie brothers, Rogers, Warren and other influential Planters had died. In fact, all of the leading "Londoners" had died except Standish and Hopkins, thereby leaving the Adventurers very poorly represented.

Under the circumstances, Cushman discovered it would be impossible to obtain an accounting for funds already spent. However, he did see that the Fortune was fully laden with a cargo of clapboards, otter skins, beaver skins and other items, and then returned to England with the ship.

[ 34 ]

It is of interest to note that Cushman while in New Plymouth on December 21, 1621, before the return of the Fortune gave a sermon in the "Common House" addressed as follows:

> "to my loving Friends and ADVENTURERS of New England" "we also have been very chargeable to many of our loving friends, which helped us hither, . . . , so that before we think of gathering riches, we should even in conscience think of requiting their charge of love, and labor, and cursed be that profit and gain which aimeth not at this."

Whether or not Cushman had in mind during his sermon, certain of the Adventurers who had died in the "first sickness" is not clear, but it does seem apparent that our Pilgrim forefathers were finding it extremely difficult to put the colony on a paying basis. As a matter of fact they had hardly, up to the arrival of the Fortune in 1621, been able to win a mere living from the soil, sea and wild life about them.

The debts were real, however, and could not be cast aside. The Mayflower Planters and the Merchant Adventurers constituted a joint stock company. Of course, some of the Planters who had put considerable cash in stock were anxious for returns on their investment. However, the money invested by the Adventurers in England, the "stay-at-homes," caused much bitterness, especially when expected profits did not show up at the end of the seven year period.

It is not clear when and how any part of the obligation was met, the matter was an open source of trouble for a number of years.

At the end of the seven-year period in 1627, it has been estimated that the Mayflower Planters owed the Adventurers 1800 pounds, and this, in spite of certain payments which had been made. Also, other obligations had been entered into. During the years of struggle with the elements, borrowings were made. One through Standish for 150 pounds at 50% interest, and one through Allerton at 30% interest for 200 pounds. This money was needed, even at the high rates, to carry on trade and meet current expenses.

Therefore at the end of the seven years the Planters owed about 2200 pounds, a heavy burden indeed, especially due to excessively high rates of interest.

Bradford in his history deals rather harshly with these creditors, but, after all, the whole matter was pure business, and sharp dealings all around seemed the common practice in those days, as it is, even unto the present generation of supposed enlightened civilization.

For instance, Allerton, acting as agent for the Planters succeeded in framing a new agreement with the Adventurers, in which all claims would be abandoned on payment of 1800 pounds, at the rate of 200 pounds per year. Eight of the Planters went as surety on this proposition. These eight, however (Bradford, Winslow, Brewster, Allerton, Standish, Howland, Alden and Prence), demanded for this surety service a monopoly of the trade of the colony, and became, more or less, dictators of financial policies. All of the Planters were to buy of them at a fixed price.

The eight Planters were not able to keep the monopoly to themselves for long. The proposition was too inviting, and four London gentlemen were soon added to the list, ostensibly, to "increase the credit of the colony and greatly facilitate business abroad." This method of getting in on the "ground floor" seems much like modern business practice.

All of these moves and counter moves, of course, created confusion and trouble. The struggle became protracted and uncertain, and the exact time when the Planters became free of debt is not known.

In 1633, however, it is stated that the various obligations had been reduced, and that within a quarter of a century the Pilgrims had liquidated the debts in one way or another. During this period various attempts were made by the Planters to straighten out misunderstandings. In 1634, Edward Winslow went to England on business, but instead of giving him a hearing, he was imprisoned in Fleet Prison for seven weeks for his "Separatist" views. On release he returned to New Plymouth, and became Governor in 1636 and again in 1644. In 1646 Winslow undertook another mission to England, and while there was prevailed upon to accept service under Cromwell, and on one expedition to the West Indies, caught the fever and died. He was buried at sea, May 8, 1655, as a fitting climax to a life of romance and adventure. Edward Winslow must be considered as one of the outstanding actors of the Pilgrim drama.

Inasmuch as the foundation of all research regarding the Mayflower Planters is "Mourt's Relations," London, 1622, and Bradford's "History of Plimouth Plantation," 1650, the verbatim statement of Bradford regarding them and their "decreasings and increasings" is given as follows:

### The Mayflower Planters

"The names of those which came over first, in the year .1620. and were by the blessing of God the first beginers and (in a sort) the foundation of all the Plantations and Colonies in New England; and their families.

Mr John Carver; Katherine, his wife; Desire Minter;
.8. and .2. manservants John Howland, Roger Wilder; William Latham, a boy, & a Maid-servant, & a child yt was put to him, called, Jasper More.

Mr William Brewster; Mary, his wife; with .2. sons
.6. whose names were Love & Wrasling; and a boy was put to him called Richard More; and another of his brothers. The rest of his children were left behind, & came over afterward.

[ 36 ]

Mr Edward Winslow; Elizabeth, his wife; & .2. men
.5. servants, caled Georg Sowle, and Elias Story; also a litle
girle was put to him, caled Ellen, the sister of Richard
More.

William Bradford, and Dorothy, his wife; having but
.2. one child, a sone, left behind, who came afterward.

Mr Isaack Allerton, and Mary, his wife; with .3. child-
.6. ren. Bartholomew, Remember, & Mary; and a servant
boy, John Hooke.

Mr Samuel Fuller, and a servant, caled William But-
.2. ton; His wife was (left) behind, & a child, which came
afterwards.

.2. John Crakston, and his sone, John Crakston.

.2. Captain Myles Standish, and Rose, his wife.

Mr Christopher Martin, and his wife, and .2. servants
.4. Salamon prower and John Langemore.

Mr William Mullines, and his wife, and .2. children,
.5. Joseph & Priscila; and a servant, Robert Carter.

Mr. William White, and Susana, his wife and one sone,
.6. caled resolved, and one borne a ship-bord, caled peri-
griene; and .2. servants, named William Holbeck and
Edward Thomson.

Mr Steven Hopkins, & Elizabeth, his wife, and .2.
.8. children, caled Giles, and Constanta, a doughter, both by
a former wife; and .2. more by this wife, caled Damaris
& Oceanus; the last was borne at sea; and .2. servants,
called Edward Doty and Edward Litster.

Mr Richard Warren; but his wife and children were
.1. lefte behind, and came afterwards.

John Billington, and Elen, his wife; and .2. sones,
.4. John & Francis.

Edward Tillie, and Ann, his wife; and .2. childeren
.4. that were their cossens Henery Samson and Humility
Coper.

.3. John Tillie, and his wife; and Eelizabeth their doughter.

Francis Cooke, and his sone John. But his wife &
.2. other children came afterwards.

Thomas Rogers, and Joseph, his sone. His other child-
.2. ren came afterwards.

.2. Thomas Tinker, and his wife, and a Sone.

.2. John Rigdale, and Alice his wife.

James Chilton, and his wife, and Mary their dougter.
.3. They had an other doughter, yt was maried, came afterwards.

.3. Edward fuller, and his wife, and Samuell, their sonne.

John Turner, and .2. sones. He had a doughter came
.3. some years after to Salem, wher she is now living.

Francis Eaton, and Sarah, his wife, and Samuell, their
.3. sone, a yong child.

[ 37 ]

Moyses Fletcher
.10. John Goodman
Thomas Williams
Digerie Preist
Edmond Margeson
Peter Browne
Richard Britterige
Richard Clarke
Richard Gardenar
Gilbert Winslow

John Alden was hired for a cooper at South-Hampton,
.1. wher the ship victuled; and being a hopefull yong man,
was much desired, but left to his owne liking to go or stay
when he came here; but he stayed, and maryed here.

John Allerton and Thomas Enlish were both hired. the
.2. later to goe mr of a shalop here and ye other was reputed
as one of ye company, but was to go back (being a seaman) for the help of others behind. But they both dyed
here before the shipe returned.

There were allso other .2. seamen hired to stay a year
.2. here in the country, William Trevore and one Ely. But
when their time was out, they both returned.

These bening aboute a hundred sowls, came over in this
first ship, and began this worke, which God of his goodnes
hath hithertoo blesed; let his holy name have ye praise.

And seeing it hath pleased him to give me to see .30.
years compleated since these beginings; and that the great
works of his providence are to be observed. I have thought
it not unworthy my paines to take a view of the decreasings & increasings of these persons, and such changes
as hath pased over them & theirs in this thirty years.
It may be of some use to such as come after; but, however,
I shall rest in my owne benefite.

I will therefore take them in order as they lye.

Mr. Carver and his wife, dyed the first year; he in ye
.15. spring, she in the somer; also his man Roger (Wilder),
and the litle boy Jaspar (More) dyed before either of them,
of ye commone infection. Desire Minter returned to her
friend, & proved not very well, and dyed in England.
His servant boy Latham, after more than .20. years stay
in the country, went into England, and from thence to the
Bahamy Ilands in ye west Indees, and ther, with some
others was starved for want of food. His maid-servant
maried & dyed a year or tow after, here in this place.
His servant, John Howland maried the doughter of John
Tillie, Elizabeth, and they are both now living, and have
.10. children, now all living; and their eldest doughter
hath .4. children, and ther .2. dougter one, all living,
and other of their children mariagable, so .15. are come
of them.

[ 38 ]

Mr Brewster lived to very old age; about .80. years he
.4. was when he dyed, having lived some .23. or .24. years
here in ye countrie; & though his wife dyed long before, yet she dyed aged. His sone Wrastle dyed a yonge
man unmaried; his sone Love lived till this year .1650.
and dyed, & left .4. children, now living. His doughters
which came over after him are dead, but have left sundry
children alive; his eldest sone is still liveing, and hath .9.
.2. or .10. children, one maried, who hath a child or .2.

Richard More his brother dyed the first winter; but he
.4. is maried, and hath .4. or .5. children all living.

Mr Ed: Winslow his wife dyed the first winter; and he
.2. maried with the widow of Mr White, and hath .2. children living by her marigable, besides sundry that are dead.
One of his servants dyed, as also the litle girle soone after
.8. the ships arivall. But his man, Georg Sowle, is still living, and hath .8. children.

William Bradford his wife dyed soone after their ariv-
.4. all, and he maried againe; and hath .4. children, .3.
whereof are maried.

Mr Allerton his wife dyed with the first and his ser-
.8. vant, John Hooke. His sone Bartle is maried in England,
but I know not how many children he hath. His doughter
Remember is married at Salem, & hath .3. or .4.
children living. And his doughter Mary is maried here
& hath .4. children. Him selfe maried againe with ye
dougter of Mr Brewster, & hath one sone living by here
but she is long since dead; and he is maried againe, and
hath left this place long agoe. So I account his Increase to
be .8. besides his sons in England.

Mr Fuller his servant dyed at sea; and after his wife
.2. came over, he had tow children by her, which are living
and growne up to years, but he dyed some .15. years agoe.

John Crakston dyed in the first mortality and about
some .5. or .6. years after, his sone dyed, having lost
himself in ye wodes. his feet became frozen, which put
him into a feaver of which he dyed.

Captain Standish his wife dyed in the first sickness,
.4. and he maried againe, and hath .4. sones liveing, and
some are dead.

Mr Martin, he and all his, dyed in the first infection,
not long after the arivall.

Mr Molines, and his wife, his sone, & his servant dyed
.15. the first winter, only his dougter Pricila survived, and
maried with John Alden, who are both living, and have
.11. children, and their eldest dougter is maried, & hath
five children.

Mr White and his .2. servants dyed soon after the
.7. landing. His wife maried with Mr Winslow (as is before

[ 39 ]

noted). His .2. sons are maried and Resolved hath .5. children, Peregrine tow, all living. So their increase are .7.

Mr Hopkins and his wife are now both dead but they lived above .20. years in this place, and had one sone and .4. dougters borne here. Ther sone became a seaman, & dyed at Barbadoes, one doughter dyed here, and .2. are maried. one of them hath .2. children, and one is yet to mary. So their increase which still survive are .4. .5. But his sone Gile is maried, and hath .4. children.

His dougter Constanta is maried and hath .12. children. .12. all of them living, and one of them maried.

Mr Richard Warren lived some .4. or .5. years, and .4. had his wife come over to him, by whom he had .2. sones before (he) dyed; and one of them is maryed, and hath .2. children. So his increase is .4. but he had .5. doughters more came over with his wife, who are all maried, & living, & have many children.

John Billington, after he had bene here .10. yers, was .8. executed for killing a man, and his eldest sone dyed before him; but his .2. sone is alive, and maried, & hath .8. children.

Edward Tillie and his wife both dyed soon after their .7. arrival; and the girle Humility, their cousen, was sent for Ento England, and dyed ther. Bot the youth Henery Samson is still liveing, and is maried, & hath .7. children.

John Tillie and his wife both dyed a litle after they came ashore, and their doughter Elizabeth maried with John Howland, and hath issue as is before noted.

Francis Cooke is still living, a very olde man, and hath .8. seene his childrens children have children; after his wife came over (with other of his children) he hath .3. still living by her, all maried, and have .5. children. So their increase is .8. and his sone John, which came over .4. with him, is maried, and hath .4. children living.

Thomas Rogers dyed in the first sickness, but his sone .6. Joseph is still living, and is maried and hath .6. children. The rest of Thomas Rogers (children) came over, & all maried, & have many children.

Thomas Tinker, and his wife and sone, all dyed in the first sickness.

And so did John Rigdale and his wife.

James Chilton and his wife also dyed in the first infec- .10. tion. But their doughter Mary is still living, and hath .9. children; and one doughter is maried, & hath a child, so their increase is .10.

Edward ffuller and his wife dyed soon after they came .4. ashore; but their sone Samuell is living, & maried, and hath .4. children or more.

John Turner and his .2. sons all dyed in the first sikness, But he hath a doughter still living at Salem, well maried, and approved of.

Francis Eaton has first wife dyed in the generall sick-
.4. ness, and he maried againe, & his .2. wife dyed, and he maried the .3. and had by her .3. children, one of them is maried, & hath a child, the others are living but one of them is an ideote. He dyed about .16. years agoe.

His sone Samuell, who came over a sucking child, is also
.1. maried, & hath a child.

Moyses Fletcher, Thomas Williams, Digarie Preist, John Goodman, Edmond Margeson, Richard Britterige, Richard Clarke. All these dyed soon after the arivall, and in the general sickness that befell. But Digerie Preist had his wife & children sent hither afterwards, she being Mr Allertons sister, But the rest left no posteritie here.

Richard Gardiner became a seaman and died in England, or at sea.

Gilbert Winslow, after diverse years aboad here, returned into England and dyed ther.

Peter Browne maried twice. By his first wife he had
.6. .2. children, who are living, & both of them maried, and the one of them hath .2. children; by his second wife he had .2. more. He dyed about .16. years since.

Thomas English and John Allerton dyed in the general sikness.

John Alden maried with priscila, Mr Mollines his doughter, and had issue by her as is before related.

Edward Doty & Edward Litster, the servants of Mr Hopkins. Litster after he was at liberty, went to Virginia, & ther dyed. But Edward Doty by a second wife hath .7. children, and both he and they are living.

Of these .100. persons which came over in this first ship together, the greater halfe dyed in the generall mortality; and most of them in .2. or three months time, and for those which survived, though some were ancient, & past procreation, & others left ye place and cuntrie. yet of those few remaining are sprunge up above .160. persons, in this .30. years, and are now living in the presente year .1650. besides many of their children which are dead, and come not within this account.

And of the olde stock (of one & other) ther are yet living this present year .1650. nere .30. persons. Let the Lord have ye praise, who is the High Preserver of men."

Bradford's list of passengers on the Mayflower, is, probably, very nearly correct. However, unfortunately, he is not clear as to many important details concerning their personal history in England, or their real status on board the ship, and in New Plymouth. His comments concerning the twenty unattached persons from London and vicinity, are especially misleading.

In this connection it should be remembered that Bradford was about thirty years old in 1620, and really had no part in planning the voyage. Brewster, Carver and Bradford were substantially the only passengers from the "North Country" in England on the ship. The others were from the vicinity of London, although some of them had resided a few years in Leyden. Naturally, they were "strangers" to Bradford, and he found it difficult to write about them in later years.

The original leaders of the Mayflower voyage, with the exception of Hopkins and Standish, died in the first sickness 1620-21, and some of these, such as Martin and Mullins were quite wealthy. Others were Merchants in the vicinity of London. Rigdale and Chilton were merchant tailors, and Rogers was a "Camlet" merchant. These Pilgrims had sold their property in England and Holland to help finance the removal to "Virginia".

Bradford comments truthfully, that "the greater halfe dyed in the generall mortality". For a time after 1621, Winslow and Allerton were quite active in New Plymouth affairs, but gradually drifted away from the colony for some reason. Brewster was elderly and more inclined toward church affairs than the Governorship, while Hopkins and Standish were not of a type to aspire to such a position, so that Bradford held undisputed the office of Governor for a period of years.

Obviously, it is not strange, perhaps, that Bradford, writing 25 years after the event should be uncertain and inaccurate concerning the personal history of many of those who died in the first sickness, especially, the Merchant Adventurers of London.

It does appear, however, that Bradford should have been better posted on the lives of those from Leyden, among whom he had lived for a number of years. Allerton and Winslow left the colony for reasons he does not fully explain. Also the important family of William Brewster, whom he should have known well, is left in a very incomplete condition, and, this in spite of the fact that Brewster, possibly Carver and himself, were the only three out of 104 passengers to hail from the vicinity of Scrooby.

It is unfortunate that he does not shed light upon the Edward Brewster of London, 1616 to 1640, and his relationship to Elder William. This Edward published twenty-five books on religious matters, mostly controversies. Also, he might have enlightened us regarding the possible financial interest that Elder William Brewster had in the Virginia Co., and his business relationship with Sir Edward Sandys, President of that Co., especially regarding the leasing of Scrooby Manor. The records of the Virginia Co. appear to show that Samuel Sandys, son of Sir Edward, leased the Manor, and that William Brewster and son Edward held shares in that enterprise in 1609. This was the year in which many of Robinson's followers removed to Leyden, Holland.

It seems strange indeed that Bradford should have been so sparing in his mention of Brewster's family and history.

The use of the prefix "Mr." by Bradford in his writings appears to have been purely arbitrary with himself, and intended to be courteous to the outstanding members of the New Plymouth Plantation.

He used "Mr." in connection with the nine heads of families in which the twenty unattached persons had been "put".

These were Martin, Hopkins, Mullins, Allerton, Carver, White, Winslow, Brewster and Fuller, and one other, Warren, ten in all.

Probably these heads of families were stockholders and members of the Merchant Adventurers in a more or less degree. Martin was the Governor and Treasurer of the Mayflower, having been appointed to that office by the Adventurers, and it is well known that Mullins was a heavy shareholder in the enterprise.

It seems clear that if Mullins and Martin had survived the first winter, the story of Plymouth Plantation might have been very different. The importance of these two individuals, and some others who died the first year have never been satisfactorily defined. Here lies a fruitful field for original research.

Bradford failed to use "Mr." in connection with his own name, perhaps through modesty, but more likely because he did not feel entitled to the term, especially in the year 1620. At that time he was still young and had not made a name for himself.

The prefix "Mr." was also omitted in connection with most of the heads of families who died in the first year, as follows, Rogers, Crakston, Edward Tillie, John Tillie, Turner, Tinker Rigsdale, Chilton, and Edward Fuller.

Evidence points to the probability that these Planters had been small tradesmen or merchants from the vicinity of London, and just as much entitled to "Mr." as the others.

For instance, Edward Fuller was brother to Dr. Samuel Fuller, and the Tillies were close friends of Thomas Weston. Rogers was a "Camlet" merchant both in London and later in Leyden, while Rigdale and Chilton were, as it appears, Merchant Tailors or the like.

However, most of these persons had died twenty-five years before Bradford wrote his history, and he was not so well informed concerning them as he was with the ten whom he called "Mr.".

The popular notion that the Mayflower Planters were "Yeomen" of England does not appear to be substantiated on a close study of the evidence.

In fact, most of these persons had been merchants of some sort near London, and persecuted for their religious views, or they were, as Capt. John Smith so aptly described them in 1624:

"Some Gentlemen, some merchants, some handicraftsmen, some adventuring great Sumes, some small . . . aiming to doe good and to plant Religion."

Bradford, Brewster and Carver were about the only Mayflower Planters from the "Yeoman" or wild country district of Notts and York, and they had lived among the Dutch in a large city for about ten years, and had become printers and business men. It is probably that they had also resided in London for a time.

Apparently, there were no very recent "farmers" or "yeomen" among the twenty-four heads of families, or the fifteen single men who finally made the voyage in the Mayflower.

It is evident, however, that they were all Separatists, and had suffered much because of their beliefs, and were seeking a haven of refuge in the colonies.

In order to clarify the personal status of the Mayflower Planters, the following groups, after considerable study, are formed from the 104 passengers:

### Mayflower Heads of Families
### (Londoners)

1. Mr. Christopher Martin, Governor and Treasurer of the Mayflower enterprise, b. Billerike, Essex Co. Eng., d. New Plymouth, Jan. 18, 1621.
2. Mr. Stephen Hopkins, a leader, probably a merchant, b. possibly in 1581, in Wortley, parish of Wotten-Under-Edge, Gloucestershire, Eng., d. New Plymouth, 1644. (See Fam. No. 1).
3. Mr. William Mullins, a merchant, b. Dorking, Surrey Co. Eng., d. New Plymouth, Mar. 3, 1621 (N.S.). (See Fam. No. 1094).
4. Capt. Myles Standish, Military Leader, b. probably London, Eng., 1584, d. Duxbury, Mass., Oct. 13, 1656. (See Fam. No. 183).
5. Mr. Richard Warren, Merchant of London, d. 1628 at New Plymouth. (See Fam. No. 257).
6. John Billington, perhaps a carpenter, d. New Plymouth, Sept., 1630. (See Fam. No. 860).
7. Edward Tillie, possibly a merchant, d. New Plymouth, Jan. 11 —Apr. 10, 1621. He was a close friend of Mr. Weston.
8. John Tillie, probably a Merchant of St. Andrews, London, d. New Plymouth, Jan. 11—Apr. 10, 1621. Brother of Edward Tillie. (See Fam. No. 220).
9. John Rigsdale, probably a Merchant Tailor, from Canterbury, Kent Co. Eng., d. in first sickness.
10. James Chilton, Citizen and Merchant Tailor of Canterbury, Kent Co. Eng., d. in first sickness. (See Fam. No. 183).
11. Edward Fuller, probably a Merchant from Redenhall, Norfolk Co. Eng., d. New Plymouth, Jan 11—Apr. 10, 1621. Brother of Dr. Samuel. (See Fam. No. 186).
12. Francis Eaton, Carpenter, d. New Plymouth, Nov. 4-18, 1621. (See Fam. No. 1105).

## Mayflower Heads of Families
## (From Leyden)

1. Mr. Isaac Allerton, Merchant Tailor from London, b. 1586, perhaps in the "North Country" of Eng., d. New Haven, Conn., before Feb. 22, 1659. (See Fam. No. 43).
2. Mr. John Carver, brother-in-law of the Rev. John Robinson, b. Doncaster, Yorkshire, Eng. Probably a merchant, and resided in London for a time. Became Governor of Plymouth Colony for a short time after the death of Governor Martin. His signature is on Mullins will. He d. New Plymouth bet. Apr. 12 and May 10, 1621 (N.S.).
3. Mr. William White, d. New Plymouth, Mar. 3, 1621. (See Fam. No. 336).
4. Mr. William Brewster, b. Scrooby, Nottinghamshire, Eng., 1566-7, d. New Plymouth, Apr. 26, 1644. He was the ruling Elder of the New Plymouth Church. (See Fam. No. 11).
5. Mr. Edward Winslow, Merchant, b. Oct. 28, 1595, Droitsrich, Eng., d. at sea about May 8, 1655. (See Fam. No. 183).
6. Dr. Samuel Fuller, Physician, b. Redenhall, Norfolk Co., Eng., Jan. 20, 1580, d. New Plymouth, Aug. 9—Sept. 26, 1633. (See Fam. No. 186).
7. William Bradford, b. Austerfield, Yorkshire Co., Eng., 1589-90, d. New Plymouth May 19, 1657. (See Fam. No. 926).
8. Thomas Rogers, Merchant of London and Leyden, d. New Plymouth bet. Jan. 11 and Apr. 10, 1621. (See Fam. No. 2).
9. John Crakston, d. New Plymouth in first sickness.
10. Francis Cooke (Francois Couck), d. New Plymouth, Apr. 17, 1663. (See Fam. No. 8).
11. John Turner, d. in first sickness.
12. Thomas Tinker, d. in first sickness.

## Single Men from London on the Mayflower

1. Peter Browne, b. Gt. Bursted, Essex Co., Eng. He was possibly a Weaver like his brother John (See Fam. No. 196). Peter d. Apr. 4—Oct. 10, 1633 in New Plymouth.
2. Richard Britterage, d. New Plymouth, Dec. 31, 1620. It was the first death at New Plymouth.
3. John Alden, b. Eng., 1599, d. Duxbury, Mass., Sept. 22, 1687 (N.S.). (See Fam. No. 1094).
4. Gilbert Winslow, b. Droitwich, Eng. He was a brother of Gov. Edward Winslow. (See Fam. No. 183).
5. Richard Gardiner. Hired as a sailor and returned to Eng.
6. William Trevor. Hired man, returned to Eng.
7. Ely. Hired man, returned to Eng.

## Single Men from Leyden on the Mayflower

1. Moses Fletcher, a "Smithy", probably native of Kent Co., Eng., d. in first sickness.

[ 45 ]

2. John Goodman. He was not a member of the "Dunham" family as claimed by some writers. See Leyden records. He d. in first sickness.
3. Thomas Williams, d. in the first sickness.
4. Degorie Priest. He was a Burgess at Leyden, and a "hatter" of London, d. New Plymouth, Jan. 11, 1621 (N.S.). See Fam. No. 950).
5. Edmund Margeson. This was probably intended for Edmund Masterson, father of Richard who came over later. d. New Plymouth in the first sickness.
6. John Alderton (Allerton). Apparently a seaman. d. in the first sickness.
7. Thomas English, Seaman, d. in the first sickness.

## Sons on Mayflower from London

1. Giles Hopkins (see Fam. No. 3).
2. Oceanus Hopkins, b. on the Mayflower, d. young.
3. Joseph Mullins, d. in the first sickness.
4. John Billington, d. soon after 1627.
5. Francis Billington (see Fam. No. 860).
6. Samuel Fuller (see Fam. No. 186).
7. Samuel Eaton (see Fam. No. 1105). A relative.
8. Henry Samson (see Fam. No. 187).

## Sons on Mayflower from Leyden

1. Love Brewster (see Fam. No. 11).
2. Wrestling Brewster, d. unmarried.
3. Bartholomew Allerton, returned to Eng.
4. Resolved White (see Fam. No. 336).
5. Peregrin White, b. on the Mayflower (see Fam. No. 336).
6. Joseph Rogers (see Fam. No. 2).
7. John Cooke (see Fam. No. 8).
8. John Crakston, Jr., d. in first sickness.
9. (          ) Tinker, d. in first sickness.
10. (          ) Turner, d. in first sickness.
11. (          ) Turner, d. in first sickness.

## Wives on the Mayflower from London

1. Mrs. Cristopher Martin, d. 1st year.
2. Mrs. Elizabeth Hopkins (see Fam. No. 1).
3. Mrs. William Mullins, d. 1st year. (See Fam. No. 1094).
4. Mrs. Rose Standish, d. Feb. 8, 1621. (See Fam. No. 183).
5. Mrs. Elen Billington (see Fam. No. 860).
6. Mrs. John Tillie (see Fam. No. 220).
7. Mrs. Ann Tillie (see Fam. No. 220).
8. Mrs. Alice Rigdale, d. 1st year.
9. Mrs. James Chilton, d. 1st year. (See Fam. No. 183).

10. Mrs. Edward Fuller, d. 1st year. (See Fam. No. 186).
11. Mrs. Sarah Eaton, d. 1st year. (See Fam. No. 1105).

## Wives on the Mayflower from Leyden

1. Mrs. Mary Allerton (see Fam. No. 43).
2. Mrs. Katherine Carver, d. 1st year.
3. Mrs. Dorothy Bradford (see Fam. No. 926).
4. Mrs. Mary Brewster (see Fam. No. 11).
5. Mrs. Elizabeth Winslow, d. 1st year. (See Fam. No. 183).
6. Mrs. Sussana White (see Fam. No. 336).
7. Mrs. Thomas Tinker, d. 1st year.

The group above of eighteen wives performed remarkably well during the voyage. It was something of a novelty for Planters to bring wives with them to the colonies. The duty of caring for their families, including the so-called "servants" on the cramped and unsanitary wine cargo ship was a health-taking task. Preparing meals must have been difficult and the smaller children had to have constant attention.

Only four of the eighteen survived the first winter of sickness.

## Daughters from London on the Mayflower

1. Constanta Hopkins, m. Nicholas Snow. (See Fam. No. 2).
2. Damaris Hopkins, d. soon after 1627.
3. Prescilla Mullins, m. John Alden. (See Fam. No. 1094).
4. Elizabeth Tillie, m. John Howland. (See Fam. No. 220).
5. Mary Chilton, m. John Winslow (see Fam. No. 183) a relation.
6. Humility Cooper, never married, returned to Eng.

## Daughters from Leyden on the Mayflower

7. Mary Allerton, m. Thomas Cushman. (See Fam. No. 43).
8. Remember Allerton, m. Moses Maversick. (See Fam. No. 43).

With the exception of Damaris Hopkins and Humility Cooper, the above group of Mayflower girls were honored in the colony for bringing up large families. They were "Londoners" in type, even the Allerton sisters, although they may have resided a short while in Leyden.

The descendants of these girls are scattered throughout the world in this year 1936.

Damaris Hopkins, the young girl who came over on the Mayflower with her parents, died in New Plymouth soon after 1627. Her sister Damaris was born in Plymouth about 1629, and married Jacob Cooke. (See Fam. No. 8).

## Unattached Persons on the Mayflower

It appears that the twenty unattached persons on the Mayflower were probably "Londoners", and were no doubt influenced to make the voyage by Thomas Weston, who considered them potentially qualified as settlers in the colonies, especially in the matter of health.

Bradford is not clear in his comments on these persons, and fails to give an account of any value concerning the auspices under which they made the voyage. His use of the word "servant" in connection with some of them must not be taken too seriously.

As a matter of fact they were not servants in the accepted modern sense of the word, but, apparently, had been "put" in certain families for voyage, thereby assuring themselves a square meal now and then, as each family group had to prepare its own food. The voyage took sixty-five days and to pay for the meals and other marks of attention from the families in which they were "put", some of them seem to have agreed to help the family heads get settled in the colony.

These agreements were not carried out in some respects. For instance, Mr. William Mullins in his will complains that Robert Cartier "hath not so approved himself as I would he should have don". Just what Robert did or did not do to merit this disapproval is far from evident, probably he was not very enthusiastic in performing certain services to pay Mr. Mullins for advancing favors on the voyage. Both Mr. Mullins and Robert Cartier died in the first winter of sickness.

The failure of the Speedwell to make the voyage caused quite a mixup in plans, and very unexpected crowding on the Mayflower. It seems probable that these unattached individuals were placed in the different family groups for mess and other favors just before or after the ship finally departed from Plymouth, England, and after the Speedwell had turned back to London.

They were "put" according to the ability and, perhaps, willingness of the groups to advance the needed meals and service for the voyage. Also, there was some economic advantage in attaching individuals to the family, as disclosed by the general agreement quoted in this work, especially in the additional allotments of land. In this regard attention is called to Par. 7 of the agreement dated July 1, 1620, as follows:

> "He that shall carie his wife and children, or servants, shall be allowed for everie person now aged .16. years and upwards, a single share in the division, or if he provid them accessaries, a doble share, or if they be between .10. year olde and .16. then .2. of them to be reconed for a person, both in transportation and division."

Bradford writing twenty-five years after the event, gives various names to these twenty persons such as "man-servant", "a boy", "maid-servant", "child that was put to", "servant boy", and other names.

However, the chances are that he was unable to marshal suitable words to describe the real situation, and, for some reason failed to

[ 48 ]

refer especially to Par. 7 of the agreement which seems clear enough.

Apparently, some of these "servants" felt their mission in that direction was about completed after the division of land in the colony was consummated, and rebelled at the tilling of the soil for their "benefactors".

Many of these unattached persons were infants under ten years. However, Par. 8 of the agreement appears to shed some light on their status and possibly real reason for being on the ship. It is quoted in part as follows:

> "That shuch children as now goe, and are under the age of ten years, have no other share in the division, but .50. acres of unmanured land."

Now, it cannot be claimed that Carver, Brewster and Winslow suffered much economic injury by having the Latham boy, and the four More children "put" in their family groups, and they were certainly too young to be "servants".

As a matter of fact, for reasons stated it is not thought any of the persons, in the unattached list, who were placed with the family units, were servants according to modern interpretation.

They were all potential Planters and ultimate sharers of the opportunities in the colony. The Merchant Adventurers of London had too much at stake to allow the transportation of any but the most promising individuals.

It is barely possible that Hopkins, Mullins and Martin may have brought Doty, Litster, Cartier, Prower and Langemore aboard with them, but this is mere conjecture. The chances are they were also attached to the respective families after boarding the ship. Mr. Weston, no doubt, had much to do with placing all of them.

Stephen Hopkins brought the largest family aboard, and became possessed of much property in the colony. Doty and Litster worked his land for him until their debt was liquidated. It cannot be said they were servants. It is recorded of Litster that,

> "after he was at liberty, went to Virginia and there dyed."

A synopsis of the twenty unattached persons on the Mayflower who were "put" with various families during the voyage is as follows:

## Unattached Persons on the Mayflower

(Placed in various family groups during voyage)

Mr. Christopher Martin, Governor and Treasurer.
  1. Solamon Prower (step-son) d. 1st year.
  2. John Langemore d. 1st year.
Mr. Stephen Hopkins, A leader from London.
  3. Edward Doty (see Fam. No. 39).
  4. Edward Litster, removed to Virginia.

Mr. William Mullins, A wealthy merchant of London.
   5. Robert Cartier d. 1st year.
Mr. William Brewster, Elder of the Church.
   6. Richard More (see Fam. No. 928).
   7. (       ) More d. 1st year.
Mr. John Carver, Governor for a short time after the death of Gov.
     Martin.
   8. Desire Minter, returned to England.
   9. John Howland (see Fam. No. 220).
  10. Roger Wilder d. 1st year.
  11. William Latham, removed to Bahamas.
  12. Maid-servant, unidentified.
  13. Jasper More d. 1st year.
Mr. Edward Winslow, Governor for a time.
  14. George Soule (see Fam. No. 1140).
  15. Elias Story d. 1st year.
  16. Ellen More d. 1st year.
Mr. Isaac Allerton, Merchant.
  17. John Hooke d. 1st year.
Dr. Samuel Fuller, Physician.
  18. William Button d. 1st year.
Mr. William White, probably a merchant.
  19. William Holbeck d. 1st year.
  20. Edward Thomson d. 1st year.

It will thus be seen that these unattached persons were placed in nine families. The detailed history of each of the family heads will appear in this series. Of these heads, Martin, Carver, Mullins, and White died in the first sickness. Winslow and Allerton left the colony, leaving only Hopkins, Brewster and Dr. Fuller of this group.

Ref. Nos. 1, 2, 3, 4, 5, 6, 7, 11, 15, 18, 26, 29, 31, 32, 33, 34, 40, 41, 46, 52, 62, 65, 67, 68.

## CHILDREN OF THE MAYFLOWER

There were thirty-four young people on the Mayflower, a third of all the passengers, and a remarkably healthy and lively group they were. Although sixty-five days were taken in making the voyage, and their quarters were necessarily cramped and unsanitary, the children remained free of any serious illness.

This wonderful record reflects great credit upon the women of the Mayflower, who prepared the meals and looked after the general needs of the children, ten of whom might be classed as infants, being under five years of age.

Some of the older girls, such as Desire Minter, Precilla Mullins and Elizabeth Tillie, no doubt were a great help to the mothers.

The boys, of course, had a wonderful time. To them it was, indeed, a great adventure. It requires little imagination to see them become acquainted with the mysteries of a sailing ship, every nook and corner of it. They explored the old wine ship from stem to stern, and from the keel in the smelly old hold, to the masthead.

To the children, the sailor with a yarn to tell, saltier the better, was a personage of importance, and assured of an appreciative audience.

The days, at times, must have passed rather tediously, especially for the boys, but they always had the man who "cund" the ship to fall back upon, and then that most interesting sailor, "the lookout man", continually fascinated them. He was likely to cry out anytime that most welcome call, "Land Oh"!

Stephen Hopkins was a never-ending source of entertainment for the children. With his delightful family near him (the largest on board), the boys and girls would gather around "Steve", and he would unfold to them wonderful stories of his trips to "Virginia", of shipwrecks, and of the time he was made "clark" to read the prayers, and how some of his old shipmates would call him "Brownist".

When the weather was good all hands would gather on deck for worship. Many were fond of singing, and the old church hymns were brought forth. This part of the program did not appeal so much to the boys. That fellow who "cunded" the ship was decidedly more interesting. However, the chances are that the children sat through the services. Their elders saw to that. It was the custom of the times.

Many of the days were exciting. There were several storms that carried away cloths and cooking dishes.

In mid-ocean a new passenger arrived. Oceanus Hopkins was born while the Mayflower was plowing its way through white-capped waves toward the promised land. Everybody was excited over this event, and Captain Jones offered the best of everything for the occasion.

[ 51 ]

And then, that "lustie yonge man", Jack Howland, lost his dignity (and nearly his life) by falling overboard, but was saved from drowning, much to the unexpressed satisfaction of the bright-eyed lass, Libby Tillie, who was looking on anxiously at the performance.

At last, after many weary weeks on the ocean, the Mayflower anchored in the snug little Cape Cod Harbor, and the children, during the next five weeks, although almost within a stone's throw of shore, had to remain on the ship while their elders were exploring the adjacent territory.

And then came the excitement of the short voyage of the Mayflower across the Bay. There were many features of mystery to the children about this move.

Christmas time is always a period of anticipation to children, and it was a typical New England day on December 26, 1620 (N.S.), that the Mayflower finally ended its memorable voyage and dropped anchor in Plymouth Harbor off New Plymouth.

The day was cold, but nevertheless, we can imagine those lively boys, Bart Allerton, Giles Hopkins, the Billington boys, John and Francis, Jack Cooke, the Dutch boy, Resolved White, Joe Rogers, Jack Crackston, Sam Fuller, Dick More and Bill Latham perched on top of deckhouses and other points of vantage in order to get good views of their future home.

They were mighty anxious to set foot on land, where they could start some explorations of their own. Their elders seemed so slow.

During the voyage, some of the men, including the sailors, had fired their imaginations with stories of adventure, and here they were right in the midst of everything. No wonder they were excited.

The girls, Remember and Mary Allerton, Constance and Damaris Hopkins, Mary Chilton, Ellen More, and Desire Minter, were clustered in a little group on deck, discussing ways and means to get things cleaned up a bit. Seventy days and more cooped up in the cramped quarters of the Mayflower had forced the girls to neglect many important matters, such as the washing of apparel and the like.

They were also, in the ancient manner of girls, making some sly digs at a couple of rather conspicuous pairs, totally oblivious to their surroundings, but plainly visible in distant parts of the deck.

Mary Chilton, one of the liveliest of the group, whispers confidentially to the girls:

"There's Jack Alden holding Pris Mullins' hand. He was hired as a cooper in Southampton, but hasn't done a barrel head of work since he boarded the ship."

The girls laughed at this sally of Mary's, for she had tried to get a little attention from Jack on her own account but with no success.

Constance Hopkins, in her quiet way, remarks:

"Well, Mary, thou hast a sharp tongue, but Pris and Jack Alden are not the only pair of love-birds on this ship. If you want to locate Libby Tillie, all you have to do is to find Jack Howland."

However, the young people were to be keenly disappointed so far as early forsaking the ship was concerned. The Mayflower lay at anchor in Plymouth Harbor until the following April, and meanwhile Captain Jones permitted the ship to be used as living quarters, until the men of the party could provide the Plantation with suitable shelter.

From the list of young people given below some interesting facts are disclosed. Humility Cooper and Desire Minter returned to friends in England. Humility was a kinswoman to Edward Tillie. She died in England after 1627. Desire Minter died in England before 1651. William Latham returned to England, then went to the Bahama Islands where he died between November 7, 1645, and March 6, 1651. Bartholomew Allerton returned to England and became a minister. They were children of destiny in the great drama.

Twelve of the children died young, most of them in the first sickness.

However, seventeen of them married and brought up 133 children, a record seldom surpassed.

It can be stated that, with the exception of the first winter, the health of the New Plymouth Colony was excellent and the children thrived.

### Young People Under Twenty Years on the Mayflower

#### CHILDREN OF PASSENGERS

1. Love Brewster b. (?) 1601 m. Sarah Collier (see Fam. No. 11) 4 ch.
2. Wrestling Brewster b. (?) 1600 unmarried.
3. Bartholomew Allerton b. (?) 1612, returned to England.
4. Remember Allerton b. (?) 1613 m. Moses Maverick (see Fam. No. 43) 7 ch.
5. Mary Allerton b. (?) 1616 m. Thomas Cushman (see Fam. No. 43) 8 ch.
6. Constanta Hopkins b. (?) 1605 m. Nicholas Snow (see Fam. No. 2) 12 ch.
7. Giles Hopkins b. (?) 1607 m. Catone Welden (see Fam. No. 3) 10 ch.
8. Damaris Hopkins b. (?) 1618 d. soon after 1627.
9. Oceanus Hopkins b. 1620 at sea d. before 1627.
10. Resolved White b. (?) 1616 m. 1st Judith Vassal m. 2nd wid. Abigail Lord (see Fam. No. 336) 8 ch.
11. Peregrine White b. 1620 on Mayflower m. Sarah Bassett (see Fam. No. 336) 6 ch.
12. Joseph Mullins b. (?) 1600 d. 1st year.
13. Prescilla Mullins b. (?) 1601 m. John Alden (see Fam. No. 1094) 11 ch.

14. John Billinton b. (?) 1604 d. soon after 1627.
15. Francis Billington b. (?) 1606 m. Christian Penn wid. of Francis Eaton (see Fam. No. 860) 9 ch.
16. Samuel Eaton b. (?) 1618 m. 1st Elizabeth m. 2nd Martha Billington (see Fam. No. 1105) 3 ch.
17. Joseph Rogers b. (?) 1607 m. Hannah (see Fam. No. 17) 8 ch.
18. John Cooke b. (?) 1612 m. Sarah Warren (see Fam. No. 8) 6 ch.
19. John Crackston, jr., b. (?) 1608 d. 1626 (?)
20. Samuel Fuller b. (?) 1612 m. Jane Lathrop (see Fam. No. 186) 9 ch.
21. Elizabeth Tillie b. (?) 1606 m. John Howland (see Fam. No. 220) 10 ch.
22. Mary Chilton b. (?) 1608 m. John Winslow (see Fam. No. 183) 10 ch.
23. (son) Tinker d. 1st year.
24. (son) Turner d. 1st year.
25. (son) Turner d. 1st year.

### RELATED TO EDWARD TILLIE

26. Humility Cooper b. (?) 1605, returned to England.
27. Henry Samson b. (?) 1608 m. Ann Plummer (see Fam. No. 187) 8 ch.

### UNRELATED

28. Desire Minter b. (?) 1600, returned to England.
29. William Latham "a boy". Removed from Plymouth.
30. Solomon Prower d. 1st year.
31. Richard More b. Nov. 13, 1614 (see Fam. No. 928) 4 ch.
32. Ellen More b. May 24, 1612 d. 1st year.
33. Jasper More b. Aug. 8, 1613 d. 1st year.
34. (son) More b. (?) d. 1st yr.

Refs. No. 59, 60, 61.

# WOMEN OF THE MAYFLOWER

The passenger list of the Mayflower was remarkable in many directions, but none more so than in the fact that twenty-nine out of a total of 104 were matrons, maidens and girls, all comparatively young and well born.

Among these were eighteen wives, worthy aids of adventurous husbands. It is true that none of the women signed the "Compact". Not being modern they probably had no thought or desire to add their names to the document. The men in those times were still heads of families in fact as well as in name.

As a matter of fact, the women of the Mayflower had just as important things to consider and do as that of signing a piece of paper. They were all efficient and cheerful home-makers, but the long voyage of sixty-five days cooped up in a small, poorly equipped and ventilated ship had taxed their strength and abilities to keep husbands and children healthy.

So far as possible during the voyage, each family (including certain unattached passengers "put in" the group by Mr. Weston or others) were supposed to prepare their own meals and maintain healthy conditions around the living quarters. These "put in" persons were not "servants" to the family, as the term is now understood, but they were there for purposes of mess and other business reasons clearly suggested by the terms of the agreement under which the Mayflower Planters were sailing.

It is feared that Bradford's use of the word "servant" has been greatly misinterpreted. Martin, Hopkins and Mullins may have brought their men with them, but apparently, the placements were made just before leaving Plymouth, or perhaps in some instances they were "put in" the various families during the voyage.

The crew had their own cook and mess. No doubt some of the fifteen single men listed among the passengers had meals with the crew, they, for the most part, being hired men, seamen and the like.

The turning back of the Speedwell resulted in a serious disruption of plans on board the Mayflower. Certain of the Leyden people shifted from the Speedwell to the Mayflower, resulting in overcrowding, and it was decided by Mr. Weston, apparently, to divide most of the twenty unattached persons among the Leyden group, according to their ability to take care of them with food and other services incidental to living on the voyage.

A few of the matrons had vivid memories of the ordeal they experienced in fleeing from England to Holland in 1609, especially Mrs. Brewster, who remembered "their little ones hanging about them and quaking with cold".

[ 55 ]

It seems that fourteen of the unattached persons on the Mayflower were placed in the families of Mrs. Carver (6), Mrs. Brewster (2), Mrs. Winslow (3), Mrs. Allerton (1) and Mrs. White (2), the other six were in the families of Dr. Fuller (1), Mrs. Hopkins (2), Mrs. Mullins (1), and Mrs. Martin (2).

While the ship was anchored in Cape Cod Harbor, and the men were foraging and exploring the adjacent territory preliminary to establishing permanent abodes on land, the women made the vessel as homelike as possible, and attended to the many important duties of wives and mothers. The children must have caused some trouble from time to time.

On December 17, 1620 (N.S.), a few days before removal to Plymouth Harbor across the Bay, Mrs. Dorothy Bradford was accidentally drowned. This was a sad event among the eighteen matrons, who had become closely attached to each other by many common hardships.

Practically from the time the Mayflower dropped anchor in Plymouth Harbor off New Plymouth on December 26, 1620 (N.S.), to the following spring, sickness and death prevailed among the matrons and their families.

Much of this sickness was probably due to lack of familiarity with the climatic conditions of New England, and attacks of scurvy caused by eating improper foods, such as too much fish, which were plentiful. At that time of year fresh vegetables and other essential foods were scarce, and they had not learned to obtain food from the Indians.

Mrs. Elizabeth Hopkins, Mrs. Mary Brewster, Mrs. Sussana White and Mrs. Ellen Billington were the only matrons to survive the winter, and they led important lives in the little colony for a number of years.

Mrs. Elizabeth Hopkins shared with Mistress White the honor of having a son born on the Mayflower. They named him Oceanus from his birthplace. She was Stephen Hopkins' second wife, and cooperated with him splendidly in the management of a large family, and an extensive estate, including servants and many cattle.

It appears that Mr. Hopkins had a number of interests including that of being proprietor of the general store and tavern, and being of a fearless and rather testy disposition, he became involved in a number of fist fights and court actions. These may have worried Mrs. Hopkins, but Stephen seems to have enjoyed them.

In his home and church life Stephen was exemplary, and he and Mrs. Hopkins brought up a fine family, and lived to see many grandchildren.

Mrs. Mary Brewster was something of a "mother" to the group of young matrons. She shared the religious faith of her husband, and cast a strong moral influence upon the women and children. She was only fifty-seven years old when she died in April, 1627, after several years of illness. Bradford says of her in appreciation,

"Her great and continuall labours with other crosses and sorrows, hastened it before ye time."

Her husband had a large library of 400 books, including sixty-four Latin texts, and her last years may have been spent browsing among these treasures.

Mrs. Sussana White was left a widow in the first sickness with two young boys, one a baby, Peregrine, born on the Mayflower. However, she was not a widow for long. To the women of the community the marriage of Mistress White to Edward Winslow on May 22, 1621, must have been a gala event. Elizabeth Barber Winslow had died only about seven weeks before. However, the marriage was quite natural under the circumstances of the place and times. In social position and worldly comforts her life became pre-eminent among the colonists. Although Edward Winslow had renounced some English wealth when he went to Holland and adopted the trade of printer, he "came into his own" again, and was in high favor with English Courts. He became agent and commissioner for Plymouth, and later for Cromwell.

Meanwhile Mrs. Sussana Winslow remained at Careswell, the estate at Green Harbor, Marshfield, with her young children. She was of graceful, aristocratic bearing, and of strong character. She was a sister of Dr. Samuel Fuller. It is thought she is buried near her estate in Marshfield, where she died October, 1680.

Mrs. Ellen Billington had more than her share of difficulties in the colony. Her husband, John Billington, was hung for killing John Newcomen in 1630, and she was accused of slandering Dea. John Doane, and sentenced to a fine of five pounds, and to "sit in the stocks and be publickly whipt". Apparently, Helen had many troubles and little sympathy in New Plymouth. The part she carried in this drama is not inviting but it is important.

The seven daughters were a remarkable group of girls. That they were healthy is self-evident. None of the seven died during that terrible first year. The record speaks for itself:

1. Mary Allerton m. Thomas Cushman. 8 ch.
2. Remember Allerton m. Moses Maverick. 7 ch.
3. Damaris Hopkins d. unmarried about 1627.
4. Constanta Hopkins m. Nicholas Snow. 12 ch.
5. Prescilla Mullins m. John Alden. 11 ch.
6. Elizabeth Tillie m. John Howland. 10 ch.
7. Mary Chilton m. John Winslow. 10 ch.

From the above it is seen that six of these girls married and had fifty-eight children. There were no "clinging vines" here. They were great home-makers, and cooperated with their husbands so well that their families were held in the highest esteem.

Constance, Prescilla, Elizabeth and Mary Chilton were old enough to have been of aid to their mothers on the Mayflower and in the early days of the New Plymouth Plantation.

Prescilla Mullins, Mary Chilton and Elizabeth Tillie became orphans during the first year of hardship, and members, for a time, of the households of Elder Brewster and Governor Carver.

Mary Allerton was one of the youngest of the seven girls. She was about ten years old when the Pilgrims landed at Plymouth, and spent her girlhood in Plymouth with other children of the new settlement.

Among her little boy friends was Thomas Cushman who had been brought to New Plymouth by his father on the Fortune in 1621. The father, Robert Cushman, returned to England on the ship, in order to report to the Merchant Adventurers in London regarding the state of affairs in the colony. He expected to return, and left his small son Thomas in charge of Governor Bradford.

However, sickness and death removed Robert Cushman from the scene, and Thomas was carefully reared by Governor Bradford.

Mary Allerton and Thomas Cushman grew up together in the stern puritanical atmosphere of New Plymouth. Friendship ripened into love and about the year 1635 they were married.

At the time of marriage they were well along in their twenties. However it was a perfect union. They lived together for fifty-five years. She survived him seven or eight years and died at the advanced age of ninety years. She is famous as the last survivor of the Mayflower passengers, dying about 1699. She was a worthy companion to her husband who was the Ruling Elder of the Plymouth Church, and a man of note. They had eight children.

Remember Allerton was very young on landing at New Plymouth, and like her sister, grew up with the community. A youngster named Moses Maverick came to Boston with his father about 1630, and it was not long before Moses and Remember met and fell in love. They were married about 1633. Mr. Maverick became a prominent man in Marblehead, Mass., where he resided for many years. His wife and he brought up a large family of children. His father-in-law, Isaac Allerton, also resided in Marblehead for some time.

Constanta Hopkins was about the same age as Elizabeth Tillie. She was a very active, efficient girl on the Mayflower and in New Plymouth. Family tradition has honored the memory of Constance. Beauty and patience has been ascribed to her by numerous writers.

A promising young man, Nicholas Snow, arrived in New Plymouth in 1623. He came in the "Anne" from Haxton, Middlesex County, England.

Constanta (Constance) married Nicholas before 1627, and built up a wonderful home and had a family of twelve children. In 1644 they removed to Eastham, Cape Cod, where the family continued to prosper. Nicholas Snow held the office of Town Clerk in Eastham for sixteen years. He was one of Governor Prence's closest associates.

Prescilla Mullins was the daughter of William Mullins, a wealthy merchant. He was a member of the Adventurers, and owned some stock in the enterprise. His death in the first sickness was a blow to the community. Just before he died he sent for Carver, and made a verbal will, which was taken down and carried to England by the Mayflower on its return voyage in April, 1621.

Prescilla was self-reliant, good to look at, and above all a skilful cook. It is not surprising that she should have taken to John Alden who "being a hopeful young man was much desired".

The story of John Alden and Prescilla can never grow old.

Their first house was at "Towne Square" in Plymouth on the site of the first school house, but by 1633 they were living upon a farm of 169 acres in Duxbury. Their first house here was about 300 feet from the present Alden house, which was built by the son, Jonathan.

Eleven children were born to them, five sons and six daughters.

John Alden "became low in his estate" because "he hath been occationed to spend time at the courts on the countryes occasion and soe hath done this many years".

In those days public servants were not paid out of taxpayers' money, to any extent. Our forefathers held to the idea that the State owed no man a living.

Elizabeth Tillie, one of the orphans of the first sickness, was the daughter of John Tillie, who must have been a man of some means. He was a close friend of Thomas Weston, and was a brother of Edward Tillie. Both of the Tillies died in the first year.

Elizabeth was of a quiet nature, nevertheless she was the only one of the seven girls who could write her own name, and in a good hand.

When her father died she was placed in the family of John Carver. He soon died, leaving the family group in charge of John Howland, or at least he assumed charge. John had been "put" in previously. On the arrival of Elizabeth in the group, the romance started right in where it had left off on the Mayflower, and the marriage of Libby Tillie to Jack Howland was celebrated about 1624.

The mother of Elizabeth was, perhaps, Bridget Van de Veldt, of Holland.

There is some evidence to indicate that John Howland was well educated. Both he and his wife were good penmen. He performed this service for many in the colony, and became prominent in numerous directions. Some writers state that he was connected with one "John Howland, Gentleman and Citizen" of London.

Mary Chilton was a lively personality. It is said she was the first woman to set foot on the Plymouth Rock. Her father was a Merchant Tailor "Freeman by Gift 1583" of the City of Canterbury, England. He was a Separatist and embarked on the Mayflower, but died during the first winter on December 8, 1620. His wife soon followed him in death, leaving Mary an orphan.

[ 59 ]

However, romance was "just around the corner" for Mary. The ship Fortune in 1621 brought her future husband, John Winslow, and they were married about 1627.

They resided at first in Plymouth, but John Winslow had visions of greater success, probably encouraged by the vivacious Mary, and they moved to Boston where he became a wealthy owner and master of merchant ships. The will of John Winslow of Boston was probated May 21, 1674, and names a very large and interesting estate.

And thus it developed, like a story from fairyland, that Mary lived a life of luxury after her hard Mayflower experience.

She also left a will of great interest, bequeathing among other things "my Best Gowne and Pettecoat and my silver beare bowl", a "silver cup with a handle", "great silver Tankard", "rugs", "my Pretty Coate with the silver Lace".

Mary (Chilton) Winslow is buried beneath the Winslow Coat-of-Arms at the front of Kings Chapel Burial Ground in Boston, a fitting resting place for a most romantic life.

Brief mention of the four unattached girls should be made. They too, were of good families, and one of them experienced one exciting adventure after another.

Desire Minter lived in the family of Governor Carver while at New Plymouth, and became a close friend of Elizabeth (Tillie) Howland. The hardships of the voyage and the New England winter undermined Desire's health and she returned to her friends in England. However, on the return voyage the ship was captured by the French, and she was held a captive for some time, which certainly was a dramatic climax to a life of adventure for any young lady. Finally, she reached her old home in England, only to die within a few years unmarried.

Desire could have written a wonderful story of her experiences on the high seas, in the colonies, in naval battles, and languishing in French prisons. The background was perfect for a moving drama.

Her old friend, Elizabeth, in far off New Plymouth, however, memorialized her name, by giving the name Desire to one of her own children.

Humility Cooper was a "cossen" to Edward Tillie, brother of John Tillie, and these brothers were friends of Mr. Weston, manager of the Mayflower enterprise for the Merchant Adventurers. According to some records Humility was closely related to the English family of Cloptons, one of whom was a cousin to Gov. John Winthrop. She returned to her friends in England and never married.

The four More children seem to have come under the special care of Thomas Weston. They were children of Samuel More of Shipton, Shropshire, England, and his wife Katherine. The Parish Register heads this family with the word "Generosus", meaning

[ 60 ]

noble birth. Ellen More was born May 24, 1612, so that she was about eight years old when she died in the first sickness.

The remaining unattached woman was the so-called "maid-servant" in John Carver's family. Bradford evidently did not remember her name.

## Women of the Mayflower

### WIVES

1. Mrs. Elizabeth Hopkins d. bet. 1640-44.
2. Mrs. Mary Brewster d. Apr. 27, 1627.
3. Mrs. Sussana White m. Gov. Edward Winslow.
4. Mrs. Hellen Billington m. Gregory Armstrong.

### DIED FIRST YEAR

5. Mrs. Christopher Martin.
6. Mrs. William Mullins.
7. Mrs. Rose Standish.
8. Mrs. Mary Allerton.
9. Mrs. Katherine Carver.
10. Mrs. Dorothy Bradford.
11. Mrs. Elizabeth Winslow.
12. Mrs. Ann Tillie.
13. Mrs. John Tillie.
14. Mrs. Thomas Tinker.
15. Mrs. Alice Rigdale.
16. Mrs. James Chilton.
17. Mrs. Edward Fuller.
18. Mrs. Sarah Eaton.

### DAUGHTERS

19. Mary Allerton.
20. Remember Allerton.
21. Damaris Hopkins.
22. Constanta Hopkins.
23. Prescilla Mullins.
24. Elizabeth Tillie.
25. Mary Chilton.

### UNATTACHED

26. Humility Cooper, returned to Eng.
27. Desire Minter, returned to Eng.
28. Ellen More d. 1st year.
29. "Maidservant", unidentified, perhaps m. Francis Eaton.

Ref. Nos. 21, 26, 33, 50, 60, 61, 97.

## VOYAGE OF THE MAYFLOWER

On Saturday, July 25, 1620 (N.S.), the Mayflower really started on its memorable voyage, weighing anchor probably off "Blackhall" or "Wapping", London, and dropping down the Thames with the tide to Gravesend.

Master Robert Cushman, London agent of the Leyden Company, and Master Christopher Martin, Treasurer agent of the Merchant Adventurers, who were backing the voyage, had come aboard at London, with about sixty other passengers. Christopher Martin had also been appointed Governor of the Mayflower.

As usual the channel pilot was taken aboard at Gravesend, and on July 29, 1620 (N.S.), the ship anchored, probably off the north end of the West Quay at Southampton.

Masters Carver, Cushman and Martin were busy for some time outfitting the ship, taking on provisions and the like.

The Leyden people had sold their possessions in order to provide Cushman with means to provision the ship, and he apparently had been quite free with the funds, especially in view of the fact that the "Londoners" seemingly consumed most of the provisions during the long delay at Southampton, and before the arrival of the Speedwell, so that the Leyden group found themselves in a difficult position.

Carver, although supposed to have been acting for the Leyden people, does not appear to have been very active in the matter.

On Wednesday, August 5, 1620 (N.S.), the "pinnace" Speedwell, Master Reynolds from Delfshaven, Holland, arrived at Southampton and anchored near the Mayflower. The larger ship transferred to the Speedwell some provisions, and certain passengers were shifted.

A great deal of dissatisfaction developed. The Leyden contingent felt that their funds had not been fairly spent, and that the "Londoners" were taking unfair advantage of them.

Master Christopher Martin was the "Governor" of the Mayflower and Robert Cushman, Assistant.

The Mayflower was ready to depart on August 8, 1620 (N.S.), but had to postpone the sailing on account of the leaky Speedwell. The larger boat now had about ninety passengers, and the Speedwell thirty.

On August 12, 1620 (N.S.), Thomas Weston came up from London. He represented the Merchant Adventurers, who were sponsoring the voyage. They stood to lose financially unless matters could be straightened out. He brought some new conditions, assented to by Cushman, but the Leyden leaders would not agree to them.

It was felt the conditions were "more fit for thieves and slaves than for honest men". Weston took offence and almost called the

[ 62 ]

voyage off, so far as the Leyden people were concerned, saying, that they could now "stand on their own legs", and he returned to London.

On Thursday, August 13, 1620 (N.S.), the Leyden Planters held a meeting and resolved to sell some stores to clear port charges, and to write a letter to the Adventurers explaining matters. The matter of agreement and subscribing thereto became quite involved, and it is not clear that one was signed by the Leyden group before the departure.

The Mayflower and Speedwell finally departed from Southampton on August 15, 1620 (N.S.), dropping down to "Southampton Water", and then from Cowes, Isle of Wight, started out in earnest on the great adventure. For several days the ships continued to beat down the channel. On August 20th, the Speedwell was found to be leaking badly, and the ships were forced back to Dartmouth where they anchored August 22nd.

No passengers were allowed ashore. Cushman states in a letter, "Will not suffer them (the passengers) to go ashore lest they should run away".

Other difficulties multiplied. It seems that differences arose between Mr. Christopher Martin of Billerike, Essex Co., Eng., who had been chosen to act with Carver and Cushman in receiving money and making provision for the voyage in England. Bradford states:

"his name was Mr. Martin, he came from Billerike, in Essex, from which parts sundrie others to goe with them, as also from London and other places, and therefore, it was thought meete and conveniente by them in Holland that these strangers that were to goe with them, should apointe one of them to be joyned with them, not so much for any great need of their help as to avoyd all susspition or jelosie."

Of course, Bradford wrote these words long after the event, about the year 1650. However, it is difficult to excuse the inference that the Holland group controlled the situation. As a matter of fact the voyage was being sponsored by the Merchant Adventurers of London under management of Thomas Weston, and Mr. Christopher Martin was a direct appointee of them, while Carver and Cushman were supposed to represent the Leyden people, but were in reality completely under the control of the Adventurers, as the records clearly show. It is unfortunate that Martin died in the first sickness, and that Carver soon followed him, while Cushman became a direct representative of the Adventurers.

Considering the fact that the Speedwell failed entirely, and that the Leyden people had to fall back on the generosity of the Mayflower "strangers", Bradford's statement that "these strangers that were to goe with them, should apointe one of them to be joyned with them" must, at least, be considered somewhat naive.

[ 63 ]

The situation of the Leyden group was desperate, owing to the unseaworthy Speedwell. Robert Cushman, writing to his friend Edward Southworth at Heniage House in Dukes Place, London, August 17, 1620, from Dartmouth, when the Speedwell had put back, says:

"and I thinke, as others also, if we had stayed at sea bot .3. or .4. howers more, shee would have sunke right downe."

The Mayflower was laid up at Dartmouth several days while the Speedwell was being overhauled. At last on September 2, 1620 (N.S.), the two ships departed from Dartmouth. On September 5, 1620 (N.S.), when about 100 leagues W.S.W. of Land's End, the Speedwell signaled "Leaking dangerously", and it was decided to put back to Plymouth. The Mayflower and Speedwell anchored in the Catwater, Plymouth, England, on September 7, 1620 (N.S.).

After some discussion it was decided to send the Speedwell back to London with eighteen or twenty passengers. Master Robert Cushman and family with others went back with the ship which sailed September 12, 1620 (N.S.).

The Mayflower was now prepared for departure. Quarters were assigned, and possibly at this time the various unattached persons were "put" in the different family groups for "mess" and the like. The families prepared their own food. Much of it they brought themselves. The ship had only one "cook", and he attended to the feeding of the crew only.

On September 16, 1620 (N.S.), the Mayflower departed from Plymouth, England. A good breeze E.N.E. started the ship on its memorable voyage, and in fact "carried them half way over the ocean".

A seaman died on October 3rd (N.S.) and was buried at sea with the usual ceremony. Soon after this a severe westerly gale arose, and then fierce storms were encountered. The Mayflower was tossed about like a floating toy boat, and that is what it really was in comparison to modern (1936) ships. A main beam in midships was bowed and cracked. For a time Captain Jones feared serious disaster, and was tempted to turn back. He consulted with the leaders of the voyage, and it was decided to continue on. There were a series of these storms during which time the ship drifted under "bare poles".

The thirty-four young people on the Mayflower must have had many conferences of their own, especially the older boys and girls, about the progress of the ship, which certainly was traveling very slowly toward "Virginia".

It never has been made quite clear why the Mayflower consumed sixty-five days in going to the colonies, and only thirty days to return.

When John Howland was washed overboard, in one of the fiercest storms, he saved himself by catching hold of a "topsail halliard", which hung over the sides. It ran out at length, yet he held on, even though "sundry fathoms under water", till he was hauled back on board with a boat hook.

The arrival in mid-ocean of a new passenger, Oceanus Hopkins, was, of course, a matter of great importance, and he was the center of interest, especially among the matrons, for the remainder of the voyage.

The distance from Plymouth, England, or from the entrance of the English Channel to Cape Cod is 2750 miles, and allowing another 250 miles for zigzagging against contrary winds, it can be stated that the Mayflower traveled 3000 miles from land to land.

The voyage took sixty-five days, an average of about forty-six miles per day, or somewhat less than two miles per hour. This was very slow indeed, especially in view of the fact that the ship made over four miles per hour on the return trip.

However, she was heavily loaded, and her hull was probably encrusted with grass and barnacles.

During the last half of the voyage, it was necessary to ease up on the ship every time the wind breezed up, and it was the season for the driving "westerlies".

Although the flow of the Gulf stream was unknown to Captain Jones at the time, yet he was, unknowingly, bucking that powerful current, and it is a wonder that the ship ever reached Cape Cod.

On November 16, 1620 (N.S.), William Button died and was buried at sea.

Two days after this sad event floating objects were observed which indicated that land was not far away.

On November 20 1620 (N.S.), Cape Cod was sighted, and the historic voyage was nearing its end.

Another act in the great drama had been completed.

---

Ref. Nos. 1, 2, 3, 4, 6, 11, 20, 21, 24, 25.

# THE LANDING

It was Wednesday, November 18, 1620 (N.S.), more than sixty days out from the shores of old England, and the Mayflower was doggedly driving through a choppy sea in the direction of New Plymouth.

It is not difficult to imagine that some of the boys, restless at being cooped up below decks, had braved the cold stiff November breeze of the north Atlantic and were wandering around the deck, hoping for something worthwhile to turn up. Giles Hopkins, Joe Rogers, and Jack Cooke were clustered together on the foredeck, acting as self-appointed "lookouts", when suddenly Giles, jumping up and down with excitement, shouted:

"Look fellows, there is a branch of a tree with leaves on it, we must be nearing Land."

And, sure enough by nightfall on Thursday, November 19, 1620 (N.S.), the good ship Mayflower was closing in with land, and on Friday, November 20, 1620, the boys were up with the rising sun to witness the view of the "promised land", after sixty-five days out from England, and over 115 days out of London.

Land being within sight, a conference of the leaders on the Mayflower was immediately called. It was not altogether harmonious. There was much "disaffection" among the Planters on account of the apparent abandonment of the location for settlement of the territory under the protection of the patent granted in their interest to John Peirce (Merchant Adventurer), by the London Virginia Co. Bradford states "observing some not well affected to unity and accord but gave some appearance of faction, it was thought good there should be an association and agreement".

The result of all this argument was that the ship tacked about and took a course "south-southwest", planning to go to a river ten leagues to the south of the Cape (Hudson), but after one-half a day, the ship fell among dangerous shoals, and at night, the wind being contrary, the ship tacked around again for Cape Cod Bay, and anchored in Cape Cod Harbor on November 21, 1620 (N.S.) (Saturday).

There was great rejoicing among all on board, and excitement prevailed among the children on seeing such a fine country, "wooded to the brink of the sea". There were "oaks, pines, juniper, sassafrass" trees clearly visible from the ship.

This day, Saturday, November 21, 1620 (N.S.) (November 11th O.S.), must be considered, always, as one of greatest historical significance. The Mayflower anchored within half a mile (or "furlong") of the end of Long Point, two miles from the present village of Provincetown (see Map).

[ 66 ]

The Pilgrims brought with them a little "shallop", of about fifteen tons, which had been stored between decks. However, it had been used as sleeping quarters on the voyage, and had become leaky, so that it had to be taken on the beach, repaired and caulked before using, a matter of two weeks or more.

However, members of the company waded ashore, although it was freezing cold weather, and obtained wood and water. A great many fowl were seen, also some whales in the Bay. Captain Jones said he could have made three or four thousand pounds by obtaining the whale oil, and that he intended to return for such a purpose.

Some of the company tried to catch fish but had no luck. They found plenty of "mucles", but for some reason they made all who ate them ill.

The fifteen or sixteen men who were sent ashore, well armed, returned at night with "juniper" (red cedar) wood for fuel.

Meanwhile, a most momentous proceeding was taking place in the cabin of the Mayflower. A "Compact" had been framed and was being signed by the men of the company.

The events leading up to this "Compact" clearly show that the Mayflower Planters were thoroughly aware that they had "voided" the patent under which they had sailed, by landing in the "Northerly" Colony of Virginia, instead of the "Southerly", and the "Compact" was, no doubt, an attempt to frame a suitable substitute under which they could live without serious difficulties with the authorities.

It is not clear where Nathaniel Morton, in 1669, obtained the list of "Signers". The arrangement of names does not indicate the true precedence of authority as it existed on the Mayflower when the "Compact" was being discussed. At that time the Merchant Adventurers, through Mr. Christopher Martin, were still in control of the situation, and he was apparently backed up in his opposition for a time by other "Londoners" such as Stephen Hopkins, William Mullins and others. Of course, they were rather reluctant to sign, but finally subscribed to the document. Most of the reluctant and tardy signers died in the first year, which brought about a complete change of leadership.

In all probability the Planters were as one so far as religious doctrines were concerned. They were all Separatists of one degree or another. From a hard-headed business point of view, however, there was a cleavage on the ship between the "Adventurers" and the Leyden group.

It is a significant fact that the first five signers (as given by Morton in 1669), are of Leyden, and they probably boarded the Mayflower after the Speedwell was abandoned.

There must have been a great argument concerning the wording of the "Compact", and it is a wonder that Martin, Mullins, Hopkins, Warren, Tillie and some others ever signed it.

Some writers have unduly stressed the precedence of names in this list. Obviously, the Leyden Planters had put the least cash into the proposition, and may have signed first. Martin, and his friends, standing to lose financially, hesitated, and signed later.

One of the big arguments on this "Compact" would appear to center around the phrase "Having undertaken . . . . a voyage to plant ye first colonie in ye Northern parts of Virginia".

In one sense this is not correct, as the voyage under their voided patent was to plant a settlement in "Southerly" Virginia, as we have shown.

However, irrespective of how it came about, the "Compact" is worthy of the high place it holds in history, and is a firm foundation stone for any government.

Following is a literal copy of the "Compact" taken from Bradford's "History of Plimouth Plantation" written about the year 1650. William Bradford was one of the signers of this immortal document. It is possible that the original may have found its way back to England.

### The Remainder of Ano: 1620

"I shall a little returne back, and begine with a combination made by them before they came ashore; being ye first foundation of their governmente in this place. Occassioned partly by ye discontented, and mutinous speeches that some of the strngers amongst them, had let fall from them in ye ship: that when they came ashore they would use their owne libertie: for none had power to command them, the patents they had being for Virginia, and not for New England, which belonged to another government with which ye Virginia Company had nothing to doe. And partly that shuch an Acte by them done (this their condition considered) might be as firme as any patent: and in some respects more sure.

The forme was as followeth:"—

"IN YE NAME OF GOD AMEN. We whose names are underwritten, the loyall subjects of our dread soveraigne lord King James, by the grace of God, of great Britaine, Franc & Ireland King, defender of ye faithe etc; Having undertaken, for ye glory of God, and advancemente of ye christian faith and honor of our king & country, a voyage to plant ye first colonie in ye Northern parts of Virginia. Doe by these presents solemnly & mutually in ye presence of God, and one another, covenant & combine our selves together into a civill body politick: for our better odering & preservation & furtherance of ye ends aforesaid: and by vertue hearof to enacte, constitute, and frame shuch just & equall laws, ordinances, Acts, constitutions, & offices from time to time, as shall be thought most meete & convenient for ye general good of ye Colonie: unto which we promise all due submission and obedience. In witness whereof we have hereunder, subscribed our names at Cap-Codd ye .11. of November, in ye year of ye raign of our Soveraigne lord

[ 68 ]

king James of England, France, & Ireland ye eightteenth, and of Scotland ye fiftie fourth.  Ano: Dom: 1620"

## Signers of the Compact

The signers were not in Bradford's History.  The earliest list is found in Nathaniel Morton's (see Fam. No. 206) "New England's Memorial", published 1669.  In the first edition of that work the names are arranged in the order given here.  Three columns of seven names each at the bottom of the page, and the others in three columns at the top of the next page.  The line dividing the columns in the list indicates the bottom of the page in the "Memorial".

| | | |
|---|---|---|
| *JOHN CARVER | SAMUEL FULLER | *EDWARD TILLEY |
| WILLIAM BRADFORD | *CHRISTOPHER MARTIN | *JOHN TILLIE |
| EDWARD WINSLOW | *WILLIAM MULLINS | FRANCIS COOKE |
| WILLIAM BREWSTER | *WILLIAM WHITE | *THOMAS ROGERS |
| ISAAC ALLERTON | RICHARD WARREN | *THOMAS TINKER |
| MYLES STANDISH | JOHN HOWLAND | *JOHN RIGDALE |
| JOHN ALDEN | STEPHEN HOPKINS | *EDWARD FULLER |
| *JOHN TURNER | *DEGORY PRIEST | *RICHARD CLARKE |
| FRANCIS EATON | *THOMAS WILLIAMS | RICHARD GARDINER |
| *JAMES CHILTON | GILBERT WINSLOW | *JOHN ALLERTON |
| *JOHN CRAKSTON | *EDMUND MARGESON | *THOMAS ENGLISH |
| JOHN BILLINGTON | PETER BROWN | EDWARD DOTY |
| *MOSES FLETCHER | *RICHARD BRITTERIDGE | EDWARD LEISTER |
| *JOHN GOODMAN | GEORGE SOULE | |

*Died first year.

There were forty-one signers.  The survivors of the first year of hardship were:

> William Bradford (see Fam. No. 926)
> Edward Winslow (see Fam. No. 183)
> William Brewster (see Fam. No. 11)
> Isaac Allerton (see Fam. No. 43)
> Myles Standish (see Fam. No. 184)
> John Alden (see Fam. No. 1094)
> Samuel Fuller (see Fam. No. 186)
> Richard Warren (see Fam. No. 1007)
> John Howland (see Fam. No. 220)
> Stephen Hopkins (see Fam. No. 1)
> Francis Cooke (see Fam No. 8)
> Francis Eaton (see Fam. No. 1105)
> John Billington (see Fam. No. 860)
> Gilbert Winslow (see Fam. No. 183)
> Peter Brown (see Fam. No. 196)
> George Soule (see Fam. No. 1140)
> Richard Gardiner (returned to England)

[ 69 ]

Edward Doty (see Fam. No. 39)
Edward Leister (removed to Virginia)

It is probable that the Mayflower was riding at anchor in the snug little Cape Cod Harbor off Provincetown, when the actors in this drama affixed their signatures to the "Compact".

Immediately after the signing, Mr. John Carver appears to have been "confirmed" Governor, although he was not chosen until March 23, 1621.

The next day was Sunday, November 22, 1620, the weather was mild and all hands were assembled for services.

Monday, November 23rd, the shallop was "unshipped", and parties went on shore to "wash". It was slow work to repair the shallop. Francis Eaton, the carpenter, was probably one of those working on it. Meanwhile sixteen men with "muskit, sword, and corslet" under Capt. Miles Standish, and including William Bradford, Stephen Hopkins and Edward Tillie, set out Wednesday, November 25th, on the First Expedition (see Map) of the adjacent country. They marched in single file about a mile by the sea, and saw five or six people, with a dog, coming toward them. The savages whistled for the dog, and ran into the woods. It appears that Captain Jones and some of his men were already ashore. Captain Standish's party followed the Indians until night about ten miles by footprints, and camped out for the night at Stouts Creek, set three sentinels, kindled a fire and turned in.

Next day, November 26th, the party started out from camp early and soon discovered Truro Springs, and Pamet River. No fresh water had been found. They walked through bushes which tore the "very armour in peces". About 10 A.M. in a "deep valley" they saw a deer, and found, finally, a spring of fresh water. The party drank deeply of the FIRST NEW ENGLAND WATER. They proceeded full south, and came to the shore. They made a fire to signal ship, and continued on, soon discovering a pond of fresh water, and signs of corn planting and a corn-hill together with some graves and an old kettle, also a basket of corn. They took the corn and kettle, and then found an old fort, and saw two canoes. The party then returned to camp where the night was spent. In the morning, November 27th, the kettle was thrown in the pond. The muskets had become wet, and had to be trimmed. The party became lost, and came to a tree "where a young sprit was bowed down over a bow". Stephen Hopkins said it was a trap to catch deer. William Bradford being in the rear, almost had his leg caught in it. Three days had been spent, on this First Expedition and they returned to the ship.

At last the shallop was repaired and on December 7, 1620 (N.S.), a large body of twenty-four men, making up the Second Expedition started out, with Captain Jones in command, in order to "gratify his kindness". They reached E. Harbor Creek and spent the night. On December 8th, they continued on to Pamet River, and

[ 70 ]

then inland for some distance and spent another night. The next day, December 9th, they revisited the corn-hill. Captain Jones and some others returned to the ship. Stopped over another night and next day, December 10th, found wigwams and graves, and returned to the ship that night, to find that Perigrine White had been born.

On December 14, 1620 (N.S.), Edward Thomson died. The next day, December 15th, Francis Billington "got hold of some gun powder, and shot off a peice or two, also there being a fowling peice charged in his father's cabbin, shot her off in the cabbin", "yet by God's mercy no harme done".

On Wednesday, December 16, 1620, the Third Expedition set out in the shallop. It was very cold. There were eighteen in the party under Capt. Myles Standish, including Carver, Bradford, Winslow, John Tillie, Edward Tillie, John Howland, Warren, Hopkins, Doty, John Alderton, Thomas English, Masters Coppin and Clarke the master gunner, and three sailors. (Twelve of these men were signers of the "Compact".) The party reached Eastham in the evening. The next day Thursday, December 17, 1620, the party explored up toward Wellfleet Bay, and inland. They passed the night at Great Meadow Creek. On Friday, December 18th, the party had their first encounter with the Indians. Then coasted along the cape and ran in under the lee of Clark's Island in Plymouth Harbor during a northeaster in the evening.

Although there was need for haste in locating the settlement, yet, it is recorded that on Sunday, December 20th, "wee rested".

However, Monday, December 21st, was a pleasant day, and the party "sounded the Harbor", "marched also into the land, and decided "a place very good for scituation" and "returned to our ship againe with good newes to the rest of our people, which did much comfort their hearts".

This date, December 21st, is known as FOREFATHERS' DAY, because members of the party "landed on the rock".

The shallop probably returned to the Mayflower on Tuesday, December 22nd, by sailing directly across the Bay, twenty-six miles. On Friday the Mayflower endeavored to sail across the Bay to Plymouth, but failed, and had to put back toward Cape Cod.

On Saturday, December 26, 1620 (N.S.), the Mayflower reached Plymouth Harbor, where it remained as the winter headquarters of the Pilgrims, and became the scene of many a tragedy in sickness and death during the following three months.

---

Ref. Nos. 1, 2, 3, 4, 5, 21, 24, 25, 27, 33, 38, 50, 52, 60, 61.

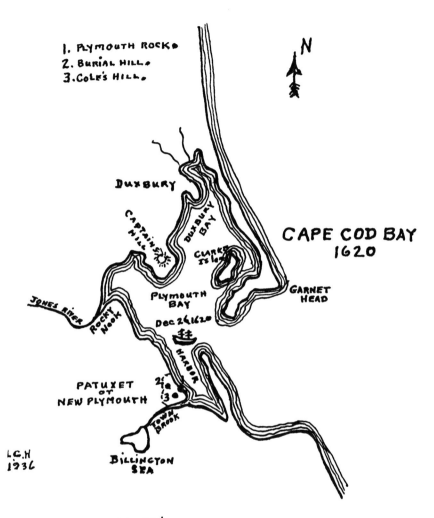

1. PLYMOUTH ROCK•
2. BURIAL HILL•
3. COLE'S HILL•

N

DUXBURY

CAPTAIN HILL

DUXBURY BAY

CLARKE IS.

CAPE COD BAY
1620

GARNET HEAD

JONES RIVER

ROCKY NOOK

PLYMOUTH BAY

Dec 26 1620

HARBOR

PATUXET
OR
NEW PLYMOUTH

2•
1•
3•

TOWN BROOK

L.C.H
1936

BILLINGTON SEA

Dec 20, 1620 N.S. 3RD EXP. SPENT SABBATH ON CLARKE ISL.

Dec 21, 1620 N.S. FOREFATHERS DAY - 3RD EXP.
LANDED ON PLYMOUTH ROCK.

Dec 25 1620 N.S. SHALLOP RETURNED TO MAYFLOWER.

Dec 26, 1620 N.S. MAYFLOWER ARRIVED PLYMOUTH HARBOR.

Mar 31, 1621 N.S. LAST PASSENGER LEFT MAYFLOWER.

Apr. 12, 1621 N.S. MAYFLOWER RETURNED TO ENGLAND.

May 6, 1621 N.S. MAYFLOWER ARRIVED IN ENGLAND.

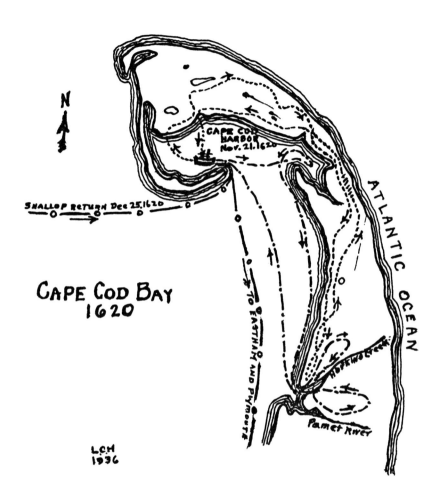

**CAPE COD BAY 1620**

N

ATLANTIC OCEAN

CAPE COD HARBOR Nov. 21. 1620

SHALLOP RETURN Dec 25.1620

TO EASTHAM AND PLYMOUTH

HERRING Creek

Pamet River

LCH 1936

Nov. 19. 1620 N.S. MAYFLOWER SIGHTED CAPE COD.
Nov. 21. 1620 N.S. SIGNED COMPACT ON MAYFLOWER.
Nov. 25. 1620 N.S. 1st EXPEDITION SET OUT. ⋯⋯⋯
Dec. 7. 1620 N.S. 2nd EXPEDITION WITH SHALLOP. —··—·—
Dec 16 1620 N.S. 3rd EXPEDITION WITH SHALLOP. —•——•—
AND DISCOVERED PLYMOUTH.

## "NEW PLIMOUTH PLANTATION"

The drama of the "Pilgrims" of 1620 has now reached the stage where the scene lies in Plymouth Harbor and New Plymouth. In 1620 the mainland of New England was still a trackless territory, except for Indian trails. Boston, Salem and other locations to the north were virgin forests.

The Dutch to the south were far away in New Netherlands (New York) and none too friendly.

It was Christmas week in New England, on a bright sunny day, December 26, 1620 (N.S.), that the Mayflower dropped anchor in Plymouth Harbor, after a short run across Cape Cod Bay from that place of refuge, Cape Cod Harbor off Provincetown.

An attempt had been made to cross the Bay the day before, but the ship had to turn back because of a change of wind.

The next day, December 27, 1620 (N.S.), was Sunday, and the whole company passed the First Sabbath in Plymouth on board the Mayflower.

Early Monday morning, December 28, 1620 (N.S.), a party left the ship to explore the vicinity of Plymouth by land. On the next day, Tuesday, one party explored by land, and another in the "shallop" discovered Jones River.

On December 30, 1620 (N.S.), it was decided to settle near "Burial Hill" in Plymouth.

Thursday, December 31, 1620, was a day of sadness. Richard Britteridge died, and was the first death after reaching Plymouth.

On Saturday, January 2, 1621, Solomon Prower died. Those on shore heard a cry of savages. Material for building the "common house" is assembled, and the construction of it is begun.

On the evening of January 4, 1621 (N.S.), it was thought Indians were heard again, and on this same date it is recorded that the party on the Mayflower began to "drink water on board". Just what they had been drinking previously is not explained.

Tuesday, January 5, 1620, was a stormy day and there was no going ashore. The next day was occupied by the women for general washing of clothes.

On Thursday, January 7, 1621 (N.S.), a communistic government was formed, the company being divided into nineteen families, in order to reduce the number of houses needed for shelter. Lots were measured out, and assigned to the family groups according to the "casting" system.

January 8th and 9th were rainy, although Indian smokes were seen.

Monday, January 10th, was a pleasant day and all hands went to work again. Before the end of the day, however, another member of the company, Degory Priest, died.

[ 74 ]

On January 13th, those who were cutting thatch saw some more Indian smokes, but no Indians.

On Thursday, January 14th, Captain Standish with a party discovered some wigwams, but failed to see any Indians. They shot an eagle, and, for some reason, expressed the idea that it tasted like mutton.

It is recorded that on Friday, January 15th, a sailor found or caught a herring. This was good news because they hoped to have success at fishing soon, although they had no cod hooks.

On Saturday, January 16th, Mr. Christopher Martin, Governor of the Mayflower, and Treasurer of the expedition, was taken with a critical illness. He was unable to leave the ship, still anchored in Plymouth Harbor, and sent for John Carver, who visited him on Sunday morning. It is quite unfortunate that details of the conference between Martin and Carver have not been found. Without doubt Carver was entrusted with the custody of certain accounts, but he died himself within a few months, and the very early financial records of the colony are somewhat confused and uncertain.

Christopher Martin was a man of means, a member of the Merchant Adventurers, and had been appointed by them Governor and Treasurer of the Mayflower, in complete charge of all expenditures, with instructions to report directly to the Adventurers in London. What became of the accounting after his untimely death is not known. On Monday, January 18, 1621, he died, and the affairs of New Plymouth passed into the hands of the Leyden group.

It happened that January 18th was a very fine day, and the shallop went out for fish and had great success, also Francis Billington, while doing a little side exploring, discovered the small lake which still bears his name.

On Tuesday, January 19th, land was finally divided by lot.

John Goodman and Peter Brown lost themselves in the woods on Friday, January 22nd, owing to the fact that it was a rainy day and a heavy mist hung over the land.

The thatch on the common-house burned on January 24th, and on January 29th the Planters began to build the storehouse.

The Company was becoming more and more familiar with their new home surroundings and on January 31st a meeting was held on land.

Rose Standish, wife of Capt. Myles Standish, died February 8th. Sickness and death prevailed.

Several shelters had now been erected in New Plymouth, among them a house for some of the numerous sick people, which unfortunately caught fire on February 19th, without, however, causing any fatalities.

On February 26th, Capt. Myles Standish and Francis Cooke inadvertently left their tools in the woods where they had been cutting thatch and felling timber for the houses. Returning for them, it was found they had been carried off by Indians.

[ 75 ]

The next day, February 27th, an important meeting was held for the purpose of formulating a military policy, and Myles Standish was chosen Captain of the militia company, and by March 3rd the "great guns were mounted on the hill". The little band of Pilgrims were in a strange country surrounded by unknown savages and it is not to be wondered at that they should take reasonable precautions.

On this same date, March 3rd, two influential members of the company died, William Mullins and William White. It is recorded that "2 others" also died, making four in one day.

Although the weather was still "wintry", yet there were distinct signs of an early spring, and snow was fast disappearing.

Sickness and death still stalked among the Pilgrims, and on March 7th Mrs. Mary (Norris) Allerton died.

The birds were chirping merrily on March 13th, and during the day a thunderstorm arose which lasted but a short time.

Those of the Pilgrims who were fortunate enough to have "garden seed" proceeded to plant it on March 17th. Green vegetables were needed by the colonists, the lack of which probably caused most of the sickness, which was a type of "scurvy".

Another meeting was held on March 26th to discuss "military orders", which was interrupted by the coming of Chief Samoset. This enabled the Planters to become better acquainted with the Indian character and desires. Stephen Hopkins was of great service in all the Indian conferences. On Sunday, March 28th, Samoset came again bringing five others.

The matter of "Laws and Orders" was taken up at a meeting March 31st. The proceedings were interrupted by the coming of the Indians, who were now seeking understandings with the "strangers".

On this date also, it is recorded that the "carpenter fitted the shallop" to "fetch all from aboard". Apparently, therefore, the Mayflower was now a "deserted ship" so far as the Pilgrims were concerned. For many of the Planters the famous ship had been a home and headquarters from July 25, 1620 (N.S.) to March 31, 1620 (N.S.), a period of eight months.

The New England spring was now in delightful evidence. On April 1st, another meeting for public business, "Laws and Orders", and the like was called, and was interrupted by the coming again of Samoset and an Indian by the name of Squanto. They announced a possible treaty with Massasoit, and one was formulated.

The important question of "Laws and Orders" for the time being was concluded on April 2, 1621 (N.S.), and at the same time John Carver was chosen Governor for the ensuing year.

Elizabeth (Barker) Winslow, wife of Edward Winslow, died April 3rd, causing another vacancy in the fast thinning ranks of the matrons.

On April 12th, Governor Carver certified a copy of the will of

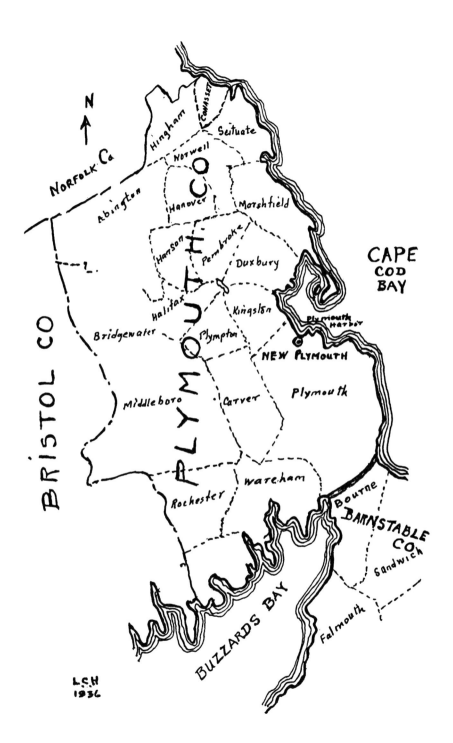

NORFOLK Co.

N

BRISTOL CO

PLYMOUTH Co.

Hingham
Cohasset
Scituate
Norwell
Hanover
Marshfield
Abington
Hanson
Pembroke
Duxbury
Halifax
Kingston
Bridgewater
Plympton
Plymouth Harbor
NEW PLYMOUTH
Middleboro
Carver
Plymouth
Wareham
Rochester
Bourne

CAPE COD BAY

BARNSTABLE Co.
Sandwich
Falmouth

BUZZARDS BAY

L.S.H
1936

William Mullins which was carried back to England on the Mayflower.

It would be of much historical value to know how many other documents Captain Jones took back with him on the Mayflower, which departed from New Plymouth on its return voyage about April 12, 1621 (N.S.), and arrived in London about May 16, 1621 (N.S.).

For instance, the records of the Merchant Adventurers kept by Gov. Christopher Martin, and the originals of the famous "Compact", and signatures attached to that mysterious and historical document, may also have been placed in the hands of Captain Jones by Governor Carver, who knew well the uncertainty of life in New Plymouth and lack of facilities for preserving valuable papers.

The little colony was now enjoying, as best it could, the May days of the Cape Cod region, and under normal conditions they were then and are now delightful. However, sickness was still prevalent, and between April 12th and May 10, 1621 (N.S.), Governor Carver died, carrying with him to the grave details of the Mayflower voyage, which had been verbally turned over to him by Governor Martin, who had preceded him in death by a few weeks.

Control of the colony now passed into the hands of younger men like Winslow and Bradford, both of the Leyden contingents. Neither Standish nor Hopkins seemed to care for officeholding, and all the other leading "Londoners" had died.

On May 22, 1621 (N.S.), a happy event occurred. Edward Winslow was married to the widow Sussana (Fuller) White. It was the first marriage in the colony.

On July 12th, Stephen Hopkins and Edward Winslow set out to visit Massasoit, and reached their destination the next day. They were cordially welcomed by Massasoit.

Rumors arose that Squanto had been killed by enemies, and Captain Standish on August 24th started out with a party of armed men to "revenge" the supposed act, but apparently it was unfounded rumor, for it is recorded that Captain Standish with a body of men, and Squanto, started out on September 28, 1621 (N.S.), to visit the Massachusetts, and for this purpose landed at Squantim in Quincy on September 30th.

It will be observed that the little band of New Plymouth Pilgrims were fast becoming acquainted with their neighbors.

The summer of 1621 in New Plymouth had given the Mayflower Planters an opportunity to adjust themselves to their new home, and with the coming of garden produce, sickness had practically ceased. Suitable shelter had been built, although of a temporary nature, and the outlook was more encouraging.

However, the need for clothing, medical supplies and the like was pressing, and the colony was anxiously awaiting the arrival of a ship from England.

Finally on November 19, 1621 (N.S.), the Fortune dropped

anchor off New Plymouth. It not only brought material things but also thirty-two or more planters, mostly young and vigorous.

## Passengers on the Fortune, 1621

This ship arrived at Plymouth on November 19, 1621 (N.S.), and, no doubt, it was a gala day for the little band of Planters still surviving after the winter of suffering. It was the first boat after the Mayflower and brought comfort and aid in numerous directions.

The ship had left London about August, and was commanded by Master Thomas Barton.

Above all it brought, for the most part, a company of "lusty yonge men", and the entire body settled in New Plymouth.

1. John Adams (see Fam. No. 1161) d. 1633 m. Elinore Newton, had 2 sons, 1 dau.
2. William Bassett (see Fam. No. 1169), Iron Monger from Bethnal County Middlesex. m. Margaret Oldham, settled in Duxbury.
3. Jonathan Brewster, son of Elder William. Age 37 at Landing. Eldest son of the Elder. Ribbon Weaver of Leyden in 1617. Removed to New London and died 1659.
4. William Beale died or removed before 1627.
5. Clement Briggs (see Fam. No. 759). Fell monger, of Southwark County Surrey. m. Joan Allen 1630-1. Settled in Dorchester, had 5 sons.
6. Edward Bompasse (Bumpas). m. Hannah (      ) removed to Marshfield, had 8 children.
7. John (Carman?) Cannon, died or removed before 1627.
8. William Conner died or removed before 1627.
9. Robert Cushman (see Fam. No. 43), Wool-carder, of Rolvenden County Kent. Returned to England.
10. Thomas Cushman (see Fam. No. 43), son of Robert. 14 yrs. old left with Governor Bradford. m. Mary Allerton 1635/6. Settled in Kingston.
11. Stephen Deane, Miller (see Fam. No. 15), probably from Southwark. m. Elizabeth Ring, had 3 daus. He built 1st Corn Mill in N.E. 1632.
12. Phillipe de La Noye, of Leyden, Holland, French. m. Dec. 19/29, 1634, Esther Dewsbury.
13. Thomas Flavell of London. His son came with him. His wife followed in "Ann". He removed or died before 1627.
14. (John?) Ford probably from Southwark, Leather Dresser.
15. Mrs. Martha Ford. She had another child right after landing. Perhaps m. 2d Peter Brown.

[ 79 ]

16. William Ford.
17. (Martha?) Ford.
18. William Hilton, Vintner? of Northwich County Chester. Wife and 2 sons came in "Ann". Removed to Dover, N. H., thence to Killery, Me., before 1661.
19. Robert Hicks (see Fam. No. 25), Fell-Monger of Southwark County Surrey. His wife came in "Ann". He died Mar. 24, 1647/8, also 2 sons and 2 daus.
20. Benedict Morgan, Mariner of St. James Clerkenwell London. d. or removed before 1627.
21. Thomas Morton (Martin), Austerfield, Yorkshire County. d. or removed before 1627.
22. Augustine Nicolas, probably of Leyden. d. or removed before 1627.
23. William Palmer, Nailer, Stepney London. His son come with him. Wife Frances came later. Removed to Duxbury. d. 1638.
24. (          ) Carvanyell.
25. William Pitt, Armorer, St. Peter London. Perhaps to Marblehead before 1627.
26. Thomas Prence, All Saints, Barking London. Son of Thomas of Lechlade, Gloucestershire. m. Aug. 15, 1624 (N.S.) Patience Brewster—5 ch.
27. Moses Simonson of Leyden. Wife probably came with him. He settled in Duxbury.
28. Hugh Stasie. He removed to Dedham then to Salem and perhaps returned to Eng.
29. James Steward. d. or removed before 1627.
30. William Tench probably of London. d. or removed before 1627.
31. John Winslow (see Fam. No. 183) brother of Edward. He m. Mary Chilton and removed to Boston in 1657. d. 1674.
32. William Wright m. Precilla (          ) died 1633—No ch.

The descendants of Stephen Hopkins, as well as those of the other Mayflower Planters, and of numerous "first comers" thereafter, resided in large percentage within the boundaries of Plymouth and Barnstable counties during the first five generations, covering a period of about 100 years, and over, and therefore the history of this section should be of decided interest to many thousands of Americans.

After landing from the Mayflower, and with the fundamental "Compact" carefully formulated and signed, the Pilgrims addressed themselves to the difficult task of settling New Plymouth, and during the first few years they suffered many severe hardships in that undertaking, but none comparable to that of the first winter.

Until the arrival of the Fortune in 1621, the little band of Mayflower Planters were forced to carry on alone. During the first winter food and shelter were difficult to provide, as they had landed in the late fall of 1620, and were not acquainted with the long hard New England season ahead of them.

Therefore, during the first year of their self exile they suffered much sickness, and grim death stalked among them. The extent of this blow may be seen from the following table:

|  | 1620 | Died 1st yr. | Survivors Nov., 1621 |
|---|---|---|---|
| Heads of Families (Males) | 24 | 13 | 11 |
| Wives | 18 | 14 | 4 |
| Sons | 18 | 6 | 12 |
| Daughters | 7 | 0 | 7 |
| Other Males | 33 | 19 | 14 |
| Other Females | 4 | 1 | 3 |
|  | 104 | 53 | 51 |

Four of the original households were completely wiped out, those of Master Christopher Martin, Thomas Tinker, John Rigdale and John Turner, twelve individuals in all.

To balance this sad picture, four households miraculously escaped any casualties. They were the fortunate families of Mr. Stephen Hopkins, Richard Warren, John Billington, Sr., and Francis Cooke (see Fam. No. 3).

However, it will be noticed that half of our little band of Pilgrims, first comers on the Mayflower, perished in that terrible first year and winter.

The arrival of the Fortune in 1621 put new life into the little community, and the matter of settlement proceeded steadily, although for several years conditions of living were far from pleasant.

In 1623 the "Anne" and "Little James" arrived in Plymouth from England with many needed articles for the settlers. These vessels also brought a number of very welcome "new comers", who found the Pilgrims sadly in need of food and clothing. In this regard Bradford states the recent arrivals were "diversely affected" to "behold their low and poor conditions". The "best dish they could present to their friends was a lobster or a piece of fish without bread or anything else but a cup of fair spring water". Some of the "new comers" wished themselves back in England again, others wept, and all were sad.

The division of land among the Planters at first was rather vague, but by the spring of 1624 "before planting season, a desire was expressed for more permanent division".

Bradford states "they began now highly to prize corne as more precious than silver, those that had some to spare began to trade one with the other for small things, by the quart, pottle and peck, for money they had none, and if any had, corne was preferred before it".

They therefore petitioned the Governor for land "given them in continuance". Accordingly suitable allotments were made, sixty-nine acres were granted to those who came over in the Mayflower.

In 1624, the colony consisted of "one hundred and eighty persons, some cattle and goats, but many swine and poultry and thirty-two dwelling houses". None of the Planters had died during the previous three years. This fact was very encouraging to the settlers in view of the heavy toll in sickness and death during the winter of 1620-21.

It may be stated that the far-sighted intelligence of the Plymouth settlers is proved from the fact that no other colony before or since can furnish such complete, exhaustive and interesting records of its acts and events. The fate of every man, woman and child is accounted for, and this, remember, in spite of cold, hunger, snow, and sickness.

The first Governor, as previously noted, was John Carver, but he was soon succeeded, in 1621, by William Bradford, who was chosen Governor annually thereafter until his death in 1657, with the exception of 1633, 1636 and 1644, when Edward Winslow was chosen, and in 1634 and 1638 when Thomas Prence was Governor.

The territory known as the "Old Colony" covered a much larger district than the section called New Plymouth. The Indian Tribes within the "Old Colony" were:

| | |
|---|---|
| Pocassetts | of Swansea, Rohoboth, Somerset and Tiverton. |
| Wampanoags | of Bristol. |
| Saconets | of Little Compton. |
| Nemaskets | of Middleboro. |
| Nausites | of Eastham. |
| Mattakees | of Barnstable. |
| Monamoys | of Chatham. |
| Saukatucketts | of Marshpee. |
| Nobsquassetts | of Yarmouth. |

Some of this territory is now in Bristol Co., Mass., and some in Rhode Island.

In 1685 Plymouth Colony was divided into three counties, Plymouth, Barnstable and Bristol. Barnstable County, or Cape Cod, had eight Towns, Sandwich, Barnstable, Yarmouth, Harwich, Eastham, Truro, Falmouth and Chatham.

The arrival of the Fortune, naturally, was a great encouragement to the Planters. Weddings were soon announced between a number of the recent arrivals in the Fortune and the Mayflower Passengers.

For instance, widow Martha Ford was soon wed to Peter Browne; Mary Chilton married John Winslow, and Thomas Cushman, then a lad of 14, became the husband of Mary Allerton, in young manhood. His father was the Robert Cushman who preached the famous sermon at Plymouth soon after the arrival of the Fortune from the text: "Let no man seek his own; but every man another's wealth." This sermon is preserved in Pilgrim Hall, Plymouth. Robert Cushman at this time was representing the Merchant Adventurers of England, and he returned to England with the Fortune, leaving his son Thomas at New Plymouth. Robert Cushman had previously, apparently, been representing the Leyden group, together with John Carver, before the Merchant Adventurers. For some reason business affiliations had become reversed.

Among the passengers brought by the Fortune were a number who became very useful to the community. William Wright, with his wife Precilla (sister of Governor Bradford's second wife) became prominent in affairs. He was a carpenter in great demand. Stephen Deane erected a mill to grind corn. Robert Hicks was followed by his wife, Margaret, in the "Anne". She taught some of the children to read and write, and was a woman of considerable influence for good in New Plymouth.

Among the outstanding young and eligible men to come over in the Fortune were Philip De La Noye, the progenitor of the Delano family in America, John and Kenelm Winslow and Jonathan Brewster.

There were many welcome additions to New Plymouth when the "Anne" and "Little James" arrived in 1623. There was the vivacious Mrs. Alice Southward, soon to wed Governor Bradford. With her came Barbara, apparently the wife of Capt. Myles Standish. Elizabeth Warren, with her five daughters, came to make a home for her husband, Richard. Mistress Hester Cooke came with three children, and Fear and Patience Brewster arrived to cheer their mother and girlhood friends. These two girls later wed Isaac Allerton and Governor Thomas Prence.

Many needed supplies were brought by the Anne and James, and among the passengers were several carpenters, cobblers, weavers and other useful and potential citizens. The ship James remained for the use of the colony.

About this time, 1623, the question of changing the form of government from a communistic state to one of individual liberty was carefully considered by the leaders.

Up to 1623 the affairs had been conducted on a pure communal basis.

The men and grown boys were expected to plant and harvest, fish and hunt, for the common use of all the households. The women also did their tasks in common.

The results were not satisfactory, for reasons that are as old as the human race. *Communism* means the rewarding of the lazy and incompetent, which is directly antagonistic to common sense, and the reasons for dropping this form of living in 1623 can never change.

A new division of land was made, allotting to each householder an acre for each member of his family. This arrangement was called "every man for his owne particular".

[ 83 ]

Bradford in his clear cut manner states regarding the reasons for making changes; and the after effects:

"The women now went willingly unto ye field, and tooke their little-ones with them to set corne which before would aledge weaknes and inabilitie; *whom to have compelled would have bene thought great tiranie and oppression.*"
"For ye yong-men that were most able and fitte for labour and service did repine that they should spend their time and strength to work for other men's wives and children without any recompense . . .. And for men's wives to be commanded to doe servise for other men, as dressing their meate, washing their cloathes etc, they deemed it a kind of slaverie, neither could many husbands well brooke it."

In spite of the lessons of history, communism is periodically attempted by governments, controlled by shrewd politicians, whose citizens have momentarily "forgotten". However, fundamentals of human nature cannot possibly tolerate communism for any length of time, for reasons brilliantly expressed by Bradford in 1650, nearly three centuries ago.

### Passengers on the Anne 1623

This ship was commanded by William Peirce, one of the most famous shipmasters of his day. During his career he brought many shiploads of passengers safely to American ports.
The entire company settled in Plymouth.

1. Anthony Annable (see Fam. No. 850), from All Saints, Cambridge, Cambridge County.
2.     Mrs. Jane Annable
3.     (    ) Annable
4.     (    ) Annable
5. Edward Bangs (see Fam. No. 620), from Panfield, Essex County, Shipwright.
6.     Mrs. Lydia Bangs
7.     Jonathan Bangs
8.     John Bangs
9. Robert Bartlett (see Fam. No. 1010).
10. Thomas Clark (see Fam. No. 7).
11. Christopher Conant (see Fam. No. 620), from St. Lawrence, Jewry, London, Grocer.
12. Anthony Dix (see Fam. 540).
13. John Faunce (see Fam. No. 224), probably from Purleigh, Essex County.
14. Edmund Flood (see Fam. No. 700).
15. Godbert Godbertson (see Fam. No. 690), from Leyden, Hat Maker.
16.     Mrs. Sarah Godbertson.
17.     Mary Priest.

18.    Sarah Priest.
19. Timothy Hatherley (see Fam. No. 815), from St. Olaves, Southwark, Surrey County, Felt Maker.
20. William Heard (see Fam. No. 900).
21. Edward Holman (see Fam. No. 1047), probably from Clapham, Surrey.
22. Manasseh Kempton (see Fam. No. 790), from Colchester, Essex County.
23. Robert Long (see Fam. No. 810).
311  24. Experience Mitchell (see Fam. No. 8), from Dukes Place, 311 London.
25. Thomas Morton, Jr. (see Fam. No. 34), son of Thomas of the Fortune.
26. Mrs. Ellen Newton.
27. John Oldham (see Fam. No. 640).
28.    Mrs. Oldham.
29.    Lucretia Oldham.
30.    Christian Penn.
2386  31. Joshua Pratt (see Fam. No. 994).
32. James Rand (see Fam. No. 550), from St. George, Southwark, Surrey County.
33. Robert Ratcliff (see Fam. No. 960).
34. Nicholas Snow (see Fam. No. 2), from Haxton, Middlesex County.
35.    Mrs. Alice Southworth, Dukes Place, London.
36. Francis Sprague (see Fam. No. 910).
37.    Anna Sprague.
38.    Mercy Sprague.
39. Thomas Tilden (see Fam. No. 248), probably from Stepney, London.
40.    Mrs. Tilden.
41.    (      ) Tilden.
42. Stephen Tracy (see Fam. No. 24), from Yarmouth, Norfolk County.
43.    Mrs. Tryphosa Tracy.
44.    (Sarah?) Tracy.
45. Ralph Wallen (see Fam. No. 480).
46.    Mrs. Joyse Wallen.
47.    Mrs. Hester Cooke, wife of Francis.
48.    Mrs. Elizabeth Flavell, wife of Thomas.
49.    Mrs. Bridget Fuller, wife of Dr. Samuel.
50.    Mrs. (      ) Hilton, wife of William.
51.      William Hilton, jr.
52.      Mary Hilton.
53.    Mrs. Margaret Hicks, wife of Robert (see Fam. No. 810).
54.    Mrs. Frances Palmer, wife of William.
2005  55.    Mrs. Elizabeth Warren (see Fam. No. 8), wife of Richard.

[ 85 ]

56.      Mary Warren.
57.      Elizabeth Warren.
58.      Anna Warren.
59.      Sarah Warren.
60.      Abigail Warren.
61.  Mary Becket.
62.  Patience Brewster, daughter of William.
63.  Fear Brewster, daughter of William.
64.  Mrs. Barbara Standish, wife of Myles.
65.  Thomas Southworth, son of Mrs. Alice.
66.  William Palmer, jr., son of William.

## Passengers of the Little James 1623

The Captain of this ship was E. Altham and the Master John Bridges. It appears to have been built by the "Plymouth Adventurers" to remain in the colony. It was small, only forty-four tons, even smaller than the Speedwell, which was intended for a similar purpose, but failed because of unseaworthiness to cross with the Mayflower. The Little James took ninety days to cross the Atlantic, and, of course, brought only a few passengers.

1. William Bridges, from London?
2. Edward Burcher from St. Saviors, Southwark.
3.    Mrs. Burcher.
4. John Jenny, Cooper.
5.    Mrs. Sarah Jenney.
6.    Samuel Jenny.
7.    Abigail Jenny.
8.    Sarah Jenny.
9. George Morton, Merchant, Harworth, Notts County.
10.    Mrs. Juliana Morton

## Passengers on the Mayflower 1629

The Master of this Mayflower was the famous Captain William Peirce. The boat left Gravesend, London, March, 1629, and arrived at Plymouth, May 15, 1629. There were something over thirty-five passengers, many of them from Leyden.

### LIST IN PART.

1. Richard Masterson.
2.    Mrs. Mary Masterson.
3.    Nathaniel Masterson.
4.    Sarah Masterson.
5. Thomas Blossom.
6.    Mrs. Anne Blossom.
7.    Thomas Blossom.
8.    Elizabeth Blossom.
9. Mrs. Bridget Robinson, widow of Rev. John.

10.     Isaac Robinson.
11.     Mercy Robinson.
12.     Fear Robinson.
13. Thomas Willett.
14. Richard Clayden.
15.     Barnabas Clayden.
16. Richard Howard.
17. Richard Ingersoll.
18.     Mrs. Anne Ingersoll.
19.     George Ingersoll.
20.     Joanna Ingersoll.
21.     John Ingersoll.
22.     Sarah Ingersoll.
23.     Alice Ingersoll.

From "Plimouth's great Book of Deeds of Lands Enrolled: From An° 1627 to An° 1651:" (pages 50-57) is obtained the following record of the Division of Cattle, made June 1, 1627 (N.S.). It includes the names of every member of the New Plymouth Colony on that date, even of the youngest children. Forty-two of the ninety-nine persons who reached Plymouth on the Mayflower were still living in 1627, which proves that the first winter was exceptional so far as sickness and death was concerned.

Over 150 persons are noted in this record, and the detailed history and family of each individual will appear in this series. The record follows:

"At a public court held the 22nd of May, 1627, it was concluded by the whole companie that the cattell wch were the companies, to wit, the cowes & the Goates should be equally devided to all the parts of the same company & soe kept until the expiration of ten years after the date above written & that every one should well and sufficiently provide for their owne pt under penalty of forfeiting the same.

"That the old stock with half the increase should remain for comon use to be devided at the end of the said terme or otherwise as ocation falleth out & the other half to be their owne for ever.

"Uppon wch agreement they were equally divided by lotte soe as the burthen of the keeping the males then being, should be borne for comon use by those to whose lot the best cowes should fall, also so the lotts fell as followeth, thirteen parts being portioned to one lot."

1. The first lot fell to ffrancis Cooke* & his Companie joyned to him his wife Hester Cooke.
*3. John Cooke
4. Jacob Cooke
5. Jane Cooke

6. Hester Cooke
7. Mary Cooke
8. Moses Simonson
9. Phillip Delanoy
10. Experience Michaell
11. John ffane
12. Joshua Pratt
13. Phinihas Pratt

To this lot fell the least of the 4 black Heyfers came in the Jacob, and two she goats.

2. The second lot fel to Mr. Isaac Allerton* & his Companie joyned to him his wife ffear Allerton.
*3. Bartholomew Allerton
*4. Remember Allerton
*5. Mary Allerton
6. Sarah Allerton
7. Godber Godbertson
8. Sarah Godberson
9. Samuell Godberson
10. Marra Priest
11. Sarah Priest
12. Edward Bumpasse
*13. John Crakstone

To this lot fell the Greate Black cow came in the Ann to which they muste keepe the lesser of the two steers and two shee goats.

3. The third lot fell to Capt. Standish* & his Companie joyned to him his wife.
2. Barbaba Standish
3. Charles Standish
4. Allexander Standish
5. John Standish
*6. Edward Winslow
*7. Sussana Winslow
8. Edward Winslow
9. John Winslow
*10. Resolved White
*11. Peregrine White
12. Abraham Peirce
13. Thomas Clarke

To this lot fell the Red Cow wch belongeth to the poore of the Collonye to wch they must keepe her calfe of this yeare being a Bull for the Companie, also to this lotte came too she goats.

4. The fourth lot fell to John Howland* & his Companie joyned to him his wife.
*2. Elizabeth Howland
3. John Howland junor
4. Desire Howland
5. William Wright
6. Thomas Morton Junor
*7. John Alden
*8. Prissilla Alden
9. Elizabeth Alden
10. Clemont Briggs
*11. Edward Dotton
12. Edward Holdman
13. Joh. Alden

To this lot fell one of the 4 heyfers came in the Jacob Called Raghorne.

5. The fift lot fell to Mr. William Brewster* & his companie joyned to him.

*2. Love Brewster
*3. Wrestling Brewster
*4. Richard More
*5. Henri Samson
6. Johnathon Brewster
7. Lucretia Brewster
8. Willm Brewster
9. Mary Brewster
10. Thomas Prince
11. Pacience Prince
12. Rebecka Prince
*13. Humillydy Cooper

To this lot fell one of the fower Hyfers Came in the Jacob Caled the Blind Heyfer & 2 shee goats.

6. The sixt lott fell to John Shaw & his companie joyned
1. to him.
2. John Adams
3. Eliner Adams
4. James Adams
5. John Winslow
*6. Mary Winslow
7. Willm Bassett
8. Elizabeth Bassett
9. Willyam Bassett Junor
10. Elyzabeth Bassett Junor
11. ffrancis Sprage
12. Anna Sprage
13. Mercye Sprage

To this lot fell the lesser of the black Cowes Came at first in the Ann wth which they must keepe the bigest of the 2 steers. Also to this lott was two shee goats.

7. The seaventh lott fell to Stephen Hopkins* & his companie joyned to him his wife.

*2. Elizabeth Hopkins
*3. Gyles Hopkins
4. Caleb Hopkins
5. Debora Hopkins
6. Nicholas Snow
*7. Constance Snow
8. William Palmer
9. ffrances Palmer
10. Willm Pallmer Jnor
*11. John Billington Senor
*12. Hellen Billington
*13. ffrancis Billington

To this lott fell A Black weining Calfe to wch was aded the Calfe of this yeare to come of the black Cow, wch fell to John Shaw & his companie, wch pveing a bull they were to keepe it ungelt 5 yeares for common use & after to make there best of it. Nothing belongeth of thes too, for ye companye of ye first stock: but only halfe ye Increase.

To this lott ther fell two she goats: which goats they posses on the like terms which others do their cattle.

8. The eaight lott fell to Samuell ffuller* & his companie joyned to him his wife.

| | |
|---|---|
| 2. Bridgett ffuller | To this lott fell A Red |
| 3. Samuell ffuller junior | Heyfer Came of the Cow |
| *4. Peeter Browne | wch belongeth to the poore |
| 5. Martha Browne | of the Colony & so is of |
| 6. Mary Browne | that consideration (vizt) |
| 7. John fford | thes psonts nominated, to |
| 8. Martha fford | have halfe the Increase, the |
| 9. Anthony Anable | other half, with the ould |
| 10. Jane Anable | stock, to remain for the use |
| 11. Sara Anable | of the poore. |
| 12. Hanah Anable | To this lott also two shee |
| *13. Damaris Hopkins | goats. |

9. The ninth lot fell to Richard Warren* & his companie joyned wth him his wife.

| | |
|---|---|
| 2. Elizabeth Warren | |
| 3. Nathaniell Warren | |
| 4. Joseph Warren | |
| 5. Mary Warren | To this lott fell one of |
| 6. Anna Warren | the 4 black Heyfers that |
| 7. Sara Warren | came in the Jacob caled |
| 8. Elizabeth Warren | the smooth horned Heyfer |
| 9. Abigail Warren | and two shee goats. |
| *10. John Billington | |
| *11. George Sowle | |
| 12. Mary Sowle | |
| 13. Zakariah Sowle | |

10. The tenth lot fell to ffrancis Eaton* & those joyned wth him his wife.

| | |
|---|---|
| 2. Christian Eaton | |
| *3. Samuel Eaton | |
| 4. Rahell Eaton | |
| 5. Stephen Tracie | |
| 6. Triphosa Tracie | To this lott ffell an |
| 7. Sarah Tracie | heyfer of the last yeare |
| 8. Rebecka Tracie | called the white belyed |
| 9. Ralph Wallen | heyfer & two shee goats. |
| 10. Joyce Wallen | |
| 11. Sarah Morton | |
| 12. Robert Bartlet | |
| 13. Tho. Prence | |

11. The eleventh lott fell to the Governor Mr. William Bradford* and those with him, to wit, his wife.
2. Alles Bradford and
3. William Bradford, Junior
4. Mercy Bradford

*5. Joseph Rogers
6. Thomas Cushman
*7. William Latham
8. Manases Kempton
9. Julian Kempton
10. Nathaniel Morton
11. John Morton
12. Ephraim Morton
13. Patience Morton

To this lott fell an heyfer of the last yeare wch was of the Greate White cow that was brought over in the Ann, & two shee goats.

12. The twelveth lott fell to John Jene & his companie joyned to him, his wife.
2. Sarah Jene
3. Samuel Jene
4. Abigaill Jene
5. Sara Jene
6. Robert Hickes
7. Margaret Hickes
8. Samuel Hickes
9. Ephraim Hickes
10. Lydia Hickes
11. Phebe Hicks
12. Stephen Deane
13. Edward Bangs

To this lott fell the greate white backt cow wch was brought over with the first in the Ann, to wch cow the keepeing of the bull was joyned for thes psonts to pvide for heere also two shee goats.

It was further agreed "that if anie of the cattel should by accident miscarie or be lost or hurt; that the same should be taken knowledge of by Indifferent men; and Judged whether the losse came by the negligence of default of those betrusted and if they were found faulty, that then such should be forced to make satisfaction for the company, as also their partners damage".

It will be noticed that there were 12 lots as follows:
1. Francis Cooke & Co.
2. Mr. Isaac Allerton & Co.
3. Capt. Myles Standish & Co.
4. John Howland & Co.
5. Mr. William Brewster & Co.
6. John Shaw & Co.
7. Stephen Hopkins & Co.
8. Samuel Fuller & Co.
9. Richard Warren & Co.
10. Francis Eaton & Co.
11. Gov. William Bradford & Co.
12. John Jene & Co.

Law and Order was a habit with the Pilgrim Planters. This was proved by the "Compact" on the Mayflower before landing. Also they did not delay in setting up a General Court in New Plymouth.

It was functioning in 1623, and the Laws were revised in 1636, 1658 and 1671.

The few extracts from the Court records which follow show that the problems facing the human race have not changed in the last 300 years, and probably never will. They all center around food, shelter and clothing, and racial differences.

It was ordained on December 17, 1623, by the Court then held, that "all Criminal facts, and also all matters of trepass and debts between man should be tried by the verdict of twelve Honest men to be Impanelled by authority in forme of a Jury upon their oaths".

It was decreed by the Court held the 29th of March, 1626, that "No handy-craftsman of what profession soever as Taylors, Shoemakers, Carpenters, Joyners, Smiths, Lawyers or whatsoever wch do or may reside or belong to this plantation of Plymouth shall use their science or trades at home or abroade for any strangers or forreigners till such time as the necessity of the colony be served".

It was ordained by the Court March 29, 1629, that "No corne, beans or pease be transported imbarqued or sold to that end to be conveyed out of the Colony without the leave and licence of the Governours Counsell".

All trials were held in General Court until 1636, when it was enacted that the Governor and two assistants might try civil causes involving an amount not exceeding forty shillings, and criminal cases involving a small fine.

During the first few years the Town meetings were held at the Governor's home, but from about 1651 to 1700 they were held in the "meeting house".

In considering this period, it should be remembered that the New Plymouth Plantation or the "Old Colony", was quite alone in its splendid isolation for fifteen years or so from the landing in 1620.

"Puritan" Boston, Salem and other localities to the north were still, for all practical purposes, Indian trails.

The manuscript volumes of Court Orders for the colony of New Plymouth, containing all the proceedings of the General Court and Court of Assistants, are six in number, and include the years 1633-1691 (except for a few years of the usurpation of Andros). It is interesting to note they are in the handwriting of Gov. William Bradford, Gov. Edward Winslow, and of the Secretaries of the colony, Messrs. Nathaniel Souther, Nathaniel Morton, Nathaniel Clarke and Samuel Sprague.

On January 1, 1623/3, the Colony chose a Court consisting of:
Edward Wynslow, Governor (see Fam. No. 183).
        Assistants:
Capt. Myles Standish (see Fam. No. 184).
William Bradford (see Fam. No. 184).
John Howland (see Fam. No. 220).
John Alden (see Fam. No. 1094).

John Doane (see Fam. No. 61).
Stephen Hopkins (see Fam. No. 1).
William Gilson (see Fam. No. 201).

Stephen Hopkins served on the Court for seven years.

## Freemen of Plymouth 1633

"The names of the Freemen of the Incorporation of Plymouth in New England An:—1633."
Edward Wynslow, Gov. (see Fam. No. 183).
  Councell:
Capt. Myles Standish (see Fam. No. 184).
William Bradford (see Fam. No. 184).
John Howland (see Fam. No. 220).
John Alden (see Fam. No. 1094).
John Done (see Fam. No. 61).
Stephen Hopkins (see Fam. No. 1).
William Gilson (see Fam. No. 201).

Isaack Allerton (see Fam. No. 43).
Thomas Prence (see Fam. No. 11).
Raph Smith (see Fam. No. 21).
William Brewster (see Fam. No. 11).
Samuell Fuller Senior (see Fam. No. 186).
John Jenny (see Fam. No. 886).
Robt. Hickes (see Fam. No. 25).
Manasseh Kempton (see Fam. No. 750).
William Wright (see Fam. No. 8).
Franc Cooke (see Fam. No. 8).
Franc Eaton (see Fam. No. 1105).
Jonathan Brewster (see Fam. No. 11).
John Wynslow (see Fam. No. 183).
John Coombs (see Fam. No. 1030).
John Shaw (see Fam. No. 33).
Anthony Annable (see Fam. No. 850).
John Adams (see Fam. No. 1161).
Stephen Deane (see Fam. No. 15).
Stephen Tracy (see Fam. No. 24).
William Bassett (see Fam. No. 1169).
Raph Wallen (see Fam. No. 480).
William Palmer (see Fam. No. 1065).
Godbert Godbertson (see Fam. No. 690).
Lieutenant Will Holmes (see Fam. No. 245).
Edward Dowty (see Fam. No. 39).
James Hurst (see Fam. No. 610).
John Dunham (see Fam. No. 991).
William Pontus (see Fam. No. 680).
Franc Weston (see Fam. No. 928).
Joshua Pratt (see Fam. No. 994).

Phineas Pratt (see Fam. No. 994).
Peter Browne (see Fam. No. 196).
George Sowle (see Fam. No. 1140).
Edmund Chandler (see Fam. No. 780).
Christopher Wadsworth (see Fam. No. 1103).
Thomas Clarke (see Fam. No. 1024).
Henry Howland (see Fam. No. 220).
Kenelm Wynslow (see Fam. No. 183).
Josias Wynslow (see Fam. No. 183).
Richard Sparrow (see Fam. No. 65).
Humphrey Turner (see Fam. No. 997).
Anthony Savery (see Fam. No. 910).
Roger Chandler (see Fam. No. 780).
Robt. Bartlet (see Fam. No. 1010).
Expience Michaell (see Fam. No. 8).
Edward Bangs (see Fam. No. 127).
Nicholas Snow (see Fam. No. 2).
John Phance (Faunce) (see Fam. No. 224).
Richard Church (see Fam. No. 836).
Joseph Rogers (see Fam. No. 2).
Henry Cobb (see Fam. No. 701).
Samuell Nash (see Fam. No. 754).
Samuell Eedy (see Fam. No. 810).
Phillip Delanoy (see Fam. No. 931).
Abraham Peirce (see Fam. No. 761).
Raph Fogge (see Fam. No. 806).
Mr. William Collier (see Fam. No. 11).
John Cooke (see Fam. No. 8).
Thomas Willett (see Fam. No. 552).
Thomas Cushman (see Fam. No. 938).

"The rest admitted afterwds"

John Barnes (see Fam. No. 1002).
George Watson (see Fam. No. 541).
Isaacke Robbinson (see Fam. No. 440).
James Coale (see Fam. No. 19).
Samuell Fowller (see Fam. No. 349).
James Cudworth (see Fam. No. 309).
Samuel Howse (see Fam. No. 732).
William Palmer junier (see Fam. No. 1065).
John Holmes (see Fam. No. 245).
William Hoskins (see Fam. No. 977).
John Cooper (see Fam. No. 410).
Henry Rowley (see Fam. No. 390).
Richard Higins (see Fam. No. 63).
Moses Simonson (see Fam. No. 381).
Richard Cluffe (see Fam. No. 463).
Thomas Atkinson (see Fam. No. 470).
Thimothy Hatherley (see Fam. No. 633).

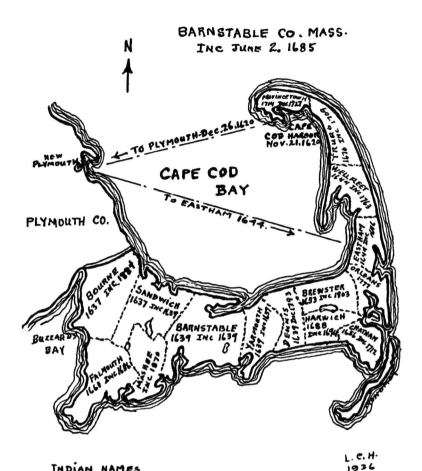

BARNSTABLE CO. MASS.
INC JUNE 2. 1685

N

TO PLYMOUTH-Dec.26.1620

PROVINCETOWN
17th Inc 1727

CAPE
COD HARBOR
Nov.21.1620

TRURO INC 1709

NEW
PLYMOUTH

CAPE COD
BAY

WELLFLEET
1644 INC 1763

To EASTHAM 1644.

PLYMOUTH CO.

EASTHAM
1644 INC 1646

ORLEANS
1797

BOURNE
1637 INC 1884

SANDWICH
1637 INC 1639

BREWSTER
1653 INC 1903

BUZZARDS
BAY

BARNSTABLE
1639 INC 1639

YARMOUTH
1639 INC 1639

DENNIS
1639 DEC 1793

HARWICH
1688
INC 1694

CHATHAM
1656 INC 1712

FALMOUTH
1668 INC 1661

MASHEE
INC 1870

INDIAN NAMES
OF TOWNS

BOURNE - COMASSAKUMXAUIT
FALMOUTH - SUCCONESSET
SANDWICH - SHAUME
MASHEE - MASSIPEE
BARNSTABLE - MATTACHEESET
YARMOUTH -
DENNIS - NOBECUSET
BREWSTER - POTANUMAQUAT.
HARWICH - SATUCKET

L.C.H.
1936

CHATHAM- MONOMOYICK
EASTHAM - NAUSET
ORLEANS -
WELLFLEET - PONONAKRNET.
TRURO - PAMET
PROVINCETOWN - MEESHAWN

MAP SHOWING DATE OF SETTLEMENT AND
INCORPORATION OF TOWNS.

John Browne (see Fam. No. 196).
Henry Samson (see Fam. No. 187).
William Hatch (see Fam. No. 920).
George Kenrich (see Fam. No. 110).
Love Brewster (see Fam. No. 11).
Nathaniel Sowther (see Fam. No. 215).

The above list is the first entry in the first volume of Court orders of the colony of New Plymouth, and from which this copy is made.

Many of these "freemen" of Plymouth of the year 1633, removed to Eastham in 1644 or soon after.

The Town Records ("Town Meetings") of Plymouth, exclusive of births, deaths, and marriages are in 9 volumes,

1—1636-1692
2—1692-1716
3—1716-1795
4—1795-1828
5—1828-1854
6—1854-1866
7—1866-1878
8—1878-1887
9—1887-

For the most part the records are in longhand and were faithfully kept by the following during the years opposite their names. The descendants of the Mayflower Planters and other first comers to New Plymouth owe these scribes an everlasting debt of gratitude.

Nathaniel Sowther, 1636—April, 1645.
Nathaniel Morton, March, 1647—June, 1685.
Thomas Faunce, July, 1685—May, 1723.
John Dyer, March, 1723/4—March, 1732/3.
Gersham Foster, March, 1732/3—March, 1733/4.
John Dyer, March, 1733/4—March, 1739/40.
Edward Winslow, March, 1739/40—January, 1741/2.
Samuel Bartlett, January, 1741/2—March, 1766.
John Cotton, March, 1766—March, 1767.
Ephraim Spooner, March, 1767—April, 1818.
Thomas Drew, April, 1818—March, 1840.
Timothy Berry, March, 1840—March, 1852.
Leander Lovell, March, 1852—March, 1878.
Curtis Davie, March, 1878—

The family records and histories of these Town Clerks will be found in this series in their proper places.

A few extracts from these records, and those of the proceedings of the colony and town from 1620 to 1696 are highly illuminating.

*March, 1637*—"William Nelson is hyred to keep the cowes this yeare at the same wages he had the last yeare which is 50

bushels of Indian Corne and is to keep them until the middle of November next."

*April, 1641*—"It is agreed that every householder within the Township shall pay a half penny for every pson in his famyly to him that shall kill a woolfe."

*September, 1642*—"It is agreed upon by the general consent of the whole towne that a fortyfycation shal be made about the ordinance and another peece mounted."

"It is agreed that every man shall bring two pieces more of viii foote long to finish the fortyfycation on the fort hill."

NOTE: Burial Hill was called Fort Hill exclusively until 1698.

"It is agreed upon that the money remaining of the poores stock shal be to by corne to releeve the psent extreme necessities of such as are ready to pish (perish) for want of bread."

*May, 1643*—"It is agreed upon that all householders within the Township shall forthwith pvide sufficient armes according to the act of the court for themselves and their servants able to beare armes within month after the 5th June next on wch day they are to trayne viz. muskett wth snaphance (flint lock), or matchlocks with match callivers (pistol)."

*September, 1643*—"It is agreed upon by the whole that there shal be a watch kept in regard of the danger of the Indians."

*October, 1643*—A council of war was appointed, consisting of

The Governor.
Mr. Prence.
Mr. Hopkins.
Mr. Jenney.
Mr. Paddy.
Nathaniel Sowther.

The committee to rate and assess for the fortification consisted of

Mr. Hopkins.
Manassah Kempton.
John Winslow.
John Cooke.
Thomas Clarke.
Richard Sparrow.
Thomas Cushman.

It will be observed that Stephen Hopkins retained his usefulness right up to the time of his death in 1644.

The modern 1936 idea, apparently, that the Government owes its citizens a living did not exist in the early days of New Plymouth. As a matter of fact the Pilgrims insisted that the citizens *give* their services from time to time to the community interests without compensation, and even fined them for not attending town meetings, as the following clearly shows:

*December 10, 1646*—It was agreed that "whosoever coms not to ye towne meeting being thereinto warned at ye time appoynted shall forfite to ye towns use for every shuch defalte 12d except to have a sufficient and lawfull excuse."

Many localities of the United States in the year 1936 are afflicted with a pest of "blackbirds" or "starlings", for instance, Washington, D. C., the Capital City. However, the problem remains unsolved because citizens do not cooperate. They leave everything up to the government.

The Pilgrims had a "blackbird" (crows) problem and solved it as follows:

*March 2, 1696*—At New Plymouth Town Meeting.

"It was acted and agreed upon by the Inhabitants of the Towne that every householder should kill 12 black birds and bring there heads to persons appointed by the Towne"

"those that neglect to kill theire proportion as above sd, shall pay a fine of 3 shillings."

Ref. Nos. 8, 10, 11, 12, 14, 18, 19, 28, 29, 30, 39, 42, 44, 45, 51, 55, 58, 63, 64, 121.

# FIRST CHURCH IN PLYMOUTH

The first few months in New Plymouth was a struggle for existence. However, Elder William Brewster saw to it that the church organization did not perish. Meetings were held. The first public building was a "Common House", about twenty feet square, which was used for both storage and worship.

In January, 1620, it was burnt to the ground, and the meetings thereafter, for a time, were held in any suitable place, and led by Elder Brewster.

In the summer of 1622, the Fort was completed on the summit of Burial Hill. Bradford states:

"they builte a fort with good timber both strong and comly, which was of good defence, made with a flatte rofe and batilmente, on which their ordnance was mounted. It served them also for a meeting-house, and was fitted accordingly for that use."

There, in a fort, on the summit of a hill, they held their meetings. The policy of the church was, broadly, copied from Calvin, and grew with the increase of population of the colony.

The church in New Plymouth did not require much space for some years. The increase in population was from less than fifty in 1620, to about 300 on the reception of the second charter in May, 1630.

In 1624 the Merchant Adventurers of London sent over a minister of their own choosing, Rev. John Lyford, but he tried to set up a Church of England form of worship and was expelled from the colony within a year, and the Plymouth Church continued under Elder William Brewster.

In 1628 Mr. Allerton on a voyage to England brought back another minister without, however, direction from the Plymouth Church. It seems that mental derangement quickly ended his service.

Finally, in 1629, Rev. Ralph Smith, of Cambridge University, England, took charge of the church at Plymouth. From this time the church was well supplied with ministerial talent. As a matter of fact, by 1641 there were seven towns in Plymouth Colony, all supplied with educated clergy of the Separatist type.

The original records of the Plymouth First Church are in three volumes—

Vol. 1—1620-1732
Vol. 2—1632-1799
Vol. 3—1799-1859

These records are, naturally, a wonderful storehouse of genealogical information, and have been freely drawn upon in the compiling of the family groups for this series.

Ref. Nos. 10, 98, 244, 253, 254.

# SCHOOLS

Naturally, home instruction of the children in the colony of New Plymouth began, or, more correctly, was continued immediately after landing, so far as the severe conditions made it possible. However, a "free school" was not mentioned in the records for some years.

New England is justly proud of its school history. Very early in the settlement of every community schools were organized. The Plymouth Colony lagged a little behind the Massachusetts Bay Colony because it was a much smaller community and weak financially.

There were many and sufficient reasons why schools were not organized in New Plymouth immediately after landing, although the Pilgrim fathers had the matter under consideration from the very beginning. Bradford mentions the training of the young as early as 1624, and the other leaders were all interested in such matters.

The question of schools in Plymouth previous to 1671 has been frequently discussed by writers. Prejudiced critics of the Pilgrims have taken pains to point out that the records are practically silent concerning schools for a period of years after landing. They assert this proves that the Pilgrims were not ambitious intellectually, and, in fact came from a very lowly class of people in England.

Of course, the critics are unfair, as they carefully avoid mentioning the severe conditions and circumstances surrounding the founding of the Plymouth Plantation in 1620.

Obviously, during the first years of the colony, little attention could be given the matter of "free schools", although it was not entirely neglected at any time. The main fight for a time was to secure a foothold in a virgin country, none too inviting.

Also, there were only a few children to be trained at the landing. It should be remembered that about twelve children of school age came over in the Mayflower, and five of these died in the "first sickness".

It is not known how many children came over in Fortune, 1621, Anne and Little James, 1623, Mayflower, 1629, and Handmaid, 1630. However, it is quite clear that there were few children of school age in the colony for some time.

Furthermore, due to their experience in Holland where they had dwelt among a foreign people, speaking a different language, the Pilgrims had become efficient in parental education, as they did not mingle freely with the Dutch. Elder Brewster had a fine library, including many Latin texts.

In his history, Bradford mentions the training of the young under the date of 1624, when he replies completely to certain criticism from England, as follows:

> "OB, children not catechised nor taught to read."
> "ANS, Neither is true; for diverse take pains with their owne as they can; indeede, we have no common schools for want of a fitt person or little too means to maintain one; although we desire now to begin."

This surely is a complete answer to all critics, both ancient and modern. As a matter of fact with such outstanding intellectual leaders as Carver, Brewster and Bradford and others in a small community, it stands to reason that the needed education was being provided.

As an example of youthful training before "free schools" it is recorded that in 1635—

> "Benjamin Eaton, with his mothers consent be put to Briget Fuller being to keep him at school two years."

Private or home instruction was the common practice in Plymouth pending more settled times.

Enactments concerning education began to appear on the statute books about 1663, at which time consideration was given to securing schoolmasters "to tran up children to reading and writing".

About 1668, John Morton, nephew of Nathaniel Morton, Secretary of the Colony (see Fam. No. 94)

> "offered to teach children and youth of the town to read and write and cast accounts, on reasonable considerations."

In 1671 this offer was accepted by the Town, and it is of record that John Morton (see Fam. No. 340) "erected and kept" the *first* "free school" of a public nature in America at Plymouth in the year 1671.

Means for supporting public schools were sought and found. The fisheries on the Cape were placed under regulation by law, and a duty was put upon mackerel and other fish caught, for a support of the "free school".

Here are samples of the care our forefathers took to provide schools. They are extracts from the Town records:

> *July 31, 1699*—"voted that the selectmen should take care to provide a scoole master for the town with all conveniant sped & should settle him as neere the senter of the Towne as may be with conveniency & that every scollar that coms to wright or syfer or to *lern latten* shall pay 3 pence pr weke."
> *March 1, 1703/4*—"Itt was voatted by ye Inhabitants that there should be a Grammer Scole master provided for ye use of ye Town for ye yeare ensueing which shall be settled in the senter of ye Town."

[ 102 ]

*September 17, 1705*—"whereas sundry of the inhabitants have subscribed themselves to become bound to pay twenty pounds per year towards the support of A Scoole in ye Town for the next 7 years."

Under the circumstances it is quite surprising to find so many "books" listed in the estates of the Mayflower Planters. They either brought them on the Mayflower, or accumulated them afterwards. In either event it discloses mental activity.

With few exceptions the Mayflower Planters left wills disposing of substantial estates in minute detail. Some of these documents are really remarkable and of themselves demonstrate the high degree of intelligence of the testator.

Stephen Hopkins left a library of "Divers Bookes" including, of course, the Bible. Nicholas Snow left some books, listing especially his "Pslm Booke". Mrs. Mary Ring left many dainty objects, including books. She must have been "genteel", perhaps closely related to Joseph Ring, a member of Parliament under Charles I. Jacob Cooke left a number of weapons of war, but his will also names various "bookes", a "bible" and the "Psalme Book". Some of the estate inventories went into detail concerning books. Elder William Brewster, being the "teacher" of the community for the first few years, left a number of books, among them being many works in Latin. One of the outstanding libraries left by the Planters, was, of course, that of Gov. William Bradford.

------

Ref. Nos. 30, 41, 51, 58, 78, 86, 91, 96, 128, 500, 501.

## SOCIAL LIFE

During the first generation or two, the social life, manners, habits and general methods of living in New Plymouth Plantation were, of course, those which the Pilgrims brought with them from England and Holland.

The "Olde England" which our Pilgrim Fathers had departed from in self exile for the sake, substantially, of religious and civil liberty had been their home for many generations, and the cradle of all their troubles, hopes, aspirations and disappointments.

The England being left behind by the Planters in 1620 consisted of a little over 400,000 people. About 230,000 resided in London and Westminster. There were twenty-five other cities. The northern counties of England were thinly populated, and infested with robbers, and this included the section around Scrooby in Nottinghamshire.

The social and economic conditions in England during portions of the 16th and 17th centuries were unfortunate. There were many reasons, other than religion, which influenced the Planters to seek new homes. The country had not grown in population for a number of causes. Among them may be cited the following:

1. Lack of sanitary safeguards.
2. An enormous death rate. Only the very hardiest survived.
3. Governmental ordinances against growth of population, to avoid starvation.
4. Dissolution of monasterism in the 16th century, the change throwing thousands of monks and nuns into need or self support.

The social problems in England which our Pilgrims were leaving behind can be defined from a census survey made on January 2, 1615, for the town of Sheffield:

Total population ................................2207

"Begging Poore" unable to live without charity... 725

Able to do something for relief of needy townspeople, yet they were poor working people, not more than 10 of, whom had grounds of their own that would keep a cow ......................................... 100

Householders who could do nothing further, who usually by the hardest labor made both ends meet, but who by the storms of a few days sickness would be down to beggary ............................... 160

Childless (half the population). These were children or servants of the 260 householders. The greater part of these were such as live on small wages, and are constrained to work some to provide necessaries........1222

The Kingdom of Great Britain was divided into fifty-three shires, thirteen being in Wales.

The English people were classed roughly into four ranks about the year 1620:

1. Gentlemen—Sovereign, Prince of Wales, King's eldest son, Dukes, Marquises, Earls, Viscounts. There were forty-three Lords or Barons, two Archbishops, and twenty-two Bishops.

   There were ninety-two in all who constituted, by right of birth or position, the House of Lords. Below these were the simple Knight Esquire bearing coats-of-arms, easily to be had for money, to those of good education, who could live without manual labor. By birth, Lawyers, Physicians and Clergy. The rank of Esquire was military, but was being used to apply to gentlemen by birth. Such gentlemen as had no special title of nobility and were not entitled to Esquire, now added "Master" or "Mr."

2. Citizens (Burgesses) were the freemen of Cities and Boroughs. They were voters and entitled to sit in the lower Houses of Parliament. It was, of course, a numerous class. Some of the Mayflower Planters were, probably, of this class.

3. Yeomen were freeborn men, who from their own land had an annual income of not less than six pounds. They were mostly thriving farmers. Once in a while they climbed to positions vacated by "decayed" gentlefolk, and educated their sons. They usually fought on foot, and were brave and fearless, a chief dependence of the King. They were addressed by Christian names, and spoken of as "Goodman". In legal papers they were "John Brown, Yeoman".

   Quite a number of this class emigrated to the colonies soon after 1620. However, it is not thought any yeomen in a strict sense were on the Mayflower.

4. Labourers included petty merchants having no free land. Copy holders who held land by grant of Lord of Manor. Artificer, carpenter, blacksmith, etc. Poor and the rabble. Several on the Mayflower were artificers or mechanics, and sailors. They became leaders in the colony.

The food of our "Pilgrim fathers" did not differ much from that of today. The Planters brought the good old English garden idea with them to the colonies, and raised melons, pumpkins, gourds, cucumbers, radishes, skirrets, parsnips, carrots, cabbage, narews, turnips, and all kinds of salad herbs.

The orchards abounded in apples, pears, plums, walnuts, filberts, cherries, apricots, and grapes.

Although the winter of 1620-21 was very hard on the Mayflower Planters, yet when spring and summer came, the vicinity of New Plymouth was found quite delightful. The birds began to sing merrily in the woods as early as March, and then came the planting time, followed by delicious strawberries and fruits.

Fresh fish, wild fowl, and larger game were plentiful.

Indeed, after the first winter, the death rate in New Plymouth was very low for a number of years.

Naturally, the Mayflower Planters brought with them the old English idea of shelter, and, in 1620, the homes of England were still crude.

The "yeoman" usually had a house of several rooms, roofed with reeds. The cottage of the "laborer" was of clay upon a timber frame, thatched with straw. There were seldom more than two rooms, and windows were latticed. Glass was unknown. With the exception of bedrooms, the floors, even in palaces, were strewn with rushes.

For the first six or seven years "thatch" was used as roofing for the shelters in New Plymouth, although the Pilgrims had already departed in some other respects from the English construction, in that logs, boards and "pale" were being used for the main body of the houses.

On January 6, 1627, at a Town Meeting

"it was agreed that from henceforward no dwelling house was to be covered with any kind of thatch, as straw, reed etc, but with either board, pale, or the like, to wit, of all that were to be new built in the town."

There had been a number of serious fires previous to 1627 in the colony, usually beginning in the thatched roofs of the dwellings.

The clothing worn by the early colonists was typical of the times, and interesting descriptions of apparel are found in the inventories of the estates of the Planters.

The material for men's clothing was of a coarse, durable type.

It has been stated that several spinning-wheels and looms were brought over on the Mayflower. There is some doubt about this tradition. They came later. The women probably found it difficult to keep apparel mended during the first two or three years.

They wore the type of garment for men and women in England.

Colors were bright and cheery, and included in 1638 "russet, purple, green, tawny, deere colour, orange colour, buffs and scarlet".

The men wore doublets and jerkins of brown and greens, and cloaks with red and purple linings.

The women wore full skirts of say, paduacoy or silk of varied colors, long, pointed stomachers, often with bright tone. Full, sometimes puffed or slashed, sleeves, and lace collars or "whisks" resting upon the shoulders.

Broadcloth gowns of russet tones were worn by those who could not afford silks and satins. Sometimes women wore doublets and jerkins of black and browns. For dress occasions the men wore black velvet jerkins with white ruffs, like those in the authentic portrait of Edward Winslow.

Velvet and quilted hoods of all colors and sometimes caps, flat on the head and meeting below the chin with fullness, are shown in portraits of English women and early colonists.

The children were dressed like miniature men and women.

Tailors, cobblers, and hatters were very essential to any community, and were held in great respect. However, the early New England Planters were inventive and industrious, valuable traits of character which have been passed down to descendants, and wherever possible they made their own hats, clothing and shoes.

The occupations of our Pilgrim forefathers were those incidental to the production of the three essentials of living, food, shelter and clothing.

There were few amusements and luxuries in the colonies for a number of generations. However, food was excellent and plentiful. The Planters were all good tillers of the soil, and many of them became successful hunters, trappers and fishermen, so that a food supply problem did not really exist. As a matter of fact, a flourishing food exporting business, such as fish, was soon built up.

Carpenters and blacksmiths were in great demand, and communities offered special inducements for them to settle in certain localities. The "village blacksmith" was a personage of high degree in colonial days. Many of them accumulated much property and became elders in the church.

Ref. Nos. 18, 28, 29, 33, 36, 40, 41, 51, 53, 55, 58, 59, 60, 62, 99, 127, 224, 245, 246, 255.

# HISTORY OF EASTHAM

To all descendants of the Pilgrims the little Town of Eastham must be considered of the greatest importance, and especially so to those many thousands who are descended from one of the early settlers, or planters, named in this history.

Nicholas Snow was among the first seven settlers of Nauset (Eastham) in 1644 (see Fam. No. 2), and was followed soon afterward by his brother-in-law Giles Hopkins (see Fam. No. 3).

In June, 1644, a committee of the New Plymouth Colony Church, consisting of "Mr. William Bradford, Mr. Thomas Prence and divers others" purchased from the Indians a territory approximately lying in what is now Orleans, Eastham and Wellfleet.

Eastham was the fourth town to be settled on the Cape. It is located across the Bay from Plymouth, a little to the southeast.

The most outstanding reason for making the purchase at the time was to break up the unity of the Indian settlements on the Cape which were still powerful, and something of a menace to the settlers of both Barnstable Co. (Cape Cod), and of Plymouth Co. A study of the map will make this clear.

Nauset, an Indian name, was applied to the whole purchase, although this name from remote times had been used by the Indians to designate some particular locality. In 1651 the Court at Plymouth ordered the name changed to Eastham. The old name, Nauset, however, still identifies the territory.

It is interesting to note that the Pilgrims had their first encounter with the Indians in 1620, near the Great Pond in Eastham, or Nauset. The Indians made this attack to gratify a revenge which had been engendered by the perfidy of Hunt in the employ of Capt. John Smith. Hunt had entrapped some of the Indians and carried them off to Spain where they were sold. Aspinet was the first Sachem of the Nauset Tribe known to the English.

This Indian Chief had joined the conspiracy in 1623 to extirpate the English, but the death of the principal actors at the hands of Capt. Myles Standish so terrified him that he concealed himself in unhealthy places and died of disease.

In the spring of the year, about March 3, 1644, the Court granted unto

"the church of New Plymouth, or those that goe to dwell at Nausett all that tractt of land lying between sea & sea from the purchasers bounds at Namseakett to the hearing brooke att Billingsgate with the saide hearing brook and all the meadows on both sides the saide brooke with the great basse pond these & all the meadows & islands lying within the saide tract."

[ 108 ]

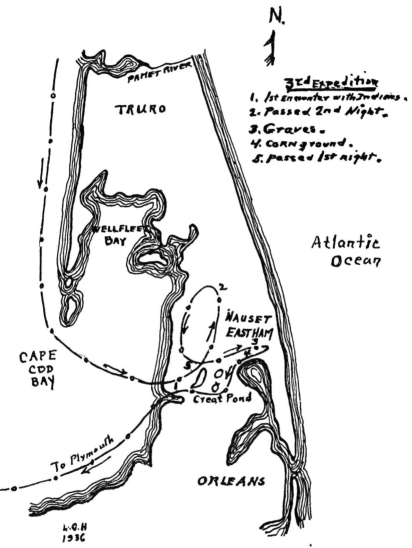

N.

### 3rd Expedition
1. 1st Encounter with Indians.
2. Passed 2nd Night.
3. Graves.
4. Corn ground.
5. Passed 1st night.

PAMET RIVER

TRURO

WELLFLEET BAY

Atlantic Ocean

2

NAUSET
EASTHAM
3

CAPE COD BAY

5

Great Pond

To Plymouth

ORLEANS

L.C.H
1936

Map of Eastham section showing
route of 3rd expedition just
before the shallop sailed for
Plymouth across the Bay, on
Dec 17th and 18th 1620 N.S.

The Eastham settlers were from among the most useful citizens of Plymouth, and the Plymouth church regretted their departure. However, owing to the urgent need for a settlement on that portion of the Cape, on or about April, 1644, seven prominent families left for Nauset, where they immediately organized a community. The first seven settlers were:

Thomas Prence (see Fam. No. 11).
John Doane (see Fam. No. 61).
Nicholas Snow (see Fam. No. 2).
Josiah Cooke (see Fam. No. 25).
Richard Higgins (see Fam. No. 63).
John Smalley (see Fam. No. 16).
Edward Bangs (see Fam. No. 127).

The family records of all of these settlers will be found in this book in the proper place.
Others, mostly from Plymouth soon followed.
Inhabitants of Eastham on May 22, 1655, were:

Henry Atkins (see Fam. No. 22).
Stephen Atwood (see Fam. No. 48).
Edward Bangs (see Fam. No. 127).
Richard Booshop (see Fam. No. 620).
Josiah Cooke (see Fam. No. 25).
Job Cole (see Fam. No. 57).
Daniel Crisp (see Fam. No. 860).
John Doane (see Fam. No. 61).
John Freeman (see Fam. No. 58).
Richard Higgins (see Fam. No. 63).
Giles Hopkins (see Fam. No. 2).
Richard Knowles (see Fam. No. 142).
John Mayo (see Fam. No. 31).
Nathaniel Mayo (see Fam. No. 27).
William Merrick (see Fam. No. 24).
Gov. Thomas Prence (see Fam. No. 11).
Thomas Paine (see Fam. No. 12).
Joseph Rogers (see Fam. No. 15).
Thomas Roberts (see Fam. No. 701).
Mark Snow (see Fam. No. 11).
Nicholas Snow (see Fam. No. 2).
Jonathan Sparrow (see Fam. No. 135).
Richard Sparrow (see Fam. No. 65).
Ralph Smith (see Fam. No. 21).
John Smalley (see Fam. No. 16).
William Twining (see Fam. No. 113).
Thomas Williams (see Fam. No. 26).
Robert Wexame (see Fam. No. 960).
John Young (see Fam. No. 76).

Many of these men held public office from time to time, and were prominent in a number of directions. The details of their history will be found in the proper place under the family group heading. Eastham prospered, and during the next twenty years many new heads of families appeared in the community. The inhabitants admitted before 1675 were:

John Bangs (for Bangs see Fam. No. 127).
Jonathan Bangs jr.
Joshua Bangs.
Ireal Cole (see Fam. No. 56).
John Doane Jr. (for Doane see Fam. No. 61).
Daniel Doane Sr.
John Freeman jr. (for Freeman see Fam. No. 12).
Thomas Freeman.
Samuel Freman Sr.
Samuel Freeman Jr.
Edmund Freeman.
Thomas Higgins (for Higgins see Fam. No. 162).
Jonathan Higgins Sr.
Jonathan Higgins Jr.
Benjamin Higgins.
Joseph Harding (see Fam. No. 100).
Stephen Hopkins Sr. (see Fam. No. 22).
Joshua Hopkins (see Fam. No. 28).
William Merrick Jr. (see Fam. No. 24).
Samuel Mayo Sr. (see Fam. No. 27).
Thomas Paine Jr. (See Fam. No. 58).
John Pains (see Fam. No. 61).
Isaac Pepper (see Fam. No. 461).
Thomas Rogers (see Fam. No. 17).
John Rogers (see Fam. No. 17).
Stephen Snow (see Fam. No. 15).
Nicholas Snow (see Fam. No. 2).
Samuel Smith (see Fam. No. 21).
Thomas Smith (see Fam. No. 21).
John Sparrow (see Fam. No. 65).
William Walker (see Fam. No. 13).

Just when public schools were established in Eastham is not known, but it was very early in the settlement, for it is recorded that in 1678 the Town voted to raise money for "CONTINUATION" of the school.

Within a period of thirty-five years, Eastham (Nausett) on the Cape, which had been purchased from the Indians for a few "moose-skins, Indian beads, wampam, little knives" and the like, developed into a thriving sea-faring village. Many of the ablest men of the colony had settled there and its future was secure.

------

Ref. Nos. 28, 69, 71, 72, 73, 74.

# CAPE CODDERS IN NOVA SCOTIA AND MAINE

The story of Nova Scotia, especially Barrington, is linked closely with that of Cape Cod. Many descendants of the Mayflower Planters settled there.

During the war between England and France 1758-59 which resulted in the taking of Louisburg and Quebec, terminating in the peace of 1763, the settlement of Nova Scotia received considerable attention in the colonies. With the complete destruction of the French power on the continent the possibility of having a loyal British population in Nova Scotia increased.

Proclamations were sent into the English colonies along the Atlantic seaboard. They appealed especially to the New England settlements. Between 1760 and 1776, a tide of English colonists began to flow into Nova Scotia, many of them from Connecticut. The first planters of Menis, Amherst, Dublin and other places in and around King's Co. came from this state, mostly from New London. The adventurers seemed anxious to take up the vacated lands of the Acadians.

On May 29, 1761, there were several hundred grantees to 65,750 acres in Horton and Cornwallis. Most of them taking a full share of 500 acres.

There were numerous reasons for this interest in Canada, especially so to Englishmen, as a brief historical narrative will show. "Acadia," a beautiful land, has been made romantic through story and song. It is the "maritime" province of Canada, consisting of Nova Scotia, New Brunswick, Prince Edward Island, and the southern portion of Quebec. Geographically the state of Maine must be considered in this section.

Long before the Pilgrims landed on Plymouth Rock, Samuel de Champlain sailed up the St. Lawrence in 1603, in the interests of fur-traders. The next year he was sailing on the Bay of Fundy, and aided in founding the first permanent French colony in North America at Port Royal (Annapolis), N. S. He began the settlement of Quebec in 1608. From this time on until his death in 1635 Champlain worked to develop Canada. He promoted trade and explored the interior. He went as far west as Lake Ontario. For many years the French and the Church ruled in Canada. They explored as far west as the Mississippi, and finally they determined to try to seize the English colonies by closing in on the English from the rear. The plan was audacious, but France wanted to rule America. They failed and the treaty of Utrecht in 1713 gave Britain claims to Hudson Bay, Newfoundland and Nova Scotia. However, France still retained the shores of the St. Lawrence, and Cape Breton to command its mouth. She wanted to control the interior of the country, and again challenged British

Settlement of Nova Scotia and Maine
By the English.

1755 Acadian French driven from Nova Scotia.
1759 Quebec fell to British under Wolfe.
1761 Barrington settled by Cape Codders.
1762 Lots in Maine began to be taken rapidly.
1763 Peace of Paris. Canada ceded to Britain.
1765 Pictou County settled by Philadelphians.
1776 Many New England families settled in N.S.

supremacy in America. She built a fortress at Louisburg. In 1701 she had settled Detroit, and her missionaries and leaders were already at Sault Ste. Marie, commanding Lake Superior, and at Mackinac, commanding Lake Michigan. In 1743 La Verendrye came in sight of mountains barring the Pacific coast. The French also crowned La Salle's work by founding New Orleans at the mouth of the Mississippi. All France had to do was to conquer the English on the coast and America could be hers.

In 1753 Virginia warned the French on the Ohio that they were on British territory. The next year, George Washington, together with Braddock, was defeated. In 1755 Britain took the stern step of deporting the Acadian French from Nova Scotia, and in 1756 the Seven Years War began. However, Louisburg was taken and Wolfe won a great victory at Quebec on September 13, 1759, causing the French to surrender a year later at Montreal, and at the Treaty of Paris, 1763, Canada was finally ceded to Great Britain, who immediately began to promote the settlement of the region by English subjects, especially from the colonies.

Other portions of Nova Scotia were soon settled by English families from the colonies as a direct result of the taking of Louisburg and Quebec. Pictou Co. was settled in 1765.

From a letter of the Lieutenant Governor of the Province to the Lord Commissioner of Trade and Plantations, dated April 30, 1765, it was stated—

"By the lots arrival of several persons from Pennsylvania, New Jersey and some of the neighboring colonies, we have the prospect of having this Province soon peopled by the accession of many settlers from these parts."

The English government desired very much to settle Nova Scotia with English families, and offered many inducements to settlers and land speculators among the American colonists along the Atlantic seaboard.

The Philadelphia Grant to portions of Pictou Co., N. S., was made and dated October 31, 1765, to the following persons:

Edmond Grawley Esq.
Rev. James Lyon
John Rhea
Richard Stockton
George Bryan
William Symonds
John Wykoff
Isaac Wykoff
Jonathan Smith
Andrew Hodge
John Bayard
Thomas Harris
Robert Harris
David Rhea

Some of the above took up actual residence in Nova Scotia, others sold their holdings, they being to a considerable degree land speculations.

Fishermen from Cape Cod began to settle in Barrington, Yarmouth Co., Nova Scotia, about 1761. Among the earliest were Solomon Smith, Archelaus Smith, Jonathan Smith and Thomas Crowell.

In November, 1761, twelve families from Chatham and Harwich, Cape Cod, came to Barrington and established homes. It appears that people from the Cape were accustomed to come down to Barrington on fishing trips, and had become familiar with opportunities there.

The first settlers were Squire Smith and Thomas Crowell, who with their families were landed at Barrington in 1761 from a vessel bound for Liverpool.

As stated previously, a charter had been granted on April 10, 1606, by James I of England to the Plymouth Adventurers, and a futile attempt was made to plant a colony on the Kennebec River (now in Maine). However, nothing came of it, and on November 3, 1620 (just about the time, it will be noted, the Pilgrims were to land at Plymouth), King James I granted what is known as the New England Charter to the Council of Plymouth, in the county of Devon, England. This charter was granted to forty lords, knights and merchants of England. They were incorporated as "The Council Established at Plymouth in the county of Devon for the planting, ruling, and governing New England in America". This interesting charter included the continent and inlands between the parallels of 40° and 48° N. Latitude.

Attempts were made by this Council to control the colonies planted in Massachusetts before 1630, but with little success, owing to the fact that they were functioning under laws more or less of their own making. Therefore, grants under this Charter were really not taken advantage of until about 1762. At this time Maine and Nova Scotia were being rapidly settled by English colonists from along the Atlantic seaboard, especially from the Cape Cod section, and many descendants of Mayflower passengers became grantees of land under the charter in the eastern and coast line counties of Maine, upon which they established their families and built homes.

The territory now called Maine suffered much during the French and Indian wars. The French were continually stirring up the Indian tribes against the English. From 1722 to 1725 the tribes of Nova Scotia and Eastern Maine waged a fierce warfare against the colonists. As a matter of fact, security in Maine was not really established until the Treaty of Paris in 1763.

Ref. Nos. 125, 236, 237, 238, 239.

# HOPKINS

1. **Hopkins, Stephen,**[1] born England about 1580, possibly bp
October 29, 1581, in Wortley, parish of Wotten-under-Edge,
Gloucestershire; died between June 6, 1644 and July 17, 1644; the
name of his first wife is unknown; married the second time Elizabeth **Fisher**, February 19, 1617/8, as recorded in St. Mary's
Church, Whitechapel, London, England. She came over with her
husband on the Mayflower, and died at Plymouth, Mass., before
1640.

Stephen Hopkins was a many-sided character. He and Miles
Standish had a number of points in common, and were close friends.
In fact, Standish was executor of Stephen Hopkins' will. They
had both been something of adventurers before making the voyage
in the Mayflower.

One historian describes him as follows:

"Stephen Hopkins was a man of weight in the Colony. Like
many another man he had faults and virtues. He was intelligent, robust, enterprising, practical, quick to see the point,
and fertile in expedients, but he was a bit touchy and not at all
averse to a setto with anybody who crossed his path."
The Pilgrims, Nobles, 1907, p. 181.

The history of his family in England is not determined, but there
can be no doubt of its respectable standing. It is known he resided in London for some time, and was probably a merchant with
some means, and a staunch "Separatist", which kept him on the
defensive with the authorities.

Some writers claim that he was a great-grandson of Stephen
Hopkins, Fellow and Professor in Kings College 1532, and Rector
of Norfolk, Eng., 1551, and that his parents were Nicholas Hopkins
and Mary Poole, sister of Sir Giles Poole.

The church register of St. Marys, Matfellon (Whitechapel),
records the marriage of Stephen Hopkins to Elizabeth Fisher,
February 19, 1617/8. This places him in the parish on the high
road entering London at Aldgate, near which Bradford, Carver,
Cushman and Southworth lived, in or near Heneage House, Aldgate
ward.

It appears he was a born fighter, leader and of an extremely
adventurous disposition.

The Mayflower voyage was not the first exploit of Stephen. As
a matter of fact, when that trip was made in 1620, he was an experienced traveler, and could be useful in many directions, especially in the founding and settlement of new lands, where hardship
and danger prevailed. He was well known to the Merchant Adventurers and Thomas Weston of London. They probably felt he was

a good type of person for the colony, and encouraged him to make the voyage.

On previous occasions Stephen had visited the Virginia Colony. In one instance, on May 15, 1609, the ship "Sea Adventure" set sail from London bound for the Virginia shores. Perhaps the name appealed to Stephen for he is on board. It was intended to make Virginia by way of the Bermuda Islands. After many days of peaceful sailing a severe storm wrecked the good ship Sea Adventure on the treacherous coast of Bermuda. Stephen immediately made himself useful.

Among other duties he was chosen to read the Psalms on Sunday, for it is recorded that he "had much knowledge of the Scripture and could reason well therein".

After some time on the Islands a certain portion of the party became restless. They desired to continue the voyage in some manner. A meeting was held of those who were not content to lead a peaceful life among the beautiful Bermudas, where the days come and go under a lazy semi-tropical sky, and no hope of anything happening.

The restless souls had a meeting, but it was marked with discord. Stephen Hopkins was a ringleader and outspoken in his opinion.

Sir George Summers, leader of the expedition, could not overlook the matter. He ordered the arrest of the leaders, and Stephen, together with his associates, was tried and found guilty of rebellion.

At last something had happened. Stephen found himself face to face with possible execution for insubordination.

Apparently the predicament did not discourage him, for he is soon petitioning for a pardon. It is recorded that—

"so penitent hee was and made soe much moane alledging the ruine of his wife and children"

that upon the plea of the rest of the party, the Governor pardoned him.

Following this exciting experience, a bark was fitted up and the company continued the voyage to Virginia.

After spending some time in the colonies Stephen returned to England, where he seemed to prosper. Probably while a small merchant in London, he became closely affiliated with the "Merchant Adventurers", that famous group of English business men who were actively engaged in promoting the settlement of the Virginia Colonies, and most of whom were "Separatists", or, at least, in sympathy with that movement.

Just when or how Stephen became attached to the contemplated Mayflower voyage of 1620 is not clear. No doubt it was due in part to the influence of Mr. Thomas Weston, manager for the "Merchant Adventurers", who were to finance the Mayflower expedition, and, naturally, were seeking substantial "Planters" for the colony.

[ 117 ]

Evidently the appeal was strong enough to convince Stephen, for bright and early on embarkation day he appeared at the wharves to board the Mayflower.

His party was the largest, and brought much baggage. Bradford in 1646 enumerates it as follows:

> "Mr. Steven Hopkins & Elizabeth his wife, and .2. children, caled Giles, and Constanta a daughter, both by a former wife. And .2. more by this wife, caled Damaris & Oceanus, the last was borne at sea. And .2. servants called Edward Doty and Edward Litster."

The embarkation of this family group must have been a lively event, and probably taxed the "touchy" temper of Stephen to the limit. Getting all parties and baggage aboard a ship in those days was a testy job, especially when the party included women and children.

No doubt, the two "servants" (Ed. Doty and Ed. Litster, boys working way over) were of some help in the matter. These two "servants", by the way, were continually quarrelling with each other, perhaps over division of duties, and soon after landing at New Plymouth fought a duel, drawing blood. It had the distinction of being the first recorded duel in the colonies. Just what part, if any, Stephen had in starting the fight is not clear. However, the records show that Stephen appeared in court at Plymouth and pleaded for the young men.

The Pilgrims were supposed to have been a peaceful group, averse to fighting. However, the record appears to show that they were quite free with fists and other weapons on occasion. This, of course, could not be otherwise, as the venture had no appeal for weaklings.

We are not informed in detail how Stephen managed to get his family and belongings, consisting of an ill wife, baby Damaris, 2 years old (there was another youngster, Oceanus, born on the Mayflower), his thirteen-year-old son Giles, and daughter Constanta, aged fifteen years, deposited in the little row-boat at the wharf, and safely transported to the Mayflower, which was lazily riding at anchor, probably off "Blackhall" or "Wapping" near London, in the Thames, on that momentous mid-July day of the year 1620.

There were eight persons in Stephen Hopkins' party, including the two "servants".

Very likely Giles and Constance, two strong, healthy children, were of great aid to the parents in getting everything snugly on board. All members of this particular party were healthy enough to survive the "first sickness" in New Plymouth, which was an exceptional record, indeed.

To the children of the Mayflower, the confusion of embarking was exciting, with wide-eyed interest they watched the preparations for departure. Neither the children nor their elders realized at the time the historical significance of the event, or the great parts they were to play in the drama of founding and building a nation.

With everybody aboard, the Mayflower, on Saturday, July 15, 1620 (O.S.), weighed anchor and dropped down with the tide to Gravesend. Owing to numerous delays at Southampton and other English ports, the ship did not leave Plymouth, England, for the New World until September 6, 1620 (O.S.), and after sixty-five days out sighted Cape Cod.

During the voyage Stephen became a great favorite of the children. He had many stories of adventure, which he was fond of telling and even the older persons were greatly interested in practical instruction which he gave in the art of building houses. He illustrated the constructions on the deck of the Mayflower by means of a series of sticks having suitable notches in them. With these sticks he made different types of "log-house" designs.

During the various landing "explorations" around Cape Cod, Stephen was much in evidence. His name and duties are frequently mentioned.

He became one of the "wealthiest" Planters of New Plymouth, and, in addition to much land, many cattle, and other possessions, he appears to have run a general store or "tavern".

For many years he was a member of the Governor's Council, but did not seek a high public office.

He built the first wharf in New Plymouth and was financially interested in shipping.

His services were called upon quite frequently in dealings with the Indians. He seemed to understand their ways and language, and had no fear of them. At one time it became essential for the colony to negotiate with Massasoit. Stephen, with an Indian named Squanto as a guide, was sent through the forest to see him. No timid man would have undertaken that job.

As previously stated Stephen made himself useful during the voyage, and in various contacts of a diplomatic nature with the Indians. He was a member of exploring parties, especially the Third Expedition which started out on Wednesday, December 16, 1620 (N.S.), to locate the place for settlement. "Mourt's Relation" 1622, states:

"So ten of our men were appointed who were of themselves willing to undertake it, to wit, Captaine Standish, Master Carver, William Bradford, Edward Winsloe, John Tilley, Edward Tilley, John Howland, and three of London, Richard Warren, Steeven Hopkins, and Edward Dotte."

Not only was Stephen in the Third Expedition, but he was an important member of the First Expedition, in which, from past experience, he identified a small tree bent over and attached to boughs and grasses woven together and covering a deep pit, as a trap used by Indians to catch deer.

When Samoset came to Plymouth to welcome the Pilgrims he was lodged over night at Stephen's house. Apparently he could understand him.

When the messenger of Canonicus brought the snake skin full of arrows to Plymouth, Standish and Hopkins had charge of him, Stephen acting as interpreter, which was his usual job.

The high position held by Hopkins in the little community, especially in "trade", and the rules governing that important occupation is shown in the following court orders, where there are appointed:

"at the general court held at New Plymouth the 3d of January 1636 in the xijth years of the Raigne of or sovaigne Lord Charles by the grace of God, of England, etc, King defendor of the faith etc before Edward Winslowe gent. Gounour, Wm Bradford, Thomas Prynce, John Alden, Steeven Hopkins, Wm Collier, Tymothy Hatherly, and John Brown Gentle. assistants"

"It is ordered by the court that Mr Collyer, Mr Hopkins, Mr Brown, Mr Done, John Jenny, Jonathan Brewster, John Winslow, Thomas Willet shall treat with those that have the trade in their hands & to prpare such conclusions concerning the same, that the Court being made acquainted therewith and approveing thereof may conclud the same with them."

Some historians have stated that Weston selected Hopkins to accompany the Mayflower Planters because of his previous experience in Virginia.

That Stephen had a fiery temper is amply borne out by the records of Plymouth. They also disclose him to be a man of wealth for that day, owning much land, many cattle, and employing considerable help, which were noted as "servants", but more aptly were plain "hired men".

He apparently maintained also a general store or tavern, and was a merchant to the colonists in some degree. His cattle and lands after a time spread into what is now Kingston and Yarmouth.

Some court orders are illuminating:

*June 7, 1636*—"John Tisdale, yeoman, entreth an accon. of battery against Steven Hopkins, assistant to the Govrn't by whom the said John was dangerously wounded, as he affirmeth."

"An accon. of battery was tried between John Tisdale, yeoman, plaintiff, & Stephen Hopkins, assistant to the goverment deft. Wherein the deft Stephen Hopkins, was cast in five pownds starling to our Sov. lord the King, whose pease he had broken, wch he ought after a special manner to have kept, and also in forty shillings to the plaintiffe, both wch he was adjudged to pay."

*October 6, 1637*—"Mr Steephen Hopkins psented for suffering servants and others to sit drinking in his house (contrary to the orders of the court), and to play at Shovell board, & such like misdemeanors is therefore fined fourty shillings.'' *January 2, 1637/8*—''William Renolds is psented for being drunck at Mr Hopkin's his house.''

''Mr Hopkins is prsented for sufferinge excessive drinking in his house.''

In this instance he was acquitted, but it clearly discloses the problem of strong drink is very old, and still unsolved in the year 1936.

That Stephen sold liquor with an eye to profit seems clear from the following court order. In those days the ''general store'' sold rum of various types, and almost everybody used or drank a fermented beverage of some kind. For the most part it was home brew, and very mild.

*June 5, 1638*—''Mr Steephen Hopkins is prsented for selling beere for ijd the quart, not worth jd a quart.'' He was fined ''for selling beere at such excessive rates to the oppressing & impoushing of the Colony.''

From this it would seem that Stephen catered to quite a large portion of the Colony.

However, Hopkins sold other things besides rum, and here again he exhibited his ''genius'' for trying to make a profit. Apparently, Stephen lost the good will of the court, and perhaps his neighbors, whenever he sold anything for much more than he paid for it.

No doubt, he developed the idea of buying at ''wholesale,'' so that he could hide some of his profits. However, even that was not a sure solution, for we have the following court order:

*October 7, 1639*—''Mr Stephen Hopkins, upon his presentment for selling a looking glasse for 16d the like whereof was bought in the Bay for ixd (9d) is referred to further information.''

Apparently, Mr. Hopkins sold the article for about twice what he paid for it. His ''misdemeanor'' occurred 300 years ago, but the lesson of the ''presentment'' seemingly has been lost, for modern merchants are still doing the same thing whenever they can get away with it.

After a busy and useful life in New Plymouth of about twenty-five years, Mr. Hopkins died, probably in June, 1644, leaving a large estate, and a very interesting will, as follows:

### WILL OF STEPHEN HOPKINS

Stephen Hopkins died at New Plymouth in 1644, between June 6, the day his will was made, and July 17, the day his inventory was taken.

The will and inventory are recorded in the Plymouth Colony Wills and Inventories, Vol. I, folios 61, 62 and 63.

[61] The last Will and Testament of Mr Stephen Hopkins exhibited upon the oathes of Mr Willm Bradford and Captaine Myles Standish at the generall Court holden at Plymouth the xxth of August Anno dm 1644 as it followeth in these wordes viz.

The sixt of June 1644, I, Stephen Hopkins of Plymouth in New England, being weake, yet in good and prfect memory, blessed be God, yet considering the fraile estate of all men, I do ordaine and make this to be my last will and testament in manner and forme following, and first I do committ my body to the earth from whence it was taken, and my soule to the Lord who gave it, my body to be buryed as neare as convenyently may be to my wyfe Deceased.

And, first, my will is that out of my whole estate my funerall expences be discharged.

Secondly, that out of the remayneing part of my said estate, that all my lawfull Debts be payd.

Thirdly, I do bequeath, by this, my will, to my sonn Giles Hopkins, my great Bull wch is now in the hands of Mrs Warren. Also, I do give to Stephen Hopkins, my sonn Giles, his sonne, twenty shillings in Mris Warren's hands for the hire of the said Bull. Also I give and bequeath to my daughter Constance Snow, the wyfe of Nicholas Snow, my mare, also, I give unto my daughter Deborah Hopkins, the brod horned black cowe, and her calf, and half the cowe, called Motley. Also I doe give and bequeath unto my daughter Damaris Hopkins, the Cowe called Damaris heiffer, and the white faced calf, and half the cowe called Mottley. Also, I give to my daughter, Ruth, the Cowe called Red Cole, and her calf, and a Bull at Yarmouth wch is in the keepeing of Giles Hopkins, wch is an yeare, and advantage old, and half the curld Cowe.

Also, I give and bequeath to my daughter Elizabeth, the Cowe called Smykins, and her calf, and thother half of the Curld Cowe wth Ruth, and an yearelinge heiffer wth out a tayle, in the keeping of Gyles Hopkins at Yarmouth.

Also I do give and bequeath unto my foure daughters, that is to say, Deborah Hopkins, Damaris Hopkins, Ruth Hopkins, and Elizabeth Hopkins, all the mooveable goods, the wch do belong to my house, as linnen, wollen, beds, bed cloathes, pott kettles, pewter, or whatsoevr are moveable, belonging to my said house, of what kynd soever, and not named by their prticular names, all wch said mooveables, to bee equally devided amongst my said daughters foure silver spoones, that is to say, to eich of them one. And, in case, any of my said daughters should be taken away by death before they be married, that, then, the part of their division to be equally devided amongst the survivors.

I do also, by this my will, make Caleb Hopkins, my sonne and heire apparent, giveing and bequeathing unto my said

[ 122 ]

sonn aforesaid, all my Right title and interest to my house and Lands at Plymouth, wth all the Right title and interrest wch doth, might or of Right, doth, or may hereafter belong unto mee, as also I give unto my saide heire all such lande wch of Right, is Rightly due unto me, and not at prsent in my reall possession, wch belongs unto me by right of my first comeing into this land, or by any other due Right, as by such freedome, or othorwise, giveing unto my said heire my full & whole and entire Right in all divisions, allottments, appoyntments or distributions whatsoever, to all or any pt of the said lande at any tyme, or tymes, so to be disposed.

Also, I do give moreover unto my foresaid heire one paire or yooke of oxen, and the hyer of them wch are in the hands of Richard Church, as may appeare by bill under his hand.

Also, I do give unto my said heire, Caleb Hopkins, all my debts wch are now oweing unto me, or at the day of my death, may be oweing unto mee, either by booke, bill, or bills, or any other way rightfully due unto me. ffurther more, my will is, that my daughters, aforesaid, shall have free recourse to my house in Plymouth, upon any occation, there to abide and re-mayne for such tyme as any of them shall thinke meete and convenyent & they single persons.

And for the faythfull prformance of this, my will, I do make and ordayne my aforesaid sonn and heire, Caleb Hopkins, my true and lawful Executor, ffurther, I do, by this my will, ap-poynt and make my said sonn, and Captaine Miles Standish, joyntly supervisors of this, my will, according to the true meaneing of the same, that is to say, that my Executor & super-visor shall make the severall divisions, parts or porcons, leg-acies or whatsoever doth appertaine to the fullfilling of this, my will.

It is also my will, that my Executor & Supervisor shall ad-vise, devise and dispose by the best wayes & meanes they cann for the disposeing in marriage, or otherwise, for the best ad-vancnt of the estate of the forenamed Deborah, Damaris, Ruth, and Elizabeth Hopkins.

Thus trusting in the Lord, my will shal be truly prformed, according to the true meaneing of the same, I committ the whole Disposeing hereof to the Lord, that hee may direct you herein.

June 6th 1644
Witnesses hereof
Myles Standish,                       By me
William Bradford                      STEVEN HOPKINS

[62] An Inventory of the Goods and the cattells of Mr Steven Hopkins taken by Captaine Miles Standish, Mr Thomas Willet and Mr John Done the xviith of July 1644 xx° Cal. Re.

[ 123 ]

This inventory is too long to insert here in detail, although exceedingly illuminating.

Broadly, the inventory shows clearly, that Mr. Hopkins must have been one of the wealthiest men of the colony, if not the richest.

He left a large herd of cattle for those days, about thirteen head, including a young "heiffer wthout a tayle". Also a yoke of oxen, pigges and poultry.

The debts "oweing unto mee, either by booke, bill, or bills" was considerable. Whether the Executor was able to collect these items is not disclosed.

The household articles included many items of interest. These went to his daughters. There was a "greene Rugg" and a "yellow Rugg", many blankets, and much bedding of all kinds. There were "pillow beares", "boulsters", "checkered blanketts", "table clothes".

There are "dymothy Caps", "wrought Caps", and the like.

He left a library consisting of "Divers Bookes", not named, however.

There are many items of clothing in the inventory, including shoes, garters, "Ruffe", "mohaire petticote", "a petticote of phillip & cheny", "a grogorm coate", "a prpetuam coate", "coate & jerkin", "a muffe".

Items for the kitchen and dining room include "a hogshead", "warming pann", "porringers", "frying pann", "quart potts", "laten candlesticks", "puter candlesticks", "bras pott", "skellets", "1 dozzen & half trenchers", "paire of bellowes", "fire shovell & tongs".

In fact, the inventory discloses that Stephen had a very comfortable home, of which he was very fond, and, as his will clearly indicates, the death of his wife was a great blow to him, as she had been, no doubt, a fine home-maker.

He requested in his will "to be buryed as neare as convenyently may be to my wyfe Deceased".

### KNOWN CHILDREN BY FIRST WIFE (UNKNOWN)

+2. Constance, b. Eng. abt. 1605, d. Eastham, Mass. Nov. 25, 1677, or about the middle of Oct. 1677; m. Nicholas[1] **Snow**.

+3. Giles, b. Eng. abt. 1607, d. abt. 1690, or after Mar. 15, 1689, and before Apr. 26, 1690; m. Catone[2] **Wheldon** (Gabriel)[1].

Stephen, bp. Dec. 22, 1609, St. Stephen, Coleman St., London, Eng. (a possibility only).

### BY SECOND WIFE, ELIZABETH FISHER

4. Damaris, b. Eng. before 1618, d. young probably.
5. Oceanus, b. on the Mayflower, d. before June 1, 1627.
6. Caleb, b. Ply. before 1623, d. single, Barbadoes, before 1651.

+7. Deborah, b. Ply. about 1625, d. after 1666; m. Andrew[1] **Ring.**
+8. Damaris, b. Ply. after 1627, d. 1665/9; m. Jacob[2] **Cooke,** son
    of Francis[1] **Cooke.**
  9. Ruth, b. Ply, ——, d. single probably.
10. Elizabeth, b. Ply., ——, d. single probably.

Reg. Nos. 17, 69, 78, 79, 93, 136, 140, 171, 184, 264, 292, 502.

# SNOW

2. **Hopkins, Constance**[2] (Stephen[1], born Eng. about 1605; died Eastham, Mass., October 1677; married **Nicholas**[1] **Snow** in Plymouth 1623-27; born Eng., died Eastham, Mass., November 15, 1676. Will dated November 14, 1676, signed November 14, 1676 (O.S.).

Nicholas[1] Snow was one of those who arrived at Plymouth in the Anne in the year 1623, and found the settlers so sadly destitute of food and clothing. He was very young, and must have felt the matter keenly on viewing the poor, ragged and half-fed Pilgrims, but he soon began to lend a helping hand, and his romance with Constance Hopkins started without much delay. He received a share of land in Plymouth in 1624, and was married before 1627.

He became a freeman and taxpayer of Plymouth in 1633, and for a number of years was a man of note in that place.

In April, 1644, he with six other prominent men of Plymouth, seven families of forty-nine persons, began the settlement of Eastham (Nauset) across the bay from Plymouth, and from the beginning became an important person in that place. He was a deputy and selectman for a number of years. (See history of Eastham.)

In 1646, it was enacted by the Court that every Town within the Government "shall have a clerk, or some one appointed to keep a register of the day and year of the marriage, birth and burial of every man, woman and child within the Township".

Eastham immediately appointed Nicholas Snow to this important office, and he held the place with honor for sixteen years, and his son Mark Snow succeeded him.

He was one of Governor Prence's intimate associates, and it was partly through his efforts that the Rev. John Mayo was prevailed upon to settle as Minister in Eastham in 1655.

Nicholas Snow became a large landowner in Harwich, Eastham and Truro. His sons Mark, Joseph and Stephen came into possession of the land in Harwich; John of Truro and Jabez received the land in Eastham including the homestead.

WILL AND INVENTORY OF NICHOLAS[1] SNOW
Ply. Col. Wills and Inv., Vol. III, Part II, p. 71-77.

A writing ordered to be Reorded Declareing the manor of Nicholas Snow his Disposing of his Estate as followeth viz Nicholas Snow of Eastham Late Deceased:

I, Nicholas Snow of Eastham being weake and Infeirme of body but of prfect Memory and understanding, not knowing the Day of my Departure but yett Dayly expecting my last change; I thinke meet to leave this behind mee as my last Will and Testament; Impr: I commend my soule into the armese of Gods Mercye through Christ Jesus in whom I hope to sleep and my body to a Decent buriall; and as Concerning my temporall estate that God of his Goodness hath Given mee; It is my last Will and Testament that after this manor it should be Disposed off.

Impr: to my son Marke Snow I Give and bequeath all that twenty acrees of upland lying att Namskekitt wher his house now stands, and two acrees of Meddow; and all that broken marsh there of mine att Namscekett; Item, two thirds of my Great lott att Satuckett lying next the Indians Ground; and that syde of my lott next the Indians land I Give to him and his heires lawfully begotten of his body forever; and what hee Can purchase more of upland and meddow of the Indians there att Satuckett I Give to him all this abovesaid lands or meddow or Marsh purchased or unpurchased I Give to him and to his heires lawfully begotten of his body forever;

Item. To my son Joseph Snow I Give that other third prte of my Great lott att Satuckett; and two acrees and an halfe of meddow lying att Namscekett neare the head and an Necke of upland lying between it lying on the westsyde of William Twinings, all this abovesaid land and meddow I Give to my son Joseph Snow and to his heires Lawfully begotten of his body forever;

Item: To my son Steven Snow I Give twenty acrees on the southsyde of my Great lott att Pachett, and ten acrees of My little lott att Satuckett lying beween Daniell Cole and Edward Banges by the side of a Little pond, an acree and an halfe of Meddow att the boat meddow, lying between Thomas Williams, and Samuel Freeman and that prte of my Meddow att the Great Meddow, That lyeth between Josiah Cooke and the Eel-creeke; all this abovesaid land and meddow I Give to my son Steven and the heires lawfully begotten of his body; forever:

Item: To my son John Snow I Give all that my land att Paomett Purchased or unpurchased whether upland or med-dow; and all my Right and title or privilidge there; all the abovesaid upland or Meddow right and Privilidge att Paomett I Give to my son John Snow; and to the heires lawfully be-gotten of his body, forever;

Item: To my son Jabez Snow I Give all this my Land lying between my house and my son Thomas Paines, and seaven acrees att the basse pond lying between Daniel Cole and Wil-liam Browne; and an halfe acree of Marsh att the end of it and six acrees of upland att the herring pond; and an acree and halfe of meddow att silver springe lying on the Northsyde of William Walkers, and the Clift of upland adjacent to the above said meddow, and all the sedge about it, to Ephraime Done; and that prte of my house hee lives in as longe as my wife or I Doe live.

Item: I Give him two acrees of Meddow att the Great Meddow lying between the Eel Creeke and Joseph Hardings;

Item: To my son Jabez I give that my four acrees of meddow att Billingsgate Due to mee yett unlayed out; All this above-

[ 127 ]

said upland and meddow I give to my son Jabez Snow and the heires of his body lawfully begotten for ever;

Item: This my meddow about my house I give to my son Jabez;

Item: I give to my Loveing wife Constant Snow all my stocks of Cattle sheep horses, swine whatsoever, to be att her Disposall for the Comfort and support of her life, with all the moveable Goods I am posessed of and after he Decease, stocke and movables to be equally Devided amongst all my children.

Item: To my wife I Give the use and Disposall of the prte of my house shee now Dwells in During her life time, and after her Decease to be my son Jabez Snowes;

Item: I give to my loveing wife that ten acrees of upland att Pachett, and 20 on Billingsgate Iland, for the Desposall for the comfort of her life, but if shee need it not, and leave it undesposed; I Give it then to my son Steven Snow;

That twenty acrees of upland att Billingsgate if my wife leave it undesposed then to be my son Jabez Snowes.

I Doe Give to the Church of Eastham for the furniture of the Table of the Lord, with pewter or other nessesaries I say I Doe Give ten shillings, out of my estate after my wifes Descease.

That this is my last will and Testament I have sett to my hand and Seale: this fourteenth Day of November one thousand six hundred seaventy and six.

Witnes
Signed & Sealled in
the presence of us
Samuel Treate                           NICHOLAS SNOW
Thomas Paine Senr                       and a (Seale)
The overseers were,
Dea. Samuel Freeman
John Mayo.

Letters of administration were granted to Constant Snow, Marke Snow and John Snow on March 16, 1676/7 (N.S.).

Nicholas Snow left a large estate which was carefully inventoried and sworn to:

"Constant Snow The Relict of Nicholas Snow late Deceased of Eastham made oathe to the truth of this Inventory before Mee John ffreeman Assistant this 22cond of March 1676/77."

In the inventory were many cooper and carpenter's tools, farm tools, and the like.

He left some live stock, including "3 hives of bees", oxen, cows, steers, young cattle, swine, etc.

There was an ample assortment of furniture, cooking utensils, etc.

[ 128 ]

There were several pounds of powder, shot, and bullets. A "smale Gun", "1 rapier", "barrell of a Gun".

A number of books were listed, including the inevitable "Psalm Booke".

## CHILDREN BORN PLYMOUTH

+11. Mark, b. May 9, 1628, d. 1695(?); m. 1st Anna² **Cooke** (Josiah¹); m. 2nd Jane² **Prence** (Gov. Thomas¹).
+12. Mary, b. 1630(?), d. Apr. 28, 1704, m. Thomas² **Paine** (Thomas¹).
+13. Sarah, b. 1632(?), m. William¹ **Walker.**
+14. Joseph, b. Nov. 24, 1634, d. Jan. 3, 1722, m. Mary (        ).
+15. Stephen, b. 1636(?), d. Dec. 17, 1705; m. 1st Sussanah (Deane²) **Rogers** (Stephen¹); m. 2nd Mary **Bigford.**
+16. John, b. 1638(?), m. Mary² **Smalley** (John¹).
+17. Elizabeth, b. 1640(?), m. Thomas³ **Rogers** (Lt. Joseph² **Thomas¹**).
+18. Jabez, b. 1642(?), d. Dec. 20, 1690, m. Elizabeth (        ).
+19. Ruth, b. 1644(?), d. Jan. 27, 1716-17, m. John² **Cole** (Daniel¹).
20. Child living unmarried in 1651.
20a. Child living unmarried in 1651.
20b. Child living unmarried in 1651.

Ref. Nos. 28, 34, 71, 125, 129, 173, 290, 501.

## ROGERS FAMILY

Sir Tancred de Hautville, b. abt. 970. d. aft. 1058, a nobleman of Hautville near Cautauces, Normandy. m. 1st abt. 992 Moriella; m. 2nd abt. 1013 Fredistand. There were a number of sons, among them Robert, Roger and William.

Robert "Guiscard," b. 1015, became a great General, commanding Norman troops in Italy, and was created Duke of Apulia 1059; King of Naples and had other honors. He d. 1085.

His brother Rogers became Grand Count Roger I 1089-1102 of Sicily. He was b. 1030, d. 1101/2.

Duke Robert and his brother Grand Count Roger were primarily responsible for the Norman conquest of Sicily, and the Fitz Roger name in South West England is alleged to have sprung from descendants of these brothers.

Conditions in Sicily of a religious nature becoming delicate, an Aaron John Fitz Rogers, a merchant of Rome, was forced to flee to London where he engaged in business. The Rogers Family have the right to bear the coat of arms accredited to Grand Count Roger I of Sicily. Aaron Rogers was b. Italy abt. 1260/70.

From this point the Rogers line to the Rev. John Rogers is quite clear.

Gen. 1. **John Fitz Roger,** b. abt. 1335 Eng. m. 1385/6 Elizabeth, b. 1330, dau. of Sir Symon de Furneaux of Ashington, wid. of Sir John Blount. She was a very wealthy heiress, sole heir of her father, and of the 9th gen. in direct line from ODO DE FORNELL b. abt. 1040 in Normandy who came to Eng. with the Conqueror.

Gen. 2. **Sir John Fitz Roger,** Knt. b. abt. 1386/7.

Gen. 3. **Thomas Rogers Gent,** b. 1408 at Ashington, Somerset, in a Furneaux mansion. m. 1st abt. 1433/4, had son Thomas; m. 2nd late in life.

Gen. 4. **Thomas Rogers,** Sergeant at Law Esq., b. 1435 probably at Benham Valence, a Furneaux mansion, d. at Bradford on the Avon, Wilts 1489. He was buried there. He was a man of influence, but of small means. m. 1st 1479 Cecilia Besill of Bradford, and had son William; m. 2nd 1483 Catherine de COURTNEY dau. of Sir Philip de Courtney, and had sons George and John Rogers. Catherine de Courtney is the 8th gen. in direct line from Edward I, King of England, through the deCourtneys, de Bohuns, etc.; and from Edward I is in direct line to King Alfred. The historian Gibson states that the House of Courtney is "one of the most illustrious races among the English nobility".

Gen. 5. **John Rogers,** of Deritend, b. 1485 at "Bradford," m. Margaret Wyatt abt. 1505/6 dau. of Sir Henry Wyatt of Abington Castle. Sir Henry was quite prominent at the Courts of Henry VII and VIII. The Sir Thomas Wyatt who led the uprising against the marriage of Queen Mary to Philip of Spain, and paid the penalty by losing his head, was a nephew. They made their home at "Deritend" in the parish of Aston, Warwick Co. They had children—

*Rev. John, b. 1507 at Deritend
William
Edward
Eleanor, m. Robert Mylward
Joan

Gen. 6. **Rev. John Rogers**, b. 1507 at Deritend near Birmingham, Co. Warwick, Eng. He was educated at Cambridge, leaving there about 1525, he took holy orders in the Roman Catholic Church about 1526, and from this time on his life was one of turmoil and strife in the religious world. He became a leader of the Anglican Reformation, and paid the penalty by being burned at the stake on Feb. 4, 1555, his children being forced to witness the ordeal. Rev. John Rogers m. abt. 1536 **Adriana Pratt, alias de Weyden,** niece of **Jacob Von Meteren.** According to Chester in his history of the Martyrs family, 1861, there were eleven children, as follows:

 I Susan, b. Brabant (Antwerp) m. John Short
 II John, b. Saxony (Wittenberg) m. Mary Leete
 III Daniel, b. Saxony abt. 1740, d. Jan., 1590
 IV· Ambrose, b. (  )
 *V Bernard, b. 1543 at Wittenberg, Saxony
 VI Samuel, b. (  )
 VII Philip, b. (  )
 VIII Augustine, b. (  )
 IX Barnaby, b. (  )
 X Elizabeth, b. (  ) m. James Proctor
 XI Hester, b. (  ) m. Henry Ball

Gen. 7. **Bernard Rogers**, b. 1543 at Wittenberg, Saxony. He was educated in Germany and returned to England, crossing over into Scotland where he resided for a time, and married there about 1564. His known issue was Thomas Mathew Rogers called after the "nom de plume" used by the martyr in publishing the "Byble".

Gen. 8. **Thomas Mathew Rogers**, b. abt. 1565 in the north of England or Scotland, m. abt. 1586 a McMurdocke. There were a number of children, among them Thomas*, Edmund, William, George, John.

Gen. 9. **THOMAS ROGERS**, b. 1587(?), d. Plymouth, Mass., Feb. 1621, m. abt. 1606(?). The name of his wife has not been determined. Thomas Rogers was a "Camlet" merchant in London and Leyden, Holland. His place in London seems to have been in the parish of St. Bartholomew the Great where he was a taxpayer, together with Christopher Martin, Governor of the Mayflower, and John Hooke. He early became interested in the Pilgrim movement, and was a member of the Leyden, Holland, Congregation on or before June 25, 1618. He seems to have been fairly well off. In order to finance his trip on the Mayflower he sold his house on Barbara Lane in Leyden Apr. 1, 1620, to a party by the name of Mordecai Cohen for 300 gilders.

Thomas Rogers may be related to George Rogers— Student at Leyden University who lived with Thomas Blossom. George Rogers matriculated in Medicine Oct. 27, 1609, then 25.

Accompanied by his youngest son Joseph, then about 12 years old, he crossed the ocean in the Mayflower, and became one of the signers of the famous compact. Unfortunately he died at an early age soon after landing at Plymouth in Feb., 1621, and his grave is on "Burial Hill" alongside those of his friends who died in that first winter of terrible hardship.

Governor Bradford in his history of Plymouth Plantation states that the other children of Thomas Rogers came over later.

Incidentally his neighbor in London, Mr. Christopher Martin, was a member of the Merchant Adventurers, and was appointed by them Governor of the Mayflower, and also Treasurer. There is good reason to suspect that Thomas Rogers was also a member of the Adventurers. He became a citizen of Leyden in 1818, guaranteed by Wm. Jepson and Roger Wilson.

POSSIBLE CHILDREN OF THOMAS ROGERS (MAYFLOWER PASSENGER), BORN ENGLAND

*I Joseph, b. 1607/8(?), m. Hannah (          ) abt. 1631.

II(?) Thomas, b. 1600/8(?). Perhaps the Thomas Rogers who died Watertown, Mass., 1638, and husband of Grace [2]Makin (Tobias[1]), widow of John Sherman of Dedham, Eng. This Grace Rogers and her husband, Thomas Rogers, with stepson, John Sherman, jr., came to Watertown, Mass., 1636. Grace, m. 3rd Roger Porter of Watertown.

III John, b. abt. 1611, d. bet. Aug. 26, 1691-Sept. 20, 1692. m. Ann Churchman, Apr. 16, 1639, dau. of Hugh Churchman.

CHILDREN BORN DUXBURY

+a. John, b. 1640(?), m. 1st Elizabeth [2]Pabodie (William[1]); m. 2d Hannah (Hobart) Brown (wid.); m. 3rd Marah (Calhoun) Browning (wid.).

+b. Abigail, b. 1642(?), d. Aug. 1, 1727; m. John **Richmond.**
+c. Anna, m. 1st John **Tisdale,** Nov. 23, 1664; m. 2nd Thomas **Terry**; m. 3rd Samuel **Williams.**
+d. Elizabeth, m. Nathaniel **Williams,** Nov. 17, 1668.
IV(?)William, b. 1613(?), d. Huntington, L. I., 1669. His will is dated Nov. 22, 1669; m. Ann (Sherman?) dau. of Edmund. This William Rogers was in Wethersfield, Conn., 1640, Hempstead, L. I., 1649/56 and then to Huntington.

CHILDREN

a. Obadiah, b. 1630/5.
b. Jonathan, b.(?) 1637, d. 1707; m. Rebecca (    ).
c. John, b. 1646(?), d. Brandford, Conn., Oct. 8, 1725; m. Elizabeth **Taintor.**
d. Mary.
e. Hannah.
V(?)James, b. 1615(?), d. New London, Conn., Feb., 1687/8; m. Elizabeth ²**Rowland** (Samuel¹).

CHILDREN BORN STRATFORD, CONN.

a. Samuel, b. Dec. 12, 1640; m. Mary **Stanton.**
b. Joseph, b. May 14, 1646; m. Sarah (    ).
c. John, b. Dec. 1, 1648; m. 1st Elizabeth **Griswold**; m. 2nd Mary **Ransford**; m. 3rd Sarah **Cole.**
d. Bathesheba, b. Dec. 30, 1650; m. 1st Richard **Smith**; m. 2nd Samuel **Fox.**
e. James, b. Feb. 15, 1652; m. Mary **Jordan.**
f. Jonathan, b. Dec. 31, 1655; m. Naomi **Burdick.**
g. Elizabeth, b. Apr. 15, 1658; m. Samuel **Beebe.**
VI dau, perhaps.
VII Noah(?)
VIII Probably other children.

NOTE: Of the above children the General Society of Mayflower Descendants has accepted as clearly established as sons of **Thomas Rogers,** the Mayflower Passenger, I Joseph, b. 1607/8(?) and III John, b. 1611(?). However, William Bradford stated other members of his family came to America, and many good arguments have been, or could be advanced, especially in the cases of IV William, b. 1613(?) and V James, b. 1615.
So far as II Thomas is concerned it must be stated that this Thomas Rogers of Watertown has been the innocent cause of much confusion. Some writers have even claimed the Thomas of Plymouth and Thomas of Watertown were identical, although one was buried in Plymouth in the spring or winter of 1620/21, and the other died in Watertown 1637. Other published statements assert that the unknown wife of Thomas of Plymouth was Grace

Makin. This is obviously wrong, as she was the wife of Thomas of Watertown.

Gen. 10. **Lt. Joseph Rogers,** b Eng. 1607/8, d. Eastham, Mass. 1677/8; m. Hannah. He was a prominent man in the community. His children were born in Plymouth and Eastham.

   a. Sarah, b. Aug. 6, 1633, d. Aug. 15, 1633.

   b. Joseph, b. July 19, 1635, d. Dec. 27, 1660; m. Sussanah **Deane,** Feb. 4, 1660.

   c. Thomas, b. May 29, 1638, d. June 16, 1678; m. Elizabeth **Snow** (Fam. No. 17).

   e. Elizabeth, b. Sept. 29, 1639, d. 1678; m. Jonathan **Higgins** his first wife.

   f.*John, b. Apr. 3, 1642, d. 1713; m. Elizabeth **Twining.**

   g. Mary, b. Sept. 22, 1644, d. (      ); m. John **Phinney.**

   h. James, b. Oct. 18, 1648, d. Apr. 13, 1678; m. Mary **Paine.** She m. 2nd Isreal **Cole.**

   i. Hannah, b. Aug. 8, 1652; m. Jonathan **Higgins.** Sister Elizabeth was his 1st wife.

Gen. 11. **John Rogers,** b. Apr. 3, 1642, d. Eastham, Mass., 1713, m. Elizabeth **Twining** Apr. 19, 1669, dau. of William Twining and Elizabeth Deane. John Rogers was a close friend and neighbor of Thomas Paine, and resided in Eastham. He and two of his sons were witness to the will of Thomas Paine. He made his will in Apr. 27, 1713, and mentioned his 5 sons, and 3 daughters, also his wife Elizabeth and grandson John Rogers, who seemed to be living with him. His children are recorded in Eastham.

   a. Samuel, b. Nov. 1, 1671, d. Dec. 3, 1671.

   b.*John, b. Nov. 4, 1672, d. (     ); m. Precilla **Hamblen.**

   c. Judah, b. Nov. 23, 1677, d. (     ); m. Patience.

   d. Joseph, b. Feb. 22, 1679; m. 1st Mercy **Crisp;** m. 2nd Sarah.

   e. Elizabeth, b. Oct. 23, 1682.

   f. Eleazer, b. May 19, 1685; m. Martha **Young.**

   g. Mehitable, b. Mar. 13, 1686/7.

   h. Hannah, b. Aug. 5, 1689; m. James **Smith.**

   i. Nathaniel, b. Oct. 3, 1693; m. 1st Elizabeth **Crosby;** m. 2nd Selena **Dimock.**

Gen. 12. **John Rogers,** b. Nov. 4, 1672, d. bf. 1739; m. Precilla **Hamblen** Apr. 3, 1696, dau. of John Hamblen and Sarah Bearse. He resided in Harwich on land probably left to him by his father under the will dated 1713. He seems to have died before 1739, for there was an agreement entered into by his heirs dated May 1, 1739, and naming children Ebenezer, John, Joseph, Rueben Nickerson, and Sarah Rogers of Harwich, Benjamin of Kingston, and Jonathan of Yarmouth.

His father by will under date of Apr. 27, 1713, stated in part "to my son John Jr. 20 acres of upland in Herwich where his dwelling house now stands—also one half of my meadow, and also that my third part of a share of sedge ground lying on pochey sedge flats which was laid out in the right of my decesed father Joseph Rogers".

The children of John Rogers and Precilla Hamblen were probably born in Harwich, as follows:

a.*Ebenezer, b. Feb. 17, 1698; m. Hannah Cooke (Fam. No. 747).

b. Thankful, b. Oct. 24, 1699, d. bef. 1739.

c. John, b. Aug. 1, 1701; 1st m. Mary Wing; 2nd m. Sarah Nickerson wid.
This John Rogers seems to have been living in the family of his grandfather John in 1713. Before 1750 he removed with members of his family to Putnam Co., N. Y. Mary Wing was a dau. of Ananias Wing, and some of this family removed to Mansfield, Conn.

d. Jonathan, b. Mar. 20, 1703; m. Elizabeth Cooke, sister of Hannah (Fam. No. 749).
In 1739 he was residing in Yarmouth, but soon after this date appears to have removed to Conn., and later to Putnam Co., N. Y., or the "Oblong", N. Y.
It appears that Richard Cooke (Fam. No. 146), father of Hannah and Elizabeth, with his cousin Amaziah Harding (Fam. No. 100), received from their grandfather Josiah Cooke (Fam. No. 25) certain rights which finally made it possible for them to obtain land in Middlesex Co., Conn.

e. Benjamin, b. Nov. 19, 1704, d. Oct. 19, 1747; m. Phebe Harding dau. of Amaziah Harding (Fam. No. 100). Benjamin was residing in Kingston in 1739. He died in 1747, leaving a young family who appear to have gone with the Hardings to Conn., and N. Y.

f. Sarah, b. July 21, 1706, unmarried in 1739.

g. Joseph, b. Sept. 20, 1708; m. Fear Bassett(?) dau. of William Bassett. Many of this family went to Windham, Conn., before 1750.

h. Precilla(?), m. Reuben Nickerson(?). The Nickerson family removed to Dutchess Co., N. Y.

Gen. 13. Ebenezer Rogers m. Hannah **Cooke** (Fam. Nos. 25, 146 and 747).

Gen. 14. Patience Rogers, m. Zacheous **Covell** (Fam. Nos. 747 and Note under Fam. Nos. 174 and 906 on the COVELL family).

Gen. 15. Hannah Covell, m. **Peter Allen** (for details see Note under Fam. Nos. 135 and 679).

Gen. 16. Jane Allen, m. Lewis **Coons** (Fam. Nos. 135 and 679).

Gen. 17. Frances Miranda Coons, m. Franklin Brutus **Hills** (Fam. Nos. 135 and 679).

Gen. 18. Leon C. Hills, m. Ina S. **King** (Fam. Nos. 135 and 679).

Gen. 19. Norma Elizabeth Hills, b. 1915.

Gen. 19. Robert Jarvis Hills, b. 1918.

NOTE: The first eight generations of the above Rogers Line may be found in Rogers Family, Underwood, 1911. The last eleven generations are found in Mayflower Index, 1932.

Among other Rogers Lines are the following two lines:

Gen. 11. Elizabeth Snow m. Thomas[3] **Rogers.**

Gen. 12. Hannah Rogers m. Amaziah **Harding.**

Gen. 13. Nathan Harding m. Anna **Brown.**

Gen. 14. Ebenezer Harding m. Huldah **Tryon.**

Gen. 15. Ebenezer Harding m. Jerusha **Fox.**

Gen. 16. Ichabod Harding m. Eunice **Camp.**

Gen. 17. Chauncey B. Harding m. Sophia H. **Klechner.**

Gen. 18. James M. Harding m. Christine **Mochler.**

Gen. 11. Elizabeth Snow m. Thomas[3] **Rogers.**

Gen. 12. Thomas Rogers m. Sarah **Treat.**

Gen. 13. Elizabeth Rogers m. Benjamin **Lewis.**

Gen. 14. Benjamin Lewis m. Pricilla **Rich.**

Gen. 15. Lucy Lewis m. James **Bickford.**

Gen. 16. Benjamin L. Bickford m. Mary E. **Knowlton.**

Gen. 17. Robert Bickford m. Lucy J. **Sloan.**

Gen. 18. Robert S. Bickford m. Ethel **Rummell.**

Further Lines of the Rogers Family will appear in future volumes of this series.

# HOPKINS

3. **Hopkins, Giles**[2] (Stephen[1]), born Eng. about 1607, died about March or April, 1690, at Eastham, Mass., or surely after March 15, 1689, and before April 26, 1690; married Catone **Wheldon** October 9, 16——, daughter of Gabriel Wheldon of Yarmouth.

Giles Hopkins was the eldest son of Mr. Stephen Hopkins of Plymouth. He came over with his father on the Mayflower in 1620, and was one of the boys on that famous voyage. With other members of the family he survived the first winter of sickness and death.

On the voyage he was one of the quieter boys, and developed a retiring disposition as he grew older, entirely unlike his father and brother Caleb.

When in 1637 the Pequots, a tribe of Indians inhabiting the eastern part of Connecticut, began war with the English in that region, and Plymouth Colony decided to send a company to assist in overthrowing the Indians, he, with his father and younger brother Caleb, volunteered to go out in the defense of their neighbors, but fortunately, before starting forth, the troops under Captain Mason had defeated the enemy, and they were not needed.

The next year, Mr. Stephen Hopkins having been allowed by the Old Colony Court "to erect a house at Mattacheese", now Yarmouth, "to cut hay there" and to winter his cattle, it is thought his son Giles went down there to look after matters, and we find him at Yarmouth in 1639, when with Hugh Tilly and Nicholas Sympkins he "deposed" to the last will and testament of Peter Warden, the elder, deceased, and also courted and married Catone Wheldon, daughter of Gabriel Whelden, who had been licensed to build at Mattacheese the year before.

The house Giles occupied while a resident of Yarmouth stood a little to the northwest of the knoll. It was probably the first house built below Sandwich, and surely was, if it was the one built by Stephen Hopkins at the order of the Plymouth Court. It was sold by Giles Hopkins in 1642 to Mr. Hallett. It would seem that he was not a resident of Yarmouth in 1643, as his name does not appear in the list of those able to bear arms that year in the township. However, evidence shows he was a resident June 6, 1644. At that date his father made his will, and several times mentions Giles as being at Yarmouth in charge of the cattle. It is probable Giles was not enrolled on account of physical disability.

In what year Giles removed to Nausett, now Eastham, is not known. He was there in 1650, a surveyor of highways, and held this position several years.

For some reason, his father, by will, made Caleb, his younger son by the second wife, the "heire apparent" and consequently all of the real estate, and the amount was large, passed into the hands of Caleb. However, Caleb, soon after his father's death in July 1644, gave up a very large tract of land to Giles, his only surviving brother, lying in what is now Brewster. Upon the death of Caleb, who was a seaman, and died at the Barbadoes before 1657, Giles came into possession of much of the land. In 1659 land was granted to him in Eastham.

## WILL OF GYLES HOPKINS

Recorded in Vol. I, p. 32, of Probate Records of Barnstable Co., Mass.

The codicil was signed March 15, 1689 (N.S.), and the will was admitted to probate April 26, 1690 (N.S.), therefore the death of Gyles Hopkins must have occurred between these two dates. The will follows:

To all Christian people to whom these presents shall com know ye that I Giles Hopkins of Eastham being sick and weak of Body and yet of perfit memory do declare this as my last will and testament on this nineteenth day of January in ye year of our Lord 1682.

I, bequeath my Body to ye grave in decent burial when this Temporal Life of mine shall have an end, and my soul to god that gave it, in hopes of a blessed Resurection at ye Last day.

2ly, my will is that my son Stephen Hopkins shall possess and Injoy all my upland and meadow. Lying and being at Satuckit, that is to say all my upland and meadow on ye southerly side of ye bounds of ye Towne of eastham, that is to say all my Right and title Intrest and claime to all those Lands from ye head of Namescakit to ye southermost part of ye long pond where mannomoyet cart way goes over to Satuckit, and from thence to ye head of mannomyet river, and so as our Line shall run over to ye south sea, all ye Lands between thos bounds and ye westermost bounds of ye purchesers at Satuckit river, all these Lands I give unto my son Stephen Hopkins and to his heirs forever; and half my stock of cattill for and in consideration of ye above sd Land, and half stock of cattel, my will is that after my decease my son Stephen Hopkins shall take ye care and oversight and maintaine my son William Hopkins during his natural Life in a comfortable manner.

3ly, my will is that all my Lands at Palmet, both purchesed and unpurchesed, both meadows and upland, and all my Lands at Pochet, and my third part of Samsons neck, and what other Lands shall fall unto me as a purcheser from ye fore mentioned Bounds of my son Stephen Hopkinses Lands and potanomacot, all these fore specified Lands I give unto my sons Caleb and Joshua Hopkins, to be equaly devided between them: further my will is that if either of my sons Joshua or Caleb Hopkins dye having no Issew that then these Lands which I have given them to be equally devided between them, fall to him that surviveth.

4ly, I give unto my wife Catorne Hopkins and to my son William Hopkins the improvement of too acres of meadow Lying at ye head of Rock Harbor during my wifes Life and ye one half of that too acres I give unto my son William during his Life and after ye decease of and after ye decease of my wife and son William I do give this above sd too acres of meadow to my son Joshua Hopkins and his heirs forever: as also after my decease I give unto my son Joshua Hopkins a parcel of meadow Lying at ye mouth of Rock Harbor according to ye bounds thereof specified in ye Towne Records of Lands; it I give unto my son Caleb Hopkins a parcel of meadow Lying at Little Nameskeket according to ye bounds thereof specified in ye Towne Booke of Records of Lands.

It. I give unto my wife my now dwelling House and halfe my Land and halfe my orchard that is by my house: by Land I mean half my Land that is about my house both fenced and unfenced during my wifes natural Life and then ye abovesd housing and Lands to fall unto my son Joshua Hopkins; the other half of my Land and orchard I give to my son Joshua Hopkins after my death that is to say ye other half of my Lands Lying about my house.

It. I give unto my son Caleb Hopkins one pair of plow irons.

It. I give unto my son Joshua Hopkins one payer of plow Irons.

It. I give unto my wife ye other half of my stock and moveables I say to my wife and my son William or what part of ye moveables my wife shall see cause to bestow on my son William Hopkins.

It. I do appointe my son Stephen Hopkins to be my true and Lawful executor of this my Last will and testament to pay what is payable and Receive what is due.

And to ye truth and verity hereof I have hereunto sett my hand and seal ye day and year above written.

Signed and sealed in
presence of us,                          ye mark of
Jonathan Sparrow                    GILES H. HOPKINS
Samuel Knowles                              (seal)

I ye abovesd Giles Hopkins do declare whereas by ye providence of God my Life has been prolonged unto me and by Reason of age and disability of Body I am Incapatiated to provide for my owne support and my wifes, my will further is that my son Stephen Hopkins from this time and forward shall possess and Injoy all my stock and moveable estate provided he take effectual care for mine and my wifes comfortable support during our natural Lives: witness my hand and seal this fifth day of March 1688/9.

| Witness | mark |
| Mark Snow | GILES H. HOPKINS (seal) |
| Jonathan Sparrow | his |

The will and codicil were finally approved on April 22, 1690.

CHILDREN BORN YARMOUTH AND EASTHAM

+21. [1]Mary, b. Nov. 1640, d. Mar. 20, 1696/7, m. Samuel[2] **Smith** (Ralph[1]).

+22. [2]Stephen, b. Sept. 1642, d. Oct. 10, 1718, m. 1st Mary[2] **Merrick** (William[1]), m. 2nd Wid. Bethia **Atkins.**

23. John, b. 1643, d. age 3 mos.

+24. [3]Abigail, b. Oct. 1644, m. William[2] **Merrick** (William[1]).

+25. [4]Deborah, b. June 1648, m. Josiah[2] **Cooke Jr.** (Josiah[1]).

+26. [5]Caleb, b. Jan. 1650/1, d. 1728, m. Mary[2] **Williams** (Thomas[1]).

+27. [6]Ruth, b. June 1653, m. Samuel[3] **Mayo** (Nathaniel[2] Rev. John[1]).

+28. [7]Joshua, b. June 1657, d. 1734/8, m. Mary[2] **Cole** (Daniel[1]).

29. William, b. Jan. 9, 1660, d. probably an invalid.

30. Elizabeth, b. Nov. 1664, d. age 1 mo.

SOME MAYFLOWER LINES FROM STEPHEN[1] HOPKINS

[1]Gen. 3. Mary Hopkins m. Samuel **Smith.**
Gen. 4. Samuel Smith m. Bathshue **Lathrop.**
Gen. 5. Samuel Smith m. Abigail **Freeman.**
Gen. 6. Martha Smith m. Reuben **Rich.**
Gen. 7. Martha Rich m. Josiah **Rich.**
Gen. 8. Hezekiah Rich m. Sarah W. **Smith.**
Gen. 9. **Zoeth Rich** m. Polly A. **Brown.**

[2]Gen. 3. Stephen Hopkins m. 1st Mary **Merrick.**
Gen. 4. Stephen Hopkins m. Sarah **Hawes.**
Gen. 5. Rebecca Hopkins m. Jonathan **Higgins.**
Gen. 6. Phoebe Higgins m. John **Taylor.**
Gen. 7. Abigail Taylor m. Nehemiah **Young.**
Gen. 8. Jonathan Young m. Eunice **Hurd.**
Gen. 9. Apphia Young m. Hiram J. **Snow.**
Gen. 10. Charles B. Snow m. Anna C. **Laney.**
Gen. 11. **Charles B. Snow** m. **Mabel A. Foster.**

[3]Gen. 3. Abigail Hopkins m. William **Merrick** (Fam. No. 24).
Gen. 4. Rebecca Merrick m. Jonathan **Sparrow** (Fam. No. 135).
Gen. 5. Hannah Sparrow m. John **Hurd** (Fam. No. 679).
Gen. 6. Sarah Hurd m. Seth **Covell.**

Gen. 7. Zacheous Covell m. Patience **Rogers.**
Gen. 8. Hannah Covell m. Peter **Allen.**
Gen. 9. Jane Allen m. Lewis **Coons.**
Gen. 10. Frances M. Coons m. Franklin B. **Hills.**
Gen. 11. Leon C. Hills m. Ina S. **King.**
Gen. 12. Norma E. Hills, b. 1915.
Gen. 12. Robert J. Hills, b. 1918.
Refs. for this Line are Mfl. Index 1932. American
Ancestry Vol. I, 1887, American Ancestry Vol. II,
1887, Mfl. Desc. Vol. 11, p. 233, Mfl. Desc. Vol. 13,
pp. 147, 148.

[4]Gen. 3. Deborah Hopkins m. Josiah **Cooke Jr.** (Fam. No. 25).
Gen. 4. Richard Cooke m. Hannah ( ? ) (Fam. No. 146).
Gen. 5. Hannah Cooke m. Ebenezer **Rogers** (Fam. No. 747).
Gen. 6. Patience Rogers m. Zacheous **Covell.**
Gen. 7. Hannah Covell m. Peter **Allen.**
Gen. 8. Jane Allen m. Lewis **Coons.**
Gen. 9. Frances M. Coons m. F. B. **Hills.**
Gen. 10. L. C. Hills m. Ina S. **King.**
Gen. 11. Norma E. Hills.
Gen. 11. Robert J. Hills.
Ref. for this Line is Mfl. Index 1932.

[5]Gen. 3. Caleb Hopkins m. Mary **Williams.**
Gen. 4. Caleb Hopkins m. Mercy **Freeman.**
Gen. 5. Constant Hopkins m. Phebe **Paine.**
Gen. 6. Constant Hopkins m. Elizabeth **Paine.**
Gen. 7. Jonathan Hopkins m. Elizabeth **Wharf.**
Gen. 8. Mary A. Hopkins m. George **Little.**
Gen. 9. Mary Little m. Samuel S. **Harris.**

[6]Gen. 3. Ruth Hopkins m. Samuel **Mayo.**
Gen. 4. Samuel Mayo m. Abigail **Sparrow.**
Gen. 5. Lois Mayo m. Barnabas **Howes.**
Gen. 6. Sparrow Howes m. Esther **Kelley.**
Gen. 7. Esther Howes m. Mulford **Nickerson.**
Gen. 8. Sparrow H. Nickerson m. Elizabeth C. **Darling.**
Gen. 9. Edward I. Nickerson m. Lyra F. **Brown.**
Gen. 10. Lyra B. Nickerson.

Many other Lines from Giles[2] Hopkins will appear
in this series of volumes.

Ref. Nos. 34, 140, 169, 288, 289, 292, 293, 294, 299, 300, 313, 512.

4. **Hopkins, Damaris**[2] (Stephen[1]), was born in England and came to America with her parents on the Mayflower. She appears to have been living in Plymouth as late as 1627 when a division of cattle was made among the settlers. She must have died soon after this. Bradford states, in commenting on the family of Stephen Hopkins, that one of his daughters "dyed here", and that he had "4 daus borne here". The one who died was, no doubt, Damaris, and one of the four daughters born in Plymouth was named after her.

5. **Hopkins, Oceanus**[2] (Stephen[1]), had the great distinction of being born at sea, on the Mayflower, between September 16th and November 11, 1620. Died, probably before 1623, in Plymouth.

6. **Hopkins, Caleb**[2] (Stephen[1]), was born in Plymouth probably before 1623, and died at the Barbadoes without issue after June 6, 1644, and before 1651. He served in the militia when very young in 1637 with his father and brother Giles. Caleb seems to have inherited much of his father's adventurous and restless spirit. In fact, he was named "heire apparent" in his father's will, and, together with Myles Standish was named executor of that document and this, in spite of the fact that his elder brother Giles was still living. However, this preference may have been due to the fact that Caleb was the only son of Elizabeth Fisher, second wife of Stephen Hopkins.

7. **Hopkins, Deborah**[2] (Stephen[1]), born about 1625 in Plymouth, Mass.; died soon after 1666. Married **Andrew Ring** April 23 to June 3, 1646, Plymouth, Mass., born England 1616; died Middleboro, Wednesday, February 22, 1692/3(?) in his 75th year. His gravestone may still be seen on Burial Hill in Plymouth. He was a son of widow **Mary Ring**, perhaps widow of **William Ring** of England. She appears early in Plymouth records. **Andrew Ring** married 2nd Lettice Morton, widow of John[2] **Morton** George[1]. She died February 22, 1690.

Andrew Ring when about thirteen years old was brought to this country by his widowed mother Mary, and was of Plymouth, Mass., as early as 1629. His mother died in 1631, leaving an interesting will stating, in part,

> "Andrew, my son, be left with my son-in-law, Stephen Deane, and do require of my son Deane he help him forward in the knowledge and fear of god, not to oppress him by any burdens, but be tender to him, as he will answer to God."

It appears, however, that after the death of his mother and when about sixteen years old, he was entrusted to the care of Dr. Samuel Fuller.

In 1640 he owned land in "Ring's" section of Plymouth, and was made a "freeman" in 1646, and was on a list of voters dated December 10, 1646.

Andrew Ring became a large property holder. He was among the first settlers of Middleboro, and served in King Philip's War from that place. In fact, he was among the "twenty six men's Purchase, and sixteen Shilling purchasers".

On October 27, 1662, his name appears among

> "the names of such as desire meddow att the new-found meddow in the south side of Turkey Swamp."

He also

> "desired a pease of meddow lying southerly from cedar bridge."

Andrew Ring m. 1st Deborah Hopkins. He survived both wives.

The Plymouth First Church records contain the following entries of the deaths of Andrew and Lettice Ring:

> "Andrew Ring dyed, february 22 (1692/3); in his seventy fifth yeare"
> "Lettice, the (second) wife of Andrew Ring, February 22 (1690), about 66 years of age."

Andrew Ring's will is in possession of the Connecticut Historical Society, at Hartford, Conn. They have had it for many years, and do not know how it was received. The will is in the handwriting of Rev. John Cotton of Plymouth. (See photostat Mfl. Desc. Vol. 4, p. 192.)

THE LAST WILL AND TESTAMENT OF ANDREW RING OF PLYMOUTH.

I Andrew Ring being now stricken in years & weake in body, but of disposing minde & memory, not knowing how neere the day of my death may be, doe make this my last Will and Testament hereby revoking all former wills.

Imprimis, I bequeath my soule unto the hands of God who made it & my body to the earth by decent buriall in hopes of a Joyfull Resurrection to eternall life by the merits of Jesus Christ my only Lord & Redeemer.

And as for the worldly estate which God has given me, my will is, it be disposed of as followeth: I give to my Elder son William, my now dwelling house & the land & housing adjoyning thereunto, excepting that portion I have taken out of it to give to my son Eliezer as hereafter expressed; also I give to my son william my twelve acres of upland lying in the New-feilds, & five acres lying at lout-swamp both within the township of Plimouth; also to my son william I give foure acres of meadow lying at Southers marsh at the East end of the Cedar swamp, and three acres of meadow in the Cove, and two acres of meadow at the oake, and one acre of meadow at Dotey's meadows, all which meadows are within the township of Plimouth; Also I give to my son william one hundred acres of upland & eight acres of meadow which I have lying within the toweship of Midlebury, all the abovementioned lands, whether uplands or meadows, lying & being either in the towne of Plimouth or Midlebury, I doe hereby freely & absolutely give and bequeath to my said son william, his heires & assignes for ever. Also to my son william, I give my plow & plowirons, all the iron worke in the cart, Horse-geares, chaine, couples, staple of the coppy-oake, working tooles, Augurs, gouges, spade, handsaw, axes, Hoe, hammer & such like. Also to my son william I give all the corne & provision laid in for the yeare.

Moreover, I give to my son Eliezer, that portion of land adjoyning to his house containing about the third part of an acre, and two acres of upland & swamp lying neere thereunto; Also, I give to my son Eliezer, my twenty acre lott of upland, and my five & twenty acre lott of upland lying in the Toweship of Midlebury. This homestead now exprest & the lands, uplands & meadows in the townships either of Plimouth or Midlebury, I doe hereby freely & absolutely give and bequeath to my said son Eliezer, his heires & assignes for ever.

Also, I give my land at Midlebury, commonly called & knowne by the name of the sixteene-shillings purchase to

[ 144 ]

my Grandson John Mayo, son of my daughter Elizabeth Mayo late of Eastham deceased, my will further is that in case said John Mayo dye before he come of age or without lawfull issue that then said land, or the value of it, be given to his surviving sisters, the daughters of my said daughter Elizabeth Mayo, by my Executor hereafter named.

Also, I give my cow, commonly called, short bob-taile cow, to my Grand-son Andrew Ring son of my son Eliezer.

Also, I give my Heifer to my granddaughter Mary Morton, daughter of my daughter Mary Morton. Also my will is that all my debts to be paid out of my moveables before division of them. Further my will is, that all the rest of my Estate in moveables of any sort whatsoever within doores or without be equally & Justly divided betwixt my son Eliezer and my three daughters Mary, Deborah & Sussana. Also I doe make & constitute my son william Ring sole Executor of this my last will & Testament. Also I doe hereby desire & appoint my loving friends Deacon Thomas Faunce and Ephraim Morton Junior to be overseers of this my will.

In witnesse whereof I have hereunto set my hand & seale this fourteenth day of December, one Thousand, six hundred, ninety and one.

ANDREW RING
Seal

Signed, sealed & declared
by Andrew Ring to be his
last will & Testament, in
the presence of us.
John Cotton
James Cole
Edward doty.

I underwritten doe attest, that Andrew Ring the Testator did divers times in September & October 1692: call upon me to cancell his will, declaring that his son william should have his whole estate both in lands & moveables (excepting the lands he had given to his son Eliezer & grandson John Mayo) in consideration of his loving & tender care of him & expence & trouble to support him in his long weaknesse:
November
19     1692                                witnesse my hand
                                                         JOHN COTTON

This Sworne to pr sd mr Cotton 22d of March 1692/3.

Before me William Bradford
Justice of peace.

From Plym. Co. Prob. Rcds. 1, p. 164, we find

"An Inventory of ye estate of Andrew Ring late of Plimouth deceased taken & apprised by us whose names are hereunto Subscribed on ye 18th day of March 1692/3."

[ 145 ]

Among the many items were wearing apparel both linnen and wollen. Books. Beds and bedding. Yarn and hemp. Pewter and brass pieces. Pot kettles, Pot hooks, hakes and tongs. Farming tools, plows, carts and the like. Furniture. Live stock. Among the debts of the estate were funeral charges and a sum for "Dyeting Nurses".

The Inventory was signed by Ephraim Morton junior and Thomas ffaunce.

The will was approved March 22, 1692/3.

CHILDREN BORN PLYMOUTH

+31. Elizabeth, b. Apr. 19/29, 1652, d. before 1692; m. William[8] Mayo (John[2] John[1]).
+32. William, b. 1653(?), d. 1731; m. Hannah Sherman (William[2] William[1]).
+33. Eleazer, b.          , d. 1748/9; m. Mary[2] Shaw (Jonathan[1]).
+34. Mary, b.      , d.      ; m. John[3] Morton (John[2] George[1]).
 35. Deborah, b.      , d.      No data.
 36. Sussanah, b.      , d.      No data.

Ref. Nos. 19, 29, 34, 125, 169, 183, 265, 266, 291, 292, 300, 510.

# RING FAMILY

The name Sigurd Ring is mentioned early in the history of Scandinavia and England.

The family name Ring appears in the register of the Parish of Hoghton, Lancaster Co., England, for more than 700 years.

A Joseph Ring was a member of Parliament in the reign of Charles I.

The earliest settlers of this name in New England were Mary Ring, widow, perhaps of William Ring of England.

It is doubtful if Mr. Ring, husband of Mary, ever arrived in America. The widow Mary, with three children, Andrew, Susan and Elizabeth came to Plymouth, Mass., 1629. Andrew was thirteen years old.

The widow Mary Ring is mentioned numerous times in the records of Plymouth. She died "15th or 19th of July, 1631", and left a will which was proved in "publick Court the 28th of Oct. 1633" (31?).

CHILDREN OF RECORD.

I Andrew m. Deborah Hopkins (see Fam. No. 7).
II Elizabeth m. Stephen **Deane** (see Fam. No. 15).
III Sussanah m. Dea. Thomas **Clark** bef. 1634.

Soon after the arrival in Plymouth of widow Ring in 1629, John and Robert Ring embarked from England in the "Bevis" and are found in Salisbury as early as 1638.

New Plymouth 1633

A Coppy of the will & Test of Mary Ring widow who dyed the 15th or 19th of July 1631. The will being proved in publick court the 28th of oct in the ninth yeare of the raigne of our Sov. Lord Charles &c.

I Mary Ring being sick in body but in prfect memory thanks be to God, doe make this my last will & Test. in manner & forme as followeth. ffirst I bequeath my soul to God that gave it me & my body to the earth from whence it was taken. Next my will is that such goods as God hath given I give also. I give unto Andrew my sonne all my brasse and pewter. I give unto my son Andrew my new bed & bolster wth the ffether (worn) to put in it wch I have ready. Item, I give to my son Andrew two white blankets, one red blanket wth the best Coverlet wch lieth upon my bed & the curtaines. Item, I give unto my sonne Andrew three pre of my best sheets & two paire of my best pillow beeres. It. I give also to him one dyapr tablecloath & one dyapr towall & halfe a dozen of napkins. It. I give unto him all my wollen cloath unmade except one peece of red wch my will is that my daughter Susan shall have as much as will make a bearing

Cloath and the remainder I give unto Stephen Deanes childe.
It. I give unto my sonne Andrew my bolster next the best.
It. I give unto him my truncke & my box & my Cubbert.
It. I give unto him all my cattle. It. I give unto him halfe
the Corne wch groweth in the yard where I dwell, And the
other halfe I give unto Stephen Deane. It. I give to Steph.
Deane, my (illegible) to make him a cloake. It. Timber
yt I lent to Mr Wynslow that cost me a pownd of Beaver,
besise a peece more that they had of me. It. I give to my
son Andrew all my shares of land that is due to me or shall
be. I give to my sonne Andrew all my tooles. It. The
money that is due to me from the Governour forty shillings.
As also the forty shillings of Comodities I am to have out
of England (worn). I give unto him also except the green
Say wch I give unto Stephen Deanes childe to make her a
Coat. It. one peece of new Linnen I give unto my sonn
Andrew. It. I give unto my daughter Susan Clarke my
bed I lay upon wth my gray Coverlet & the teeks of the two
pillows; but the ffethers I give unto my son Andrew. It. one
Ruffe I had of goodman Gyles I give to my daughter Eliz.
Deane.

All the rest of my things not menconed I give unto my
daughters to be equally divided between them. I give unto
my son Andrew all my bookes my two pr of potthooks & my
tramell, one course sheet to put his bed in, & all the money
that is due to me from goodman Gyles. And my will is that
he shall have the peece of black stuffe. The goods I give
my two daughters are all my wearing cloathes, all my wearing linnen. It. I give unto Mrs Warren one woodden cupp
wth a foote as a token of my love. It. my will is that the
Cattle I give my sonne be kept to halfes for him by Stephen
Deane, or at the discretion of my overseers to take order
for them for the good of the childe. It. I give to Andrew
my sonne all my handkerchers buttoned or unbuttoned. It.
I give to Andrew one silver whissell. It. I give him one
course kercher & one fine kercher. It. my will is that Andrew my son be left wth my son Stephen Deane; And doe
require of my son Deane to help him forward in the knowledge & feare of God, not to oppresse him by any burthens
but to tender him as he will answere to God. My overseers
of my will I institute & make my loving ffriends Samuel
ffuller & Thomas Blossom, whom I entreate to see this my
will pformed according to the true intent of the same. And
my will is that my son Andrew have recourse unto these two
my loving friends for councell & advice & to be ruled by
them in anything they shall see good & convenient for him.
Also my will & desire is that my overseers see that those
goods wch I have given unto my sonne Andrew be carefully
preserved for him, until such time as they shall judge it meet
to put them into his own hands. My will also is that if my

overseers shall see it meet to dispose of my sonne Andrew otherwise then wth his Brother Deane that then my son Deane shall be willing to consent unto it, & they to dispose of him, provided it be alwaies wth the good will of my sonne Andrew. I give unto Andrew a linnen Capp wch was his ffathers, buttons for his hankercher unbuttoned I leave for him. My will is that Andrew my sonne shall pay all my debts & chargs about my buriall. In witness whereof I set my hand before witnes.

Mary Ring.

Witnesses
Samuel ffuller
Thomas Blossom

# CLARK FAMILY

Dea. Thomas **Clark** came to Plymouth in the Anne 1623. His stone on Burial Hill, Plymouth, still stands. He was a man of influence in the community.

Dea. Thomas Clark m. 1st Sussana Ring before 1634. She died before 1664. He m. 2d wid. Alice Nichols 1664.

CHILDREN

a. Andrew, b. 1639, m. Mehitable **Scottow.**
b. James, b. 1636(?), m. 1657 Abigail **Lathrop.**
c. Sussana, m. Barnabas **Lathrop.**
d. William, b. 1656, m. 1st 1678, Hannah **Griswold**; m. 2nd Abiah Wilder.
e. John.
*f. Nathaniel, m. Dorothy Lettice widow of Edward **Gray.** No ch.

>*Nathaniel Clark became one of the Council of Andros, and served several years as Secretary of Plymouth Colony. Many early records are in his handwriting.

8. **Hopkins, Damaris**[2] (Stephen[1]), born after 1627 in Plymouth, Mass.; died after January, 1665/6, and before November 1, 1669, at Plymouth. Married as the 1st wife of **Jacob**[2] **Cooke** shortly after June 10/20, 1646. He was born in Holland about 1616, the son of **Francis**[1] **Cooke,** the Mayflower Planter, and his wife Hester Mahieu. The 2nd wife of Jacob[2] Cooke was Elizabeth (Lettice) Shurtleff, whom he married on November 18/28, 1669. No record of the death of Jacob[2] Cooke has been found. He died at Plymouth between December 21, 1675, the day his will was made, and December 28, 1675, the day his inventory was taken.

Jacob Cooke resided in a substantial dwelling located on the south side of "Smelt Brooke" in Plymouth. His place included suitable barns and outhouses for his livestock. However, his landed interests were many in other portions of the Town, including property at Rocky Nooke left to him by his father Francis[1] Cooke.

He held a number of the usual Town offices from time to time, in common with all active citizens of those days, and such service was performed without remuneration of any kind except the honor of holding the position or office.

### JACOB[2] COOKE'S WILL AND INVENTORY.

He made his will December 21, 1675 (N.S.), and died before December 28, 1675 (N.S.), when the inventory was taken.

His will and inventory is found in Vol. III, Part II, pp. 1-4 of the Plymouth Colony Wills and Inventories. The record is badly worn, as indicated in the following copy:

(p. 1) The last Will and Testament of Jacob Cooke, senir: of Plymouth in New England late Deceased exhibited to the Court held att Plymouth aforesaid the 8th Day of March 1676 on the oathes of Mr Edward Gray and Leift: Joseph howland as followeth:

Know all men to whom these prsents shall come that I Jacob Cooke senir of the Towne of Plymouth in New England: being att this prsent very weake in body through many Infeirmities and Deseas; that are upon mee; but of sound and prfect understanding and memory; Doe make and ordaine this to be my last Will and Testament to Continewe for ever feirme and Inviolable; Imprimis my will is that my engagement unto my Deare and loveing wife Elizabeth Cooke att or before my marriage with her be truly and honestly prformed unto her; Item. I will and bequeath unto my said wife Elizabeth Cooke one yoake of oxen and one cow, towards the bringing up of my three youngest Daughters; and for her and theire more comfortable subsistence; I Give unto her, my said wife Dureing her widdowhood; the use benifitt and Improvement of the orchyard that is by my Now Dwelling house; and the orchyard that I planted by or in the place I lived in att my first Marriage; alsoe During her widdowhood I Give her free Comonage for her stocke of Cattle of all sorts to Depasture in and upon those my lands att Rockey nooke; and my will is that my said wife take into her Costody the portions of my three youngest Daughters; To Cecure them untell they are of Capassitie to receive them; if shee please; Item I will and bequeath unto my eldest son Caleb Cooke; a Double portion of all my lands; that is to say one halfe of them for quantitie and quallitie; and my will is that hee shall have in his prte of them, the one halfe of my meddow that lyeth att Pyny point alsoe three quarters of my two Great Lotts of meddow that lyeth in Joneses River meddow; and all my meddow that lyeth att home on Jonses River and the remainder of his proportion of lands; hee shall have them out of my Lands that I now live on; and my lands in Rocky Nooke; and my thirty acrees of wood land that lyeth att the head of my lotts; onely what meddow or Grasse I have engaged unto my wife aforesaid; shee shall have it of his lott and halfe of meddow att Joneses River Meddow; and hee shall not Deney my said wife but lett her have ffree egresse and regresse for Pastureing on those lands in Rockey nooke which shalbe Considered to him when (worn)n is made; Item, I will and bequeath unto my son Jacob Cooke one share of (worn) lands, that is one quarter prte of them for quantitie and quallitee; and my (worn) at hee shall have in his prte of them; my sixty acres of upland that lyeth (worn) all that my meddow and upland that lyeth next unto (worn) Gave and possessed, by my brother John Thomson (worn)nd in Rocky nooke; alsoe hee shall have the one half (worn) lyeth next unto John Dunhames meddow att (worn) of meddow that lyeth in Joneses river meddow; and (worn) amount to his proportion for quantitie (worn) payed by one of his brothers (worn) that in mony, soe hee to alow them if otherwise (worn) on ffrancis Cooke one share of all my lands (worn) contitie and quallitie; and my will is that in his (worn) my forty five acrees of upland (worn) rother Wrights land; Alsoe the one halfe of my (worn) Winnatucksett next John Dunhames Meddow (worn) meddow; that lyeth att Joneses River meddow and (worn) what these several prsells shall want of (worn)mainder out of the land I live upon or (worn)es of age; by his brother Caleb; if those to (worn)s is my will see cause; that my son ffrancis (worn) ny; and that they; att the Division Determine (worn) prformance; Item I will and bequeath unto (worn)s having Don fomerly, according to (worn)th unto my six Daughters viz Mary (worn)kah Cookes my Debts and legacyes (worn)s monyes Debts Goods Cattle Chattells and whatsoever moveable estate appertaineth unto mee to be equally Devided

[ 152 ]

betwixt them six onely what corne and provision shalbe found in being shal(worn) be Devided; but spent by my wife and children that are with her; and my Desire is that my executors take the best course they can, to Cecure theire portions, to the time of theire marriage or that they Come of age; And I Doe by these prsents appoint make and ordaine my Deare and loveing wife Elizabeth Cooke; and my loveing son Caleb Cooke my executors of this my Last Will; and testament; to Adminnester upon my said estate to receive all such Debtes as are Due to mee and to pay all such debts and legacyes as I owe or are Given by these prsents; and I Doe alsoe Impower and Authorise my said executors by these presents to give unto my Cozen Daniell Wilcockes a Deed of that land att Punckateesett; which I sold him, and hee hath payed mee for; Alsoe to Give & take a Deed of my brother John Thompson for the land and meddow that hee and my selfe exchanged, one with the other; alsoe that my executors see that my body be Decently buried, and out of my estate to Defray the charge thereof; and my will is that my loveing frinds my brother John Thompson and William Crow; Doe see the prformance of this my last Will, and settlement of my estate; and I Doe therefore Desire order and Impower them; for to be healpfull to my wife and children in all theire Devisions above mensioned; and to Determine what and how any matter shalbe between them; as neare as they Can according to the true intent of this my last will and testament; and by these prsents I revoake all former wills; thus hopeing that this my last will and Testament wilbe kept and prformed according to the true intent and meaning thereof;

I comitt my body to the Dust and my soule to God that Gave it mee; In witness whereof, I Jacob Cooke Senir: have sett to my hand and seale this eleventh Day of December one thousand six hundred seaventy and five; alsoe for my fifty acrees of Land att or about Joneses river meddow; I would have it Devided to my sonnes as my other lands, either to all of them or else to one of them hee paying his brothers for their prtes:

Signed and sealed
in the presence of us                    JACOB COOKE SENIR.
to be his last will                          his I c marke
and Testament                              and a (seale)
   Joseph Howland
   Edward Gray his marke
   Isaake Wright his marke.

"an Inventory of the Estate of Jacob Cooke Senir of the Towne of New Plymouth Deceased taken and apprised the 18th Day of December 1675, by Mr Thomas Cushman, Leiftenant Joseph Howland, and serjeant Ephraim Tinkham; and exhibited to the Court of his Matie etc aforsaid the 8th of March Anno Dom: 1675, 76 on the oath of Elizabeth Cooke.''

This inventory is very interesting, and shows that Jacob[2] Cooke was a large and prosperous farmer.

He left a yoke of oxen, four cowes, two steers, one heiffer, three calves, a mare and colt, one mare and a ''yonge'' horse. There were also fifty-nine sheep and lambs, seven sowes and four piggs.

It will be noticed, therefore, that the farm was well supplied with live stock, far above the average.

The tools for carrying on the farm work included "winch for a Grindstone'', ''carte and wheeles with theire Iron worke'', ''Cappe yeoke and one stinge yoake with theire Iron work'', ''plow share with a Coulter and bee'', ''Dunge forke'', hoes, spades, axes, ''hooke and exe'', ''hoop and a paire of pince'', ''Cow Bells'', and many other items.

Among the many items ''in the house'' were, ''a longe fowling peece'', ''1 short muskett'', ''1 carbine'', ''1 Rapier'', ''1 backe sword'', ''6 pound of bulletts'', ''2 hornes with powder'', and other warlike items.

Although well equipped with weapons of war, Jacob was a man of peace, for he left a ''bible'', ''Psalme book'' and other ''bookes''.

The items of household furniture were many, and likewise ''Apparrell''.

Jacob died possessed of considerable land, including a dwelling-house with the out-houses standing upon his two lots of land that lay on the ''southsyde of the smelte brooke'', in the Town of Plymouth with the additions belonging thereto. Also, a portion of land and meadow, which belonged to his father Francis[1] Cooke, lying in Rocky Nook, in Plymouth. Also sixty acres of upland at Moonponsett pond; forty-five acres of upland at ''Winnetucksett Neare Richard Wrights''; fifty acres of upland in another portion of the Towne; and about eighty-one acres in smaller lots located in various sections of Plymouth.

CHILDREN BORN PLYMOUTH BY FIRST WIFE DAMARIS HOPKINS

+39. Elizabeth, b. Jan. 18/28, 1648/9, d. Nov. 21, 1692; m. John[2] **Doty** (**Edward**[1] of the Mayflower).

+40. Caleb, b. Mar. 29-Apr. 8, 1651, d. Apr. 24, 1747; m. Jane ( ).

*+41. Jacob, b. Mar. 26, 1653, d. Apr. 24, 1747; m. Lydia[3] **Miller** (John[2] Rev. John[1]).

+42. Mary, b. Jan. 12, 1657/8, d.          ; m. Deacon John[3] **Rickard** (Giles[2] Giles[1]).

*+43. Martha, b. Mar. 16, 1659/60, d. Sept. 17, 1722; m. Deacon Elkanah[2] **Cushman** (Thomas[2] Robert[1]).

+44. Francis, b. Jan. 5, 1662/3, d.          ; m. Elizabeth[3] **Latham** (Robert[2] William[1]).

45. Ruth, b. Jan. 17, 1665/6, d.
    There were two other children, Rebecca and Sarah
    by the 2nd wife, but they were not descended from
    Stephen Hopkins.

Ref. Nos. 28, 34, 290, 291, 292, 294, 503.

# FRANCIS[1] COOKE

In view of the fact that the children of Damaris (Hopkins) Cooke are grandchildren of both Stephen[1] Hopkins and Francis[1] Cooke, it appears desirable to go into detail concerning the history of Francis[1] Cooke, and his descendants.

3748     **Francis[1] Cooke** was born, either in England or Holland before 1582, probably 1580. He lived to a very old age. According to records "he hath seen his childrens children have children". He died in Plymouth, Mass., April 7, 1663, leaving a will dated December 7, 1659. He was residing in Leyden, Holland, long before the other Pilgrims. At the time of his marriage he was called "woolcomber, bachelor, from England". The marriage entry in the Betrothal Book at Leyden is dated June 30, 1603. His bride was Hester Mahieu "spinster from Canterbury in England." At the marriage she was attended by her mother Jenny Mahieu and sister Jenny. Hester was a "Walloon", of which sect there was a large group in Canterbury, many of whom had been driven out of Southern Belgium during the wars of the Reformation and the terrors of the Inquisition. The Separatists while in Holland, as well as in New England, allowed the interchange of the courtesy of offering communion to the French (Walloon), and the Dutch Reformed Churches.

Francis and his eldest son, John, a boy of about eight years, were on the Mayflower during its famous voyage. John, especially, must have had the thrill of his boyish life, playing pirates with Giles Hopkins aged about thirteen, and the other children. Francis signed the Compact with the others. Having resided so many years in Holland, perhaps, in fact, being of Dutch lineage himself, and marrying a "Walloon" of French extraction, he must have appeared somewhat foreign to the "Londoners" on the Mayflower.

It seems Francis was a quiet, reserved man, and he can readily be imagined standing at the rail of the Mayflower with his boy John beside him. A stiff cold wind is howling across the ship, and Francis has his broad high hat pulled well down over his eyes, while his short cloak is gathered closely about the body, and his feet and legs, encased in stout boots with long wide uppers, are firmly planted on the deck. John, bundled up to the chin, has a close hold of his father's hand, and looks every inch the little Dutch boy that he is.

There are numerous reasons for thinking that Francis was not of English descent. In the first place his English home has not been located. Then there is the stubborn fact that he was residing in Leyden at least seven or eight years before the arrival of Robinson and his followers.

He is recorded in the Betrothal Book on June 9, 1603, which makes his birth sometime before 1582. The witnesses were two Walloons. His name is recorded "FRANCHOIS COUCK", his bride Hester Mahiew, and both appeared to have been living for a time in England.

Francis[1] Cooke died at Plymouth on the seventh of April, 1663, and his Will and Inventory were recorded in Plymouth Colony Wills and Inventories, Vol. II, Part II, Folios 1 and 2:

The last will and Testament of ffrancis Cooke of Plymouth late Deceased: exhibited before the Court held att Plymouth aforesaid the fift day of June 1663 on the oathes of Mr John Aldin and Mr John Howland.

The last will and Testament of ffrancis Cooke made this seaventh of the tenth month 1659.

I being att prsent weake and Infeirme in body yett in prfect memory throw mercy doe comitt my soule unto god that gave it and my body to the earthe: which my will is should bee Intered in a decent and comly manner.

As for such goods and lands as I stand posessed of I Doe will and bequeath as followeth:

1. My will is that hester my Dear and loveing wife shall have all my movable goods and all my Cattle of all kinds; viz: Neat Cattle, horsekind, sheep and swine to be att her Dispose.

2. my will is that hester my wife shall have and Injoy my lands both upland and meddow lands which att prsent I possess. During her life.

3. I Doe ordaine and appoint my Deare wife and my son John Cooke Joynt exequitors of this my said will.

Witness
John Alden                                    FFRANCIS COOKE.
John Howland

From the Inventory taken on May 1, 1663, by Ephraim Tinkham and William Crow, it is noted that Francis Cooke had accumulated quite an estate during the forty-three years of his residence in New Plymouth. Among the items were "Iron Potts, Skilletts, Pott Hookes, Pewter Dishes, Basons, Powter Potts, Porringer, salt seller, Candlesticks, Aloemy spoones, Lanthorn, gally pot, Trenchers, Stone Bottle, a great Brass Kettle, a small kettle, warming pan, etc."

There were "Feather beds, Vallences, curtaines, sheets etc."

Among the live stock were "two mares, one yearling mare, two cowes, one calfe, three Heiffers, sixteen sheep, five lambs, four swine."

There were "Hatts, Long Coates, a short coate, Jerkins, Briches, shooes, linens, etc."

In addition to the above Francis possessed many acres of upland and meadow, mostly at Rocky Nook, which eventually went to his children and their heirs.

3750 I. John, b. Holland abt. 1612, d. Nov. 23, 1695; m. Sarah[2]
2009 **Warren** (Richard[1]) Mar. 28, 1634.

ch.

   a. Sarah, m. Arthur **Hathaway** Nov. 20, 1652.
   b. John(?).
   c. Elizabeth, m. Daniel[2] **Wilcox** (Edward[1]).
   d. Esther, b. 1650, m. Thomas[2] **Tabor** (Philip[1]).
   e. Mary, b. 1652, m. 1 Philip **Tabor**; m. 2 (Davis).
   f. Mercy, b. 1655, m. Stephen **West.**

II. Jane, d. before June 8, 1666; m. **Experience**[1] **Mitchel,** aft.
1627/8. He d. Bridgewater 1689 age 80(?). He m. 2 Mary.

ch.

   a. Elizabeth, m. John[2] **Washburn** (John[1]).
   b. Thomas(?).
   c. Mary, m. James[2] **Shaw** (John[1]).
   d. Edward, m. 1st Mercy **Hayward**; m. 2nd Alice[4]
     **Bradford** (John[3] William[2] William[1]).
   e. Sarah, m. John[2] **Hayward** (Thomas[1]).
   f. Jacob, m. Sussana[2] **Pope** (Thomas[1]).
   g. John, m. 1st Mary **Bonnay**; m. 2nd Mary **Lathrop**;
     m. 3rd Mary **Prior.**
   h. Hannah, m. Joseph[2] **Hayward** (Thomas[2]).

III Jacob (see Fam. No. 8).

IV Hester, d. after June 8, 1666; m. **Richard Wright,** Nov. 21,
1644. He d. June 9, 1691.

ch.

   a. Adam, m. 1 Sarah **Soule**; m. 2 Mehitable **Barrows.**
   b. Esther, m. Ephraim **Tinkham.**
   c. Marey, m. (Hugh?) **Price.**
   d. John, d. young.
   e. Isaac, d. young.
   f. Samuel(?), d. young.

V Mary, b. 1624/27, d. Mar. 21, 1714, age 88; m. **John**[1] **Thompson,** Dec. 26, 1645; b. Wales 1616, d. June 16, 1696. They
are buried in the 1st burying ground at Middleboro, Mass.

ch.

   a. Adam, b.     , d. young.
   b. John, b. Nov., 1647, d. young.
   c. John, b. Nov. 24, 1649, d.   ; m. Mary **Tinkham.**
   d. Mary, b   , d.   ; m. Thomas **Tabor.**
*e. Esther, b. July 28, 1652, d.   ; m. William **Reed.**
   f. Elizabeth, b. Jan. 28, 1654, d.   ; m. William
     **Swift.**
   g. Sarah, b. Apr. 7, 1657, d.   ; m. (   ).
   h. Lydia, b. Oct. 5, 1659, d.   ; m. James **Soule.**

[ 158 ]

i. Jacob, b. Apr. 24, 1662, d.          ; m. Abigail
    **Wadsworth.**
  j. Thomas, b. Oct. 19, 1664, d.     ; m. Mary **Morton.**
  k. Peter, b.          , d.          ; m. Rebecca **Sturtevant.**
  l. Mercy, b. 1671, d.

## SOME LINES FROM FRANCIS[1] COOKE

Gen. 3. Jacob Cooke m. Lydia **Miller** (Fam. No. 41).
Gen. 4. William Cooke m. Tabitha **Hall.**
Gen. 5. Elisha Cooke m. 1st Rebecca **Edgerton.**
Gen. 6. Levi Cooke m. Mary **Corwin.**
Gen. 7. Sarah Cooke m. Rev. Jacob **Rice.**
Gen. 8. Margaret R. Rice m. Rev. Lyman **Mumford.**
Gen. 9. Charlotte Mumford m. Jesse W. **Dann.**
Gen. 10. Mary E. Dann m. Rev. James W. **Magruder.**
Gen. 11. **Kenneth D. Magruder.**

Gen. 3. Jacob Cooke m. Lydia **Miller** (Fam. No. 41).
Gen. 4. William Cooke m. Tabitha **Hall.**
Gen. 5. Lydia Cooke m. Moses **Bassett.**
Gen. 6. Precilla Bassett m. Ebenezer **Dawes.**
Gen. 7. Abraham Dawes m. Deborah **Darling.**
Gen. 8. Josephus Dawes m. Sally H. **Freeman.**
Gen. 9. Frank H. Dawes m. Addie E. **Holmes.**
Gen. 10. **Sally F. Dawes.**

Gen. 3. Martha Cooke m. Dea. Elkanah **Cushman** (Fam. No.
    43).
Gen. 4. Allerton Cushman m. Mary **Buck.**
Gen. 5. Allerton Cushman m. Alethea **Soule** (Fam. No. 1140).
Gen. 6. Allerton Cushman m. Harmony **Allen.**
Gen. 7. Minerva Cushman m. Precilla **Collins.**
Gen. 8. Alonzo Cushman m. Matilda C. **Ritter.**
Gen. 9. Angelica B. Cushman m. Gustavus **Faber.**
Gen. 10. ∫**Mathilda C. Faber.**
Gen. 10. ⎠**Rudolph B. Faber.**

Gen. 3. *Esther Thompson, m. William **Reed.**
Gen. 4. Sarah Reed, m. Hezekiah **King.**
Gen. 5. Capt. Hezekiah King, m. Abigail **Adams.**
Gen. 6. Elijah King, m. Mary **Baker.**
Gen. 7. Joseph King, m. Almira (          ).
Gen. 8. Ebenezer King, m. Savilla **Benedict.**
Gen. 9. Jerome Baxter King, m. Elizabeth **Sonn.**
Gen. 10. Ina Savilla King, m. Leon C. **Hills.**
Gen. 11. ∫Norma Elizabeth Hills, b. 1915.
Gen. 11. ⎠Robert Jarvis Hills, b. 1918.

NOTE: The above line may be found in the D.A.R. Lineage
Book, Vol. 117 (1915), p. 237, No. 116,759, and in the Mayflower

Descendants Index, 1932, Vol. 1, p. 442, No. 20595; also Dau. Am. Colonists Lin. Bk., Vol. 3, p. 15, No. 2047.

Many other Lines from Francis[1] Cooke will be found in the series of volumes to follow. Also numerous Lines from Stephen[1] Hopkins and Thomas[1] Rogers, as well as the history and genealogy of the other first comers mentioned in this volume No. I.

# INDEX

[ 163 ]

CUSHMAN—Continued
Angelica 159
Elkanah 154, 159
Minerva 159
Robert 6, 12, 15, 19, 26, 27, 28,
    29, 30, 32, 33, 34, 35,
    58, 62, 63, 64, 79, 82,
    83, 116, 154
Thomas 22, 47, 53, 57, 58, 79,
    82, 83, 91, 94, 97, 153,
    154

CRACKSTON (CRAKSTON)
John 22, 29, 37, 39, 43, 45, 46,
    52, 54, 69, 88

CRISP
Daniel 110
Mercy 134

CROMWELL
36, 57

CROSBY
Elizabeth 134

CROW
William 153, 157

CROWELL
Thomas 115

DANN
Jesse W. 159

DARLING
Deborah 159
Elizabeth C. 141

DAVIE
Curtis 96

DAWES
Abraham 159
Ebenezer 159
Frank H. 159
Josephus 159
Sally F. 159

DEANE
Elizabeth 147, 148
Stephen 79, 83, 91, 93, 129,
    143, 147, 148, 149
Sussanah 129, 134

DEWSBURY
Esther 79

DE BOHUNS (BOWNS)
130

DE COURTNEY
Catherine 130
Sir Philip 130

DE FURNEAUX (DE FURNELL)
Elizabeth 130
Sir Symon 130

DE HAUTVILLE
Robert 130
Roger (Duke) 130
Sir Tancred 130
William 130

DE LA NOYE (DELANO)
Phillipe 79, 83, 88, 94

DE WEYDEN
131

DIMOCK
Selina 134

DIX
Anthony 84

DOANE
Daniel 111
Ephraim 127
John 57, 93, 110, 111, 120, 123

DOTY (DOTEN)
Edward 6, 20, 29, 37, 41, 49,
    69, 70, 71, 88, 93, 118,
    119, 144, 145, 154
John 154

DUNHAM
John 93, 152

DREW
Thomas 96

DYER
John 96

EATON
Benjamin 102
Christian 90
Francis 21, 29, 37, 41, 44, 54,
    69, 70, 90, 91, 93

[ 167 ]

**HOOKE**
John 21, 29, 37, 39, 50, 132

**HOSKINS**
William 94

**HOWARD**
Richard 87

**HOWES (HAWES)**
Barnabas 141
Esther 141
Samuel 94
Sarah 140
Sparrow 141

**HOWLAND**
Desire 60, 88
Elizabeth 60, 88
John 21, 29, 36, 38, 40, 47, 50,
    52, 53, 54, 57, 59, 64, 69,
    71, 88, 91, 92, 93, 94,
    119, 157
John jr. 88
Joseph 151, 153, 154

**HUNT**
108

**HURD**
Eunice 140
John 140
Sarah 140

**HURST**
James 93

**HOPKINS**
Abigail 140
Caleb 89, 122, 123, 124, 137,
    138, 139, 140, 141, 142
Constance 20, 37, 40, 47, 52,
    53, 57, 58, 61, 118,
    122, 124, 126
Constant 141
Damaris 6, 20, 37, 47, 52, 53,
    57, 61, 90, 118, 122,
    123, 124, 142, 151,
    156
Deborah 6, 89, 122, 123, 124,
    140, 141, 143, 147

**INGERSOLL**
Alice 87
Anne, Mrs. 87
George 87
Joanna 87
John 87
Richard 87
Sarah 87

**JAMES I**
King 14, 68, 69, 115

**JENNY**
Abigail 86, 91
John 86, 91, 93, 97, 120
Samuel 86, 91
Sarah 86, 91
Sarah, Mrs. 86, 91

**JEPSON**
William 132

[ 168 ]

POOLE
Sir Giles 116
Mary 116

POPE
Sussana 158
Thomas 158

POPHAM
Sir George 14, 26
John 26

PORTER
Roger 132

POTANUMAQUAT
95

PRATT
Adriana 131
Joshua 85, 88, 93
Phinehas 88, 94

PRICE
Hugh 158

PRENCE
Jane 129
Patience 80, 89
Rebecca 89
Thomas, Gov. 3, 36, 58, 80,
82, 83, 89, 90,
93, 97, 108,
110, 120, 125,
129

PRIEST
Degory 22, 29, 38, 41, 46, 69,
74, 84
Marra 88
Sarah 85, 88

PRIOR
Mary 158

PROCTOR
James 131

PROWER
Solomon 20, 29, 37, 49, 54, 74

RAND
James 85

RANSFORD (RAINSFORD)
Mary 133

RATCLIFF
Robert 85

REED
Sarah 159
William 158

REYNOLDS
Master 62
William 121

RHEA
David 114
John 114

RICE
Jacob, Rev. 159

RICH
Hezekiah 140
Josiah 140
Martha 140
Precilla 136
Reuben 140
Zoeth 140

RICHARD
the Lion Heart 11

RICHMOND
John 133

RICKARD
Giles 154
John Dea 6, 154

RIGDALE (RIGSDALE)
Alice 37, 46
John 21, 29, 37, 40, 42, 43, 44,
69, 81
Mrs. 21, 37, 46, 61

RING
Andrew 6, 124, 143, 144, 145,
147, 148
Deborah 146
Eleazer 144, 145, 146
Elizabeth 79, 144, 146, 147
John 147
Joseph 103, 147
Lettice 143
Mary, Mrs. 103, 143, 147, 148,
149
Mary 145, 146
Robert 147

[ 172 ]

**SPRAGUE**
Anna 85, 89
Francis 85, 89
Mercy 85, 89
Samuel 92

**STACIE**
Hugh 80

**STEWARD**
James 80

**STANDISH**
Alexander 88
Barbara, Mrs. 83, 86, 88
Charles 88
John 88
Myles, Capt. 6, 18, 21, 29, 34,
   35, 36, 37, 39, 42,
   44, 69, 70, 71, 75,
   76, 78, 88, 91, 92,
   93, 108, 116, 119,
   120, 122, 123,
   142
Rose, Mrs. 21, 37, 46, 61, 75

**STANTON**
Mary 133

**STOCKTON**
Richard 114

**STORY**
Elias 21, 29, 37, 50

**STURTEVANT**
Rebecca 159

**SQUANTO, INDIAN**
76, 78, 119

**SUCCONESSET**
95

**SUMMERS**
Sir George 117

**SWIFT**
William 158

**SYMPKINS**
Nicholas 137

**TABOR**
Philip 158
Thomas 158

**TAINTOR**
Elizabeth 133

**TAYLOR**
Abigail 140
John 140

**TENCH**
William 80

**TERRY**
Thomas 133

**THOMPSON (THOMSON)**
Adam 158
Edward 6, 21, 29, 37, 50, 71
Elizabeth 158
Esther 158, 159
Jacob 159
John 152, 153, 158
Lydia 158
Mary 158
Mercy 159
Peter 159
Sarah 158
Thomas 159

**TILDEN**
Mrs. 85
Thomas 85

**TILLY (TILLIE)**
Ann, Mrs. 21, 37, 46, 61
Edward 21, 34, 37, 40, 43, 44,
   53, 59, 60, 67, 69, 70,
   71, 119
Elizabeth 21, 37, 38, 40, 47,
   51, 53, 54, 57, 58,
   59, 60, 61
Hugh 137
John 21, 34, 37, 38, 40, 43, 44,
   59, 60, 69, 71, 119
Mrs. 21, 37, 46, 61

**TINKER**
Mrs. 22, 29, 37, 47, 61
Thomas 22, 29, 37, 40, 43, 45,
   47, 69, 81
Son 22, 29, 37, 46, 54

**TINKHAM**
Ephraim 154, 157, 158
Mary 158

[ 175 ]

# CAPE COD

## SERIES

### Vol. II

## HISTORY AND GENEALOGY

#### OF THE

## MAYFLOWER PLANTERS

#### AND

## FIRST COMERS

#### TO

## YE OLDE COLONIE

By
LEON CLARK HILLS

# FOREWORD

The author of this series has spent many happy hours during the past thirty years or more in the study of colonial history, especially that pertaining to the New England States, and, particularly, the characteristics and genealogy of the people from the earliest times. He has found the subject a vast and fascinating one in numerous directions.

From a genealogist's point of view, Plymouth County and Barnstable County (Cape Cod) may rightfully be considered the most important cradle of New England genealogy and history, or, at least, the most interesting one.

Within the confines of these two counties for several generations, the ancestors of many thousands of individuals now scattered around the United States, and, in fact, the world, struggled to obtain food, shelter and clothing under the most trying conditions of climate and circumstance.

However, a people capable of framing and subscribing to a document such as the immortal "MAYFLOWER COMPACT" must ultimately succeed.

In the midst of untold difficulties, town and county governments were formed, churches and schools were organized. Stern discipline was established. Respect for law and order was demanded and insisted upon. Slackers were not tolerated.

The early church, town and court records of Plymouth Plantation might well be read with profit by present day "voters" and "government" officeholders, as well as citizens in general.

The problems which our fathers faced 300 years ago, resemble our difficulties of today, but were dealt with in a more direct manner. There were no frills. The public servant was paid little or nothing for services. Economy was a habit. The tax payer and the thrifty ran the communities in "ye olden tyme." Today, the order of command appears reversed.

Throughout his study and investigation during these many years, the author has been made conscious of the confusion and scattered condition of the records as they bear upon these two counties, especially pertaining to genealogical matters. Much time was consumed in locating authorities which might have been saved through the availability of a book of ready reference having suitable maps of Barnstable and Plymouth Counties, and a list of resources commonly referred to.

In an attempt to provide a reference of general usefulness for all those interested in tracing Cape Cod lineages, it has been decided to base this work substantially on the genealogy of the London Mayflower Planter Stephen Hopkins, including both

[5]

male and female lines through a number of generations. Descendants of four of his children intermarried with descendants of most of the "first comers" to Plymouth and the Cape.

It will be noted that the scope of the work, so arranged, is considerably more than a Hopkins genealogy. There are, in fact, a number of genealogies involving important and far reaching Cape Cod family groups, such as the families of Snow, Cole, Ring, the Cookes—Francis and Josiah, Paine, Walker, Rogers, Smith, Mayo, Merrick, Williams, Cushman, Holmes, Rickard, Doty, Bartlett, Morton, Standish, Thomson, Sturdevant and many others.

Detailed stories and genealogies will be found in this work of the Mayflower Planters including those from whom descent is positively proved, or whose lines have been approved by competent authority, such as the Mayflower Society.

The author has found that the first few generations from Stephen Hopkins may be divided into two general groups. Andrew Ring and Jacob Cooke with their wives Deborah and Damaris Hopkins remained in Plymouth or vicinity, while Giles Hopkins and Nicholas Snow, with his wife Constance settled in Eastham on the opposite side of Cape Cod in Barnstable County.

It will be observed that the maps in this work, with their legends, cover a large field of some interest.

These maps together with several hundred group records, involving many old Cape Cod families and the citation of numerous references, cannot help but be of great aid to any investigator in this field.

The author, through force of circumstance, and other reasons, being compiler, editor, and publisher, assumes full responsibility for all errors of commission or omission in this work. There were many conflicting references, and a work of this kind can never be complete or free from errors. However, if brought to his attention they can be corrected in future publications, which it is hoped will follow this, within frequent intervals, dealing especially in later generations of the families mentioned in this work, and many other Cape Codders.

In releasing the second volume of this series, the author wishes to thank the many who have purchased Volume One, and, especially, the numerous well-wishers who were kind enough to write words of encouragement.

The six special articles, and seven maps in this volume, have been framed with the idea of presenting, rather crudely and inexpertly, it is feared, the political, economic and social background of the Mayflower Planters. The subject is very large and these articles must be considered sketchy.

Everybody is familiar with the religious background of the "Pilgrims" in Europe, through the writings of numerous brilliant theological historians. However, there were many other

[6]

deep seated reasons why the Mayflower Planters came to America.

Many family groups with much detailed information will be found in this volume. It is hoped these records may be useful and helpful.

LEON CLARK HILLS.

Washington, D. C.
August 21, 1941

# CONTENTS

Page

# THE MERCHANT ADVENTURERS OF ENGLAND
## 1500?-1605

Some students of history claim that man inhabited this earth at least 500,000 years ago, yet 450 years ago "America" had not been usefully "discovered." People in Europe thought that the unknown ocean to the west harbored terrible monsters. Their entire world comprised a section of Europe, and certain Mohammedan peoples across the Mediterranean. It all seems so incredible, especially when compared to the assumed new and clever accomplishments of modern times. However, it is quite possible that many "lost" civilizations of still higher achievements may be scattered throughout the dark past of 495,000 years, more or less, about which present man has little or no information.

Soon after 1490 daring adventurers and navigators with crude instruments and ships began to make long voyages to the south and west on the high seas. Although unanticipated at the time, it was the beginning, not only of a new trade development, but of a vast colonizing movement. The monarchs of Spain, Portugal, and merchants of these countries were seeking merely to establish new trade routes to India so that they could compete successfully with the rich and powerful trading countries of Germany and Italy. From the dawn of history, Britain especially had been on the western fringe of civilization, with no possible opportunity for the coveted "favorable trade balance," and England must have this in order to live comfortably. The weak trading position of England for centuries, and to a lesser extent of Spain, Portugal and France, is shown on the maps, No. I and No. II.

Much of the serious misunderstanding between the nobles, the clergy, the merchants and plain people during the 16th century was due to the struggle between these forces to claim and control the vast trading possibilities that were opening up. It should be remembered that high churchmen in those stormy days were not backward in affiliating with the society of Merchant Adventurers. Rev. John Rogers was a member, and chaplain of a company, before 1555 when he was burned at the stake in London. In fact, many merchants were developing a great desire for liberty, not only in religious matters but also in business. The idea of "free enterprise" was beginning to circulate. Meanwhile, Spain, backed up by the all-powerful church, was in death grips with England for mastery of the situation, while France was waking up to the main chance. Everywhere confusion stalked.

The general movement of the 16th century is called by historians "The Commercial Revolution." It started Europe on her wild scramble for world conquest, and the struggle still continues.

The "Mayflower Planters" and other first comers to America before 1636 were a part of this great struggle for trade supremacy, and were well acquainted with many of the leading actors in the drama.

For hundreds of years Germany and Italy had been the chief far western trading points for caravan trade from India, China and way places. Trade between Europe and Asia was flourishing even before the time of ancient Greeks and Romans. Occasionally, it was slowed up by barbarian invasions, such as those of the 5th century, and by the vicious conflicts between Mohammedans and Christians. During many centuries the old trade routes were traveled principally by Jews and Syrians.

Several centuries B. C. certain towns in southern Italy began to send ships to the eastern Mediterranean. Venice, Genoa and Pisa soon followed. Much to the financial advantage of the shrewd Italians these towns were used by the "Crusaders" between 1095-1270 as bases for transportation and provisions. During this period Venice laid the foundations of her maritime empire in the Aegean Sea and privileges in Constantinople. The "Crusaders" returned to England with fantastic stories of riches in the East. They brought back silks, spices, and jewels which they had stripped from the "infidels." In this manner extravagant taste in dress and ornament was established in Britain, to the great advantage of European merchants for several generations.

The Italians traded through the German merchants, who purchased commodities in Venice, and sent them back into the Germanies, England, and Scandinavian countries. Commerce was difficult. There were no roads. Pack animals were used. Expense of travel was heavy. Feudal lords demanded excessive tolls. The nobles did not desire good roads. They feared loss of toll-rights. For instance between Mainz and Cologne on the Rhine, toll was exacted in thirteen different places. Local market privileges were expensive, especially to a "foreigner." Then, there were those mysterious weights, measures and coinage to contend with, always of uncertain value.

Trade was seriously obstructed by robbers crowding the highways, and pirates roaming the seas. Needy nobles did not hesitate to become romantic highwaymen. Travelers were wise to carry arms, and move in groups. Even fleets of merchantmen, under convoy, and protected by a war vessel, were frequently attacked by roving Corsairs, defeated, robbed and sold as prizes to the Mohammedans. The black flag of piracy waved over large fleets in the Mediterranean, and in the Baltic.

There was another type of pirate wandering about on the seas, very real, but difficult to explain. For instance, a ship would

MAP No 1

# ANCIENT TRADE ROUTES.
### Before 1500.

Modern air-plane traffic will
reestablish many of these
old overland routes.

| | |
|---|---|
| A Bruges | 1 Venice |
| B Hamburg | 2 Constantinople |
| C Lubeck | 3 Antioch |
| D Genoa | 4 Beyrut |
| E Norgorod | 5 Bagdad |
| F Moscow | 6 Rosetta |
| G Azar | 7 Suez |
| H Astrakhan | 8 Tor |
| I Bokhara | 9 Medina |
| J Samarkand | 10 Mecca |
| K Pekin | 11 Massowa |
| L Canton | 12 Cairo |
| M Pegu | 13 Diu |
| N Malacca | 14 Goue |
| P. Treblzona | 15 Canaher |
| P Basra | 16 Calicut |
| R Ormuz | 17 Cochin |
| S Mascat | 18 Ouilon |
| T Aden | 19 Jiddah |

L.C.H
1941

proudly sail from a port in England, commanded by a gallant navigator. The mission is one of simple trade or exploration. For protection a little brass cannon is mounted on deck. A day out and a well loaded cargo ship is sighted. After some persuasion by the little brass cannon the cargo ship is "captured." It is soon safe at anchor in the English port, and the brave navigator is raised to the exalted rank of "Knighte" by a grateful sovereign for adding materially to a depleted treasury.

In order to protect themselves traders and merchants found it necessary to combine their forces. For this reason the Germans organized the powerful Hanseatic League as the confederation of Cologne, Brunswick, Hamburg, Lubeck, Dantzig, Konigsburg and other cities.

The German trading post at Venice received metals, furs, leather goods, and woolen cloth from the north, and sent back spices, silks, glassware, fine textiles, weapons, and paper of Venetian manufacture.

Baltic and Venetian trade-routes had a main trading post at Bruges, in the Netherlands, which was the center of trade for western Europe during the 14th century. The raw wool from England and Spain, the woolen cloth from Flanders, the wines from France and other commodities of Sweden, Norway and the British Isles were traded for eastern luxuries and the like.

For nearly 200 years the German city of Hamburg was the principal seaport on the continent with which the Society of Merchant Adventurers of London traded. Here they "stapled" the woolen industry of England. The relations between the city and Adventurers began in 1567 and continued to the dissolution of the Society in 1807.

The exact origin of the Adventurers cannot be determined. The Society began back in the obscure and unsettled conditions of English commerce of the Middle Ages. The romantic story may be considered to embrace a period of six hundred years from about 1200 to 1800. The Fellowship may have originated among "some few mercers of London" called the Brotherhood of St. Thomas a' Becket of Canterbury. They received special privileges for trade from John, Duke of Brabant in the 13th century. Edward III confirmed the grant, and Henry IV in 1399 "gave to the company a very beneficial charter of privileges."

Furthermore, they may be considered as beginning in 1296, when Edward I incorporated the Merchant Adventurers of England and they "established a factory at Antwerp and employed themselves in the manufacture of woollen cloths." No doubt they grew out of an earlier company called the Merchants of the Staple, which, in turn, comprised a combination of the principle of the "guild" and the royal privilege of establishing fairs and markets.

Up to the year 1526 the minutes of the "Adventurers" and of the "Guild of Mercers" were kept in the same books, and prior to the great fire of 1666, the premises of the "Mercers" were the headquarters of the "London Merchant Adventurers." Apparently, out of the municipal guild grew the great company for trading beyond the seas.

Of course, in the towns and town life of the middle ages there were always master craftsman and hired journeymen. The master craftsman was the central figure in the guild. The trade unions came later.

Craft guilds were common in the Norman, Flemish and German towns of the 12th century. They were more especially introduced into England as royally authorized organizations among the alien artisans settled in English towns, for the purpose of encouraging local manufacture of cloth.

The Guilds became powerful and were sometimes in conflict with authorities. In 1300 the Mayor of London had succeeded in establishing authority over the "Weavers" guild. As a rule they were an aid to law and order in the community. In the 14th century English merchants formed separate organizations such as the Grocers, Mercers, Drapers and Vintner's companies, but the craft guilds had taken root long before. A baker's guild was organized in Coventry in 1208, and it is still existing.

The craft guild system of England originated in the woolen industry, because wool and cloth were the foundation of the wealth of England. In the Middle Ages wool was the one important article of export from England through the great trading towns of Europe. She determined to manufacture cloth and imported alien artisans to start the business. At the end of the 17th century woolen manufactured goods were two-thirds of England's exports.

Food and clothing being two essentials of life, the guilds of the bakers and weavers were among the first organized in England. Before the 12th century each family, as a rule, made its own cloth, mostly in the winter evenings, after a day of toil in the fields. In France and Germany weaving was a business carried on by great nobles and the clergy, ordinarily on their vast estates by poorly paid mass labor, or "villiens."

As a matter of plain fact, most of England's commerce before 1500 was in the hands of the Italians, merchants of the Hanse League, or the Staplers. Early Britain never had much trade. The communities were primitive and hostile to any complicated system of exchange. Under the Romans the products of the mines and corn lands were in demand, but this trade ceased at the Saxon invasions. Even internal trade was difficult. No sales were made without witnesses. There was no standard of weights and measures. Attempts to sell stolen goods were common. Foreign trade was quite dead.

Saxon England was wholly agricultural. Connection with the mainland of Europe was so difficult that the government promoted all merchants successful in three voyages to the nobility.

After the conquest in 1066, some crude roads and bridges were built, and the highways were cleared of a few bandits and "gentlemen" robbers.

Something like a guild-merchant was mentioned in the Domesday Book. One outstanding feature was a monopoly of internal trade, but not less important was the exemption from all manner of taxes and petty imposts.

Ordinary persons of mediaeval England were subjected to every form of tax extortion. Nobles and clergy had to be supported. There were feudal aids, royal taxes, "trinoda necessitas," duties on imports, taxes on passengers, customs on ship's lading, charges for landing, tolls on bridges, internal navigation, wagons whether on roads or in the forest, payments for maintaining walls, and breaking turf for the market booths and for putting up the stalls themselves. Finally plain blackmail was common in the form of forced taxes or contributions as hush-money for imaginary offenses.

Naturally, merchants going from town to town had to be free of these burdens. Thus in Bristol "the members of the guild merchant buy and sell freely from all tolls and customs." They had another privilege called the "hansa," which permitted them to establish their guilds in foreign ports and trade as merchants.

In 1497 the adventurers were officially recognized by Parliament. The charter of 1505 seems, for the first time, to have limited them to a special group called "Merchant Adventurers." They now controlled the woolen manufacturing trade to the coast of the North Sea. In 1499 Henry VII granted the Society a private coat of arms. Two years later he confirmed the previous charter, and in 1505, when the disputes with Burgundy led to the removal of the English to Calais, he gave the company a new charter.

The charters were confirmed in turn by Henry VIII, Edward VI and Elizabeth. They did not differ much from the early charters of private companies for trade of 1407 and 1462, until 1564, when Elizabeth permitted the Fellowship to incorporate into a company comprising a "Body Politick." It was incorporated as "Governor Assistants and Fellowship of the Merchant Adventurers of England," with extensive rights and privileges. The words of the grant declared its purpose to be "for the good Government, Rule and Order x x x x x of the Fellowship of Merchant Adventurers x x x x x as also of all and every other of the subject of our heirs x x x x x using the seate of trade of the said Merchant adventurers." Monopoly rights were secured and absolute control over the admission of merchants to the privileges of their society guaranteed. This charter was for trade only and not for exploration and settlement.

However, in 1555 a company had been incorporated both for discovery and trade called the Muscovy or Russian Company,

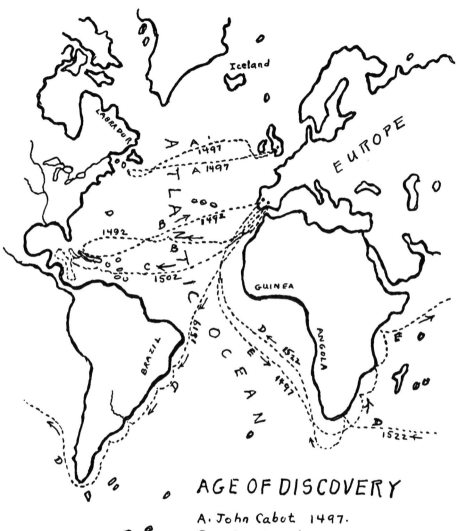

AGE OF DISCOVERY

A. John Cabot 1497.
B. Columbus 1st voyage 1492
C. Columbus 4th voyage 1502
D. Magellan 1519.
E. Vasco da Gama 1497

BEGINNING OF THE COMMERCIAL REVOLUTION

L.C.H
1941

MAP No 2

and known as the "Merchant Adventurers of England for the discoveries of lands and territories unknown." It was established with a joint stock of £6,000. Sebastian Cabot was appointed governor for life. There was a board of directors consisting of four consuls and twenty-four assistants. The company had rights of exploration, of conquest, of acquiring lands, and of seizing the ships of any who should infringe on their monopoly of trade.

In 1583 a committee from the Muscovy merchants drew up resolutions regarding an "intended discoverie and attempt into the hithermost parts of America." This was similar to the plan of Sir Walter Raleigh. It proposed to send forth 100 men for one year, providing £4,000 for the adventure, in order to gain a "knowledge of the particular estate of the country and gather what commodity may hereafter be looked for." A joint stock was provided consisting of two groups, one of "Adventurers" and one of "Enterprisers."

There was another company, the Eastland, trading in the Baltic, the Levant, Turkey, Syria and Asia Minor. In fact, at the close of Elizabeth's reign in 1603, France was about the only country with which English merchants could trade without belonging to a company.

Economic conditions in England during the reign of Elizabeth were terrible, and thoroughly familiar to the "Mayflower Planters," the leaders of whom were either "Merchant Adventurers" or "Enterprisers."

Elizabeth fell heir to an empty treasury in 1558, and it was several years before England could get even in sight of stability. A compromise in religion helped a little, but the merchants and industry were more encouraged by the apparent desire of the government to promote and reward private initiative and thrift.

Poverty and sickness prevailed. Crime increased. Men of rank became robbers, fifty at one time were hanged at Oxford, and Lord Stourton was hanged at Salisbury in a halter of silk to mark his dignity.

Various attempts to build up local trade in cloth items took on an aspect of humor. In London 1558

"Citizen's wives who are not alderman's wives nor gentlewomen by descent, are obliged to wear minever caps, being white woolen, knit three cornered, with peaks fore heads. Alderman's wives wear theirs made of velvet."

In 1562 an act is passed "requiring the mayors of the towns and church wardens to draw up lists of all inhabitants able to contribute for the relief of the poor, and enforce payment."

In 1566 two marshals are appointed to clear the streets of London of "vagrants," including the sick, blind and lame.

About this time the first recorded lottery in England was held at the western door of St. Paul's. There were 40,000 "lots at 10s each." The prizes were pieces of plate, the profits are intended for repair of harbors.

Great excitement attends the introduction of carriages, and the awful plague becomes a scourge in London in 1563.

In 1567 Flemish dyers, cloth drapers, linen-makers, silk-throwers and the like are encouraged to settle at Canterbury, Norwich, Colchester, Southampton, and other places.

Although excess in dress is restrained by law in 1570, it appears that in 1572, masks, muffs, fans and false hair for the women, devised in Italy, are brought to England from France.

At this time a statute requires justices and mayors to make registers of the impotent poor, and find them habitations at the expense of the inhabitants of their locality.

About 1586 a young man named Shakespeare, walked out on his home town, Stratford, and was forced to hike all the way into London, because in those times a "hitch-hike" was unknown. He soon became part owner of a horseshoe shaped playhouse in London, mostly covered with thatch (1594).

Camden assigns the rise of Puritanism in England to the year 1568. However, as early as 1165 the Council of Oxford was summoned to deal with thirty weavers of Worcester, whose "heretical" opinions were similar to those of later times. There seems to be a relationship between freedom of religion and enterprise.

In 1558 Elizabeth found the credit of the government so low that it had to pay 14% for loans. Every branch of the government was absolutely insolvent in thought and action. England was at war, but deficient in all military and naval appliances. Domestic trades were dying. Vagrancy and pauperism was spreading.

The currency had depreciated greatly. This question was more pressing than the religious turmoil. No trade and prosperity was possible while the currency was in such a condition. No one could determine the real value of a coin. In 1559 there were three different kinds of shilling in circulation, and four types of "tester," or six penny pieces. They not only had an original difference in size and quality, but clever "clippers" and "sweaters" had sapped their value. Similar difficulties prevailed among the lesser coins.

Finally, by proclamation, Sept. 27, 1560, Elizabeth called in the old currency and issued new currency. The holders of the currency, of course, took a beating on the exchange.

However, the operation did result in a fairly sound currency for a time, and gave the merchants a little encouragement.

Elizabeth wanted money with which to bribe Scotch and French rebels, to embarrass her external enemies, to maintain internal order, to provide for national defence. Law and order at home was necessary for the growth of English industry.

New navigation laws were framed to encourage the construction of home built ships, and to promote seamanship. During the reign of Elizabeth, the English foreign trade gradually fell into the hands of the great companies described above. The earlier companies were simply associations of merchants, each of whom might trade with his own capital, and at his own risk, provided he was a member of the company and conformed to the rules. The stock companies were a later development as described.

Previous to 1556 the exchange transactions had been conducted in the open air in Lombard Street. Soon after this date the new Royal Exchange Building was completed, and the London merchants, at last, had a permanent home in which to trade.

Richard Hakluyt informs us that the Newfoundland fisheries were very prosperous in 1577, at which time there were engaged in the business 15 English ships, 150 French ships, 100 Spanish ships and 50 Portuguese ships. Just how many of these fishermen dropped off to settle on the adjacent shores will never be known.

As a typical Elizabethan charter the one for Exeter can be commented upon. This charter was granted by Queen Elizabeth a few months after her accession to the throne, and signed by her June 17, 1560. There were Guilds and Merchant Adventurers in Exeter for several hundred years previous to this date. For instance one signed by "Bloody Queen Mary" in 1556, but none of these earlier charters stimulated "commercial adventure" to any extent. Practically, the Exeter Society begins with the Elizabeth charter, which was granted to the Merchants of Exeter as a part reward for their loyalty and defense of their brethren within the walls of the city in a siege about 1549.

It appears that in the summer of 1549 the city of Exeter was beset by "rebel fanatics" whose minds were affected owing "to the sun being in Cancer and the midsummer moon at full." Lord Russell had been sent down by King Henry VIII to suppress the rebellion, and was at "Honiton" in an "agony and of a heavy cheer" for want of men and money, especially money. Fortunately, three merchants of Exeter "understanding of his lordship's heaviness and grief, did procure such a mass of money" that Lord Russell was able to raise the siege on Aug. 6, 1549.

This charter differs from most, in that Elizabeth makes direct reference to a certain service to the Crown.

The original charter, until recently, was in possession of the Master and Wardens of the Ancient Society of Weavers, Fullers and Shearmen of Exeter.

Toward the end of Queen Elizabeth's reign a great impetus was given to the settlement of Englishmen in America. To Richard Hakluyt England owes much, although seldom, if ever, making a voyage of any moment, he became by close study, a noted historiographer. As a boy he became interested in the stories of travel and geography. When a pupil in the old Westminster School in London, he would visit the Middle Temple and pour over the crude books of travel and maps of the world there spread upon a table. The vast unchartered spaces on the map fascinated him. On entering the University he determined to specialize in geography, and grew to be the best authority of the time on climate, products and races of the known world, although a "devine" by profession.

The Merchant Adventurers made a practice of calling Hakluyt into conference before undertaking an expedition, or in considering the formation of a new company.

He was a Queen's scholar at Westminster, and in 1570 entered Christ Church, Oxford, where he read all existing prints on voyages and discoveries. He received his A. B. in 1573 and M. A. in 1577.

In 1583 he was appointed chaplain to the English Embassy at Paris under special instructions of Sir Francis Walsingham, to report on everything he saw and heard. While there he learned that Sir Francis Drake was about to fit out his expedition to America, and forthwith expressed a wish to give up his "spying" job and fly to England "with wings of Pegasus," to help prepare the expedition.

Hakluyt became well known to all the great seagoing captains of the time, the greatest mariners and merchants. He was a rapt listener to the tall tales of seamen on their return from long voyages.

During the later part of the 16th century much consideration was given by the Adventurers to the best method of developing a lucrative colonial trade. Chartered commercial companies were finally decided upon.

Soon after 1600 the East India Company was formed and a charter granted by Elizabeth. It is not surprising to note in the minutes of this company under date of Jan. 29, 1601-2, that Richard Hakluyt was a guiding spirit in the proposition.

Before the American Company could be formed and the charter granted, Elizabeth died in 1603.

When King James ascended the throne he began to rave against the Puritans and Separatists, and as many of the Merchant Adventurers were of these groups the Society became a shining target. After some violent opposition James finally confirmed their charters in 1605 and again in 1607.

Meanwhile active attempts were under way to round up associates willing to engage in founding an English colony in America. Captain Bartholomew Gosnold, a man of fine character and ability, spent one year in this connection, and a second year in obtaining prospective colonists, ships and supplies. He was the driving force in the undertaking and held the confidence of the Adventurers.

However, Gosnold was having some unexpected cooperation from James in promoting emigration to America. The King now seemed anxious to get rid of the vast army of idle men over-running England by sending them to distant parts. Many were ex-soldiers returned from the Spanish wars. The streets of London were crowded with veterans of the wars in Ireland and the Netherlands. They had been pressed into military service and unwilling or unable to earn an honest living. They became beggars and robbers.

Ex-army officers, of course, were hoping that their services would be requested. Swords were swinging in rusty idleness on the walls of homes and castles.

Preachers were becoming urgent in advising parishioners to emigrate, and above all else, the Merchant Adventurers appeared willing to risk their capital in the enterprise. They had even interested the writers and poets, Marston, Chapman, and Ben Jonson to collaborate on a play which would present tempting reasons for sailing to the Virginia plantations immediately.

The three old friends got together and wrote a play called "Eastward Ho," based upon some gossip of the day, as overheard, probably, around the Royal Exchange in London where the burning question of plantations was a common topic.

The stage must not be taken too seriously, yet it reflects in some degree the spirit of the period.

The play was quite the rage in London during 1605.

The following portions of the play include some conversation between "Sea-Gull," "Drawer," "Spend All," and "Scape-thrift."

"**Sea Gull**—Come, Drawer, pierce your neatest hogshead, and let's have cheer, not fit for your Billingsgate tavern, but for our Virginia Colonel, he will be here instantly."

"**Drawer**—You shall have all things fit, sir; please you have any more wine?"

"**Spend All**—More wine, slave! Whether we drink it or no; spill it and draw more."

"**Scapethrift**—But is there such treasure there, Captain, as I have heard?"

"**Sea Gull**—I tell thee, gold is more plentiful there than copper is with us, and for as much red copper as I can bring I'll have thrice weight in gold. Why, man, all their dripping-pans and chamber-pots are pure gold; and all the chains with which they chain up their streets are massive gold; all the prisoners they take are fettered in gold; and for rubies and diamonds they go forth in holy days, and gather them by the sea-shore to hang on their children's coats and stick in their children's caps as commonly as our children wear saffron-gilt brooches and groates with holes in them."

"**Scapethrift**—And it is a pleasant country withal?"

"**Sea Gull**—As ever the sun shin'd on; temperate and full of all sorts of excellent viands; wild boar is as common there as our tamest bacon is here; venison as mutton. And then you shall live freely there, without sargeants or courtiers, or lawyers or intelligencers. Then for your means to advancement—there it is simple, and not preposterously mixt. You may be an alderman there, and never be a scavenger; you may be any other officer, and never be a slave. You may come to preferment enough, and never be a pander; to riches and fortune, and have never the more villany nor the less wit. Besides, there we shall have no more law than conscience, and not too much of either."

The above fascinating bit of propaganda might be an inspiration to modern novices in the art of gently, but firmly guiding the public mind. For complete appreciation the entire play should be read. Jonson was probably the master mind. He was at odds with James I from time to time, and occasionally imprisoned for short periods.

At last, Gosnold had aroused sufficient interest among influential persons, including Sir Ferdinando Gorges, to warrant a petition to the King for a "Virginia Company" and patent. He himself was thoroughly informed concerning the proposition, having been commander of the "Concord" in 1602, when it visited the coast of New England from what is now Maine to Martha's Vineyard, even landing at and naming Cape Cod and returning to England with a cargo of furs, sassafras and other items.

Gosnold had a great liking for the Cape Cod section, and expressed this sentiment quite freely among his friends in England, which included Sir Edwin Sandys, and, probably, William Brewster.

No doubt the glowing accounts of Gosnold had much to do with the decision to plant a colony at Plymouth some years later.

On April 10, 1606, James granted a patent, the story of which is told under the heading of the Virginia Company and the Mayflower Planters.

The "Merchant Adventurers" should be assigned a high place in English history. They had a colorful existence from the central years of the Middle Ages to the beginning of the nineteenth century, when the "Fellowship" and "Society" of merchants withered up with age and died, to be replaced by a more modern, but less romantic form of organization.

Refs. 398, 399, 400, 402, 472, 473, 474, 475, 476, 477, 478, 480, 482, 403, 407, 408, 409, 410, 411, 442, 413, 418, 412.

# SNOW

II. **Snow, Mark**[3] (Constance[2] **Hopkins**, Stephen[1]) ; born May 9, 1628, died 1695? ; married 1st Anna[2] **Cooke** in Eastham Jan. 18, 1654-5; she died July 24, 1656; daughter of Josiah[1] **Cooke**; married 2nd Jane [2] **Prence** in Eastham Jan. 9, 1660-1; born Plymouth Nov. 1, 1637; died Harwich 1710-2; daughter of Gov. Thomas[1] **Prence**.)

He was able to bear arms in Aug. 1643 in Plymouth, and with his father removed to Eastham. He succeeded his father as town clerk for 14 years from 1663, served as a selectman for 18 years from 1667, and a deputy to the General Court 6 years from 1675. He was also Captain of the militia company in 1659. In many other ways he served his community efficiently.

CHILDREN BORN EASTHAM

48. Anna, b. July 7, 1656, d.      ; m. Eldad **Atwood.**
49. Mary, b. Nov. 30, 1661, d.      ; m. William **Nickerson.**
50. Nicholas, b. Dec. 6, 1663, d. 1754; m. Lydia **Shaw.**
51. Elizabeth, b. May 9, 1666, d. Jan. 18, 1675-6; m.
52. Thomas, b. Aug. 6, 1668, d.      ; m. 1st Hannah **Sears.**
                                     ; m. 2nd Lydia ˉ (Sears) **Hamblin.**
53. Sarah, b. May 10, 1671, d.      ; m.
54. Lt. Prence, b. May 22, 1674, d.      ; m. Hannah **Storrs.**
55. Elizabeth, b. June 22, 1676, d. Mar. 22, 1677-8; m.
56. Hannah, b. Sept. 16, 1679, d.      ; m.

---

Refs. 171, 291, 294, 161, 129, 261.

# BREWSTER

The name William Brewster, usually with an "Elder" in front, is among the very earliest and most worthwhile recollections of the author of this work. A New England home some years ago without a picture book or story for youngsters dealing with the landing of the Pilgrims on Plymouth Rock would have been hard to find. To the youthful mind the Pilgrims seemed rather severe, always going to or from some church meeting with a gun in one hand and a Bible in the other. There was a meekness yet a set purpose and power in the scene that fascinated and left a lasting impression. The religious atmosphere may have been a little overdrawn, yet the self-imposed high standards of life set by the early settlers in New England have been an everlasting inspiration to following generations.

After spending many years, as time permitted, in getting more intimately acquainted with the Mayflower Planters, especially their background in Europe, and real reasons for planting a colony at Cape Cod in 1620, it is a very great pleasure to report an ever increasing respect for this really remarkable body of men and women.

There is every reason to think that the Merchant Adventurers of London through the Virginia Company, under the critical management of Sir Edwin Sandys, exerted every means to obtain the best possible men and women adapted for planting colonies in a new world, for the six ships, sent out 1619-20. Everybody on those vessels was most carefully picked for health, character and prospective usefulness. The Company had to make good, and could take no chances with failures in life, idlers, or worthless members of the "nobility."

However, the Mayflower happened to have a special distinction in having among its passengers a number of close personal friends of Sir Edwin. They were all seeking a new haven for self-expression, not alone in a method of worship, but also, and more especially, in a political, economic and social freedom. Unfortunately, several outstanding members of the party died soon after landing at Plymouth, but others lived to carry on, among them two extraordinary individuals, Master William Brewster of Scrooby and Cambridge, sometime member of Queen Elizabeth's Court, soldier, teacher and tutor, and his pupil and friend William Bradford. Among their great accomplishments was the writing of the History of the Plymouth Plantation, most of which was done between 1630-1644, when Brewster may have been somewhat infirm in body, but certainly not in spirit and memory. William Brewster had been an active character in some of the exciting moments of history, and at four score years the hand that holds the pen may have been shaky, but, fortunately for generations to come, there by his side, was his old pupil William Bradford, who had developed into a very able man, and was a penman of no mean ability, according to his manuscript.

Now, who was this William Brewster, and what was his background that he should have felt it so essential to remain in such almost total obscurity during the twenty-four years of his life in Plymouth? Why did he fail to make a will or leave any personal writings? Why did friends, seemingly, have to be so discreet in discussing his affairs? Even Bradford in the last chapters of the "History" right after the death of his friend in 1644 seemed to hesitate, stating "I should say something of his life, if to say a little were not worse than to be silent."

Most of the word pictures of Brewster disclose him as supremely religious, meek and humble. However, among the assets of his estate were some rather assertive items such as two swords, a pistol, dagger and armor, headpiece, and "corselet." Then again, the clothing he wore such as a violet colored cloth coat, black silk stockings and a ruff do not seem to square with the traditional severity attributed to the "Pilgrims."

Under a separate heading in this volume entitled "The Sandys and Brewsters of Scrooby Manor" will be found some facts concerning William Brewster and his connections to the time he left Scrooby for Cambridge in December, 1580.

William had probably been spending much of his boyhood at the old Manor House, twelve years of it, at least, in happy association with boys of the neighborhood of his own standing, and the Brewsters were neither socially obscure or poor. It is not known what schools William attended, but there were good ones at Retford, Gainsboro and Lincoln. Then again William Brewster of Bury St. Edmunds, probably connected with the Brewsters of Wrentham, may have been his grandfather. If so he could have spent some years there, studying at the famous grammar school founded by Edward VI, and having the rights of two scholarships at Cambridge. Or, if at home, he could have been prepared for the University under the Vicar Henry Brewster, perhaps his uncle. Latin was the prime entrance requirement for Cambridge. A beginner had to make himself familiar with William Lyly's grammar, first published in 1513 for the scholars of St. Paul's and so enjoined by Henry VIII as to make it "penal for any publicly to teach any other." Writing and speaking of Latin were subjects of special drill.

Apparently, his progress encouraged his parents to proceed with William's education, and, after the usual consultations with the parish vicar and schoolmaster in regard to the boy's capacity, he was sent to Cambridge, according to the custom of that district, rather than to Oxford.

No doubt there was some excitement in the household at

Scrooby Manor when William was packed off to college. His mother, "Prudence," must have felt distressed, as mothers do at such times, to watch the departure of her 17-year-old son, knowing that she would see him but seldom in the future. However, a feeling of pride helped to temper the sadness at parting. Was not her boy to be a collegian?

There were the usual leave takings in the village among his friends, and perhaps presents of money from certain of his father's friends.

He was up early to join other hopeful scholars on the Great North Road, all bound on the long journey to Cambridge.

The students arranged to travel up to the University in groups, both for company and safety, as they often carried with them the allowance for a whole term, and numerous highway robbers were well aware of that fact.

Journeying southward through Newark, Grantham, Stamford and Peterborough by easy stages, they came to the old Roman Road, the "Via Devana," which ran across country from Chester to Colchester. Following this ancient line of traffic, they soon reached Huntingdon, and continued on to Cambridge.

As they came over the hill by Cambridge Castle, the town on the far side of the river, with its noble buildings was spread out before them. To a young lad coming up to the University this view must have been impressive, with its assemblage of collegiate buildings, hostels and churches.

He glanced eagerly about as they came down Castle Hill, on through Monk's Place to the Great Bridge. Crossing the river they soon reached the heart of the town, and on Dec. 3, 1580, William Brewster of Scrooby matriculated at St. Peters, more commonly called Peterhouse, the oldest of the fourteen colleges at the time grouped into the University of Cambridge. Along the same route from Sturton, a neighboring town to Scrooby in Notts, twelve years later, John Robinson made the journey to Cambridge, and in 1604-5 these two men met in a common cause of freedom which was the guiding influence of their future activities.

Peterhouse was founded on Mar. 3, 1284. In 1309 it had gained possession of the property of the friars of the order "De Poenitentia Jesu."

In Brewster's time there were "fellows," who lived from the revenues of the colleges; "fellow-commoners," who sat at the table and could converse with the "fellows"; "scholars" or students partly supported by institution funds; "Bible-clerks," whose duty was to read the Scriptures aloud at meals; "pensioners," who paid a pension, or rent, for lodging in the college; and "sizars," or poor students, who performed menial, or semi-menial, services. Detailed records of Peterhouse for some years after 1580 are missing, but there were probably about 100 in residence during his time, the majority being "pensioners," or.

students whose families paid the cost of living. No doubt, Brewster was a "pensioner," his family being in comfortable circumstances, and able to pay the needed fifty pounds a year. The master of Peterhouse was the famous Dr. Andrew Perne, and, of course, Brewster was directly influenced by him, during his three years or more at the college. Perne, in 1580, had been for twenty-six years master of Peterhouse, and although a "Puritan" at heart, had managed to survive during the reign of Mary, by sheer ability in fast mental and verbal shifting. He became affectionately known by the students as "Dr. Turncoats" and the "Old Turner," due to the fact that he was twice "Papist," and twice "Protestant," sometimes "Puritan," but generally strong for the established church. It can be said of Perne that he never made a rash change, it was always done at the right time, not alone to save himself, but also to protect the "fellows" under him in the University. Brewster never forgot Perne or his teaching.

Naturally, other great teachers and preachers of his college day profoundly stirred and inspired Brewster, among them William Perkins, who published many works, eleven copies of which were in Brewster's library. Then there were Dr. John Copcot and Peter Baro, both rather advanced thinkers of the time.

One of Brewster's close Cambridge friends, George Johnson, entered the University at the same time. He went through banishment and shipwreck to Amsterdam, was excommunicated with his father, and died in prison at Durham in 1605, but not before he had published a work on the English Church in Amsterdam. Brewster brought a copy of this work to New England with him on the Mayflower. It is possible that the persecution and death of his friend Johnson in 1605 may have spurred Brewster to take the course he did after this date.

Robert Devereux, Earl of Essex, about the same age as Brewster, was a Cambridge man, and later events proved that they were friends, politically and otherwise. A work about his friend Essex was found in Brewster's library.

Then, there were Christopher Marlowe, Richard Harvey, Robert Greene, and others too numerous to mention, all known to Brewster.

Among his fellow students at Peterhouse were: Edmund Coote, Robert Priest, James Scruby, Abraham Fleming, Reginald Bainbrigg, John Morden, Robert Bownd, Charles Horne, Miles Sandys, Mark Sadlington, Nicholas Deane, John Penry and others.

The path to learning in 1580 was not one strewn with roses. Two students were assigned to each apartment, consisting of a common room about eighteen by twenty, and two small studies. The two beds were in the large room, the furniture consisted of two beds, a leaden jug, a rude bowl, a plain wooden table, two forms or a few stools or a settle, a cupboard, and wooden shutters for the windows, and in each small study a desk for writing, and a shelf or so for books.

It must be remembered that the plan of an English college within an University, was patterned after the monastery. It consisted of a cluster of buildings within an enclosure, including courts, refectory, kitchen, offices, chapel and master's lodge. About the one difference from a monastic arrangement was the lodging of the scholars in chambers, instead of a grand dormitory.

A college in those days, and for several hundred years previously, was essentially a foundation "endowed by private munificence for the complemental work of lodging and boarding poor young men, who desired university privileges but lacked means."

Peterhouse in the time of Brewster was about 300 years old, quite a ripe age. Old Bishop Balsham in 1284 secured two inns near the little church of St. Peter. These were called "hostels, or literary inns." From time to time additions were made, a library was built in 1431-48, a kitchen in 1450, a hall sometime before.

Some scholars roomed in the "hostels," others in chambers or dormitories, the living conditions being about the same.

The large "stone parlor," or Combination Room, boasted the only fireplace in the college. There were no chimneys in the students' rooms, and no heat. They dined in a hall next to the kitchen and "buttery." The floors were strewn with rushes. The furniture of the halls was simply "a fayre long table of waynscott," with a number of benches. There was a table on a dias for the master and fellows.

Petty robbery was quite common among all classes of people. Therefore the books reserved for the library use were chained to cases and placed on shelves with backs inward. The unchained volumes could be used by students, but were carefully guarded in chests having two locks, one key kept by the master, the other by the senior dean. This is the library that Brewster consulted.

The master's quarters were above the "stone parlor." He ate with the students in the hall, sitting at the middle of the long table on a dias.

The college funds were stored in an oaken chest, strapped with bands of iron, and having several different kinds of locks so that it could be opened simultaneously in the presence of several officials, each with his own key. "The common seal, the charters, royal letters-patent" and similar valuables were guarded in the same manner. In Peterhouse the special "strong" room for the chests was over the buttery.

A college, at the outset, was a sectarian community, most of the scholars were preparing for holy orders. Attending a chapel was habitual even in Brewster's time, although all scholars were not preparing for the ministry in the established church.

The Peterhouse house chapel had about sixty "superstitious pictures, some popes and crucifixes, with God the Father sitting in a chair and holding a globe in his hand." These were all removed in 1643.

The daily grind was about as follows: At 5 A. M. the college bell tolled, and the students attended morning service at Little St. Mary's, followed by a "bit" of advice from one of the fifteen "fellows," lasting about an hour. Then came various studies, university exercises, lectures by professors, or public disputations. At 10 or 11 A. M. they dined in the hall, on a joint of roast beef, mutton or veal, varied occasionally by a meat soup, "havyng a fewe porage made of the brothe of the same byefe, wyth salte and otemell, and nothynge els." On Fridays nothing but fish. After dinner there would be declamation and dispute, then prayers in St. Mary's, and supper at 5 P. M. "not much better than theyr dyner."

It is quite possible that Davison contacted with William Brewster, then about 19 years old, at Cambridge through mutual friends such as Essex, and Sandys in 1583, when returning to London from a mission to Scotland for the Queen, who considered Davison "a man of abilities and address," and was about to appoint him personal ambassador to the Low Countries for the purpose of forming a treaty with them. A good language student was needed on his staff, and apparently Brewster was chosen, for from this time he became closely affiliated with Davison, both as friend and aid in some degree, up to the death of Davison in 1608.

Early in 1585 the states of the Low Countries became obliged to throw themselves on the Queen's protection, and after Antwerp was seized by the Spaniards, she found it necessary to adopt some decided action. Elizabeth determined to assist them in their resolution of defending their freedom by force of arms, and Mr. Davison was selected as Her Majesty's ambassador.

In Aug., 1585, Davison and staff, including Brewster, went into Holland. The Queen's instructions were countersigned by Walsingham, and consisted of nine articles. On Sept. 5, 1585, the Queen ordered him to take possession of Flushing in her behalf; and to put Brill into the hands of the person whom Gen. Norris should appoint.

After suitable arrangements were made, Sir Philip Sydney was put in charge of Flushing, Mr. Thomas Cecil, son of Lord Treasurer Burghley, in charge of Brill, and the Earl of Leicester arrived in Holland Dec. 12, 1585, to take over general command.

During the next few months members of Davison's staff, including William Brewster, experienced some exciting moments, even to the extent of a skirmish or two in actual combat.

When Sir Philip Sydney arrived to take charge of Flushing, he immediately urged his commander, the Earl of Leicester, to some resolute action against Spain. Sir Philip had married

Frances, daughter of Sir Francis Walsingham, and both of these men were not only good friends of Davison, the ambassador, but had distinct Puritan leanings. Sydney was a fighter and wanted to attack Philip II in Spain itself, and was at Plymouth ready to sail with Drake in his Spanish expedition of 1585, when the Queen recalled him and ordered him to join Davison in Flushing.

Not being able to move his elegant military commander, the Earl, to activity, Sydney made a successful raid of his own on a place near Flushing, and soon joined the force of Sir John Norris who was operating against Zutphen. On Sept. 22, 1586, while in command of a small force sent out to intercept a convoy of provisions, a fight took place, and Sir Philip was mortally wounded; although able to ride back to camp, he died at Arnheim on Oct. 17, 1586. His body was taken to England and buried in St. Paul's. His widow in 1590 married another "Puritan," and leader of the "Liberal" or "Patriot" party, no less a person than Robert Devereux, Earl of Essex. All of these characters were well known to William Brewster.

That Brewster had some part in all these happenings seems quite evident, for Bradford, writing fifty-five years later in far away New England, relates how Brewster wore a gold chain, presented by the Netherlands. On return to England he was commanded "to wear it as they rode through the country until they arrived at Court."

It is not clear whether Brewster took a personal part in Sir Philip Sydney's affair at Zutphen in Sept., 1586, but he certainly had full official knowledge of it, and quite likely was on the spot as Davison's agent, or, perhaps, that of Walsingham.

Before the middle of September Davison was back in London and elevated to one of the "Principal Secretaries." His formal commission as such is dated Westminster, Dec. 12, 1586. In October, George Cranmer, friend of Sir Edwin Sandys of Scrooby Manor, joined Davison's staff. Several months of exciting and history making work followed. Brewster, Cranmer and Davison must have been extremely busy. They probably did business at Davison's house in London, and were more or less in daily attendance at Court, which rotated between Whitehall, Richmond, Hampton Court, Nonesuch, Oatlands and Greenwich, where the Queen liked to be, especially in summer.

Some historians claim that Davison was appointed Secretary of State solely to be made the instrument of Mary's death, and then to be sacrificed to the selfish policy of Elizabeth in persuading the world that the event was without her knowledge, and against her inclination.

There is good reason, however, to suppose that she merely saw a chance, at the moment, to shift the odium from herself, and the poor victims happened to be Davison and his staff.

Sir Francis Walsingham, for the asserted purpose of protecting the Queen, had organized an elaborate spy or espionage system. He had agents in the College of Cardinals, the Jesuit Seminaries, the French embassy, the Spanish Court, and in the mansions of the chief Romanists. Spies of all sorts roamed the courts in London, and were scattered throughout England. However, information obtained in this manner was not reliable, and Walsingham was finding it difficult to prove that Mary was a menace to the Queen, so far as her life was concerned.

From a political point of view it was highly desirable to remove the menace of Mary entirely, although Elizabeth could not be convinced of danger.

The advisors of the Queen, Walsingham especially, decided to lay a trap for Mary. She was removed from Tutbury Castle to Chartley Manor to be more accessible, and after much intrigue concerning intercepted letters of a threatening nature on the life of the Queen, a case was framed and Mary the Queen of Scots was removed to Fotheringay Castle in Northamptonshire, and on Sept. 28, 1586, the commission to try her met at Windsor, and made plans for the trial, one of the most famous in history.

They left London Oct. 8, 1586, for on that day Davison wrote to Lord Burleigh a note, intended for him and Walsingham only, requesting advice about some procedures at the trial, ending "I do here, with remembrance of my duty, most humbly and in haste to take my leave, at the Court at Windsor, this 8th of October, 1586."

The cavalcade of horsemen formed and the eventful journey to Fotheringay on that October day in 1586 began the eighty mile ride to the Castle where Mary was imprisoned. It was an imposing company of high ranking officials of the realm, there were the commissioners, with their aids, Secretary Davison, and staff including probably his "trusted" assistant Brewster, and retainers of high and low degree.

The wretched Mary was waiting for them. On Oct. 11, 1586, the commissioners assembled for the trial, which was carried through with considerable pomp and ceremony. Before this tribunal the Queen of Scots did not have a chance for life. The stage was set. The trial over, the doomed Mary was left with her ladies in waiting, and the cavalcade returned to London.

On Oct. 25, 1586, the Commissioners met in the star chamber at Westminster, and pronounced sentence, which they confirmed by their seals and signatures. On Oct. 29th, Parliament met, and on Nov. 12, 1586, both houses addressed the Queen, requesting the execution of the sentence passed against the Queen of Scots.

Elizabeth had a distasteful job thrust upon her. She had to sign the death warrant which was prepared. Somebody had to present it to her for signature, but her chief ministers hesitated to undertake the ticklish duty, Burghley and Walsingham knew Elizabeth and how uncertain, but outspoken she could be at times.

Furthermore she put herself on record promptly with a letter in reply to Parliament, in part:

> "the act of Parliament had brought her into a great strait, by obliging her to give directions for her own kinswoman's death, which was to her a most grievous and irksome burthen."

Even if the tears were false, this was a mighty clever thing for Elizabeth to put forth, and certainly did not make it any easier for the bearer of the warrant.

The warrant had to be executed, however, and somebody had to brave the tempest and carry it to Elizabeth.

The sentence was published Dec. 21, 1586, and proclaimed with great pomp and solemnity. The Lord Mayor, attended by several noblemen, the aldermen and principal officers of the city, the majority of the gentry in the neighborhood, and about eighty citizens dressed in velvet, and wearing gold chains, all on horseback, assembled at about 10 o'clock in the forenoon, when the sentence was publicly read by the town clerk at the cross in Cheapside; at the end of Chancery Lane; at Leadenhall Corner; and at St. Magnus Corner near London Bridge.

Now, everything was set for the execution, but still no warrant. Burghley and Walsingham had become rather suddenly ill. Meanwhile, the warrant had been handed to Davison, who being the secretary and in frequent consultation with Elizabeth could present it at any time.

After a day or two of hesitation, Davison, or perhaps Brewster, as his aid, handed the warrant to the Queen. She took one glance at it and went into a towering rage, refusing to sign it for some weeks.

Finally, pressed by the Court officers, Davison most humbly begged the Queen to sign the warrant so that it could be delivered to the proper authorities immediately.

Right then and there Elizabeth decided to shift the odium from her own shoulders to Davison, and perhaps Brewster was there. She went into the usual rage, refused to sign, then changed her mind, signed the warrant and threw it onto the floor.

Davison, greatly troubled, picked up the warrant, glanced at the Queen, but she, with an imperious wave of hand, dismissed him without further comment.

There was nothing for Davison to do except to hand the signed warrant to the "Great Seal," from where it would be passed on to the proper officials. However, he must have had some unpleasant misgivings owing to the actions of Elizabeth. He wondered what her real motive was in throwing the warrant on the floor at his feet. Although she had "swore" and raved at him from time to time, a stunt like that had never been tried before on him.

[ 33 ]

The warrant reached Fotheringay on Feb. 7, 1587, and the next morning at 8 A. M., the Queen of Scots was executed. When Elizabeth heard about it, she immediately, on Feb. 11, 1587, convoked the Council, berated them soundly, and even denounced her friend and advisor Burghley. Davison had become ill and could not attend the Council meeting, perhaps Brewster was there in his place. Anyway she became violent about Davison before the Council, charging that she did not direct him to take the warrant to the Great Seal, and forthwith ordered him to the Tower, although the Council begged her to pause.

When news reached Davison about this action on the part of Elizabeth, he was, possibly, not surprised. She had merely shifted the responsibility of Mary's death from herself, so far as the warrant was concerned, and he just happened to be the medium.

On Feb. 14, 1587, William Davison was taken to the Tower of London. State prisoners, however, with private means were permitted to have one or two secretaries or assistants, and, no doubt, Brewster continued to serve, even to the extent of living in the Tower. Many high ranking officers and their staffs resided at the Tower for years, most of them political prisoners.

If lodged in the place as an assistant, Brewster would have had a room in the famous Beauchamp Tower, whose windows looked down Great Tower Street as far as All Hollows, Barking.

At that time the Tower was in charge of a constable of high rank, and Davison, as Secretary of State, could eat with the Lieutenant Sir Owen Hopton, if he could pay for it.

On entering the Tower in 1587 as a prisoner, a room is assigned, absolutely bare, cold and uninviting, having a stone floor, an iron clamped door, and a grated window. Everything else, including food, must be obtained by the occupant. Brewster probably fitted their rooms up with a table, benches and a few books. Sir Walter Raleigh lived for thirteen years in a place like this, making experiments in chemistry and writing.

A Tower prisoner having no private means, or friends willing to aid with food and other human needs, simply died of neglect and starvation.

Of course, Davison went through the formality of a trial. He was found guilty, and sentenced to imprisonment in the Tower, at the Queen's pleasure, and fined 10,000 marks ($150,-000), which he could never hope to pay.

His friends at Court, including the Earl of Essex, interceded from time to time for him. They all felt that he had been unjustly treated. He probably remained in the Tower two or three years.

Brewster, naturally, did not have to reside in the Tower to assist Davison. He probably went in and out of the place at will, and might very well have lived in a home of his own in

London, and probably did, with a young family of his own, however, all the time under something of a cloud.

Just what part Brewster played in the great drama leading up to the execution of Queen Mary may never be known in detail, but he was an active associate at the time of William Davison, Secretary to Queen Elizabeth, in fact, a member of his staff, and must have been well informed concerning the rather confused and remarkable story of the famous death warrant. It is possible he may have performed some very important service in connection with the delivery of the warrant, which in later years he did not feel free to discuss.

William Bradford tells us all too little about the political, social and economic life of William Brewster, his benefactor and friend, his teacher and guide for nearly fifty years. However, the death of Brewster in Plymouth on April 18, 1644, seemed also to mark the practical completion of the "History of the Plymouth Plantation" upon which they had been working since 1630. Among Bradford's final words about his friend are some very suggestive phrases. Apparently the real story of Brewster was never released.

These few sentences carry many implications, "I should say something of his life if to say a little were not worse than to be silent, but I cannot wholly forbear, though perhaps more may be written at some later time."

"After he had attained some learning, viz., the knowledge of the Latin tongue and some insight into Greek, and had spent some little time at Cambridge x x x x he went to Court, and served that religious and godly gentleman, Mr. Davison, for several years, when he was Secretary of State."

That Brewster was a very useful diplomat in difficult times, associated with such men as Essex, Walhingham, Burghley, Sydney, Sandys and others seems to be amply endorsed by Bradford, who states that Davison

"found him so discreet and faithful, that he trusted him more than all the others who were round him, and employed him in all matters of greatest **trust and secrecy**. He esteemed him rather as a son x x x x x and knowing his wisdom and godliness he would converse with him in private more as a friend. x x x x He accompanied him when he was sent as ambassador by the Queen into the Low Countries, in the Earl of Leicester's time, besides other important affairs of state, to receive possession of the cautionary towns, in token of which the keys of Flushing were delivered to him in her majesty's name. Mr. Davison held them some time, handing them over to Mr. Brewster, who kept them under his pillow the first night. On his departure, the Netherlands honored Mr. Davison with a gold chain; he gave it into the keeping of Mr. Brewster, and when they arrived in England commanded him to wear it as they rode through the country, until they arrived at Court. He remained with him through his troubles, when later, he was dismissed in connection with the death of the Queen of Scots, and for some good time after, doing him much faithful service."

The plain inference is that Brewster was the personal and confidential assistant or secretary to Davison throughout all of the exciting times, and probably to a more or less extent right up to the death of Davison in 1608, after which time Brewster made plans to leave England as soon as possible. His two older sons William and Edward departed for Virginia immediately, while he, although purchasing shares in the Virginia Company, went over to Leyden, where he opened up a school; teaching, apparently being his main profession, together with the printing and selling of books.

Bradford remarks that Brewster was "nearly fourscore years, if not quite, when he died," and the events of his life would make a birth date around 1563-4 very reasonable. He probably married soon after leaving Cambridge, or about 1585-6, and perhaps resided in the vicinity of London for a number of years, to be near the Courts, and his many friends around Heneage House, Duke's Place.

There is reason to suspect that a son William was born about 1586 and a son Edward about 1588, and possibly other children in the territory near or in London, during the period of his active service at Court under Davison, which probably extended in some degree to about 1594, and perhaps later.

Bradford does not state just when "Mr. Brewster went and lived in the country, much respected by his friends and the gentlemen of the neighborhood." His father had died in 1590, and the "Post" at Scrooby had been assigned to Samuel Bevercotes, a cousin to Lord Stanhope. Apparently, after his father's death, young Brewster appeared in no hurry to occupy the position, usually handed down from father to son. He was still, no doubt, serving under Davison in one way or another at Court, and, perhaps doing some tutoring in or around London. However, he decided after a while, that it would be expedient for him to take up his residence again at the Manor, and William Davison interceded for him in the matter with Lord Stanhope, Post-master-general. Other friends, such as the Earl of Essex came to his aid, and by Apr. 1, 1594, he was in full possession of the Post and Scrooby Manor, and continued in that status for the next thirteen years. The position at Scrooby was that of a "living" for a "gentleman," and, of course, included the very substantial Manor House, possibly shared by members of the Sandys family. The real work was probably delegated, the income of the Post to Brewster was about $760 per year in modern money, and he probably added to this by teaching. During the period from 1594 to 1607, he probably kept in close contact with his friends in London, and at Court, in fact, possibly, possessing a city residence or address near that of Sir

Edwin Sandys or Heneage Place. It might be mentioned that when Brewster was cited before the High Court of Commission in Notts Dec. 1, 1607, he was described officially as "William Bruster of Scrowbie, gen. (gen. meaning "generosas" or well-born),' and this by the way was the official designation of his son, a member of the first expedition to Virginia in 1607.

There are good reasons to suspect that Brewster was not a very active dissenter up to the death of Queen Elizabeth on Mar. 24, 1602-3. It is true his leanings were Puritan, along with those of his Cambridge friends, and in politics he followed Sir Edwin Sandys, who was a leader in the "Patriot" or "Liberal" Party. However, his life at the Manor was that of a country gentleman, and he enjoyed the confidence and esteem of the neighborhood, and religiously attended St. Wilfreds, near the old Manor-house, the church of the beautiful spire.

James I was crowned, and his personality immediately began to stir up smoldering hates and antagonisms, political, economic, social and religious. He was puffed up with an enormous self-conceit, and forthwith adopted the notion of the divine right of Kings in its most extravagant form. He was fond of saying, "No bishop, no King." Under him only one form of worship was to be tolerated, and that was the established form over which he had control, and, incidentally the power to tax, and the treasury was empty, always bare.

Well, here was a challenge and it came right to Brewster's doorstep, at Scrooby Manor, in the person of his younger but old neighbor at Sturton Notts, the young Rev. John Robinson, who had been but recently, in 1603, married, and, because of King James, had found it impossible to keep his first pastorate at Norwich. He was without a "living," and a place to preach. Here was a fellow Cambridge man sorely distressed. Brewster did the obvious. He offered the Manor House as a place to preach, and meet. By the autumn of 1606, the meetings were well organized, being held every Sabbath "in the manor-house chapel, notwithstanding all the dilligence & malice of their adversaries." Of course, when the King heard of this, Brewster had to resign from the Post, which he did before Sept. 30, 1607-8, Francis Hall succeeding him at the post.

Naturally the surrender of his position under the government forced him to withdraw from the Manor, although Sandys and his London friends probably exerted themselves in his behalf. All of this, no doubt, influenced his determination to seek a new home in the Colonies, and the sending of his son William on the first expedition to Virginia in 1607. Brewster, Robinson and his brother-in-law Carver, were from the beginning interested in the Virginia Company, in which the Sandys family of Scrooby were very influential.

In addition to various other difficulties, about the time Brewster arrived in London to adjust his accounts at Scrooby, his old

[ 37 ]

friend William Davison died and was buried Dec. 24, 1608. This must have been a severe blow to Brewster, and, very likely, hastened his desire to leave England.

In May, 1609, Brewster appears to have been settled in Leyden with his family, or that portion of it still at home, and, no doubt, he was quite busy teaching, and perhaps had already entered into the business of printing and selling books, an occupation which his son Edward in later years followed in London.

Bradford at this time was about twenty years old, and probably was enjoying the full advantage of Brewster's teaching. He states

> "Being thus setled x x x they continued many years in a comfortable condition, injoying much sweete & delightfull societie x x x x under x x x the prudent governmente of Mr. John Robinson & Mr. William Brewster, who was an assistante unto him in ye place of an Elder."

One of the problems the Leyden congregation under Robinson had to contend with was the difficulty in finding work. The lowest kinds of labor were free to them, if they could find employers, but skilled labor had to submit to conditions.

To become a citizen one had to be twenty-five, at least two guarantors, themselves citizens, were required, and the payment of three florins and twenty stivers. The "Poorter's" oath, also had to be taken before two magistrates.

Of course, Brewster knew Holland better than most of his associates, and perhaps could understand the language, having served at Court there.

In 1610 Leyden enjoyed much additional prosperity. Much new industry was being developed, and the least skillful of the Englishmen could find work.

For seven or eight years the Leyden congregation struggled along, during which time there was very little excitement, just the daily grind with the regular meetings under Pastor Robinson to relieve the monotony.

On June 12, 1617, it is observed that William Bradford borrowed 400 gilders from Jan Van Griecken, a goldsmith, at six and a quarter percent interest, on his house in the "Achtergracht" as security, and on June 17 Thomas Brewer bought the "Groenehuis (Green House) for 600 gilders down and agreed to pay 131 and a quarter gilders annually.

Just when Brewer and Brewster started as printers is not recorded, but it must have been as early as 1616, for, at least four volumes can be traced to their press at this time, two in Latin and two in English.

Many of the English people were beginning to get thoroughly discouraged concerning social and enonomic conditions in Holland. Bradford states some were unwilling to "endure ye great labor and hard fare x x x x yea, some preferred & chose ye prisons in England, rather than this liberties in Holland, with these afflictions."

At last they decided to leave Holland, and seek the social and economic freedom so much desired in the new colonies. How Brewster started his famous "Pilgrim Press" in "Choir Alley," Leyden, is not known. Probably his numerous influential friends among the Merchant Adventurers in London, especially those residing around Heneage House, Duke's Place, had something to do with it and, of course, John Robinson. His immediate partner in Leyden seems to have been Thomas Brewer, another Cambridge man, who functioned as a sort of silent partner, buying the type and other essentials, while Brewster hustled around hunting up material for printing, and, incidentally, laying the foundation for another major misunderstanding with the King of England.

It appears that James I was finding his beloved "Scots" rather unruly and independent of his imperial will, and blamed this state of affairs upon their new form of worship, which was not of his choosing, and which he did not control. James forthwith determined to destroy the "Kirk" of Scotland, and force upon that unwilling people his own Church of England. He had his plans all set in this direction when Brewster, perhaps, unintentionally, planted a bomb right in the heart of everything. The fury of James can be imagined when he discovered that the "Pilgrim Press had printed between Oct., 1616, and June, 1619, the arguements against Episcopacy in the volumes of David Calderwood." Those works were "Perth Assembly," and "De regimine ecclesae Scoticanae brevis Pelatio."

The King immediately exerted every pressure to have the "Pilgrim Press" suppressed and the type seized by the University of Leyden. Brewer was imprisoned by the town and University, but William Brewster removed his family and goods to London and was a hunted man thereafter for a year or more, by the University, by Sir Dudley Carleton, the English ambassador in Holland, and by Sir Robert Naunton, the Secretary of State in London. Incidentally, Carleton and Naunton were really good friends of Brewster, and inclined toward the Puritan idea themselves.

Brewster, apparently, was a good teacher of languages, for he had built up, in Leyden, a school to which "many gentlemen, both Danes and Germans, resorted x x x x as they had time from other studies, some of them being Great Men's sons," and Bradford, himself, probably took full advantage of the opportunity.

In May, 1619, Brewster was living among his friends, probably in London, perhaps, with or near his son Edward Brewster, who had recently returned from Jamestown, Virginia, and was engaged in trying to iron out some misunderstandings with the

Virginia Company. Young Brewster had been back since Nov., 1618, and Sir Edwin Sandys was doing his best to smooth over Edward's difficulty with Gov. Argall of the Colony.

In the midst of this confusion, including, of course, the active pending negotiations for the removal of his Leyden friends and himself to Virginia, William Brewster was under a serious handicap with King James, in fact, was a hunted and hounded man.

Apparently, because of the many complications which had arisoned, Brewster had become discouraged and ill. In fact, he may have been, more or less, infirm for the rest of his life, which would explain the absence of any written items by his own hand left to posterity, not even a will. One or two of his supposed authentic signatures seem a little ragged and shaky, and possibly he found it necessary for the rest of his life to avail himself of the services of his old friend and pupil William Bradford, as a sort of secretary. Bradford states in his own will three years after the death of Brewster, in part:

"I commend unto youer wisdome and descretions some smale bookes written by my owne hand to bee improved as you shall see meet."

However, it is known that Brewster had left Leyden and was residing in London in 1619, for his good friend, Robert Cushman, writing from that city to the people in Leyden under date of May 8, 1619, makes this very interesting comment:

"Master Brewster is not well at this time, wether he will come back to you, or go into the north (Scrooby or Sturton)I yet know not. For myself, I hope to see an end of this business ere I come x x x x. Thus, having summarily pointed at things which Master Brewster I think hath more largely writ of to Master Robinson, I leave you."

In this letter of Robert Cushman, which has been so carefully preserved, certain features establish some important facts. We learn that "Master Brewster" is not well, and might retire to Scrooby? ("into the north"), and that he "hath more largely writ" of all these interesting things. It is extremely unfortunate that none of Brewster's letters or writings have been located, and, somewhat strange, forsooth, when so many lesser ones have been preserved.

Attention should be called to the title "Master" before Brewster's name. In those days it implied an occupation of a teacher, tutor, college instructor or the like.

It is apparent that a number of Robinson's followers (Separatists) resided in London much of the time, probably for business reasons. This they could do safely at Heneage House in Duke's Place, Aldgate Ward, London. For instance, Southworth married Alice Carpenter on May 28, 1613, at Leyden, and later on went to reside in London at this famous place. Rogers,

Fuller, Cushman, Southworth, Allerton, Martin, Hopkins, and many other Separatists and Puritans made Duke's Place their London headquarters, and many of Sir Edwin Sandys' closest friends resided there. This place was really quite a large parish or section, having many dwellings. It appealed to the dissenters because it stood in the old parish of the Priory of Holy Trinity. This religious house was dissolved in 1531 and granted to Sir Thomas Audley, through whose daughter it came to Thomas, Duke of Norfolk. Hence the name Duke's Place. Those dwelling there were without a parish church, therefore, of course, escaped indictment under the Act enforcing attendence on the parish church. In fact, London was probably the real cradle of dissension in politics and religion.

The dwellers within Duke's Place had worshipped about as they pleased for some time, much to the disgust of James, who gnashed his teeth in vain. There being no parish church, the people organized meetings to their own liking. No doubt Robinson was a frequent visitor.

It is fortunate that Brewster did not go "north" in May, 1619, but that he carried on in London, together with his many friends, until finally the expedition in the Mayflower to New England was an accomplished fact, and the little group of Colonial Planters were securely settled at New Plymouth.

Perhaps, after all, it does not matter so much how the many complications were overcome. Above everything towers the fact that an exceptionally fine body of English men and women left England and Holland, with a high resolve to be English colonists and English freemen in a country where it might be possible to obtain a free hold on land for themselves, and to be passed down to their children, a very great privilege which had been denied to them in England for centuries.

In Plymouth, Brewster for twenty-four years assumed a position of quiet power and dignity, permitting the details of government to be carried on by the younger men, and of course his main aide was William Bradford, whom he had probably tutored and advised, more or less, since at the age of seven years the orphaned lad roamed the fields around Scrooby Manor.

With Master Brewster around, the small Plymouth Colony had no need of a primary school for several years. The youngsters must have had wonderful times, sitting in silent awe as he told them of the English court life, of the wars in the Lowlands, of the Armada, trial and execution of Queen Mary and of the great personages. They knew that he had taken part in many of them, and that even he, quiet, studious and dignified though he was, must be considered as a sort of "exile" from the officers of the Crown.

His wonderful library was open to the community, and might be called the "First Public Library" of New England. In the midst of friends, books, and wonderful Cape Cod surroundings the years slipped by with moccasined feet.

In 1622, an old Cambridge friend, John Pory, dropped in at Plymouth, on one of his trips along the coast. He was an agent of King James, but also a good friend to Brewster, and before the visit was over the King's business seems to have been lost in the fascinating recesses of that library of books.

Pory spent much more time that summer in 1622 digging into Brewster's books than he intended. He dipped into some of the books that had come from the press in "Choir Alley." Whether or not he had time to read "Seyrge of Drunkerds," "Politike Diseases," or more weighty volumes, is not known, but he did write a letter of appreciation when he returned to London, dated Aug. 28, 1622, addressed to Gov. Bradford, stating in part:

> "To yourself and Mr. Brewster I must humbly acknowledge myself many ways indebted. Whose books I would have you think very well bestowed x x x x my haste would not suffer me to remember, much less to beg Mr. Ainsworth's elaborate work on the five books of Moses x x x x.

> Your unfeigned and firm friend,

> John Pory."

In 1630 Brewster and Bradford seem to have begun collaborating on the "History of Plymouth Plantation." It is possible that during the writing of this comprehensive work, the original notes and letters of Brewster's were destroyed, as the substance was made a part of the final draft of the history. However, in 1644, the work was quite complete, and Brewster's death failed in any way to affect the situation. The wonderful manuscript was an accomplished fact.

Master William Brewster, teacher, printer, pioneer planter of a great state, soldier, diplomat and statesman, "dyed at Plymouth in New England the 10th of Aprill, 1644."

---

Refs. 193, 267, 271, 273, 284, 285, 286, 339, 475, 476, 478, 489, 290, 291; 564, 128, 230, 334, 335, 33, 508, 362, 383, 4. 3470

3461  I. **Brewster,** William[2] (William[1]), born England, perhaps, in Nottinghamshire, about 1564?; died Plymouth, Mass., April 20, 1644; age about 80 years according to Bradford, married 1st or 2nd before 1593 Mary (    ); some writers have suggested Mary Wentworth. She died at Plymouth, Apr. 27, 1627.

He failed to make a will, and on June 5, 1644, his "onely two sonnes surviveing," Jonathan and Love, were appointed administrators of the estate, which was quite interesting.

Jonathan, the eldest son, was given the arms consisting of two swords, pistol, dagger and armor, head piece and "costlett" (corselet). One sword was presented to the Mass. Hist. Soc.

[ 42 ]

in 1798. These items are probably more definitive of William Brewster's real character than that of "Elder" in a church.

CHILDREN—NO DEFINITE LIST AVAILABLE

3463 IIa. William, b. England 1585-6 (?); killed by Indians Jamestown, Va., 1608.
3464 IIIb. Cept. Edward, b. England 1587 (?); d. England.
3452 IVc. Jonathan, b. England Aug. 12, 1593; d. Preston, Conn., Aug. 7, 1659; m. 1st (    ) ; m. 2nd Lucretia **Oldham.**
3469 d. Child, b. England    ; d. Leyden, buried June 20, 1609.
3466 Ve. Love. b. England 1595 (?); d. Duxbury, Mass., 1651; m. Sarah **Collier.**
3468 f. Wrestling, b. England    ; d. after 1627; unmarried.
3467 VIg. Fear, b. England    ; d. Dec. 1, 1634; m. Isaac **Allerton** (2nd wife).
3465 VIIh. Patience, b. England    ; d.    ; m. Gov. Thomas **Prence.**

Refs. 171, 290, 291, 472, 473, 478, 479, 480.

IIa. **Brewster,** William[3] (William[2], William[1]), born, probably, in or near London about 1586, died Virginia "Aug. 10, 1608, the tenth day died William Bruster gentleman, of a wound given by the savages, and was buried the 11th day." (See letter from this William to Robert Cecil, Earl of Salisbury, in this volume under the article on the Virginia Company). Although Robert Cecil was a friend of Elder William Brewster, the young William who died 1608 may be of another family. It is an interesting problem. He may have been of Suffolk County.

IIIb. **Brewster,** Capt. Edward[3] (William[2], William[1]), born England about 1587, died, probably in London after 1635. His family record, if any, may be in London, or vicinity.

Probably, through the influence of his father, Edward subscribed to the Virginia Company in the amount of 30 pounds, and sailed from England during March with the expedition, which, apparently, included Stephen Hopkins and Christopher Martin, later of the Mayflower, arriving in Jamestown, Va., June, 1610, although some of the fleet had been delayed by shipwreck in the Bermudas (see the story of Stephen Hopkins in Volume I of this series).

Edward arrived at Jamestown in the service of Lord De La Warr, being Captain of the Lord's own company or body guard.

After spending eight years in the Colony, Lord De La Warr died, and Captain Edward Brewster, forthwith, severely criticized Governor Argall's handling of his friend's estate.

Argall, being Acting-Governor, judge and plaintiff in the case, tried Edward by court martial and sentenced him to death, but, on petition of the local ministry and other friends in the Colony, commuted his sentence to banishment, under oath never to return.

Captain Brewster sailed for England Nov., 1618, just about the time his father was busy trying to make arrangements to come to Virginia himself, and getting into trouble with King James over printing and selling certain books.

Arriving in London, Sir Edwin Sandys and other good friends of the Brewsters, immediately appealed the case for Captain Edward. It was tried and retried in London Courts from 1618-23, with Sir Edwin acting as counsel and peace maker. At last he was exonerated, but, at the same time, Argall and his associates, none too honest, were whitewashed.

Evidently Edward was not a fighting "Puritan" or a "Separatist," for it was stated in London in Aug., 1619: "Brewster's sonne of his ffather' sect within this halfe yeare, now comes to church," and in commenting on William Brewster, who was then probably living among his friends in Duke's Place, safe from the wrath of James, it was stated "Captain Edward Brewster, his sonne also returned this year from Virginia and conformed to the church." Then again another comment, "Brewster frightened back into the low countries, his son has conformed and comes to church."

Of course, during this period, Captain Edward was under the strain of trying to clear himself in the London Courts from Argall's Jamestown conviction, and attending the established church probably strengthened his case.

He seems to have remained in London, and may possibly be the Edward Brewster, bookseller, in 1635 near the north door of St. Paul's, and at a later period treasurer of the Stationer's Company.

It is possible that Edward was still living in 1656, for Jonathan Brewster on this date seemed about ready to return to England, perhaps to join his brother.

There may have been two contemporary Edward Brewsters in London, one a descendant of Humphrey Brewster of Wrentham Hall.

This matter will be more thoroughly discussed in future volumes. There were Brewsters in the Company of Drapers before 1620.

3452    IVc. **Brewster**, Jonathan³ (William², William¹), born Scrooby, England, Aug. 12, 1593; died Preston, Conn., Aug. 7, 1659; married 1st Leyden (?); married 2nd Plymouth, Apr. 10, 1624, Lucretia **Oldham**, died Mar. 4, 1678/9, she was a sister of John **Oldham** who came to Plymouth, 1623, from "Darby" England. The 1st wife of Jonathan, name unknown, seems to have been buried in Leyden, May 10, 1619. A child may have been buried there Nov. 27, 1610. He came to Plymouth in the "Fortune," Nov., 1621.

[ 44 ]

Jonathan, in the Leyden records, is mentioned several times in connection with his father. On June 25, 1609, "William Brewster, Englishman, Mary Brewster, wife of the same, and Jonathan Brewster, their son."

They seem to have lived in Leyden on the "Pieterskerkhof," in the little colony of houses on the Robinson estate.

At the betrothal of one John Reynolds on July 28, 1617, an employe of his father William, Jonathan acted as a witness.

He was admitted into full citizenship at Leyden, June 30, 1617. On Aug. 27, 1618, he witnessed the betrothal of Edward Winslow.

About 1630 Jonathan removed his family to Duxbury, from which place he was a deputy to the General Court 1639, '41-'44. In 1649 he removed to New London, where he was admitted as an inhabitant Feb. 25, 1649-50. Here he soon became deputy to the General Court of the Colony of Connecticut, 1650-'55-'58.

It is probable that Jonathan was not entirely pleased with his life in New England, and that he may have been in correspondence with his brother Edward, or other relatives in England, for under date of Sept. 1, 1656, he wrote a letter to his sister-in-law, Sarah, widow of Love Brewster, stating that he and his whole family "resolved for old England" the following year, and two of his sons, William and Jonahan, did go. The facts leading up to this decision would be highly illuminating. The Allertons and Brewsters, at times, appear to have been in disagreement with their friends at Plymouth Plantation, probably due to economic causes, rather than religious differences.

CHILDREN

a. William, b. Mar. 9, 1625; d. England (?); m. Mary **Peime** of London.
b. Mary, b. Apr. 16, 1627; d.        ; m. John **Turner**.
c. Jonathan, b. July 17, 1629; d. England (?); m.
d. Ruth, b. Oct. 3, 1631; d. New London, Ct., May 1, 1677; m. 1st John **Pickett**; died at sea; m. 2nd Charles **Hill** of London.
e. Benjamin, b. Nov. 17, 1633; d. Norwich, Ct., Sept. 14, 1710; m. Ann (**Addis**) **Darte**.
f. Elizabeth, b. May 1, 1637; d. New London, Ct., 1708; m. 1st Peter **Bradley**; m. 2nd Christopher **Christophers**.
g. Grace, b. Nov. 1, 1639; d. New London, Ct., Apr. 22, 1684; m. Daniel **Wetherell**.
h. Hannah, b. Nov. 3, 1641; d. New London, Ct., after 1691; m. Samuel **Starr**.

Refs. 309, 310, 311, 293, 290.

Ve. **Brewster**, Love[3] (William[2], William[1]), born England about 1595, perhaps in Scrooby, because his father appears to have returned to the "country" (Scrooby) in 1593; died Duxbury

1650 (?); married Sarah **Collier**, May 15, 1634, daughter of William **Collier**. She married 2nd Richard **Parke** of Cambridge, Mass., who died there in 1665. She returned to Plymouth and died Apr. 26, 1691.

He came to Plymouth on the Mayflower with his parents and brother Wrestling, and became a member of the Duxbury Company in 1643.

CHILDREN

a. Sarah, b.   ; d.   ; m. Benjamin **Bartlett**.
b. Nathaniel, b.   ; d. 1676; m. Sarah **North**.
c. Dea William, b.   ; 1645; d. Nov. 3, 1723; m. Lydia **Partridge**.
d. Wrestling, b.   ; d. Jan. 1, 1696/7; m. Mary (   ).

VIg. **Brewster**, Fear[3] (William[2], William[1]), born England died Plymouth, Dec. 12, 1634, married Isaac **Allerton**, his 2nd wife before May 22, 1627. He died New Haven, Conn., between Feb. 1st and 12th, 1658-9.
(See Allerton Family)

VIIh. **Brewster**, Patience[3] (William[2], William[1]), born England, died 1634 Plymouth, married Gov. Thomas **Prence**, Aug. 5, 1624, his 1st wife, born England 1600/1, died Mar. 29, 1673.
(See Prence Family)

## COLLIER

I. **Collier**, William[1], born England before 1590, died Plymouth 1670 (?); married 1st (   ); married 2nd Jane (   ).

He was a Merchant Adventurer of London, and very active in support of the New England settlers. In fact, he was one of those to subscribe for special aid to the Plymouth colonists on Nov. 15, 1626. He finally decided, like so many other merchants, to remove himself and family to America. It is not surprising to find him, his four daughters and apprentices (not servants), among whom were the brothers John, Job and Daniel Cole, disembarking from the good ship "Mary and James," together with 190 other passengers when it arrived at Plymouth in 1633. His wife probably had died, leaving him with the children.

He was an able man and soon took a high position in the Colony, especially in the matter of final settlement of accounts with the London Adventurers. He was a commissioner at the first meeting of the United Colonies in 1643, and served as Governor's Assistant from 1634 to 1665, a period of 31 years. The Court ordered a special aide for him in 1659, on account of "age and much business."

[ 46 ]

CHILDREN BORN ENGLAND

a. Rebecca, b. 1610 (?); d. 1698, age 88; m. Job **Cole.**
b. Sarah, b. 1615 (?); d. Apr. 26, 1691; m. 1st Love **Brewster;** m. 2nd Richard **Parke.**
c. Mary, b.   ; d. before Dec., 1662; m. Thomas **Prence.**
d. Elizabeth, b.   ; d.   ; m. Constant **Southworth.**

Refs. 171, 288.

## BARTLETT

1943

I. **Bartlett,** Robert[1], born in England; died at Plymouth between 19-29 Sept., 1676, the date of his nun-cupative will, and the 29 Oct. to 8 Nov. 1676, the day his will was probated; married Mary **Warren** after 1627, died between 1678-83, daughter of Richard **Warren.**

The "Barttelot" family is old in England, probably coming there with William the Conqueror.

Robert was in his "teens" when the ship "Anne" safely unloaded him on a July day in 1623, at Plymouth. He was listed as a "cooper." Before being permitted to sail for America he had to be healthy, and show some evidence of possessing a useful occupation. He had both qualifications in abundance. On the same boat coming over was Mary Warren, a girl about 15 years old, daughter of Richard Warren, a Mayflower passenger. That fact probably did not make the trip any more unpleasant. They were married later. Robert received one acre on the south side of Plymouth, and became a very useful citizen of the Colony.

CHILDREN BORN PLYMOUTH

a. Benjamin, b.   1632; d.   ; m. 1st Sussana **Jenny;** m. 2nd Sarah **Brewster;** m. 3rd Cecilia (   ).
b. Joseph, b.   (?) 1639; d.   ; m. Hannah **Pope.**
c. Rebecca, b.   ; d.   ; m. William **Harlow.**
d. Mary, b.   ; d.   ; m. 1st Richard **Foster;** m. 2nd Jonathan **Morey.**
e. Sarah, b.   ; d.   ; m. Samuel **Rider.**
f. Elizabeth, b.   ; d.   ; m. Anthony **Sprague.**
g. Lydia, b. June 8, 1648; d.   ; m. 1st James **Barnaby;** m. 2nd John **Nelson.**
h. Mercy, b. Mar. 10, 1650; d.   ; m. John **Ivey.**

Ref. 290, 577.

## PRENCE

I. **Prence,** Gov. Thomas[1], born (?) Lechlade Co., Gloucester, England, 1600-1, died Mar. 29, 1673, will dated Mar. 13, 1672-3, proved June 5, 1673; married 1st at Plymouth (it being the 9th marriage in the Colony), Patience[2] **Brewster,** Aug. 5, 1624, died 1634, daughter of William[1] **Brewster;** married 2nd Mary[2] **Collier,**

Apr. 1, 1635, died before Dec., 1662, daughter of William[1] **Collier** of Duxbury; married 3rd Apphia (Quicke) **Freeman** before Dec. 8, 1662, she was the widow of Samuel **Freeman**, Sr.; married 4th Mrs. Mary **Howes** 1665-68, died Dec. 9, 1695, widow of Thomas **Howes** of Yarmouth.

He was another able business man to arrive in Plymouth on the "Fortune" in 1621, and became Governor of Plymouth Colony for 20 years, serving at times from 1634 to 1673. He followed his father-in-law, William Brewster, to Duxbury in 1632, and finally removed to Nauset (Eastham) in 1644 with six other families, returning later to Plymouth where he died.

CHILDREN BY PATIENCE BREWSTER

a. Rebecca, b. before 1627; d. before July 18, 1681; m. Edmund **Freeman.**

b. Merey, b. (?) 1631; d. Sept. 28, 1711; m. John **Freeman.**

c. Hannah, b.       ; d. before Nov. 23, 1698; m. 1st Nathaniel **Mayo**; m. 2nd Jonathan **Sparrow.**

d. Thomas, b.       ;       ; d. before Mar. 13, 1672; m. had family in England.

CHILDREN BY MARY COLLIER

e. Jane, b. Nov. 1, 1637; d.       ; m. Mark **Snow.**

f. Mary, b.       ; d.       ; m. John **Tracy.**

g. Sarah, b.       1643-6; d. Mar. 3, 1706-7; m. Jeremiah **Howes.**

h. Elizabeth, b.       ; d.       ; m. Arthur **Howland.**

i. Judith, b.       ; d.       ; m. 1st Isaac **Barker**; m. 2nd William **Tubbs.**

Ref. 171.

## FREEMAN

I. **Freeman**, Edmund, buried June 6, 1623, Pulborough, Essex, England, married Alice **Coles.**

He made a will dated May 20, 1623, proved June 8, 1623, disposing of about 800 pounds. His wife, Alice, was a sister of George Coles of Amberly, Essex. She spent her last years at Reigate, Surrey, in the home of her daughter and son-in-law, Alice and John Beauchamp, who was one of the London merchants aiding Plymouth Colony by financial assistance, which was not wholly liquidated in his case until 1641 or later.

CHILDREN BORN PULBOROUGH, ENGLAND

Baptized St. Mary's Church.

IIa. Edmund, bp. July 25, 1596; d. , 1682; m. Elizabeth **Graveley** (?).

b. Alice, bp. Apr. 15, 1601; d. ; m. John **Beauchamp**.

c. William, bp. ; d. ; m. 1st Christian **Hodsoll**; m. 2nd Jane **Gratwick**, widow.

d. Eleanor, bp. ; d. ; m.

e. John, bp. ; d. ; m.

f. Elizabeth, bp. ; d. ; m. John **Coddington**.

IIa. **Freeman**, Edmund[2] (Edmund[1]), born Pulborough, Essex, England, 1594 (?); died 1686 (?) Sandwich, Mass. (?); married Oct. 13, 1617, Elizabeth **Graveley** (?), Herts, England, died Sandwich (?) Feb. 14, 1676. This was probably his second marriage.

He arrived in New England 1635, from the ship "Abigail" and took up abode at Saugus (Lynn). He was there but a short time, removing to Plymouth, where he was made a freeman Jan. 2, 1637. A few months later, with nine others, he obtained permission to found the first English town on the Cape, that of Sandwich. His portion was the largest, and he became a person of some influence in the community. He was Deputy for Plymouth Colony in 1641, assistant to Gov. Prence 1640-46, and a member of the Council of War in 1642, and later served as a judge.

CHILDREN BORN ENGLAND

a. Alice, bp. Apr. 4, 1619; d. Apr. 24, 1651; m. William **Paddy**.

IIIb. Edmund, bp. Nov. 26, 1620; d. Mar. 29, 1673; m. 1st Rebecca **Prence**; m. 2nd Margaret **Perry**.

c. Bennett, bp. Jan. 20, 1621; d. 1633-4; m.

d. Elizabeth, bp. Apr. 11, 1624; d. ; m. John **Ellis**.

IVe. John, bp. Jan. 28, 1626-7; d. Oct. 28, 1719; m. Mercy **Prence**.

f. Nathaniel, bp. Sept. 2, 1629; d. 1629; m.

g. Mary, bp. ; d. ; m. Edward **Perry**.

IIIb. **Freeman**, Edmund[3] (Edmund[2], Edmund[1]), bapt. Nov. 26, 1620, in England, died Mar. 29, 1673, and was buried in Plymouth; married 1st Rebecca **Prence** Apr. 22, 1646, daughter of Gov. **Prence** and Patience **Brewster**; married 2nd Margaret **Perry** July 18, 1651.

He resided in Sandwich, Mass.

[ 49 ]

CHILD BY 1ST WIFE

a. Rebecca, b.      ; d.      ; m. Ezra **Perry.**

CHILDREN BY 2ND WIFE

b. Margaret, b. Oct. 2, 1652; d.      ; m.      .
c. Edmund, b. Oct. 5, 1655; d.      ; m. Sarah (    ).
d. Alice, b. Mar. 29, 1658; d.      ; m.      .
e. Rachel, b. Sept. 4, 1659; d.      ; m. John **Landers.**
f. Sarah, b. Feb. 6, 1662; d.      ; m. Richard **Landers.**
g. Deborah, b. Aug. 9, 1665; d.      ; m. Thomas **Landers.**

IVe. **Freeman,** John[3] (Edmund[2], Edmund[1]), born England 1625 (?); bapt. Jan. 28, 1626-7; died Eastham, Oct. 28, 1719; married Mercy **Prence** Feb. 14, 1649, daughter of Gov. **Prence.** He came to New England with his father in 1635, when about 8 years old. He was prominent in the affairs of Eastham, being one of the planters of the town, and a deacon in the church for many years. He was a major of militia and saw service in the Indian wars, and was a member of the Bench of the Court of Common Pleas. His estate, consisting of land holdings, became extensive.

CHILDREN BORN EASTHAM

a. John, b. Feb. 2, 1650; d. young; m.
b. John, b. Dec., 1651; d. July 27, 1721; m. 1st Sarah **Merrick;** m. 2nd Mercy (**Hedge** (?)) **Watson.**
c. Thomas, b. Sept., 1653; d. Feb. 9, 1715-6; m. Rebecca **Sparrow.**
d. Patience, b.      ; d. Feb. 15, 1745; m. Samuel **Paine.**
e. Hannah, b.      1654; d. Feb. 15, 1743-4; m. John **Mayo.**
f. Edmund, b. June, 1657; d. Dec. 10, 1717/9; m. 1st. Ruth **Merrick** (?); m. 2nd Sarah **Mayo.**
g. Mercy, b. July, 1659; d.      1744; m. Samuel **Knowles.**
h. William, b.      1660; d.      , 1686; m. Lydia **Sparrow.**
i. Prence, b. Feb. 3, 1665-6; d. young; m.      .
j. Nathaniel, b. Mar. 20, 1669; d. Jan. 4, 1760; m. Mary **Howland.**
k. Bennett, b. Mar. 7, 1670; d. May 30, 1716; m. John **Paine.**

Refs. 147, 171, 299, 295.

## PAINE

12. **Snow,** Mary[3] (Constance[2] **Hopkins,** Stephen[1]), born 1630 (?), Plymouth, died Eastham Apr. 28, 1704; married Thomas[2] **Paine** 1650 (?); born England, died Eastham, Aug. 16, 1706; probably son of Thomas[1] **Paine** who appears to have resided quite early in Yarmouth where he was a Deputy in 1639 to the Old Colony Court at Plymouth.

It is thought Thomas[2] was about ten years of age when brought over from England, but we know little about him previous to 1653, when he appears in Eastham, where he became a highly respected citizen, holding many public offices. He removed to Boston in 1695 for business reasons, but soon returned to Eastham. He was a builder of grist mills.

Thomas[2] was well educated, and a splendid penman. He wrote his name "Tho. Paine."

Mary was a good wife and mother. Her son Dea. John[3], states in his diary that she was "a careful mother," a "quiet neighbor" and a "diligent reader of God's Holy Word."

### CHILDREN BORN EASTHAM

57. Mary, b.    ; d.    ; m. 1st James **Rogers**; m. 2nd Israel **Cole**.
58. Samuel, b.    ; d. Oct. 13, 1712; m. Patience **Freeman**.
59. Thomas, b.    1656-7; d. June 23, 1721; m. 1st Hannah **Shaw**; m. 2nd Mrs. Elizabeth (    ) **Eairs**.
60. Eliezer, b. Mar. 10, 1658; d. young; m.
61. Elisha, b.    ; d. Feb. 7, 1735-6; m. Rebecca **Doane**.
62. John, b. Mar. 14, 1660; d. Oct. 26, 1731; m. 1st Bennett **Freeman**; m. 2nd Alice **Mayo**.
63. Nicholas, b.    ; d.    1733; m. Hannah **Higgins**.
64. James, b. July 6, 1665; d. Nov. 12, 1728; m. Bethia **Thatcher**.
65. Joseph, b.    ; d. Oct. 1, 1712; m. Patience **Sparrow**.
66. Dorcas, b.    ; d. Oct. 30, 1707; m. Benjamin **Vicherie**.

Ref. 130, 146, 129, 147, 132, 163.

## DOANE

I. **Doane**, John[1], born England, married 1st Ann (    ); married 2nd Lydia (    ).

John Doane was of Plymouth before 1631, and removed to Eastham with other leaders, where he proved his genuine worth as a citizen in many ways. He was a deacon in the church for many years, and one of the seven planters of Eastham in 1644.

### CHILDREN

a. Lydia, b. England    ; d.    ; m. Samuel **Hicks**.
b. Abigail, b. Plymouth, Jan. 13, 1631-2; d. Jan. 23, 1734-5; m. Samuel **Lothrop**.
c. John, b.    (?) 1635; d. Mar. 15, 1708; m. 1st Hannah **Bangs**; m. 2nd Rebecca **Pettee**.
IId. Dr. Daniel, b.    (?) 1636; d. Dec. 20, 1712; m. 1st (    ); m. 2nd Hepzibah (**Cole**) **Crispe**.
e. Ephraim, b.    before 1645; d.    1700; m. 1st Mercy **Knowles**; m. 2nd Mary (**Smalley**) **Snow**.

[ 51 ]

**IId. Doane,** Daniel[2] (John[1]), born Plymouth, 1636 (?), died Eastham, Dec. 20, 1712; married 1st ( ) ; married 2nd Hepzibah (**Cole**) **Crispe.**

He was the first physician of Eastham, and practiced the profession as long as health permitted. He accumulated considerable lands. Most of the acreage was near Orleans. He made a will dated Sept. 18, 1711, and proved Oct. 9, 1712.

CHILDREN BORN EASTHAM

a. Son, b.    (?), 1664; d. Sept. 20, 1667.

b. Daniel, b.    (?), 1666; d. Sept. 1, 1743; m. 1st Mehitable **Twining**; m. 2nd Mary **Yates.**

c. Joseph, b.    (?), 1668; d. July 27, 1757; m. 1st Mary **Godfrey**; m. 2nd Desire **Berry.**

d. Constant, b. Mar. 7, 1669; d.    ; m. George **Shaw.**

e. Rebecca, b.    1672-3; d.    ; m. Benjamin **Merrick.**

f. Israel, b.    ; d.    ; m.

g. Abigail, b.    ; d.    ; m. Timothy **Dimock.**

h. Nathaniel, b.    1680-3; d.    1758; m. Mary (    ).

i. Ruth, b.    (?), 1685; d. before 1722; m. Nathaniel **Mayo.**

j. Hepsibah, b.    ; d.    ; m.

Refs. 132, 290.

## WALKER

13. **Snow,** Sarah[3] (Constance[2] **Hopkins,** Stephen[1]), born 1632 (?); died Eastham, married William[1] **Walker** Jan. 25, 1654-5, in Eastham, born 1620 (?). His will was proved 1703. She was the daughter of Nicholas[1] **Snow.**

Wiliam Walker received a grant of land in 1639 in Hingham, Mass., and was among the first settlers there. He may be the William, who with Richard, James and Sarah Walker came to New England in the "Elizabeth" in April, 1635. He later removed to Eastham where he was admitted to freedom June 3, 1656. He was one of two to check up on liquor coming into Eastham. In one report he states:

"Trustram Hull, of Barnstable, brought a barrel of rum to the town of E. and sold it, but gave noe account of it to either of us, and we thought it good to give the Court notice of it. June 9, 1655."

William Walker.
John Doane."

[ 52 ]

CHILDREN BORN EASTHAM

67. John, b. Nov. 24, 1655; killed by Indians 1676.
68. William, b. Oct. 12, 1657; d. before Aug. 16, 1659; m.
69. William, b. Aug. 2, 1659; d. Jan. 1743-4; m.
70. Sarah, b. July 30, 1662; d.          ; m.
71. Elizabeth, b. Sept. 28, 1664; d.          ; m.
72. Jabez, b. July 8, 1668; d.          1742; m. Elizabeth (    ).

Refs. 131, 129.

## SNOW

14. **Snow, Lt. Joseph**[3] (Constance[2] **Hopkins,** Stephen[1]), born Plymouth, Nov. 24, 1634; died Eastham Jan. 3, 1722; married Mary (    ), died after 1717.
He was long a useful citizen of Eastham, and was chosen Lieut. of the Eastham militia company on Oct. 2, 1689.

CHILDREN BORN EASTHAM

73. Joseph, b. Nov. 24, 1671; d.      ; m. Sarah **Smith.**
74. Benjamin, b. June 9, 1673; d.     ; m. Thankful **Bowerman.**
75. Mary, b. Oct. 17, 1674; d.        ; m.        .
76. Sarah, b. Apr. 20, 1677; d.       ; m. Benjamin **Young.**
77. Ruth, b. Oct. 14, 1679; d.        ; m. James **Brown.**
78. Stephen, b. Feb. 24, 1681; d.     ; m. Margaret **Elkins.**
79. Llydia, b. July 20, 1684; d.      ; m.        .
80. Rebeca, b. Dec. 4, 1686; d.       ; m.        .
81. James, b. Mar. 31, 1689; d.       ; m.        .
82. Jane, b. Mar. 27, 1692; d.        ; m.        .
83. Josiah, b. Nov. 27, 1694; d.      ; m.        .

Refs. 290, 71, 72, 69, 129, 294.

## SNOW

15. **Snow, Stephen**[3] (Constance[2] **Hopkins,** Stephen[1]), born 1636 (?); died Eastham Dec. 17, 1705; married 1st Sussanah **(Deane) Rogers** Oct. 28, 1663; died before 1701, daughter of Stephen **Deane** and Elizabeth **Ring,** and widow of Joseph **Rogers;** married 2nd Mary **Bickford** Apr. 9, 1701.
He was a freeman of Eastham in 1684.

CHILDREN BORN EASTHAM
All by 1st Wife.

84. Bethshua, b.     ; d.      ; m. John **King.**
85. Hannah, b.       ; d.      ; m. William **Cole.**
86. Micajah, b.      ; d.      ; m. Marey **Young.**
87. Bethia, b.       ; d.      ; m. John **Smith.**
88. Ebenezer, b.     ; d.      ; m. Hope **Horton.**

Refs. 129, 171, 133, 134, 145.

[ 53 ]

# DEANE

I. **Deane,** Stephen[1], born England, married Elizabeth **Ring,** daughter of Mary **Ring,** widow. She married 2nd 1635 Josiah **Cooke.**

Stephen Deane came over in the "Fortune," 1621, and built the first corn mill in New England, 1632.

### CHILDREN

a. Elizabeth, b.      ; d.      ; m. William **Twining**.
b. Miriam, b.         ; d.      ; m.         .
IIc. Sussanah, b.     ; d. before 1701; m. 1st Joseph **Rogers;** m. 2nd Stephen **Snow.**
　　　　IIc. (see Fam. No. 15)

Refs. 171, 289.

# SNOW

16. **Snow,** John[3] (Constance[2] **Hopkins,** Stephen[1]), born 1638 (?), at Plymouth, died 1692 (?); married Sept. 19, 1667, in Eastham. Mary[2] **Smalley,** born Dec. 11, 1647, died 1703 (?); daughter of John[1] **Smalley.** She married 2nd Ephraim **Doane.**

His father, Nicholas, had given John all the family lands at "Paumett" (Truro), with "all my Right and title or privilege there," but except for a short residence at Piscataway, N. J., he resided in Eastham until his death.

Some of his children removed to Duck Creek, Delaware.

### CHILDREN BORN EASTHAM

89. Hannah, b. Aug. 26, 1670; d. before 1717; m. Hezekiah **Doane.**
90. Mary, b. Mar. 10, 1671-2; d.      ; m.
91. Abigail, b. Oct. 14, 1673; d.      ; m.
92. Rebecca, b. July 23, 1676;      ; m. 1st Benjamin **Smalley;** m. 2nd John **Porter.**
93. John, b. May 3, 1678; d.      ; m. Elizabeth **Ridley.**
94. Isaac, b. Aug. 10, 1683; d. To Duck Creek, Dela.; m. Alice (    ).
95. Lydia, b. Sept. 29, 1685; d.      ; m.
96. Elisha, b. Jan. 10, 1686; d. to Duck Creek, Dela.; m. Elizabeth (    ).
97. Phebe, b. June 27, 1689; d.      ; m.      .

Refs. 73, 194, 129, 149, 132.

# SMALLEY

I. **Smalley,** John[1], born England, died Piscataway, N. J., July 30, 1692; married Ann **Walden,** Nov. 29, 1638, at Plymouth.

[ 54 ]

John Smalley arrived in New England with Edward Winslow in the "William and Francis," sailing from London Mar. 9, 1632, arriving in New England June 5, 1632.

He was granted in 1637-40 several acres of land in Plymouth County, which he sold in 1644. In April, 1644, he was among the group from Plymouth to remove to Eastham, far down on Cape Cod. At Eastham he helped to organize the place, and then about 1667, with his wife and two sons he removed to Little Compton, R. I., but soon afterward with Richard Higgins and others he removed to Piscataway, Middlesex Co., N. J., where he was among the earliest of pioneer freeholders.

### CHILDREN

a. Hannah, b. June 4, 1641; d.    ; m. John **Bangs.**
b. John, b. Sept. 4, 1644; d.    ; m. Lidia **Marten.**
c. Isaac, b. Dec. 11, 1646; d.    ; m. 1st Esther **Wood;** m. 2nd Mary **White.**

IId. Mary, b. Dec. 11, 1647; d.    1703; m. John **Snow.**
IId (See Fam. No. 16)

Refs. 194, 149.

## BANGS

I. **Bangs,** Edward[1], born Chichester, England, died Eastham, Mass., 1678; age 86; married Rebecca ( ).

He arrived at Plymouth in 1623 in the "Ann." He was made a freeman 1633, and removed to Eastham in 1644 with the planters of that town, where he served as a Grand-Juryman, overseer of the Board. He was a Deputy to the Colony Court for four or five years. The first vessel built in Plymouth was a barque of 40 or 50 tons, and Edward Bangs had charge of the construction.

### CHILDREN

a. John, b.    ; d.    ; m. Hannah **Smalley.**
IIb. Capt. Jonathan, b.    1640; d. 1728, age 88; m. Mary **Mayo.**
c. Lt. Joshua, b.    ; d. Jan. 14, 1709; m. Hannah **Scudder.**
d. Bethia, b. May 28, 1650; d.    ; m.    .
c. Apphia    b. Oct. 15, 1651; d.    ; m. John **Knowles.**
f. Mercy    b. Oct. 15, 1651; d.    ; m. Stephen **Merrick.**
g. Lydia, b.    ; d.    ; m. Benjamin **Higgins.**
h. Hannah, b.    ; d.    ; m. John **Deane.**
i. Rebecca, b.    ; d.    ; m. Jonathan **Sparrow.**

IIb. **Bangs,** Capt. Jonathan[2] (Edward[1]), born 1640, died Harwich 1728, age 88; married Mary[3] **Mayo** July 16, 1664, bapt. Feb. 3, 1650, at Barnstable; died 1711, age 66; daughter of Samuel[2] **Mayo** (Rev. John[1]).

[ 55 ]

He was a Deputy to the Colony Court at Plymouth 1674,
1676, 1682, 1683 and 1687, and was Representative to the General
Court at Boston, 1692.

CHILDREN BORN EASTHAM

a. Capt. Edward, b. Sept. 3, 1665; d. May 22, 1740; m.
  1st    ; m. 2nd Mrs. Ruth **Mayo.**
b. Jonathan, b. 1670; d. same year; m.
c. Capt. Jonahan, b.    1673; d.    ; m 1st Elizabeth
  (   ); m. 2nd Experience (   ); m. 3rd Mrs. Ruth
  **Young**.
d. Capt. Samuel, b.    ; d. June 11, 1750; m.
e. Rebecca, b.    ; d.    ; m.    .
f. Mary, b.    ; d.    ; m.    .
g. Hannah, b.    ; d.    ; m.    .
h. Thomasin, b.    ; d.    ; m.    .
i. Mercy, b.    ; d.    ; m. (   ) **Hatch.**
j. Elizabeth, b.    ; d.    ; m.    .
k. Sarah, b.    ; d.    ; m.    .
l. Lidia, b.    ; d.    ; m. Shubal **Hinckley**.

Refs. 159, 171.

## ROGERS

17. **Snow,** Elizabeth[3] (Constance[2] **Hopkins,** Stephen[1]), born
1640 (?); died June 16, 1675; married Thomas[3] **Rogers** at Eastham, Dec. 13, 1665; born Mar. 29, 1638; died Mar. 15, 1670; son
of Lt. Joseph[2] **Rogers** (Thomas[1]).

CHILDREN BORN EASTHAM

98. Elizabeth, b. Oct. 8, 1666; d.    ; m.    .
99. Joseph, b. Feb. 1, 1667; d.    ; m. Prudence (   ).
100. Hannah, b. Feb. 20, 1669; d.    ; m. Amaziah **Harding.**
101. Thomas, b. Mar. 6, 1670; d. Mar. 16, 1670-1; m.    .
102. Thomas, b. May 6, 1672; d.    ; m. Sarah **Treat.**
103. Eleazer, b. Nov. 3, 1673; d.    ; m. Ruhmah **Willis.**
104. Nathaniel, b. Jan. 18, 1675; d.    ; m.    .

Refs. 135, 129, 256, 148, 152.

## SNOW

18. **Snow,** Lt. Jabez[3] (Constance[2] **Hopkins,** Stephen[1]), born
1642 (?); died Dec. 27, 1690; married Elizabeth[3] **Smith** before
Oct. 29, 1670; daughter of Ralph[2] **Smith** (John[1]).
  He served on the grand jury June 1, 1680, on which day he
was made a freeman, and took the oath of fidelity. On June 5,
1690, he was chosen one of the lieutenants for the expedition to
Canada.

[ 56 ]

His wife had a martial temperament and was in occasional wordy conflict, even with the minister, for on Mar. 5, 1684, she was fined ten shillings for "using railing expressions on a Lord's Day to the Rev. Samuel Treat."

CHILDREN BORN EASTHAM

105. Jabez, b. Sept. 6, 1670; d.        ; m. Elizabeth **Treat.**
106. Edward, b. Mar. 26, 1672; d.        ; m. Sarah **Freeman.**
107. Sarah, b. Feb. 16, 1673; d.        ; m    .
108. Grace, b. Feb. 5, 1675; d.        ; m. 1st Samuel **Hedge;** m. 2nd George **Lewis.**
109. Thomas, b.        ; d. Apr. 2, 1697; m.        .
110. Elizabeth, b.        ; d.        ; m. Edward **Kenrick.**
111. Deborah, b.        ; d.        ; m. Stephen **Merrick.**
112. Rachel, b.        ; d.        ; m. Thomas **Huckins.**

Refs. 292, 129, 147, 148, 153, 154, 136, 550.

## COLE

19. **Snow,** Ruth[3] (Constance[2] **Hopkins,** Stephen[1]), born 1644 (?); died Eastham, Jan. 27, 1716-7; married John[2] **Cole** Dec. 12, 1666, born July 15, 1644, died June 6, 1725, at Eastham, son of Daniel[1] **Cole.**

John Cole was a useful citizen and a lieutenant in the militia. He had been at Groton in 1672, but probably returned, driven out by Indians, as he is on the freeman list in Eastham of 1695.

CHILDREN BORN EASTHAM

113. Ruth, b. Mar..11, 1668; d.        ; m. William **Twining.**
114. John, b. Mar. 6, 1670; d.        ; m. Mary (        ).
115. Hepzibah, b. June 20, 1672; d.        ; m.        .
116. Hannah, b. Mar. 27, 1675; d. June, 1677; m.        .
117. Joseph, b. June 11, 1677; d.        ; m. 1st Elizabeth **Cobb;** m. 2nd Mercy **Hinckley.**
118. Mary, b. Oct. 27, 1679; d.        ; m.        .
119. Sarah, d. June 10, 1682; d.        ; m.        .

Refs. 292, 133, 129, 134.

## TWINING

I. **Twining,** William[1], born England, died Eastham, April 15, 1659; married Anne **Doane** about 1652, died Feb. 27, 1680. She may have been a sister to John[1] **Doane.**

He resided in Eastham near the Town Cove, probably coming there from Plymouth where he is of record as early as 1641, although at that time he may have been living at Yarmouth, where he was able to bear arms in 1643. He held minor town offices in Eastham.

[ 57 ]

CHILDREN

IIa. Isabel, b.      ; d. May 16, 1706; m. Francis **Baker.**
IIIb. William, b. Eng. 1625 (?); d. Nov. 4, 1703; m. Elizabeth
**Deane.**

## BAKER

IIa. **Twining,** Isabel[2] (William[1]), born England, died May
16, 1706; married Francis[1] **Baker,** born Hertfordshire, England,
1611.
Francis came to New England in the "Planter," 1635.

CHILDREN

a. Nathaniel, b.    1642; d.    1691; m.    .
b. John, b.    ;    ; d.    ; m. Alice **Pierce.**
c. Samuel, b.    1648; d.    ; m. Martha.
d. Daniel, b.    1650; d.    ; m. Elizabeth **Chase.**
e. William, b.    ; d.    ; m. Mercy.
f. Thomas, b.    ; d.    ; m. Bathsheba.
g. Elizabeth, b.    ; d.    ; m. John **Chase.**
h. Hannah, b.    ; d.    ; m.    .

## TWINING

IIIb. **Twining,** William[2] (William[1]), born England 1625 (?);
died, probably at Newtown, Bucks Co., Pa., Nov. 4, 1703. His
will is on file at Philadelphia. He married Elizabeth[2] **Deane**
about 1650; died Dec. 8, 1708; daughter of Stephen[1] **Deane.**

He was very young when brought to New England by his
father about 1635. In 1677 he was a deacon at the Eastham
church. In 1659 Eastham granted him three and one-half acres
for a house lot adjoining William Twining, Sr.

In 1695 he had to leave Eastham because he had joined the
Quaker meetings, and removed to Newtown, Bucks Co., Pa.
His name appears in the Middletown Meeting Records in 1699,
together with that of his son, Stephen.

CHILDREN

*a. Elizabeth, b.    ; d.    ; m. John **Rogers.**
b. Anne, b.    ; d.    ; m. 1st Thomas **Bills;** m. 2nd David
**Kelly.**
c. Sussana, b. Jan. 25, 1654; d. young.
d. William, b.    ; d.    ; m. Ruth **Cole.**
e. Mehitable, b.    ; d.    ; m. Daniel **Doane.**
f. Joanna, b. May 30, 1657; d.    ; m.    .
g. Stephen, b. Feb. 6, 1659; d.    ; m.    .

* See Family record of John[3] Rogers (Lt. Joseph[2], Thomas[1]),
Vol. I, p. 134, of this series.

Refs. 155, 223.

# COLE

The origin of the surname Cole may be a contraction of "Agricola," a tiller of the soil, as Cola occurs in the Domesday Survey. Like many early settlers of New England, the Cole family had a strong "dissenting" background. For instance, Thomas Cole, a divine who died in 1571, and his brother William, who had to leave England when Mary came to the throne in 1553. He was one of a large group of scholars, like John Rogers, Edwin Sandys and others to seek refuge in Germany and Switzerland. Cole, however, was more fortunate than Rogers, and remained in Zurich until Elizabeth ascended the throne, when most of the exiled divines returned to England.

Three brothers, Job, John and Daniel **Cole**, came to Plymouth with William Collier, a merchant of London in 1633. Probably James Cole of Plymouth was also a brother.

In 1634 Job married Rebecca **Collier**, daughter of William **Collier**, and removed to Duxbury, but in 1643 he settled in Eastham, where he was chosen a deputy several times for the town.

CHILDREN OF JOB **COLE** AND REBECCA **COLLIER**

a. John, m. Elizabeth **Keiler** Nov. 21, 1667.
b. Job, m. .
c. Daniel, m.
d. Rebecca, m. .

I. **Cole**, Daniel[1], the younger brother married Ruth **Chester** and removed to Yarmouth, but joined Job at Eastham in 1650. He was deputy ten times and held other positions.

CHILDREN OF DANIEL **COLE** AND RUTH **CHESTER**

a. John, b. July 15, 1644; m. Ruth **Snow** (see Fam. No. 19).
b. Timothy, b. Sept. 4, 1646.
c. Hepsebah, b. Apr. 16, 1649; m. 1st Daniel **Doane**; m. 2nd George **Crisp**.
d. Ruth, b. Apr. 15, 1651; m. John **Young**.
e. Israel, b. Jan. 8, 1653; m. Mary (**Paine**) **Rogers**.
f. James, b. Nov. 3, 1655; m. .
g. Mary, b. Mar. 10, 1658; m. Joshua **Hopkins** (see Fam. No. 28).
h. William, b. Sept. 15, 1663 (?); m. Hannah **Snow** (see Fam. No. 85).

Refs. 133, 134, 145, 310.

# SMITH

I. **Smith**, Ralph[2] (**John**[1]), born England, married 1st (    ), married 2nd Grace **Hatch**, widow of Thomas **Hatch**.

A John Smith was probably the father of Ralph. The early settlers of Hingham, Mass., were mostly from Hingham County, Norfolk, England, from which place Ralph came to New England in 1633. He drew a lot on Batchelor Street in 1637. He removed to Eastham about 1653, where he held several town offices at various times.

CHILDREN BORN HINGHAM, MASS.

IIa. Samuel, bp. July 11, 1641; d.     ; m. Mary **Hopkins.**
 b. John, bp. July 23, 1644; d.     ; m. Hannah **Williams.**
 c. Daniel, bp. Mar. 2, 1647; d. Mar. 1720; m. Mary **Young.**
IIId. Elizabeth, bp.     1648; d.     ; m. Lt. Jabez **Snow.**
 e. Thomas, bp.     1650 (?); d.     1720; m. Mary     .
 f. Deborah, bp. Mar. 8, 1654; d.     ; m.     .
IIa.—See Fam. No. 21, Mary Hopkins).
IIId.—(See Fam. No. 18, Lt. Jabez Snow).

Refs. 135, 158, 742.

## SMITH

21. **Hopkins,** Mary[3] (Giles[2], Stephen[1]), born Yarmouth, Nov. 1640; died Eastham, Mar. 20, 1696-7; married Samuel[2] **Smith** Jan. 3, 1665; bapt. Hingham, Mass., July 11, 1641; son of Ralph[1] **Smith.**

CHILDREN BORN EASTHAM

120. Samuel, b. May 26, 1668; d.     ; m. Bathshua **Lathrop.**
121. Mary, b. Jan. 3, 1669; d.     ; m. Daniel **Hamilton.**
122 Joseph, b. Apr. 10, 1671; d.     ; m.     .
123. John, b. May 26, 1673; d. before 1717; m. Bethia **Snow.**
124. Grace, b. Sept. 5, 1676; d. Dec. 1, 1691; m.     .
125. Deborah, b. Dec. 10, 1678; d     ; m.     .

Refs. 135, 158, 264, 742, 163, 218.

## LOTHROP

I. **Lothrop,** Rev. John[4] (Thomas[3], Robert[2], John[1]), born Etten, Yorkshire, England, bapt. Dec. 20, 1584, died Barnstable, Mass., Nov. 8, 1653; married 1st Hannah **Howes,** died 1633, married 2nd Ann **Hammond** Feb. 17, 1636-7.

The Lo-Lathrops are descendants of the Lowthrops of Lowthrope, East Riding, Yorkshire, England. John[1] Lothrop, of Cherry Burton, England, was a fairly prosperous citizen in 1545. He had a son Robert[2] who died in Cherry Burton in 1558, leaving a son Thomas[3], who had Rev. John[4].

Rev. John[4] attended Queen's College, Cambridge, where he seems to have acquired the usual "dissenting" spirit of that University. In 1611 he became Vicar of Egerton, Kent Co., England, but resigned in 1623 and went to London, where he became pastor of the first independent Congregational church in London. It was broken up in 1632. He was tried by the Star chamber, and imprisoned for two years in Newgate. He was released in 1634, and sentenced to "banishment." He sailed from England with his family in the ship "Griffin," and landed at Boston in 1634-5. He settled at Scituate and Barnstable, being the first minister who preached at either place.

## CHILDREN

a. Dau., b.　　　; d.　　　; m.
b. Dau., b.　　　; d.　　　; m.
c. Joseph, b.　　　; d.　　　; m. Mary **Ansol.**
d. Samuel, b.　　1620; d.　　　; m.
e. Thomas, b.　　　; d.　　　; m. (　　) **Evans,** wid.
f. John, b.　　　; d.　　　; m.
g. Hopestill, b.　　　; d.　　　; m.
h. Barnabas, b.　　　; d.　　　; m.

Refs. 569, 570, 298.

## HOPKINS

22. **Hopkins,** Stephen[3] (Giles[2], Stephen[1]), born 1642 (?); died Oct. 10, 1718; married 1st Mary[2] **Merrick,** born Nov. 4, 1650, daughter of William[1] **Merrick;** married 2nd Bethia **Atkins,** widow of Henry **Atkins;** died Mar. 25, 1726, in Brewster, Mass., daughter of (　　) **Linnell.**

Stephen removed to Harwich, now Brewster, his father Giles having willed to him all the family possessions there.

### CHILDREN BORN EASTHAM

126. Elizabeth, b. June 1668; d.　　　; m.　　　.
127. Stephen, b. July 1670; d.　　　; m. Sarah **Howes.**
128. Ruth, b. Nov. 1674; d.　　　; m.　　　.
129. Judah, b. Jan. 1677; d.　　　; m. Hannah **Mayo.**
130. Samuel, b. Mar. 1682; d.　　　; Lydia (　　).
131. Nathaniel, b. Mar. 1684; d　　　; m. Mercy **Mayo.**
132. Joseph, b.　　1688; d.　　　; m. Mary **Mayo.**
133. Benjamin, b. Feb. 1690; d.　　　; m. Rachel **Lincoln.**
134. Mary, b. Apr. 15, 1692; d.　　　; m. John **Maker.**

Refs. 132, 136, 143, 147, 171, 550, 264, 163, 185.

## ATKINS

I. **Atkins,** Henry[1], born England, married 1st Elizabeth **Wells;** married 2nd Bethia **Linnell** Mar. 25, 1664; she married

[ 61 ]

2nd Stephen **Hopkins** and resided in Brewster where she died Mar. 25, 1726.

He removed from Plymouth to Eastham before 1655. He purchased some real estate from John Mayo on Apr. 21, 1659, and added to his property from time to time. He was a quiet man, taking slight interest in town affairs.

CHILDREN BY 1ST WIFE

a. Mary, b. Mar. 13, 1647; d. young; m.———.

CHILDREN BY 2ND WIFE

b. Isaac, b. June 15, 1665; d.　　; m.　　.
c. Desire, b. May 7, 1666; d.　　; m.　　.
d. John, b. Dec. 15, 1667; d. young; m.———.
e. Nathaniel, b. Dec. 25, 1668; d.　　; m.　　.
f. Joseph, b. May 4, 1669; d.　　; m.　　.
g. Thomas, b. June 19, 1671; d.　　; m.　　.
h. John, b. Aug. 1, 1674; d.　　; m. Elizabeth **Newcomb**.
i. Mary, b. Nov. 24, 1676; d.　　; m.　　.
j. Samuel, b. June 25, 1679; d.　　; m. Emlen **Newcomb**.

Refs. 573, 288.

## MERRICK

24. **Hopkins**, Abigail[3] (Giles[2], Stephen[1]), born Oct. 1644, married William[2] **Merrick** May 23, 1667; born at Eastham Sept. 15, 1643; died at Harwich Oct. 30, 1732; son of William[1] **Merrick**.

William Merrick was admitted a legal voter of Eastham in 1675. Sometime later he removed to Harwich, where he was one of the original members of the church there in 1700. His wife was admitted in 1704. He was an Ensign in the Militia, and represented the town in the General Assembly in 1719.

CHILDREN BY ABIGAIL HOPKINS

135. Rebecca, b. Nov. 28, 1668; d.　　; m. Jonathan **Sparrow**.
136. William, b. Aug. 1, 1670; d. Mar. 20, 1671; m.———.
137. Stephen, b. Mar. 26, 1673; d. Mar. 11, 1732; m. Deborah **Snow**.
138. Nathaniel, b.　　1675; d.　　; m. Alice **Freeman**.
139. Hannah, b.　　; d.　　; m. John **Snow**.
140. Benjamin, b.　　; d.　　; m. 1st Rebecca **Doane**; m. 2nd Wid. Rachel **Lincoln**.
141. John, b.　　; d.　　; m. Anna **Sears**.
142. Joshua, b.　　1680; d.　　1740; m. Lydia **Mayo**.
143. Ruth, b.　　1684; d.　　; m. 1st Samuel **Sears**; m. 2nd Chillingworth **Foster**.

Refs. 292, 136, 550, 297.

[ 62 ]

# SPARROW

I. **Sparrow,** Richard, born England; died New England Jan. 8, 1660-; married Pandora ( ) England. (See Americana Vols. 1925, 1928, 1932, 1933).
Certain members of the Sparrow family of England owned shares in the Virginia Company, and were probably among the early planters of Jamestown, but had become discouraged about conditions in that settlement previous to 1630, therefore, it is not surprising to find Richard Sparrow, his wife and son Jonathan residents of Plymouth as early as 1632.
The will of Richard is dated Nov. 19, 1660.

### CHILDREN (KNOWN)

IIa. Jonathan, b. England ; d. Mar. 21, 1706-7; m. 1st Rebecca **Bangs**; m. 2nd Hannah **(Prence) Mayo**; m. 3rd Sarah **(Lewis) Cobb.**

IIa. **Sparrow,** Jonathan[2] (Richard[1]), born England, died Eastham Mar. 21, 1706-7; married 1st Oct. 28, 1654, Rebecca[2] **Bangs** (Edward[1]); married 2nd Hannah[2] **(Prence) Mayo**, daughter of Governor Thomas[1] **Prence**, and granddaughter of William[1] **Brewster**; married 3rd 1698 Sarah **(Lewis) Cobb**, daughter of George **Lewis** and widow of James **Cobb.**
He held numerous public offices, including that of schoolmaster, and acted as an attorney for townsmen. He was a deputy at 19 sessions of the Colonial Court, and commanded a troop of horse. He left a will, and much land.

#### CHILDREN BY REBECCA BANGS, BORN EASTHAM

a. Rebecca, b. Oct. 30, 1655; d. Feb. 1740; m. Thomas **Freeman.**
b. John, b. Nov. 2, 1656; d. Feb. 23, 1734-5; m. Apphia **Tracy.**
c. Priscilla, b. Feb. 13, 1658; d. ; m. Edward **Gray.**
d. Lydia, b. ; d. ; m. 1st William **Freeman**; m. 2nd Jonathan **Higgins.**
e. Elizabeth, b. ; d. ; m. Samuel **Freeman.**
f. Jonathan, b. July 9, 1665; d. Mar. 9, 1739-0; m. Rebecca **Merrick.**

#### CHILDREN BY HANNAH (PRENCE) MAYO

g. Richard, b. Mar. 17, 1669; d. young.
h. Patience, b. ; d. Oct. 25, 1745; m. 1st Joseph **Paine**; m. 2nd John **Jenkins.**
i. Richard, b. (?) 1675; d. Apr. 13, 1728; m. Merey **Cobb.**

Refs. 171, 299, 575.

# TRACY

I. **Tracy**, Stephen[1], born England, died Great Yarmouth, England, 1630; will dated Oct. 25, 1630, proved Oct. 25, 1630-1; married Agnes **Endley**, Feb. 23, 1585-7.

He was a freeman of Yarmouth, England, 1606, and resided at Great Yarmouth, County Norwolk, England. His occupation was that of a mariner.

The Tracy family is old in England, going back in some lines to "Woden," 300-400 A. D. However, the parents of this Stephen have not been definitely identified.

## CHILDREN BORN GREAT YARMOUTH

  a. William, b.      ; d.      ; m.      .
  b. Thomas, b.       ; d.      ; m.      .
  c. Christopher, b.      ; d.      ; m.      .
  d. Agnes, b.      ; d.      ; m.      .
IIe. Stephen, b.      ; d.      ; m. Tryphosa **Lee**.
  f. Margaret, b.      ; d.      ; m.      .
  g. John, b.      ; d.      ; m.      .
  h. Margaret, b.      ; d.      ; m.      .

IIe. **Tracy**, Stephen[2] (Stephen[1]), born Great Yarmouth, England; married at Leyden, Holland, Jan. 2, 1620-1, Tryphosa **Lee**.

He followed the dissenters to Leyden, probably coming from the locality of Great Yarmouth, England, since he returned there. While in Leyden he was recorded as "Sayworker" from England.

In March, 1652, Stephen Tracy, Francis Cooke and others acquired a large tract of land to the west, later called Dartmouth. These two men had one share each in the venture. For some reason about this time Stephen decided to leave the country. He returned to England before 1654, and signed a power of attorney in London directing his "loving friend" John Winslow of Plymouth to dispose of his property and divide it among his five children.

## CHILDREN

  a. Sarah, b.      ; d.      ; m. George **Partridge**.
*b. Rebecca, b.      ; d.      ; m. William **Merrick**.
  c. Ruth, b.      ; d.      ; unmarried.
  d. Mary, b.      ; d.      ; m.      .
*e. John, b.      1633; d. May 3, 1710; m. Mary **Prence**.

---

*b. See (Merrick).
*e. See (Prence).

---

Refs. 171, 137.

# MERRICK

I. **Merrick,** op. Llewellyn (Meuric) was a Captain of the Guard at the coronation of Henry VIII, April 25, 1509. He was the first High Sheriff of the County Anglesey, which office he held until his death. From him the name "Meyrick," signifying "Guardian," is derived as a surname, in pursuance to an act of Henry VIII, requiring that the name of every man at the time should be borne by his descendants as a surname, there being no surnames before that time in Wales. He married Margaret, daughter of Roland, Rector of Aberffraw, Anglesey, Wales. His will is dated Nov. 30, **1538.**

## CHILDREN (MERRICK)

a. Richard of Bodorgan, Anglesey, Wales, succeeded to High Sheriff.
b. Rt. Rev. Roland, b. 1505, Bishop of Bangor, Wales.
c. William, d.      ; unmarried.
d. Owain, d.      ; unmarried.
IIe. Rev. John, Rector of Llandachya, Wales.
f. Rev. Edmund, Arch-Deacon of Bangor, Wales.
g. Rev. Reynault, Rector of Llanlechid, Wales.
h. Alice.
i. Sionedd.
j. Agnes.

All of the above children except William and Owain appear to have married and left descendants.

IIe. **Merrick,** Rev. John[2] (Meuric[1] op. Llewellyn), born about 1513, became Rector of Llandegai (Llandachya). It is understood that John left the navy to enter the ministry, which seemed to appeal to members of this family.

## CHILDREN (OF RECORD)

IIIa. Rev. William, Rector of St. Davids[1], Pembrokeshire.
b. Rev. Owain, a minister at Llangylle.
c. Maud; m. Powell.

IIIa. Rev. William[3] **Merrick.** Had a son.
IVa. John.

IVa. Rev. John[4] **Merrick,** b. 1579. Had four sons.

Va. William, b. 1601-5 (?); m. Rebecca **Tracy.**
b. John.
c. James.
d. Thomas.

Va. **Merrick,** William[5] (John[4], William[3], John[2], Meuric op. Llewellyn[1]) born Wales about 1615, made his will Dec. 3, **1686,** proved Mar. 6, 1688-9, married Rebecca **Tracy** about 1642, died after 1688-9, daughter of Stephen **Tracy**. He seems to have been the oldest of the four brothers to reach Charlestown in the "James" in the spring of 1636, and was a soldier serving for six years in the Colonial Militia under Capt. Standish as an Ensign and Lieutenant. At the end of his service he married, very likely, in Eastham. He married late in life.

CHILDREN

VIa. William, b. Sept. 15, 1643; d. Oct. 30, 1732; m. 1st Agigail **Hopkins**; m. 2nd Wid. Elizabeth **Snow.**
  b. Stephen, b. May 12, 1646; d.    1705; m. 1st Mercy **Bangs**; m. 2nd Anna **Wilbur.**
  c. Rebecca, b. July 28, 1648; d.   ; m.   .
VIId. Mary, b. Nov. 4, 1650; d.   ; m. Stephen **Hopkins.**
  e. Ruth, b. May 15, 1652; d.   1680-1; m. Edmund **Freeman.**
  f. Sarah, b. Aug. 1, 1654; d.   ; m. John **Freeman.**
  g. John, b. Jan. 15, 1656; d.   ; m.   .
  h. Isaac, b. Jan. 6, 1660; d.   ; m.   .
  i. Joseph, b. June 1, 1662; d. June 15, 1737; m. 1st Elizabeth **Hawes**; m. 2nd Elizabeth **(Freeman) Remick.**
  j. Benjamin, b. Feb. 1, 1664; d.   ; m. 1st Rebecca **Doane**; m. 2nd Rachel (  ) **Lincoln.**

VIa. William (see Fam. No. 24, Abigail Hopkins).
VIId. Mary (see Fam. No. 22, Stephen Hopkins).

Refs. 136, 550, 297.

## SEARS

I. **Sears**, Richard[1], born England, died Yarmouth, Mass., buried Aug. 26, 1676; married Dorothy (  ); buried Yarmouth Mar. 19, 1678-9.

He is found at Plymouth in 1633, but soon removed to Marblehead, being taxed there 1637, and was granted four acres of land in 1638. Many of the settlers at Marblehead were from Guernsey and Jersey in England. He appears in Yarmouth 1643, where he served on the Grand Jury and as constable, also was a deputy to the General Court at Plymouth in 1662. His occupation was farming.

CHILDREN

IIa. Capt. Paul, b.    1637-8; d. Feb. 20, 1707; m. Deborah **Willard.**
IIIb. Lt. Silas, b.   ; d. Jan. 13, 1697; m. Anna (  ).
IVc. Deborah, b. Sept. 1639; d. Aug. 17, 1732; m. Zachary **Paddock.**

IIa. **Sears,** Capt. Paul[2] (Richard[1]), born Marblehead (?) 1637-8, died Feb. 20, 1707-8; married Deborah **Willard** 1658, at Yarmouth, bapt. Scituate Sept. 14, 1645; daughter of George **Willard**; died Yarmouth May 13, 1721.

He was a Captain of Militia and a highly respected man in the community.

CHILDREN BORN YARMOUTH

a. Mercy, b. July 3, 1659; d.     ; m.     .
b. Bethia, b. Jan. 3, 1661-2; d. July 5, 1724; m. John **Crowell,** Jr.
c. Samuel, b. Jan. 1663-4; d. Jan. 8, 1741; m. Mercy **Mayo.**
d. Lydia (?), b. Oct. 24, 1666; d.     ; m; Eleazur **Hamblen.**
e. Paul, b. June 15, 1669; d. Feb. 14, 1739; m. Mercy **Freeman.**
f. Mary (?), b. Oct. 24, 1672; d.     ; m. Col. John **Knowles.**
g. Ann, b. Mar. 27, 1675; d. Nov. 14, 1745; m. John **Merrick.**
h. John, b.     1677-8; d. Apr. 9, 1738; m. Pricilla **Freeman.**
i. Richard, b.     1680-1; d. May 24, 1718; m. Hope **Howes.**
j. Daniel, b.     1682-3; d. Aug. 10, 1756; m. Sarah **Howes.**

IIIb. **Sears,** Lt. Silas[2] (Richard[1]), born Marblehead; died Yarmouth Jan. 13, 1697-8; married Anna (**Bursell** (?), daughter of James **Bursell** of Yarmouth, who died a widow Mar. 4, 1725-6.

CHILDREN BORN YARMOUTH AND EASTHAM

a. Silas, b.     1661; d.     ; m. 1st Sarah **Crosby;** m. 2nd Elizabeth **Killey.**
b. Richard, b.     ; d.     ; m. 1st Bashua **Harlow;** m 2nd Sarah (**Graham**).
c. Hannah, b. Dec. 1672; d.     1701; m. Thomas **Snow.**
d. Joseph, b.     1675; d. May 7, 1750; m. Hannah **Hall.**
e. Josiah, b.     1676; d.     1727; m. 1st Mercy **Howes;** m. 2nd Judith **Gilbert.**
f. Elizabeth, b.     ; d.     ; m. John **Cooke.**
g. Dorrity, b.     1687; d.     ; m. Joseph **Staples.**

## PADDOCK

IVc. **Sears,** Deborah[2] (Richard[1]), born Yarmouth Sept. 1639; died Aug. 17, 1732; married Zachary **Paddock;** born Plymouth Mar. 20, 1636; died Yarmouth May 1, 1727; son of Robert **Paddock** of Plymouth.

[ 67 ]

CHILDREN

a. Ichabod, b. Feb. 2, 1661; d.      ; m.
b. Zachariah, b. Apr. 14, 1664; d. Apr. 8, 1717-8; m. 1st
   Bethia (    ); m. 2nd Mary (Hedge) Thatcher.
c. Elizabeth, b. Aug. 1, 1666; d.      ; m. John Howes.
d. John, b. May 5, 1669; d. Feb. 18, 1717-8; m. Pricilla Hall.
e. Robert, b. Jan. 17, 1671; d.      ; m.      .
f. Joseph, b. Sept. 12, 1674; d.      ; m.      .
g. Nathaniel, b. Sept. 22, 1677; d.      ; m.      .
h. Judah, b. Sept. 15, 1681; d. Mar. 31, 1770; m. Alice Alden.

Refs. 143.

## COOKE

25. **Hopkins**, Deborah[3] (Giles[2], Stephen[1]), born June 1648 (?);
married Josiah[2] **Cooke** July 27, 1668; born 1645 (?); died Jan. 31,
1731-2, son of Josiah[1] **Cooke.**

Josiah[2] **Cooke** resided in Eastham, but together with others
had land allotted to him in 1675 at Little Compton, R. I. This
territory was then claimed by the Plymouth Colony. The land
was certified to him in 1698. Some of his children, including
Josiah and Joshua, removed to Connecticut.

CHILDREN BORN EASTHAM

144. Elizabeth, b. Oct. 12, 1669; d.      1670; m.——.
145. Josiah, b. Nov. 12, 1670; d. after 1727; m. Mary (    ).
146. Richard, b. Sept. 1, 1672; d. Apr. 25, 1754; m. Hannah
     (    ).
147. Elizabeth, b. June 16, 1674; d. after 1727; m. Thomas
     **Newcomb.**
148. Caleb, b. Nov. 15, 1676; d. after 1727; m. Deliverance
     (    ).
149. Deborah, b. Feb. 15, 1678; died      ; m. Moses **Godfrey.**
150. Joshua, b. Feb. 4, 1683-4; d. after 1727; m. Patience
     **Doane.**
151. Benjamin, b. Apr. 28, 1686-7; d. after 1727; m. Mercy
     **Paine.**

Refs. 161, 162, 171, 197, 264.

## NEWCOMB

I. **Newcomb**, Capt. Andrew[1], born England about 1618; died
Boston, Mass., Nov. 1686; married 1st (    ); married 2nd 1663,
Boston, Grace **Ricks,** widow of William **Ricks,** born 1620-5.

He probably came to America as a captain of a sailing vessel.
He became a resident of Boston after 1663.

## CHILDREN BY 1ST WIFE

a. Andrew, b. 1640; d. 1706-8; m. .
b. Sussanah, b. 1645-50; d. ; m. .

## CHILDREN BY 2ND WIFE

c. Grace, b. Oct. 20, 1664; d. Aug. 1713; m. 1st James Butler; m. 2nd Andrew **Rankin.**

Refs. 197, 162.

## COOKE

I. **Cooke**, Josiah[1], born about 1610 in England; died in Eastham Oct. 17, 1673, aged about 63 years; married Sept. 16, 1635, at Plymouth; Elizabeth (**Ring**) **Deane**, daughter of widow Mercy Ring, and widow of Stephen **Deane.**

His relationship, if any, to Francis Cooke has not been established. He is first of record in Plymouth, January, 1633-4, but removed to Eastham about 1645, where he was an original proprietor, along with Thomas Prence, John Doahe, Edward Bangs and others. In 1658 with Richard Sparrow and several other men he received a grant of lands between Bridgewater and Weymouth.

### KNOWN CHILDREN

IIa. Ann, b. ; d. July 24, 1656; m. Mark **Snow.**
IIIb. Josiah, b. (?) 1645; d. Jan. 31, 1731-2; m. Deborah **Hopkins.**
IVc. Bethia, b. ; d. ; m. Joseph **Harding.**

IIa.—See Fam. No. 11, Hopkins Line.

IIIb.—See Fam. No. 25, Hopkins Line.

Refs. 171, 161, 291.

## HARDING

IVc. **Cooke**, Bethia[2] (Josiah[1]) married Joseph **Harding** at Eastham, Apr. 4, 1660. He had been left an orphan when his mother died in 1633, and no record is available of the history of his parents. He was brought up by John **Doane**, who removed to Eastham in 1644, and Joseph became, in due time, a respected citizen of that place. His mother's name was Martha, and in 1633, the inventory of her estate was taken by Francis Cooke, John Doane and James Hurst.

[ 69 ]

## CHILDREN BORN EASTHAM

a. Martha, b. Dec. 13, 1662; d.　　; m. Samuel **Brown.**
b. Mary, b. Aug. 19, 1665; d.　　; m.　　.
c. Joseph, b. July 8, 1667; d.　　; m.　　.
d. Josiah, b. Aug. 15, 1669; d.　　; m.　　.
e. Amaziah, b. Nov. 1, 1771; d.　　; m. Hannah **Rogers.**
f. John, b. Oct. 9, 1673; d. June 14, 1697; m. Sussana.
g. Joshua, b. Feb. 15, 1675; d.　　; m.　　.
h. Nathaniel, b. Dec. 25, 1676; d.　　; m. 1st Hannah **Collins**; m. 2nd Hannah **Young.**
i. Abiah, b. Jan. 26, 1679; d.　　; m. Rebecca **Young.**

Refs. 256.

## HICKS

I. **Hicks,** James[2] (Baptist[1]), born England, married Phebe **Alyn,** daughter of Rev. Ephraim **Alyn** and Nancy **Evarts.**
He probably resided in Southwark, London.

### CHILDREN BORN ENGLAND

IIa. Robert, b.　　(?) 1583; d.　　; m. 1st Elizabeth **Morgan**; m. 2nd Margaret **Winslow.**
IIIb. Thomas, b.　　; d. Scituate, 1653; m. Margaret **Atwood.**

IIa. **Hicks,** Robert[3] (James[2], Baptist[1]), born England 1575-83; died Plymouth, Mass., Mar. 24, 1647; married 1st Elizabeth **Morgan** 1596, in England; she died 1607; married 2nd in London, 1610, Margaret **Winslow,** who became the first woman teacher in America. She was a sister of the Winslow brothers of the "Mayflower."
Robert Hicks resided in the Plymouth Colony twenty-six years, sharing in the division of cattle in 1627.
He had come to Plymouth in the "Fortune," 1621. His wife and daughter following him in the ship "Ann," arriving in June, 1622.

### CHILDREN BY 1ST WIFE

a. Elizabeth, b.　　; d.　　; m. John **Dickinson.**
b. Thomas, b.　　; d.　　; m.　　.
IVc. John, b.　　(?) 1607; d. L.I., N.Y., May 1672; m. Herodia **Long.**
d. Stephen, b　　; d.　　; m.　　.

### CHILDREN BY 2ND WIFE

e. Samuel, b.　　; d.　　; m.　　.
f. Ephraim, b.　　; d.　　; m. Elizabeth **Howland.**
g. Lydia, b.　　; d.　　; m.　　.
h. Phebe, b.　　; d.　　; m.　　.

[70]

IIIb. **Hicks**, Thomas³ (James², Baptist¹), born England, died Scituate 1653; married Margaret **Atwood** of Gloucester, England. He resided at Scituate, coming probably from Southwark, London, where his brother Robert had lived before he came to New England in 1621. Thomas made his will Jan. 10, 1653, appointing his wife Margaret executrix, and mentions sons Zachariah, Daniel and Samuel.

### CHILDREN

a. Zachariah, b. 1628; d. Aug. 5, 1702; m. Elizabeth **Sills**.
b. Daniel, b. ; d. before 1694; m 1st. Rebecca **Hanmer**; m. 2nd Elizabeth **Hanmer**.
c. Samuel, b. ; d. Dorchester; m. Hannah **Evans**.

IVc. **Hicks**, John⁴ (Robert³, James², Baptist¹), born England 1607; died on Long Island, May, 1672; married in England Herodia **Long**.

He came to New England in 1635, and resided for a while at Weymouth, Mass., then to Newport, R. I., and finally moved to Hempsted, L. I., in 1642, where he became quite active as an adjuster of Indian claims to land. He was a delegate from Long Island in 1663 to a Council called by Governor Nicoll of New York "to make additions and alterations to existing laws." Representative from Flushing to Convention called by Governor Stuyvesant in New Amsterdam 1653. Justice of the Peace 1666. Grantee of Patents of land in town of Hempstead, Mar. 6, 1666, and the first patent for Flushing granted by Governor Keith to English emigrants included John Hicks.

### CHILDREN BY HERODIA LONG

Va. Thomas, b. Weymouth, Mass., 1640; d. L. I., 1740; m. 1st Mary **(Butler) Washburn**; m. 2nd Mary **Doughty**.
b. Hannah, b. ; d. ; m. William **Haviland**.
c. Elizabeth, b. ; d. ; m. Josias **Starr**.

Va. **Hicks**, Thomas⁵ (John⁴, Robert³, James², Baptist¹), born in Weymouth, Mass., 1640; died Long Island, N. Y., 1740; married in Long Island 1st Mary **(Butler) Washburn**; married 2nd 1677 Mary **Doughty**.

He was a Justice of the Peace, High Sheriff of Queens County, 1702-3, Captain in the Queens County Troop 1686, member of the Assembly, appointed by Governor Andros, Judge of Common Pleas in Queen's County, 1691-1699. "In 1666 he obtained from Governor Nicoll a patent for about four thousand acres of land near Little Neck, L. I., where he built a good house and lived like a 'Lord of the Manor,' for many years." He was an outstanding personality, and lived to the age of 100 years. The newspapers of the times state that he left behind more than three hundred descendants.

## CHILDREN BY 1ST WIFE

a. Thomas, b.　; d.　; m. Deborah **Valentine.**
b. Jacob, b.　1699; d.　1755; m. Hannah **Carpenter.**

## CHILDREN BY 2ND WIFE

c. Isaac, b.　; d.　; m.　.
d. William, b.　; d.　; m.　.
e. John, b.　; d.　; m.　.
f. Charles, b.　; d.　; m.　.
g. Benjamin, b.　; d.　; m.　.
h. Charity, b.　; d.　; m.　.
i. Mary, b.　; d.　; m.　.
j. Elizabeth, b.　; d.　; m.　.
k. Stephen, b.　; d.　; m.　.
l. Phebe, b.　; d.　; m. Samuel **Seaman.**

Refs. 288, 295, 298, 553.

# THE SANDYS AND BREWSTERS OF SCROOBY MANOR

Sherwood Forest and the shades of Robin Hood are in constant communion with the little parish of Scrooby Notts, which came very early into the possession of the See of York. At the time of William the Conqueror, 1086, a survey, commonly called the Domesday Book, clearly describes it as one of the properties of the northern archbishops. No palace then existed on the land. A century later there appears to have been a residence there of no mean proportions. In 1207 King John ordered "three tuns of Vascon wine and one of Massac to be conveyed thither." At that time his half brother was the archbishop, and the King was making provision for a protracted visit. He spent some time there, signing orders which went to distant parts of England. From the size of the wine order it would seem that the palace must have been very commodious, and that the parties held there were far from small.

Although it was truly in a remote and lonely section of the wild "North Country," yet as early as 1301 the palace had a chapel of its own, where homage could be extended "to the Archbishop in the Chapel of Scrooby for the Manor of Muskham."

On Dec. 19, 1486, six years before the so-called discovery of America, the archbishop conferred a benediction upon Thomas Thurne, abbot-elect.

Then, on June 12, 1503, the beautiful Margaret, eldest daughter of Henry VII, on her way to Scotland to become the second wife of King James IV of Scotland, made a stay at Scrooby. In her cavalcade on this occasion were the great and near-great of England. There was the Earl of Surrey, Lord Treasurer of England, "varey nobly arayed and all his Trayne," "my Lady his Wyffe, accompaned of many Ladys and Gentlyllwomen varey nobly arayed." Then came "Ladyes mounted upon fayre Pallefrays, many Squyers before them."

In its prime Scrooby manor house was a noble building, standing on ground given by John, Earl of Chester, in 1170, to the Archbishop of York of his day and was intended as a place of enjoyment to his successors forever. It was used by them as a resting place when they traveled between York and London, or when they desired a change.

During the sixteenth century it was a very popular manor house consisting of two courts, built of timber, having thirty-nine chambers, with a banqueting hall, ceiled and dressed with "waynscot," a chapel with "one lectionary and superellers, a payer of organs, a clock without plometts and ropes."

The great north road to Scotland wound through the little village by the quaint and peaceful stone church of St. Wilfrid with its crenelated tower and lofty spire. It was here that William Brewster used to worship, before King James ascended the throne in 1603, and Rev. John Robinson, an old friend and neighbor, came back to his home in Sturton a few miles distant, without a "living" and no place to hold a meeting.

It is doubtful if Brewster was a very enthusiastic "Puritan" or "Separatist" before 1603-4. In fact, he may have stumbled into a series of events which, rather unintentionally, changed the even and peaceful course of a country gentleman, and reshaped the destiny of his life.

Within the little stone church, beautifully covered with spreading ivy, may still be seen the Brewster pew having a richly carved seat and back of dark oak, a very fitting seat, indeed, for Master William Brewster, sometime assistant Secretary at the Court of Elizabeth.

In Sept., 1529, Cardinal Wolsey removed from Southwell to Scrooby, evading various attentions that would have been paid him on the journey by the Earl of Shrewsbury and the country gentlemen, lest it should be said that he was courting favor. He remained at Scrooby some time, doing many deeds of charity in the neighborhood.

Strange as it may appear Scrooby was not lost to the archbishops because of the Reformation, but that fate befell the Manor at the hands of Archbishop Sandys, who had a large family and considered it his duty to provide for them out of the estates of the church. The rather elastic customs of the times seemed to tolerate this sort of practice. Therefore, he devised a lease of four livings—including Scrooby Manor—to his eldest son Sir Samuel Sandys, and the ancient house remained in the lay hands of the Sandys family until 1676, and lost, forever, all connection with the See of York.

With the Sandys, came the Brewsters, one brother Henry Brewster was Vicar of Sutton-cum-Scrooby or Loud in 1565, while another brother, William Brewster, became a bailiff to Sir Samuel Sandys and was appointed "Post." His official duty was to keep two horses ready to take the road between Doncaster and Tuxford and convey the "two bags of leather," which served the purpose of the mail.

The family of Archbishop Sandys had much to do with the Virginia Company and the planting of the first English colonies in America. In fact if it had not been for the stubborn perseverance of Sir Edwin Sandys the whole project would have fallen through, and America would have been overrun with the Spanish, Dutch and French.

Scrooby Manor has several claims to distinction. Among the least known and appreciated, but of the highest importance, is its close connection with the Sandys family, certain members of whom nursed the dying Virginia Company along until an English plantation was an assured success on American soil, both in North and South Virginia (Plymouth and Jamestown).

[ 74 ]

MAP No 3

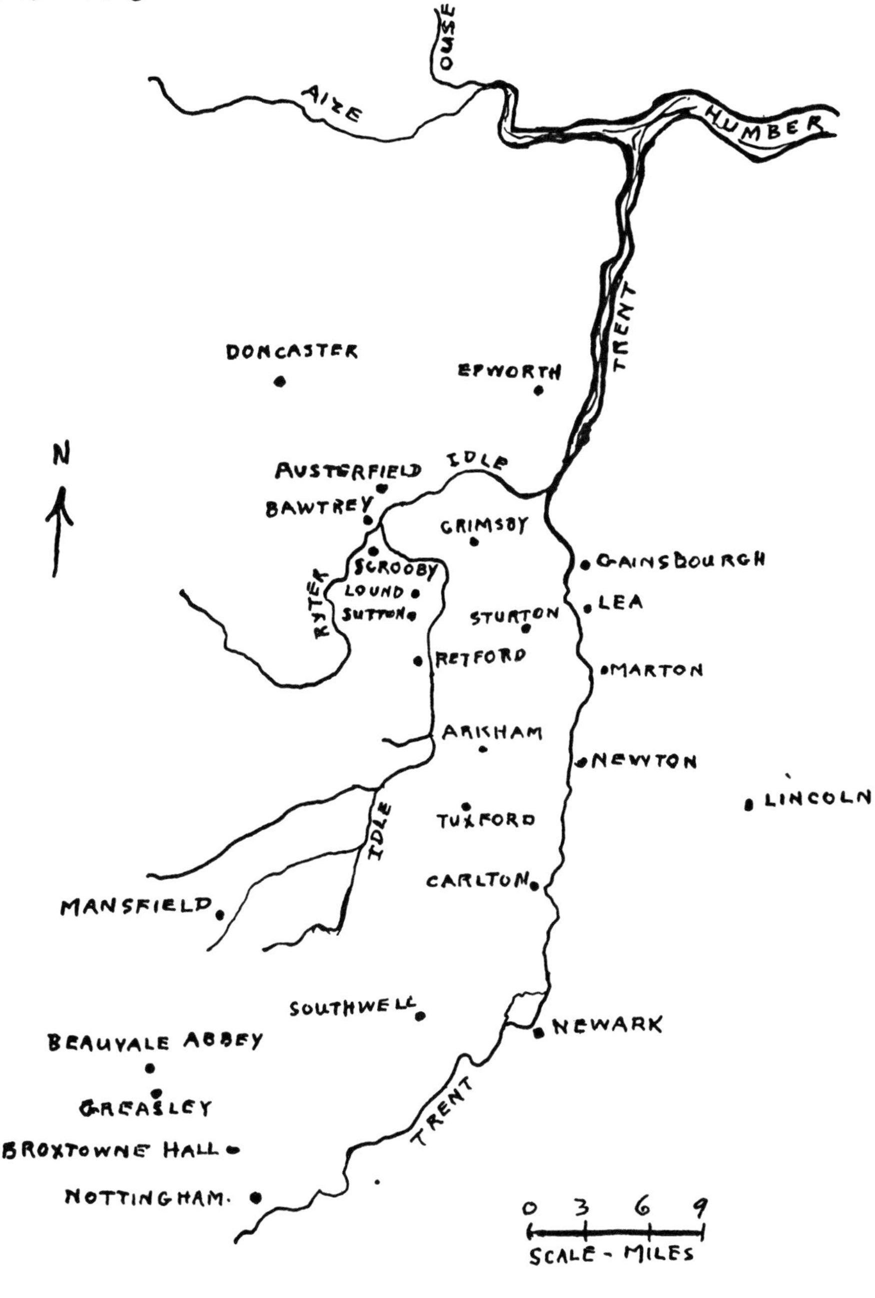

OSSE

AIZE

HUMBER

TRENT

DONCASTER

EPWORTH

N

AUSTERFIELD

IDLE

BAWTREY

GRIMSBY

GAINSBOURGH

RYTER

SCROOBY
LOUND
SUTTON

LEA

STURTON

RETFORD

MARTON

ARKHAM

NEWTON

LINCOLN

IDLE

TUXFORD

MANSFIELD

CARLTON

SOUTHWELL

NEWARK

BEAUVALE ABBEY

GREASLEY

TRENT

BROXTOWNE HALL

NOTTINGHAM.

0    3    6    9
SCALE - MILES

LGH
1941

SCROOBY MANOR AND VICINITY

# SANDYS

I. **Sandys,** Edwin, D. D. Archbishop, born England; married 1st Mary **Sandes,** daughter of John **Sandes;** married 2nd Cicely **Wilford;** died 1588, daughter of Thomas **Wilford.**

He was one of the first reformers, and was committed to the Tower by Queen Mary, but released and fled to Germany where he lived at Strasburgh until accession of Elizabeth in 1558, when he returned to England and became Bishop of Worcester, then of London and finally Archbishop of York.

### CHILDREN

IIa. Sir Samuel, b.      ; d.      ; m. Mercy **Culpeper.**
IIIb. Sir Edwin, b.      ; d.      ; m. Katherine **Bulkley.**
  c. Sir Myles, b.      ; d.      ; m. Elizabeth **Cooke.**
  d. William, b. Sept. 13, 1565; d.      ; m.      .
  e. Thomas, b.      ; d.      ; m. Margaret **Tyas.**
  f. Henry, b. Sept. 30, 1572; d.      ; m.      .
  g. Margarel, b.      ; d.      ; m. Sir Anthony **Aucher.**
  h. Anne, b.      ; d.      ; m. Sir William **Barne.**
  i. George, b.      ; d.      1643; m. unmarried.

IIa. **Sandys,** Sir Samuel[2] (Edwin[1]), born England, married Mercy Culpeper, daughter of Martin **Culpeper.** He died Aug. 18, 1623, and probably resided at Scrooby Manor much of the time. Member of His Majesty's Council for Virginia 1612, and of Somers Island Company 1615.

### CHILDREN BORN (SCROOBY ?)

  a. Sir Edwin, b.      1590; d.      ; m. Penelope **Bulkley.**
  b. Sir Martin, b.      1597; d. at Scrooby; m. Frances **Egiot.**
  c. John, b.      1604; d.      ; m. Winifred **Chambers.**
  d. William, b.      ; d.      ; m.      .
  e. Cecily, b.      ; d.      ; m. John **Brace.**
*f. Margaret, b.      ;d.      ; m. Sir Francis **Wyatt.**
  g. Anne, b.      ; d.      ; m. Sir Francis **Wenman.**
  h. Mary, b.      ; d.      ; m. Richard **Humphreys.**
  i. Mercy, b.      ; d.      ; m. (      ) **Ewbank.**
  j. Joyce, b.      ; d.      ; m. Edward **Dingley.**
  k. Elizabeth, b.      ; d.      ; m. Edward **Pytt.**

IIIb. **Sandys,** Sir Edwin[2] (Edwin[1]), born Dec. 9, 1561, died Oct., 1629; married 1st Margaret **Eveleigh;** married 2nd Anna **Southcott;** married 3rd Elizabeth **Nevinson;** married 4th Katherine **Bulkley,** daughter of Sir Richard **Bulkley.**

Sir Edwin was about three years older than William Brewster. They must have known each other well since boyhood. He became renowned as an author, member of Parliament, leader of the "Patriot" or "Liberal" party, a fighter for a representative assembly. Although a bitter enemy, James knighted him in 1603. From 1617-24 he was the moving spirit in the Virginia Company. Without his encouraging actions English colonies on the Atlantic seaboard of America would have been failures. The whole country would have been left to Spanish, Dutch and French planters.

CHILD BY 1ST WIFE

a. Elizabeth, b.　　; d.　　; m. Sir Thomas **Wilford.**

CHILD BY 3RD WIFE

b. Anne, b.　　; d.　　; m. Thomas **Engeham.**

CHILDREN BY 4TH WIFE

c. Henry, b.　　; d.　　; m. Margaret **Hammond.**
d. Edwin, b.　　; d.　　; m. Catherine **Champneys.**
e. Richard, b.　　; d.　　; m. Hester **Aucher.**
f. William, b.　　; d. before 1629; m.　　.
g. Sir Thomas, b.　　; d.　　; m.　　.
h. Francis, b.　　; d. before 1629; m.　　.
i. Penelope, b.　　; d.　　; m. Nicholas **Lechmore.**
j. Frances, b.　　; d.　　; m.　　.
k. Catherine, b.　　; d.　　; m. Gerard **Serimshire.**
l. Mary, b.　　; d.　　; m. Richard **Spencer.**

Several members of the Sandys family were early in New England, among them Captain James Sandys of Portsmouth, R. I., where he had a land grant in 1643-44, and in 1661 settled on Block Island.

Refs. 339, 591.

The ecclesiastical affairs of Scrooby were really under the guidance of members of the Brewster family for many years.

Among the Bishop's Certificates of persons presented to Benefices within their dioceses by the Archbishop of York for 1565 was:

**Brewster,** Rev. Henry, "Sutton-super-Loude." He held the "living" till his death in Feb. 1597-8. He was married to Agnes (　　), who was buried at Sutton on Mar. 15, 1597-8, a month after her husband. No records of any children have been found, unfortunately.

I. Rev. James **Brewster** succeeded him as Vicar of Sutton, and held the living until his death Jan. 1613-4; buried at Sutton 14th of that month; married Mary **Welbeck**; buried Apr. 7, 1637. From the register at Sutton is obtained:

[ 77 ]

a. Grace, bp. 1600; m. William **Glaive**, Oct. 22, 1620.
b. Eliabeth, bp. 1603; m.
c. Sussana, bp. 1606; m. unmarried.
d. Judith, bp. 1609; m. Edward **Oldfield**, Nov. 5, 1633.

The Rev. James Brewster, either a cousin or brother of William, performed a good service for the parish of Sutton (about three miles from Scrooby). He transcribed all baptisms, marriages and burials from the oldest book of 1538 to his own time. In 1604, about the time that William Brewster loaned the Manor to his friend Rev. John Robinson for independent meetings, the Rev. James was "instituted" to the Vicarage of "Gringley-on-the-Hill," on the highroad between Bawtry and Gainsboro, but this did not draw him from his beloved Sutton.

There is reason to consider, also, Humphrey Brewster of Wrentham Hall or Manor, Suffolk Co., England, as a possible uncle of William Brewster. This Manor in the Great Survey was held by William de Warrene, and before that time by Edric the Saxon. The manor eventually came into the Dacre family, well known in Nottinghamshire. In 1570 Lord Dacre, by various proceedings as trustee, "vested" the Manor in Lord Norris of Rycot. They held court there in 1572, but in 1575 it was "alienated" to Humphrey Brewster, which alienation was effected by fine levied in 1576.

At this time Rev. Henry Brewster was Vicar of Sutton in Notts, and William Brewster, Sr., was just taking over Scrooby Manor from Sir Thomas[20] Wentworth (see Wentworth family, 20th generation from Reginald[1] 1066).

Some writers suggest that the wife of William Brewster of the "Mayflower" may have been Mary Wentworth. This is quite possible.

The Wentworths were of an ancient Yorkshire family. Thomas Wentworth, 1st Baron of Nettlestead, Suffolk, was of this family, and St. John's Cambridge was the favorite place of schooling for the clan, so that they had as a matter of course, accumulated some more or less "Puritanical ideas."

The Scrooby Manor Wentworths descend from

---

Refs. 339, 591.

## WENTWORTH

I. **Wentworth**, Sir Thomas[19] (from Reginald[1] of 1066), died Dec. 5, 1548; married Beatrix **Woodruff**, widow of John **Drax**, daughter of Sir Richard **Woodruff** of Woolley, Yorkshire.

This Sir Thomas was enormously wealthy for the times, being called "Golden Thomas." He paid Henry VIII a large fine to be excused from accepting the "Order of the Bath," and in 1528 obtained a license from the King to remain covered in the royal presence. This cost him a small fortune, but it must have given him a lot of personal satisfaction.

## CHILDREN

a. William, b.    ; d.    ; m.    .
b. Gervase, b.    ; d.    ; m.    .
c. Michael, b.    ; d.    ; m. Isabel **Whitley.**
IId. Thomas, b.    ; d. Scrooby 1574; m. Grace **Gascoigne.**
e. Bryan, b.    ; d.    ; m.    .
f. Elizabeth, b.    ; d.    ; m. Ralph **Denham,** Esq.
g. Isabel, b.    ; d.    ; m. Nicholas **Womwell.**
h. Beatrice, b.    ; d.    ; m. Thomas **Warrell,** Esq.

IId. **Wentworth,** Thomas[20] (Sir Thomas[19]—Reginald[1]), died Scrooby 1574; married Grace **Gascoigan.**

Thomas Wentworth of "Scrowbie Manor" died (will dated Mar. 27, 1574) and then William Brewster, Sr., took over the tenancy of the historic Manor.

## CHILDREN BORN SCROOBY

a. Thomas, b.    ; d.    ; m.    .
*b. Mary, b.    ; d.    ; m.    .
c. Grace, b.    ; d.    ; m.    .
d. Elizabeth, b.    ; d.    ; m.    .

* Did Mary marry William Brewster? Some historians think so. Without marriage and birth dates, however, it cannot be proved. It may have been one later generation. We only know that the widow of William, Sr., was called Prudence, and the widow of William, Jr., Mary.

When Sir Edwin Sandys decided to take over control of the Virginia Company affairs and attempted to organize a representative assembly in the Colonies, he had a very able and sincere friend as an assistant to report on the matter, Mr. John Pory, a Cambridge man, well acquainted with Brewster. Sandys was a leader of the "Liberals" or "Patriot" party in the Commons, and a representative government was his hobby.

The assembly was organized in Jamestown, July 30, 31, August 2, 3, 4, 1619, much to the disgust of King James. John Pory "covered" this epoch-making proceeding in a manner that would do credit to any modern correspondent, in "A Reporte of the Manner of Proceeding in the General Assembly Convened at James City," to the Virginia Company in London.

Pory's letters to Sir Edwin Sandys are extremely interesting, but too numerous to mention here.

In July, 1621, Sir Francis Wyatt was sent by Sandys to Virginia as Governor, and young Christopher Davison, as his secretary. It will be noticed that Wyatt was a son-in-law of Sir

Samuel Sandys of Scrooby, England, brother of Sir Edwin, and that Christopher Davison was a son of William Davison, close friends of Brewster.

Under these circumstances, it is not strange to learn that Pory made a visit on his old friend, Master William Brewster, and others at Plymouth in 1622, and found everybody, more or less, contented. It was on this visit that Pory became so interested in Brewster's library.

---

Refs. 493, 495, 487, 491, 339, 508, 4, 273, 281, 362, 383, 591, 489, 592.

# DAVISON

I. **Davison,** William, born England; buried at Stepney, Dec. 24, 1608; married Katherina **Spelman** about 1570, daughter of Francis **Spelman** and Mary **Hill.**
He was related to the families of the Earl of Leicester, Lord Burghley, Sir John Cheke and other outstanding lines, and held many positions of trust at the Court of Elizabeth, until the time of the famous "misunderstanding" with the Queen.
From 1584 to the time of his death in 1608, William Brewster was, in one way or another, no doubt, his aide, confidant and friend. There is good reason to suspect that Davison was connected with the East India Company and the early period of the Virginia Company. Anyway, Robert Cecil, Earl of Salisbury, son of Lord Burghley, friend of both Davison and Brewster, appears to have sent young William Brewster, Gent, to Virginia in 1607, on the first expedition.

### CHILDREN
```
a. Francis, b.    1575; d.    1620; m.
*b. Christopher, b.    ; d.    ; m.
c. William, b.    ; d.    ; m.    .
d. Walter, b.    ; d.    ; m.    .
e. Daughter, b.    ; d.    ; m. (    ) Townley.
f. Catherine, b.    ; d.    ; m. (    ) Duncombe.
```
* Secretary 1621 to Sir Francis Wyatt of Scrooby, and Governor of Virginia.

Ref. 489.

# HOPKINS

26. **Hopkins,** Caleb[3] (Giles[2], Stephen[1]), born Jan. 1650-1; died 1728 (?); married Mary[2] **Williams**; died before 1728; daughter of Thomas[1] **Williams** of Eastham.
Caleb was born in Eastham, and died in Truro intestate not long before May 22, 1728, when his son Caleb was appointed administrator. He appears in the first entry in the first book of records in possession of the town of Truro. It bears date June 17, 1690, and shows that he with six others were then proprietors of Pamet (Truro).

### CHILDREN BORN EASTHAM OR TRURO
```
152. Caleb, b.    ; d.    ; m. Mercy Freeman.
153. Nathaniel, b.    ; d.    ; m. Lydia (    ).
154. Thomas, b.    ; d.    ; m. Deborah Bickford.
155. Thankful, b. May 27, 1709; d. Aug. 1, 1785; m. Ambrose Dyer.
```

Refs. 149, 194, 147.

# DYER

I. **Dyer,** William[1], born England, and seems to have gone directly to Sheepscot, on landing in New England. He was there in 1662, and appears to have resided in that vicinity of Massachusetts continually thereafter.

The Dyer Family was ancient in Somerset County, England. There are pedigrees of it in the Visitations of that county. It has produced many able men, among whom are Sir James Dyer, Knight, Lord Chief Justice of the Common Pleas 1558. He died in 1581-2. Sir Edward Dyer, Knight, Chancellor of the Garter, a poet of Elizabeth's time, who was buried at St. Saviour's, Southwark in May, 1607, and Sir Thomas Dyer, Knight, Sheriff of Somerset 1558.

The Dyer family was severely persecuted by King James, and was especially condemned for loyalty to Charles I, which possibly influenced some members of the clan to settle in New England.

## CHILDREN

IIa. Christopher, b. 1640 (?); d. New Dartmouth 1689; m. 1st ( ); m. 2nd Ruth ( ).

b. John, b. 1648 (?); d. ; m. 1st Mary ( ); m. 2nd Sarah ( ); m. 3rd Anna **Holbrook.**

c. Mary, b. ; d. ; m. Samuel **Bowles.**

d. Giles, b. ; d. ; m. Hannah ( ).

IIIe. William, b. 1653 (?); d. Truro July 27, 1738; m. Mary **Taylor.**

f. Jonathan, b. ; d. ; m. .

g. Henry, b. ; d. ; m. Hannah **Riddan.**

h. George, b. ; d. ; m. .

i. Anthony, b. ; d. ; m. .

IIa. **Dyer,** Christopher[2] (William[1]), born 1640 (?); died 1689 (?); married 1st ( ); married 2nd Ruth ( ). He resided last at New Dartmouth and was killed by Indians 1689.

### BY 1ST WIFE (?)

a. William, b. 1663-4; d. 1749; m. 1st Joanna ( ); m. 2nd Mary **Whitman.**

b. John, b. ; d. ; m. Abigail **Ball.**

c. Grace, b. 1666; d. ; m. John **Allicet.**

### BY 2ND WIFE

d. Ebenezer, b. ; d. ; m. Martha ( ).

IIIe. **Dyer,** Dr. William[2] (William[1]), born New England 1653 (?); died Truro, Mass., July 27, 1738; married Mary **Taylor**

Dec., 1686; daughter of Henry **Taylor** of Barnstable; she died
Oct. 8, 1738.

Dr. Dyer resided in Barnstable and Truro, and lived a long
and useful life.

### CHILDREN

a. Lydia, b. Mar. 30, 1688; d.    ; m.   .
IVb. William, b. Oct. 30, 1690; d.    ; m. Hannah **Strout.**
c. Jonathan, b. Feb., 1692; d.    ; m.   .
d. Henry, b. Apr. 11, 1693; d.    ; m. Ann **Small.**
e. Isabel, b. July, 1695; d.    ; m. Samuel **Small.**
f. Ebenezer, b. Apr. 3, 1697; d.    ; m. 1st Sarah **Doane;**
   m. 2nd Ruth **Arey,** wid.
g. Samuel, b. Oct. 30, 1699; d.    ; m. 1st Mary **Brown;**
   m. 2nd Mary **Paine.**
h. Judah, b. Apr., 1701; d.    ; m. Phebe **Young.**

IVb. **Dyer,** William[3] (Dr. William[2], William[1]), born Oct. 30,
1690, Barnstable; married Hannah **Strout** in Eastham Apr. 15,
1709. She became the mother of ten sons, and three daughters.

He removed from Truro to Falmouth about 1736, and was a
cordwainer by trade.

### CHILDREN BORN TRURO

Va. Ambrose, b. Dec. 22, 1709; d. May 10, 1792; m. Thankful
   **Hopkins.**
b. John, b. Dec. 27, 1711; d.    ; m. Mary **Bickford.**
c. William, b. Mar. 27, 1715; d.    ; m.   .
d. Hannah, b. Jan. 29, 1717; d.    ; m. Timothy **Eldred.**
e. Joseph, b. Jan. 4, 1718; d.    ; m.   .
f. Anthony, b. Dec. 8, 1720; d.    ; m.   .
g. Christopher, b. Dec. 29, 1722; d. Oct. 2, 1759; m. Mercy
   **Smalley.**
h. Samuel, b. Nov. 29, 1724; d.    ; m. Thankful **Delano.**
i. Mary, b. Aug. 29, 1727; d.    ; m. Moses **Plummer.**
j. Isabel, b. July 10, 1729; d.    ; m. 1st Vincent **Roberts;**
   m. 2nd John **Fickett.**
k. Levi, b. July 15, 1731; d.    ; m.   .
l. Benjamin, b. Dec. 1, 1733; d.    ; m. Elizabeth **Higgins.**
m. George, bp. Sept. 7, 1735; d.    ; m.   .

Va. **Dyer,** Ambrose[4] (William[3], William[2], William[1]), born
Truro Dec. 22, 1709; died Truro May 10, 1792; married Thankful
[4]**Hopkins** Jan. 22, 1729-30; daughter of Caleb[3] **Hopkins** (Giles[2],
Stephen[1]). She died Aug. 1, 1783.

Ambrose was one of the Proprietors of Truro.

a. Ambrose, b. Jan. 29, 1730; d.          ; m.
b. Thankful, b. Apr. 16, 1733; d.          ; m. James **Lombard**, Jr.
c. Hannah, b. Apr. 5, 1736; d.          ; m.
d. Abigail, b. Jan. 9, 1738; d.          ; m.
e. Naphtali, b. Dec. 29, 1741; d.          ; m. Elizabeth (      ).
f. Mary, b. Sept. 9, 1744; d.          ; m.
g. Jerusha, b. July 9, 1747; d.          ; m.
h. Reuben, b. May 25, 1753; d. Apr. 13, 1780; m.

Refs. 149, 194.

## MAYO

27. **Hopkins**, Ruth[3] (Giles[2], Stephen[1]), born June, 1652; married Samuel[3] **Mayo**; born Eastham Oct. 12, 1655; died Oct. 29, 1738; son of Nathaniel[2] **Mayo** (John[1]).

### CHILDREN BORN EASTHAM

156. Samuel, b.     1690; d.     ; m. Abigail **Sparrow**.
157. Jonathan, b.     ; d. May 17, 1768; m. Thankful **Twining**.
158. Rebecca, b.     ; d.     ; m.     .
159. Mercy, b.     ; d.     ; m. Nathaniel **Hopkins**.
160. Mary, b.     ; d.     ; m.     .
161. Hannah, b.     ; d.     ; m. Judah **Hopkins**.
162. Sarah, b.     ; d.     ; m. James **Higgins**.
163. Anne, b.     ; d.     ; m. Benjamin **Hamblin**.

Refs. 163, 223, 155, 158, 135, 742, 164, 138, 139, 264.

## MAYO

I. **Mayo**, John[1], born England, buried Feb. 17, 1634-5, married Elizabeth (      ); buried 1645.
Rector of Cattistock, England.
The Mayo family has a long and distinguished past in England. It is claimed that Rev. John Mayo, the first pastor of the Old North Church in Boston, was the son of the John Mayo of Cattistock, England, the author of the famous black letter book or pamphlet entitled, "The Pope's Parliament, containing a pleasant and delightful historie wherein."

### CHILDREN BAPTIZED CATTISTOCK

a. Bridget, bp.     ; d.     ; m. Walter **Dawe**.
IIb. John, bp.     ; d.     ; m.     .
c. Edward, bp. Aug. 14, 1614; d. Eng. 1689; m. Anne **Dyke**.
d. Thomas, bp. Apr. 11, 1619; d. Eng. 1660-4; m. Joanne **Bunter**.

[ 84 ]

IIb. **Mayo**, Rev. John[2] (Rev. John[1] ?), born England 1590-00; died May, 1676, a very old man at Yarmouth, Mass.; married in England, Tamison ( ); born England; died Yarmouth, Feb. 26, 1682.

Arriving in New England 1638, he settled in Barnstable, being a "teacher" in the church there from its beginning until 1644. He was ordained Apr. 15, 1640. He removed to Eastham in 1646, and was pastor of the church there until 1654, when being "discouraged" he moved to Boston, and became Nov. 1655, the first pastor of the "Old North Church." In 1673 with his own consent he was retired for age, and was succeeded by the famous Dr. Increase Mather. While in Boston he lived on Middle, now Hanover Street.

After retirement he removed to Yarmouth and resided there with his daughter Elizabeth Howes, until his death.

KNOWN CHILDREN BORN ENGLAND

IIIa. Samuel, b. 1615 (?) ; d. Boston (?) 1664; m. Thomasin **Lumpkin.**
IVb. John, b. ; d. Eastham 1663; m. Hannah **Reycroft.**
Vc. Nathaniel, b. ; d. 1661 (?) ; m. Hannah **Prence.**
d. Elizabeth, b. ; d. Yarmouth 1701; m. Joseph **Howes.**
e. Hannah, b. ; d. ; m. Nathaniel **Bacon.**

IIIa. **Mayo**, Samuel[3] (John[2], John[1]), born England; died Boston (?), 1664; married Thomasin **Lumpkin**, daughter of William **Lumpkin** and Thomasin ( ).

Of the children, Joseph and John were born in Oyster Bay, L. I.

CHILDREN

a. Mary, b. 1645; d. ; m. Jonathan **Bangs.**
b. Samuel, b. 1647; d. ; m. no issue.
c. Hannah, b. Oct. 20, 1650; d. ; m.
d. Elizabeth, b. May 22, 1653; d. ; m. Rev. Samuel **Treat.**
e. Joseph, b. 1654; d. ; m.
f. John, b. 1656; d. ; m.
g. Nathaniel, b. Apr. 1, 1658; d. ; m. no issue.
h. Sarah, b. Dec. 19, 1660; d. ; m.

IVb. **Mayo**, John[3] (John[2], John[1]), married Hannah **Reycroft** (**Lecraft**) Jan. 1, 1651.
He resided in Eastham.

CHILDREN BORN EASTHAM

a. John, b. Dec. 15, 1652; d. Feb. 1, 1724; m. Hannah **Freeman.**
b. William, b. Oct. 7, 1654; d.    1691; m. Elizabeth **Ring** (see Fam. No. 31).
c. James, b. Oct. 3, 1656; d.    ; m. 1st    ; m. 2nd Sarah (   ).
d. Samuel, b. Aug. 2, 1658; d.    ; m.    .
e. Elisha, b. Nov. 7, 1661; d.    ; m.    .
f. Daniel, b. Jan. 24, 1664; d.    1715; m. Sarah **Howes.**
g. Nathaniel, b. Apr. 2, 1667; d.    ; m. 1st    ; m. 2nd Mary **Brown.**
h. Thomas, b. June 29, 1670; d. Aug. 11, 1670; m.——.
i. Thomas, b. July 15, 1672; d.    ; m.    .

## MAYO—SPARROW

Vc. **Mayo,** Nathaniel[3] (Rev. John[2], Rev. John[1]), born England; his will was proved Mar. 4, 1661; married Hannah **Prence** Feb. 13, 1649-50; she married 2nd Capt. Jonathan **Sparrow,** son of Richard and Pandora **Sparrow.** Hannah was the daughter of Thomas **Prence** and Patience [2]**Brewster** (William[1]).
Nathaniel Mayo was a prominent man in Eastham.

CHILDREN BORN EASTHAM (MAYO)

a. Thomas, b. Dec. 7, 1650-1; d. Apr. 22, 1729; m. Barbara **Knowles.**
b. Nathaniel, b. Nov. 16, 1652; d. Nov. 3, 1709; m. 1st Eliza **Wixam;** m. 2nd Mercy **Young,** widow.
VIc. Samuel, b. Oct. 12, 1655; d. Oct. 29, 1738; m. 1st Ruth **Hopkins;** m. 2nd (   ).
d. Hannah, b. Oct. 17, 1657; d.    ; m.    .
e. Theophilus, b. Dec. 12, 1659; d.    ; m. Rebecca **Smith.**
f. Bathsheba, b.    ; d.    ; m. Thomas **Freeman.**

CHILDREN (SPARROW)

g. Richard, b. Mar. 17, 1669; d. young.
h. Patience, b.    ; d.    ; m. 1st Joseph **Paine;** m. 2nd John **Jenkins.**
i. Richard, b.    (?) 1675; d. Apr. 13, 1728; m. Mercy **Cobb.**

VIc. Samuel **Mayo** (see Fam. No. 27, Ruth **Hopkins**).

Refs. 163, 301.

[ 86 ]

# HAMBLEN

I. **Hamblen** (Hamlin), James, born England, married **Ann** ( ). His will is dated Jan. 23, 1683, and proved Oct. 22, 1690. This name was probably introduced into England by William the Conqueror. It is very old in France. He was probably residing in London for some time before coming to America, and sailed for New England before 1639 when he is recorded in Barnstable. He seems to have been a follower of Rev. John Lothrop who came to New England in 1634. James resided in Barnstable near a pond now called Coggin's Pond.

The first four children are recorded at St. Lawrence, Reading, Berkshire, England. The last five at Barnstable.

## CHILDREN

a. James; bp. Oct. 21, 1630; d.　　; m.　　.
b. Sarah; bp. Sept. 6, 1632; d.　　; m.　　.
c. Mary; bp. July 27, 1634; d.　　; m.　　.
d. James; bp. Apr. 10, 1636; d. Tisbury, Mass., May 3, 1718; m.　　.
e. Bartholomew; bp. Apr. 24, 1642; d.　　; m.　　.
f. John; bp. June 30, 1644; d.　　; m.　　.
g. Child; buried Dec. 2, 1646.
h. Sarah; bp. Nov. 7, 1647; d.　　; m.　　.
i. Eleazer; bp. Mar. 17, 1649; d.　　; m.　　.

Refs. 164.

# HOPKINS

28. **Hopkins**, Joshua[3] (Giles[2], Stephen[1]), born June 1657; died 1734-8; married Mary[2] **Cole** May 26, 1681; died Mar. 1, 1734; daughter of Daniel[1] **Cole.**

He resided on the east side of Town Cove, near his father's house, and became quite a landowner, much of it being inherited. His land holdings were in Eastham, Harwich and Chatham.

## CHILDREN

164. John, b. Apr. 16, 1683; d. June 24, 1700; m.——.
165. Abigail, b. March 9, 1686; d.　　; m. John **Taylor.**
166. Elisha, b. Dec. 17, 1688; d.　　; m. Eperience **Scudder.**
167. Lydia, b. Apr. 1, 1692; d.　　; m.　　.
168. Mary, b. Jan. 20, 1695; d.　　; m. Joseph **Smith.**
169. Joshua, b. Feb. 20, 1698; d.　　; m. Priscilla **Curtice.**
170. Hannah, b. Mar. 25, 1700; d. Oct. 24, 1793; m. Ebenezer **Paine.**
171. Phebe, b. Mar. 11, 1702; d. New York; m. Moses **Byxbee.**

Refs. 133, 134, 145, 158, 135, 742, 291, 158, 135, 742, 146, 264.

# LYMAN

The **Lyman** Family is entitled to arms, crest and motto. The name is Anglo-Saxon. From our Teutonic ancestors came the roots which developed into "Lyman," "Leaf" "dear and beloved," "man," "beloved man." The name is spelled Leman, Lemmon, Lemon, Leeman, Leemon, Leaman, and Liman. It is very old in England and occurs in the Doomsday Book.

1. John **Lemon,** citizen and merchant of London 1314-22, afterwards at Navistoke, Wethersfield and Norton Mandeville, Co. Essex.
2. John **Lemon**—surety in 1432 for Thomas **Mireton.**
3. Thomas **Lyman** married Elizabeth **Lambert,** daughter of Henry **Lambert** of High Ongar, Essex. The Estate came into the **Lyman** family. (Some writers claim that Henry **Lambert** was a son of Robert **Lambert** of Owlton).
4. Henry **Lyman** married Alicia, daughter of Simon **Hyde** of Wethersfield, resided Navistoke 1487; living 1517.
5. John **Lyman,** eldest son, in 1546 possessed Navistoke and High Ongar estates, married Margaret **Gerard,** daughter and heiress of William **Gerard** of Beauchamp, Co. Essex.
6. Henry **Lyman,** m. 1st Elizabeth (      ); buried Navistoke Apr. 15, 1587; m. 2nd Phillis (      ), either daughter of Richard **Stane,** or John **Scott.**

CHILDREN BORN HIGH ONGAR 1ST WIFE

a. Judith, bp. Nov. 2; buried Nov. 24, 1578.
b. Jane, bp. Oct. 20; buried Oct. 2, 1579.
7c. Richard, bp. Oct. 30, 1580; d. Hartford, Conn., Aug. 1640; m. Sarah **Osborn.**
d. Henry, bp. Nov. 19, 1581; buried Mar. 13, 1582.
e. Agnes, bp. Nov. 28, 1585.
f. Sarah, bp. Jan. 18, 1587.

CHILDREN BORN 2ND WIFE

g. Henry, bp. June 6, 1591; d. New England.
h. William, bp. Mar. 2, 1594.
i. Phillis, bp. May 12, 1597.

7c. Richard **Lyman,** bapt. High Ongar, Essex, Eng., Oct. 30, 1580; died Hartford, Conn., Aug. 1640; married Sarah **Osborn,** daughter of Roger **Osborn** of Halstead, County Kent, England.

In 1629 he sold his lands, orchards and gardens in the parish of Ongar to John **Gower** and sailed with his wife and children on Aug. 1631 in the ship "Lion," William Pierce, master, for New England. On this same vessel were Martha **Winthrop,** 3rd wife of Gov. **Winthrop,** William and Thomas **Hills,** and many others.

They landed at Boston. Richard **Lyman,** William **Hills** with others in 1635 joined **Hooker's** removal to Hartford, Conn., where they became original proprietors.

CHILDREN BORN HIGH ONGAR

      a. William, bp.   ; buried Aug. 28, 1615.
Gen. 8\*b. Phillis, bp. Sept. 12, 1611; d.   ; m. William **Hills.**
      c. Richard, bp. July 18, 1613; d. young; m.——.
      d. William, bp. Sept. 8, 1616; d. Nov. 1616; m.——.
    \*e. Richard, bp. Feb. 24, 1617; d. June 3, 1662; m. Hepsibah **Ford.**
    \*f. Sarah, bp. Feb. 8, 1620; d.   ; m.   .
      g. Anne, bp. Apr. 12, 1621; d. young; m.——.
    \*h. John, bp.   1623; d. Aug. 20, 1690; m. Dorcas **Plumb.**
    \*i. Robert, bp. Sept. 1629; d.   ; m. Hepzibah **Bascom.**

\* These five children came with their father and mother to New England. All born and baptized at High Ongar about 25 miles east of London, near Upminster, birthplace of William Hills.

  Gen.  9. William Hills, Jr., m. Sarah (**Risley?**).
  Gen. 10. John Hills, m. Margaret **Dix.**
  Gen. 11. John Hills, m. Deliverance **Crow.**
  Gen. 12. Joseph Hills, m. Eunice **Kibbee.**
  Gen. 13. Oliver Hills, m. Polly **Soper.**
\*Gen. 14. Oliver S. Hills, m. Mary Ann **Clark.**
  Gen. 15. Franklin B. Hills, m. Frances M. **Coons.**
  Gen. 16. Leon C. Hills, m. Ina S. **King.**
  Gen. 17. Norma, b. 1915.
          Robert, b. 1918.
  ' \* (See Browne Xe).

Refs. 571, 544.

## MAYO

31. **Ring,** Elizabeth[3] (Deborah[2] **Hopkins,** Stephen[1]), born Apr. 19, 1652; died before 1692; married William[3] **Mayo** of Eastham; born Oct. 7, 1654; died 1691; son of John[2] **Mayo** (John[1]).

CHILDREN

172. Thankful, b.   ; d.   ; m.   .
173. Merey, b.   ; d.   ; m.   .
174. Hannah, b.   ; d.   ; m. Samuel **Tucker.**

Refs. 85, 163, 266.

# TUCKER

**Tucker,** Samuel[2] (John[1]), born Tisbury (?), Mass., about 1683 (?); married Hannah **Mayo** 1706; daughter of William **Mayo** and Elizabeth **Ring.**
He settled at Monomoit (Chatham) soon after 1706, and joined the church at Harwich, May 17, 1713. His daughters Keziah, Thankful and Elizabeth were baptized there July 3, 1715. He had the care of the church for many years, receiving a small amount from the town for "his panes of swepen the meten hous."

### CHILDREN BORN MONOMOIT

a. Keziah, b. Nov. 1707; d.　　; m. Nathaniel **Covell.**
b. John, b. Sept. 1709; d. Sept. 1709; m.——.
c. Thankful, b. Sept. 1710; d.　　; m.　　.
d. Elizabeth, b. Sept. 1712; d.　　; m.　　.
e. Hannah, b. Sept. 1714; d.　　; m. Isaac **Hawes,** Jr.
f. John, b. Mar. 20, 1715; d.　　; m.　　.
g. Samuel, b. Mar. 16, 1719; d.　　; m.　　.
h. Eunice, b. June 12, 1722; d.　　; m.　　.

Refs. 79, 512.

# NICKERSON

I. **Nickerson,** William[1], born Norwich, Norfolk Co., England; married Anne **Busby,** born Norwich, daughter of Nicholas **Busby** and Bridget **Cooke,** who were married at St. Mary's, Norwich, June 24, 1605.
William Nickerson, a weaver, aged 33 years, and Anne, his wife, aged 28 years, together with four children, Nicholas, Robert, Elizabeth and Anne, were among those expressing a desire to go to Boston in New England, there to settle. They were examined Apr. 8, 1637, and set sail for the great adventure on the ship "John and Dorothy" of Ipswich, William Andrews, master, and the "Rose" of Yarmouth, William Andrews, Jr., master. They arrived in Boston June 20, 1637.
Incidentally, it was in Norwich that Rev. John Robinson held his last pastorate in the established church in 1603-4, and had to return to his home town, Sturton, Notts, out of a "living" and a place to preach.
The father-in-law, Nicholas Busby, came over at the same time.
William took the oath of freeman before the Massachusetts Court May 2, 1638. He was proposed as freeman to the Plymouth Colony Court Dec. 1, 1640, and took the oath of fidelity June 1, 1641. He was of Yarmouth at this time, and apparently

had ideas of his own about religion and other matters, and not averse to expressing them for "he was complained of in Mar., 1642, as a jeerer and scoffer at religion, and as making disorder at the town meeting in Yarmouth." However, his genuine ability was acknowledged and he became a deputy from Yarmouth to the Court at Plymouth in 1655.

Nickerson was progressive and determined to become a large land holder for himself and family. In England the people of importance were landlords, and his own family had been denied the right to own land for centuries.

Prior to 1656 he had bought of the Indian chief Mattaguason, and John Quason, his son, a tract of land at Monomoy (Chatham) without the consent of the authorities.

He was not able to obtain a deed for it, and the matter was, of course, brought before the Court. Nickerson was a fighter in Court and out, and had no intention of giving up that large territory if he could help it. Members of his family were also of that stubborn variety. After all, what did they come to New England for? Who really did own, and who was going to possess the vast domain of unsettled territory all about them?

After much consideration and no definite decision in any official direction, Nickerson decided the land was his without further parley, and on July 4, 1663, presented a petition to the Court for leave "to settle a township att Mannomoyett (Chatham), or thereabouts."

The Court was so shocked by this audacity and enterprise, that they failed to act promptly. The petition had been signed by the whole Nickerson clan, including William Nickerson, Sr., his sons and sons-in-law, Nicholas Nickerson, Robert Nickerson, Samuel Nickerson, John Nickerson, William Nickerson, Jr., Joseph Nickerson, Robert Eldred, Trustrum Hedges, and Nathaniel Covell

There was considerable fighting and business talent in this group, and the Court rather hesitated so long that Nickerson and his clan simply went in and took possession. As a result the Court issued a warrant to the Marshall of the Colony to serve notice on Nickerson that his alleged purchase was not legal, and "to the prejudice of many of the more ancient inhabitants." The Marshall was also expected to collect £200 as a part penalty.

However, for reasons not entirely clear, the Marshall failed to serve the notice, or obtain any satisfaction.

The court voted to dispossess on June 8, 1664, but the matter was not so easily disposed of, and was the topic of discussion and actions for some years, until settled, more or less, to the satisfaction of all concerned.

The first English settlers in New England had to struggle with a difficult problem, that of proper consideration for a legal deed, and to whom. Who owned the land and what was it worth?

## CHILDREN

a. Nicholas, b. Eng.    ; d. before Mar. 26, 1681; m. Mary **Darby.**
b. Robert, b. Eng.    ; d.    ; m.   .
c. Elizabeth, b. Eng.    ; d.    ; m. Robert **Eldred.**
d. Anne, b. Eng.    ; d.    ; m. Tristam **Hedges.**
e. Samuel, b.    ; d. before Sept. 3, 1719; m. Mary **Bell.**
f. John, b.    ; d.    ; m. Sarah **Williams.**
IIg. Sarah, b.    ; d.    ; m. Nathaniel **Covell.**
IIIh. William, bp. June 1, 1646; d.    ; m. Mercy **Williams.**
i. Joseph, b.    ; d.    ; m. Ruhamah **Jones.**

## COVELL

IIg. **Nickerson,** Sarah[2] (William[1]), (see Covell I).

## NICKERSON

IIIh. **Nickerson,** William[2] (William[1]), bapt. June 1, 1646; married Mercy **Williams,** daughter of Thomas **Williams.**
He resided in Chatham on part of the Nickerson estate.

### CHILDREN BORN CHATHAM

a. Thomas, b.    ; d.    ; m. Mary **Bangs.**
b. William, b.    ; d.    ; m. Deliverance **Lambert.**
c. Nathaniel, b.    ; d.    ; m. Catherine **Stuard.**
d. Robert, b.    ; d.    ; m. Rebecca **Jones.**
e. Elizabeth, b.    ; d.    ; m. William **Cahoon.**
f. Mercy, b.    ; d.    ; m. 1st William **Mitchell;** m. 2nd James **Griffiths.**
IVg. Judith, b.    ; d.    ; m. Nathaniel **Covell.**
h. Dau. (?); b.    ; d.   .
i. Dau. (?), b.    ; d.   .

## COVELL

IVg. **Nickerson,** Judith[3] (William[2], William[1]), (see Covell IIa).

## COVELL

I. **Covell,** Nathaniel[1], born England, married Sarah[2] **Nickerson** (William[1]).
There were Covells in Suffolk County, England, very early. A John Covell was Master of Christ College, Cambridge, in 1660, and a marriage license was issued to Thomas Covell and Martha

Pecocke in 1610. Some of the Covell family were Merchant Adventurers, on the list of shareholders in the Virginia Company, 1608-1624.

KNOWN CHILDREN BORN CHATHAM

IIa. Nathaniel, b.　(?) 1670; d.　; m. Judith **Nickerson.**

IIIb. William, b.　(?) 1673; d. Jan. 18, 1760; m. Sarah ( ).

IVc. Joseph, b.　; d.　; m. 1st Lydia **Stuard**; m. 2nd Hannah **Bassett.**

Vd. Ephraim, b.　; d.　; m. 1st Mercy ( ); m. 2nd Mrs. Abigail **Ellis**; m. 3rd Mrs. **Taylor.**

e. Dau., b.　; d.　; m. Benjamin **Phillips.**

IIa. **Covell,** Nathaniel[2] (Nathaniel[1]), born Chatham 1670 (?), married Judith[3] **Nickerson** Mar. 5, 1696-7, daughter of William[2] **Nickerson** and Mercy[2] **Williams.**

He resided on or near his father's farm between Crow's Pond and Ryder's Cove at Chathamport. He was a selectman, and treasurer of the town. His will is dated Sept. 19, 1746, and was proved Mar. 13, 1746-7. He had previously disposed of his real estate to his children.

KNOWN CHILDREN BORN CHATHAM

a. Jane, b.　; d.　; m. Jonathan **Nickerson.**

b. John, b.　1700; d. Dec. 1, 1760; m. Thankful **Bangs.**

c. Nathaniel, b.　; d.　; m. Keziah **Tucker.**

*d. Seth, b.　; To Ridgefield, Ct., 1747; m. Sarah **Hurd.**

e. Hannah, b.　; d. before 1741; m. Alexander **Cunningham.**

f. Simeon, b.　; To Ridgefield, Ct., 1747; m. Thankful **Robbins.**

g. Elizabeth, b.　; d.　1776; single.

* Seth Covell (see Vol. I, p. 140).

IIIb. **Covell,** William[2] (Nathaniel[1]), born Chatham (Monomoit) about 1673; died Wellfleet Jan. 18, 1760, age 87; married Sarah ( ).

His homestead, bought of Joseph Nickerson about 1695, was at Chathamport, and contained about 60 acres. He sold out at Chatham in 1716, and removed to Harwich, then to Wellfleet in 1725, where he died.

## KNOWN CHILDREN

a. Nathaniel, b.      ; d.      ; m. Esther **Atwood.**
b. Ephraim, b.      ; d.      ; m. Mercy **Brown.**
c. William, b.      ; d.      ; m. 1st Joanna **Atwood,** Wid.;
  m. 2nd Elizabeth **Webber.**
d. Son, b.      ; d.      ; m. Mary (      ).
e. Dau., b.      ; d.      ; m. Daniel **Eldredge.**

IVc. **Covell,** Joseph[2] (Nathaniel[1]), born Chatham, married 1st Lydia **Stuart,** 1700, daughter of Ensign Hugh **Stuart;** married 2nd Hannah **Bassett** Mar. 1, 1703-4; daughter of Nathaniel **Bassett** of Yarmouth.

His farm was on the east side of Muddy Cove. It was a part of the old William **Nickerson** farm.

### CHILDREN BY 1ST WIFE

a. Lydia, b. July 12, 1701; d.      ; m. Thomas **Nickerson,** Jr.

### CHILDREN BY 2ND WIFE

b. Sarah, b.      ; d.      ; m. William **Nickerson.**
c. James, b.      ; d.      ; m. 1st Mehitable **Nickerson;**
  m. 2nd      .
d. Nathaniel, b.      ; d.      ; m. Mary **Chase.**
e. Joseph, b.      ; d.      ; m.      .
f. ? Constant, b.      ; d.      ; m. Ebenezer **Nickerson.**
g. ? Dorcas, b.      ; d.      ; m. James **Nickerson.**

Vd. **Covell,** Ephraim[2] (Nathaniel[1]), born Chatham, Mass.; married 1st Mercy (      ); died Feb. 1, 1727-8; married 2nd Abigail **Ellis,** Feb. 4, 1729-30; married 3rd Mary **Taylor.**

### KNOWN CHILDREN

a. Thankful, b.      ; d.      ; m. Edward **Nickerson.**
b. Mercy, b.      ; d.      ; m. Samuel **Burge.**
c. Sarah, b.      ; d.      ; m. Benjamin **Nickerson.**
d. Mary, b.      ; d.      ; m. Thomas **Burge.**

Refs. **79, 512.**

## RING

32. **Ring,** William[3] (Deborah[2] **Hopkins,** Stephen[1]), born 1653 (?); died 1731; married July 13, 1693; Hannah[3] **Sherman;** born Marshfield, Feb. 21, 1668; daughter of William[2] **Sherman** (William[1]), and Desire[2] **Doty** (Edward[1]).

[ 94 ]

175. Deborah, b. Jan. 24, 1695; d. May 29, 1696.
176. Hannah, b. May 26, 1697; d.          ; m. no children.
177. William, b. July 25, 1699; d.          ; m. no children.
178. Elizabeth, b. Feb. 15, 1701; d.          ; m. Joseph **Pearce.**
179. Eleazer, b. Jan. 16, 1704; d.          ; m. no children.
180. Deborah, b. Feb. 5, 1708; d.          ; m. Caleb **Sherman.**

Refs. 85, 167, 266.

## CLARKE

I. **Clarke,** Richard[1]; born England; died Plymouth Plantation Jan. 11 to April 10, 1621.

Certain members of the Clarke (Clark) family are listed as owners of shares in the Virginia Company, and no doubt some of the early Clarke settlers of New England are related in some degree to this Richard, the Mayflower Planter.

Refs. 214, 215.

## LAZELL

I. **Lazell,** John[1], probably born England 1620 (?); died Hingham, Mass., Oct. 21, 1700; married Nov. 29, 1649, Elizabeth **Gates,** daughter of Stephen and Ann **Gates,** who came to New England with her parents on the ship "Diligent" in 1683; she died Hingham, Aug. 3, 1704.

John Lazell was a resident of Hingham as early as 1647, and resided there until his death.

His will is dated Sept. 2, 1695, and proved in Boston, Jan. 11, 1700-1.

### CHILDREN BORN HINGHAM

a. John, bapt. Sept. 8, 1650; d. May 14, 1665.
b. Thomas, b. Sept. 15, 1652; d. Windham, Ct., May 1, 1725; m. Mary **Allen.**
IIc. Joshua, b. Nov. 17, 1654; d. Hingham, Feb. 12, 1689; m. Mary ( ? ).
d. Stephen, b. Oct. 6, 1656; d. Hingham, Jan. 16, 1717; m. Sarah ( ? ).
e. Elizabeth, b. Feb. 28, 1658; d. Apr. 7, 1676; unmarried.
f. Isaac, b. July 10, 1660; d. Hingham, Oct. 20, 1690; m. Abial **Leavitt.**
g. Hannah, b. Aug. 31, 1662; d. Andover, May 22, 1717; m. 1st James **Turner;** m. 2nd William **Johnson.**
h. Mary, b. Sept. 2, 1664; d.          ; m. Simon **Burr, Jr.**
i. Sarah, b. Nov. 29, 1666; d.          ; m. Peter **Ripley.**
j. John, b. Apr. 25, 1669; d. Windham, Ct., Dec. 2, 1755; m. Deborah **Lincoln.**
k. Israel, b. Sept. 24, 1671; d. Hingham, Dec. 30, 1755; m. Rachel **Lincoln.**

IIc. **Lazell,** Joshua[2] (John[1]), born Hingham, Nov. 17, 1654; died Feb. 12, 1688-9; married Mary (    ). She m. 2nd Benajah **Pratt.**

CHILDREN BORN HINGHAM

a. Elizabeth, b. Dec. 20, 1681; d.    ; m. Micajah **Dunham.**
b. Martha, b. Feb. 23, 1683-4; d.    ; m. Joseph **Pratt.**
c. Joshua, b. Nov. 15, 1686; d. York, Maine; m. Catherine **Brown.**
IIId. Simon, b. Sept. 12, 1688; d. Middleboro, 1747; m. 1st Margaret **Cooke**; m. 2nd Joanna (**Tilson**) **Wood.**

IIId. **Lazell** Simon[3] (Joshua[2], John[1]); born Hingham, Sept. 12, 1688; died at Middleboro in 1747; married 1st at Plymouth, Apr. 5, 1716; Margaret[4] **Cooke,** born Plymouth, Nov. 3, 1695; died Middleboro before Dec. 20, 1742; daughter of Jacob[3] **Cooke** and Lydia **Miller** (Jacob[2], Francis[1]), Mayflower Passenger. Jacob[2] **Cooke** married Damaris[2] **Hopkins** (Stephen[1]), another Mayflower Passenger. He married 2nd Dec. 20, 1742, Joanna **Tilson,** born at Plymouth, Oct. 9, 1696; died at Middleboro 1747; daughter of Edmund **Tilson** and widow of David **Wood.**

CHILDREN BY MARGARET COOKE

a. Joshua, b. Plymouth May 5, 1717; d. July 9, 1718.

b. Joshua, b. Plymouth Sept. 30, 1719; d. Middleboro Feb. 11, 1748-9; m. Elizabeth **Ames.**

c. Lydia, b. Plymouth Jan. 4, 1722-3; d. Middleboro Apr. 6, 1749; m. John **Alden.**

d. Mary, b.    ; d. Middleboro before 1752; m. Ephraim **Wood.**

e. Jacob, b. Middleboro Mar. 25, 1729; d. Bridgewater July 25, 1751; m. Elizabeth **Davenport.**

f. William, b. (Twin) Apr. 30, 1732; d.    ; m. Eunice **Davenport.**

g. Sarah, b. (Twin) Apr. 30, 1732; d.    ; m. Elkanah **Ellms.**

h. Abner, b. Middleboro Aug. 22, 1734; died French and Indian wars.

Ref. 190.

## RING

33. **Ring,** Eleazer[3] (Deborah[2] **Hopkins,** Stephen[1]), died 1748-9; married Mary[2] **Shaw,** daughter of Jonathan[1] **Shaw.**

181. Eleazer, b. Nov. 7, 1688; d. Dec. 3, 1688; m.——.
182. Andrew, b. Nov. 14, 1689; d. young; m.——.
183. Phebe, b. Jan. 26, 1691; d.      ; m. Ichabod **Standish.**
184. Samuel, b. Mar. 12, 1694; d.      ; m. Ruth (**Sylvester**) **Cooke,** wid.
185. Andrew, b. Mar. 28, 1696; d.      ; m. Zurich **Standish.**
186. Deborah, b. July 10, 1698; d.      ; m. John **Fuller.**
187. Mary, b. Dec. 9, 1700; d.      ; m. Peleg **Samson.**
188. Jonathan, b. Dec. 23, 1702; d.      ; m. Sarah **Mitchell.**
189. Sussanah, b. Apr. 9, 1705; d.      ; m. Nehemiah **Bosworth.**
190. Elkunah, b. Oct. 19, 1706; d.      ; m.      .
191. Elizabeth, b.      ; d.      ; m. James **Claghorn.**
192. Lydia, b. Nov. 20, 1710; d.      ; m. Ephraim **Sturtevant.**

Refs. 85, 182, 183, 185, 170, 184, 266.

## CLAGHORN

I. **Claghorn,** James[1], born 1628-30 at Corstorphine, near Edinburgh, Scotland; died Oct. 1683; married Abia **Lumbard** Jan. 6, 1653-4; daughter of Lt. Bernard **Lumbard.** She died Aug. 21, 1677.
"Glegerne" is old and of Celtic origin. The Cleghornes who resided in Edinburgh and vicinity were mostly merchants. James Claghorn resided in Yarmouth, and seems to have been a professional soldier.

### CHILDREN

a. Ens. James, b. Jan. 29, 1654; d. Mar. 27, 1723; m. Experience **Bowerman.**
b. Mary, b. Oct. 26, 1655; d.      ; m. Joseph **Davis.**
c. Thomas, b.      ; d.      ; m.      .
d. Shubel, b.      ; d.      ; m. Jane **Lovell.**
e. Sarah, b. Jan. 3, 1659; d.      ; m.      .
f. Experience, b.      ; d.      ; m.      .
g. Elizabeth, b. Apr. (?), 1660; d.      ; m.      .
h. Robert, b. Oct. 27, 1661; d. Aug. 1715-23; m. Bethia **Lothrop,** wid.

Ref. 180.

# SOUTHWORTH

The family name seems to originate from the Manor of Southworth in South Lancashire, England, in the parish of Wirwick. It was confirmed at Westminster, Jan. 20, 1326, to Sir Gilbert de'Southworth, and was originally called Samlesbury Hall. The Line follows:

1. Sir Gilbert de'Southworth.

2. Sir John.

3. Sir Thomas.

4. Sir Richard.

5. Sir Christopher.

6. Sir John.

7. Sir Thomas.

8. Sir John came into possession of Samlesbury and many other estates during the difficult times of 1546. During Elizabeth's reign he was in constant misunderstandings with Sir Francis Walsingham about his "Romanism," and questionable loyalty to Elizabeth. To add to his misery the eldest son and heir had become a "Protestant," the first of the family to leave the established church. In 1584 Walsingham, hearing that young Thomas was to be disinherited, had old Sir John placed under detention in London. In 1594, he was allowed to return to Samlesbury, after spending several years in Fleet Prison, broken in spirit and health, and died Nov. 3, 1595. He made a will "Weake in Bodie but of perfect remembrance," and what he remembered must have been bitter, indeed.

9. Sir Thomas was born 1561, a few years before William Brewster. Of course, his father's estate had been heavily loaded up with debts, legal costs, and fines, placed there by Elizabeth.

Sir Thomas married Rosamond Lister, daughter of William Lister of Thornton, in Craven, York County. Perhaps Edward Lister or Litser, the Mayflower passenger, was related to this family.

Sir Thomas had a large family, seven sons and four daughters, all living in 1595 when Sir John made his will. Two of these sons, Thomas and Edward, were of Leyden as early as 1613. The seven sons were:

a. John, b.          .
b. Thomas, b. of Leyden 1613.
c. William, b.          .
d. Richard, b.          .
e. Michael, b.          .
f. Christopher, b.          .

10g. Edward, b. of Leyden 1613.

10g. **Southworth**, Edward[10], of Leyden before 1613, and a frequenter of the famous Duke's Place in London, where he seems to have been residing in 1620, perhaps near William Brewster, while the Mayflower voyage was being arranged. At this time his address was Heneage House, a noted rendezvous for dissenters against selfish arbitrary laws of James 1, and advocates of a new order of religious toleration, and more liberal form of government under the leadership of Sir Edwin Sandys of the Virginia Company, and outstanding merchants of London. Bradford also frequented this district.

Duke's Place included several streets in the same district. In fact, it was a whole section. Heneage House was on three streets, Heneage Lane, Bevis Marks, and Berry Street. Sir Francis Walsingham had lived across the street for some years previous to his death.

Samlesbury, the old Southworth estate, is within a few miles of the Standish family residence, probably related to Capt. Myles Standish.

Edward was born about 1590, and died 1621 (?), married May 28, 1613, Alice **Carpenter**, born 1590 (?), died Plymouth Mar. 26, 1670; daughter of Alexander **Carpenter** of Wrington, England. She married 2nd William **Bradford** at Plymouth Aug. 14, 1623, whose 1st wife Dorothy **May** had drowned in Cape Cod Bay.

Edward was a silk worker in Leyden, and, of course, a member of Robinson's church. On Nov. 4, 1611, he witnessed in Leyden the marriage of Isaac **Allerton** and Mary **Norris**. Again, on Apr. 30, 1613, he served the same way for his friend Samuel **Fuller** and Agnes **Carpenter**. At his own wedding brother Thomas was a witness.

KNOWN CHILDREN

11a. Constant, b. Leyden 1615 (?); d. Mar. 10, 1678-9; m. Elizabeth **Collier**.
11b. Thomas, b. Leyden 1616 (?); d. Dec. 8, 1669; m. Elizabeth **Reynor**.

11a. **Southworth**, Constant [11] (Edward[10]), born Leyden 1615; died Duxbury. Mass., Mar. 10, 1678-9; married Elizabeth **Collier** Nov. 2, 1637; daughter of William **Collier**.

[ 99 ]

He was a real estate dealer and owner in Duxbury, Tiverton and Little Compton. His will, dated Feb. 27, 1678, is witnessed by John Alden, Sr., and William Crow.

CHILDREN

a. Mercy, b.     1638; d. Nov. 25, 1712; m. Samuel Freeman.
b. Edward, b.    ; d.    (?), 1727; m. Mary Pabodie.
c. Alice, b.     1646; d. Mar. 5, 1719; m. Col. Benjamin Church.
d. Nathaniel, b.    ; 1648; d. Jan. 14, 1711; m. Desire Gray.
e. Mary, b.    1650; d.    1719; m. David Alden.
f. Elizabeth, b.    ; d.    ; m. Lt. William Fobes (?).
g. Priscilla, b.    ; d.    ; m. 1st Samuel Talbot; m. 2nd John Irish.
h. William, b.    1659; d. June 25, 1718; m.

11b. Southworth, Thomas[11] (Edward[10]), born Leyden 1616 (?); died Dec. 8, 1669; married Elizabeth Reynor, daughter of Rev. John Reynor.
His will is dated Nov. 18, 1669, and witnessed by John Morton and George Bonum.

CHILD

a. Elizabeth, b.    ; d.    ; m. Joseph Howland.

# CHILTON

I. **Chilton, James**[1], born probably Canterbury, Kent Co., Eng., about 1563; died on the Mayflower in Cape Cod Harbor Dec. 18, 1620; his wife died at Plymouth early in 1621, after Jan. 11.

In 1593 he was a citizen and tailor of Canterbury, England, and active in the affairs of the Merchant Adventurers. The Chilton family was, no doubt, of French descent, but were very early settlers in England. The name may originate from the chalk cliffs of Dover, or more likely from the Crusaders, for when Robert of Normandy embarked for the Holy Land, names were then bestowed which have been retained by their descendants in America.

In 1066 William of Normandy set sail for the conquest of England, and inscribed on his banner roll was Sir John Chilton. No doubt, he shared the spoils bestowed by the conqueror.

CHILDREN ST. PAUL'S, CANTERBURY, ENG.

IIa. Isabella, bp. Jan. 15, 1586; d.      ; m. Roger **Chandler.**

CHILDREN ST. MARTIN'S, CANTERBURY, ENG.

b. Elizabeth, bp. July 14, 1594; d.      ; m.      .
c. James, bp. Aug. 22, 1596; d. young; m.——.
d. Mary, bp.      ; d. about 1593; m.——.
c. Joel, bp.      ; d. about 1593; m.——.

CHILDREN ST. PETER'S, SANDWICH

f. Christian, bp. July 26, 1600; d.      ; m.      .
g. James, bp. Sept. 11, 1602; d.      ; m.      .
IIIh. Mary, bp.      (?) 1607; d. before May 11, 1679; m. John **Winslow.**

# CHANDLER

IIa. **Chilton, Isabella**[2] (James[1]), bapt. Jan. 15, 1586; married Roger **Chandler** at Leyden July 21, 1615; she is called "Isabella **Tgrilton**" in the Leyden Records.

CHILD

a. Sarah, b.      ; d.      ; m. John **Leonard.**

# WINSLOW

IIIh. **Chilton, Mary**[2] (James[1]), born 1607 (?), Canterbury, Eng.; died in Boston, Mass., before May 11, 1679; married John

**Winslow** Oct. 12, 1624; born Droitwich, Eng.; died Boston, 1674. Her will is interesting and is on record in Suffolk County Registry of Probate, Vol. VI, p. 300, 301. The original will is preserved, together with bond of administration, signed by her son John, and son-in-law Richard **Middlecott.** The original inventory is missing, but a copy is in Vol. XII, p. 314-315 of the Probate Records.

### CHILDREN

a. John, b.　　; d.　　; m. 1st Elizabeth　　; m. 2nd Judith

b. Sussanah, b.　　(?) 1628; d.　　(?) 1688; m. Robert **Latham.**

c. Mary, b.　　(?) 1630; d.　　(?) 1663; m. Edward **Gray.**

d. Sarah, b.　　; d.　　1727; m. 1st Myles **Standish;** m. 2nd Tobias **Paine;** m. 3rd Richard **Middlecott.**

e. Edward, b.　　(?) 1634; d.　　1682; m. 1st Sarah **Hilton;** m. 2nd Elizabeth **Hutchinson.**

f. Joseph, b.　　; d.　　1679; m. Sarah　.

g. Samuel, b.　　(?) 1641; d.　　1680; m. Hannah **Briggs.**

h. Isaac, b.　　(?) 1644; d.　　1670; m. Mary **Norvell** ——.

i. Anne, b.　　; d.　　; m. (　　) **Le Blond.**

j. Benjamin, b. Aug. 12, 1653; d.　　1673; m.——.

k. Mercy, b.　　; d.　　; m.　　.

# BRADFORD

The surname is derived from a place, Broadford or Bradenford in England. There are two ancient towns of this name. Wiltshire has one, and Yorkshire near Leeds.

During the sixteenth century members of the family developed a strong desire for liberty of self expression and opportunity. They became active dissenters, some of them encouraged in that direction by progressive teaching at Cambridge. For instance, John Bradford, Prebend of St. Paul and a noted preacher, born in Manchester, 1510, was executed for dissenting opinions by Queen Mary on July 1, 1555. A number of his friends and associates including Rev. John Rogers a few months before suffered the same fate.

The close relationships of the early families have not been established, but it is known that they were residing in Bentley, five miles from Austerfield, just north of Doncaster, during the time of Henry VI, and probably before. They were, apparently, of good sound yeomanry stock possessing comfortable estates for that period, although suffering very severe tax restrictions on the part of both "nobles" and "clergy," who were constantly demanding means of support from "their people" without performing any useful service whatsoever. Now and then, a member of the "clergy". close enough to the "people" would perform a needed duty, but, for the most part, the "nobles" were a dead load on society, doing nothing at all for their food, shelter and clothing. The following line seems to be accepted:

I. **Bradfuth,** Robert[1] of Bentley, England, b. 1450; d. 1523.

II. **Bradfouth,** Peter[2] (Robert[1]), b. 1475; d. 1542.

III. **Bradfouth,** Robert[3] (Peter[2], Robert[1]), b. 1500; d. 1552-3.

IV. **Bradford,** William[4] (Robert[3], Peter[2], Robert[1]), removed to Austerfield about 1557, and became a tenant of the Manor there. In 1576 he bought a free-hold estate. At this time he and John **Hanson** were the only subsidiaries there. He was taxed twenty shillings on land, and **Hanson** the same amount on goods. His grandson, the future Governor of Plymouth, resided with him after the death of William **Bradford,** Jr., in 1591. William[4] was buried in Austerfield (Osterfeldt) on Jan. 10, 1595-6, at that time located in West Riding, Yorkshire.

Va. **William,** b.     1560 (?); buried July 15, 1591; m. Alice
**Hanson.**
  b. **Thomas,** b.   ; d.   ; m.   .
  c. **Elizabeth,** bp. July 16, 1560; d.   ; m. James **Hill.**
VId. **Robert,** bp. June 25, 1561; buried Apr. 23, 1609; m.
Alice **Waigestafe.**

Va. **Bradford, William**[5] (William[4], Robert[3], Peter[2], Robert[1]),
born before 1560; buried at Austerfield July 15, 1591; married
Alice **Hanson,** daughter of John **Hanson,** July 21, 1584. She was
baptized Dec. 8, 1562, and married 2nd Robert **Briggs** Feb. 23,
1593.

CHILDREN BORN AUSTERFIELD

  a. Margaret, bp. Mar. 8, 1585; d. 1586.
  b. Alice, bp. Oct. 30, 1587; d. Jan. 30, 1607.
VIIc. William, bp. Mar. 19, 1589; d. Plymouth, Mass.

VId. **Bradford, Robert**[5] (William[4], Robert[3], Peter[2], Robert[1]),
bapt. June 25, 1561; buried Apr. 23, 1609; married Jan. 31, 1585,
Alice **Waigestafe.**
This Robert Bradford appears to have resided near Scrooby,
a few miles from Austerfield, and when the grandfather, William,
died in 1595, young William went to live with his uncle Robert
in Scrooby, or near there. At this time he was about six years
old, and no doubt his uncle started him in some of the schools
nearby. As a matter of fact, Master William Brewster had
recently returned to Scrooby Manor, about 1594, from his
duties at Court and otherwise in London, and quite possibly
was taking on a few pupils at the Manor, and young William
Bradford may have been one of the aspiring scholars.
About 1604, an old friend and neighbor of Robert Bradford
and William Brewster came back to his home and relatives in
Sturton a few miles from Scrooby. This friend was the Rev.
John Robinson, who had found it "impracticable to retain his
pastorate in Norwich owing to the restrictive policies of King
James, and found himself out of a "living," and a place to preach.
Brewster was not only an old neighbor, but also a brother
Cambridge alumnus of Robinson, and of course encouraged him
to use the Manor as a meeting place. At these meetings, Robert
Bradford and his young nephew were no doubt, attentive lis-
teners, and very sympathetic.
Robert Bradford died in 1609, leaving four minor children, and
his nineteen year old nephew William Bradford, if not apprenticed according to custom already, perhaps to William Brewster,
had to shift for himself. This may have been one of the main
reasons for his going to Holland. Several friends left for Amsterdam about this time.

CHILDREN

a. Robert, minor in 1609.
b. Mary, minor in 1609.
c. Elizabeth, minor in 1609.
d. Margaret, minor in 1609.

VIIc. **Bradford**, William[6] (William[5], William[4], Robert[3], Peter[2], Robert[1]), bapt. Austerfield, England, Mar. 19, 1589; died Plymouth, Mass., May 19, 1657; married 1st Leyden, Holland, Dorothy **May**, Nov. or Dec. 1613; born 1597 (?); accidentally drowned in Cape Cod Harbor, Dec. 17, 1620; daughter of Deacon Henry **May** of the Leyden Church; married 2nd Plymouth, Mass., Aug. 24, 1623, Alice **Carpenter**, one of the famous sisters and widow of Edward **Southworth**, born after 1590; died Plymouth Apr. 5-6, 1670. She was the daughter of Alexander **Carpenter** of Wrentham, England, and Leyden, whose family is described in this volume.

Only two and one-half miles north of Scrooby, by a path along the rich meadows of the Idle River, lies the delightful old Yorkshire village of Austerfield in the north of England. So extremely poor were the few inhabitants that in the subsidy of 1575, the only laymen having sufficient property to be rated were William Bradford, the grandfather of the Governor, and John Hanson, and these ratings were low. John **Hanson** had married Margaret **Gresham** on July 23, 1560, and the Greshams, although not of the Herald's visitations, were of a higher social status, also **Bradford** and **Hanson** were in some degree, according to the standards of the time, above their neighbors, except the vicar of the chapel, who was not subject to tax.

Old William Bradford had a son William, and Hanson had a daughter Alice, and in due time "William Bradfourth and Alice Hanson" were married June 28, 1584, and their son, the future Governor, was baptized by the Rev. Henry Fletcher at St. Helen's, the ancient and quaint little chapel of Austerfield. It is still standing.

When only about 18 months old William lost his father, who was buried July 15, 1591, and it is generally thought his mother died soon afterward, leaving him an orphan in a world of social turmoil.

The infant William was taken care of by his grandfather William until his death in 1596, when the seven-year-old lad was taken into the family of his uncle Robert, who resided on the line of, if not in Scrooby.

Brewster was now spending most of his time "in the country" (Scrooby), and it is possible that he was doing some tutoring of the boys in the neighborhood. Teaching was one of his occupations.

Robert Bradford is said to have been a man of culture, possessing a small library of English and Latin books, and his

[ 105 ]

nephew, no doubt, was encouraged in his studies, and like other English boys having relatives with sufficient means, was probably sent to some one of the numerous primary schools in the neighborhood.

However, at Scrooby Brewster had a good library and was an excellent teacher, with a fascinating background, so that the chances are that the boy from the age of seven years came under the spell of Master Brewster's teaching and personality.

Bradford, of course, was too young to have been a leader in the removal to Leyden, Holland, and then to Plymouth Plantation. However, the unexpected deaths of Gov. Christopher Martin, and then Gov. John Carver, together with the deaths of most of the Merchant Adventurers from London, during the winter of 1620-21, placed a rather heavy responsibility on Master William Brewster, who probably was not very strong physically, and most certainly did not care to assume the burden of detailed management.

Therefore, Bradford assumed the Governorship of Plymouth Plantation and Colony for many years, with his old friend and teacher William Brewster, at his side to extend needed advice and counsel.

In 1630, according to Bradford, he began to "scribble" on the writing of the "History of Plymouth Plantation," which naturally must have been with the full knowledge and active collaboration of his teacher and guide, whose notes and testimony must have been freely used throughout the history.

It is impossible to establish the part that Brewster had in the writing of this famous history, but it must have been a very important one indeed. For some reason none of Brewster's many writings, notes and papers have been preserved. Not even a will was found. For that matter, the Bradford manuscript is about the only writing preserved by either one.

So far as the contents of the history is concerned, no one could have known more about them than Bradford's teacher, and without doubt full advantage was taken of that fact.

When Brewster died in 1644, the history was about complete, and when Bradford died in 1657, very little was noted in his will about the manuscript, unless this is supposed to cover the item:

"I commend unto youer Wisdome and Descretions some smale bookes written by my owne hand to bee improved as you see meet."

Of course, this was a "Nunckupative" will taken down in the presence of Thomas Cushman, Thomas Southworth and Nathaniel Morton.

Now, this Nathaniel Morton forthwith conformed to the above suggestion, and took unto himself probably every scrap of paper, from which he evolved his "New England's Memorial,"

1669, which cannot be said to be an improvement over the original, although adding an important fact or so, for some reason omitted from the Bradford work.

The will and inventory of Governor William Bradford are recorded in the Ply. Col. Wills and Invs., Vol. II, Pt. I, p. 53-59.

P. 53. The last Will and Testament Nunckupative of M^r William Bradford seni^r: Deceased May the Ninth 1657 and exhibited to the court held att Plymouth June 3d, 1657.

Mr. William Bradford seni^r: being weake in body, but in prfect memory haveing Defered the forming of his Will in hopes of haveing the healp of M^r Thomas Prence therein; feeling himselfe very weake and drawing on to the conclusion of his mortall life spake as followeth: I could have Desired abler then myselfe in the Deposing of that I have; how my estate is none knowes better than youerselfe, said hee to Lieftenant Southworth; I have Deposed to John and William alreddy theire proportions of land which they are possessed of;

My Will is that what I stand Ingaged to p^rforme to my Children and others may bee made good out of my estate that my Name Suffer not;

ffurther my Will is that my son Joseph bee made in some sort equall to his brethern out of my estate;

My further Will is that my Deare & loveing Wife Allice Bradford shalbee the sole Exequitrix of my estate; and for her future maintainance my Will is that my Stoeke in the Kennebecke Trad. be reserved for her Comfortable Subsistence as farr as it will extend and soe further in any way such as may bee Judged best for her;

I further request and appoint my welbeloved Christian ffrinds M^r Thomas Prence, Captaine Thomas Willett and Lieftenant Thomas Southworth to bee the Supperrissors for the Desposing of my estate according to the p^rmises Confiding much in theire faithfulnes.

I comend unto youer Wisdome and Descretions some smale bookes written by my owne hand to bee Improved as you shall see meet: In special I Comend to you a little book with a blacke cover wherein there is a word to Plymouth, a word to Boston and a word to New England with sundry usefull verses. These pticulars were expressed by the said William Bradford Gov^r the 9th of May 1657 in the p^rsence of us, Thomas Cushman, Thomas Southworth, Nathaniell Morton: whoe were Deposed before the court held att Plymouth the 3rd of June 1657, to the truth of the abovesaid Will that it is the last Will and Testament of the abovesaid M^r William Bradford sen^r.

(P. 54). "A Trew Inventory"

[ 107 ]

A very complete and interesting inventory of the estate was placed before the court at Plymouth June 3, 1657. It was taken May 22, 1657, by Thomas Cushman and John Dunham, and signed by them on the same date. This was only 18 days after the death of Bradford.

The inventory included many items of "beding and other thinges in y$^e$ old parler" such as a "feather bed," a "canvas bed," "green rugg," "blanketts," "old curtaines Darnickes & an old paire of say curtaines," "Court Cubbard," several "lether chaires," "Table & forme and 2 stooles," "Case with six knives," "3 matchcock musketts," "a Snaphance Muskett," "a birding peece and an other smale peece," "a pistoll and Cutlas," and numerous other items in the room called "ye old parlor."

A number of items were found "in the great rome" such as several "Carved Chaires," "3 striped Carpetts," "10 Cushens," "a Causlett and one headpeece," "1 fouling peece without a locke, 3 old barrells of guns, one paire of old bandeleers and a rest."

There were a large number of "Linnin" and "pewter" items, while in the "Kitchen" were, "ffrench kittles," "brasee kittles," "Duch pan," "brasse skimmer," "iron skilletts," "4 Dozen Trenchers," "Juggs" and the like. Bradford's wardrobe shows that he was a neat dresser, for the items "in the New Chamber his clothes" include such articles as "a stuffe suite with silver buttons & a Coate," "cloth cloake faced with Taffety and lineed throw with baies," "a sad coullered cloth suite," "a Turkey Grogorum suite an cloake," "a paire of black briches and a rid wast coat," "an old green goune," "an old vidett coullered cloake," "2 hattes a blacke one and a coullered one," "a great chaire," and other items. The items of "the plate" include, "one great beer bowle," "2 wine cupps," "a trencher salt and a Drame cup," "9 silver spoones and the like."

The takers of the inventory found "In the Studdie" the usual "Deske," "2 Cases with some emty bottles," and other items, but the most informing of the articles were, of course, "his bookes," about 100 in all. They include "Mr. Perkins workes," "the Guiciardin," "Peter Martire on the Romans," "Cottons Concordance," "Speeds general Description of the world," "the method of phisicke," "Gouges Domesticall Dutyes," "Dike or the Deceitfulness of mans hart," "2 bibles," "history of the Netherlands," "bodins Comons wealth," "B. Babbingtons workes," and many others.

The inventory lists a number of sheep, "a rame lambe," several horses and colts," "4 bullockes," "7 Cowes," "a bull," a number of "Calves," "hoggs," "shoats," and other live-stock.

There was quite an item of debt due the estate from "the Kennebeck Stocke Consisting in goods and Debts both English and Indians."

The inventory mentions "the house and orchyard and some smale pcells of land about the towne of Plymouth," also "2 spining wheeles & a wether."

---

NOTE: The Ms. "History of Plimouth Plantation," was in Bradford's possession, at least, until 1651 (although he did not die until 1657).

It passed to his son Major William, then to his grandson Major John Bradford, who died in 1736. The later story is well known.

Aside from the History few writings of Bradford are known to exist. There may be some hidden away in England like this Ms. was for so many years.

CHILD BORN HOLLAND 1ST WIFE

a. (?) John, b. Holland, Leyden; d. Norwich (?) 1678 (?); m. Martha[2] **Bourne** (Thomas[1]), no issue.

CHILDREN BORN PLYMOUTH 2ND WIFE

VIIIb. William, b. June 17, 1623-4; d. Feb. 20, 1703-4; m. 1st Alice[2] **Richards** (Thomas[1]); m. 2nd Mary (    ) **Wiswell**, wid.; m. 3rd Mary (**Atwood**) **Holmes**, wid.

IXc. Joseph, b. May 1630; d. July 10, 1715; m. Jael[2] **Hobart** (Rev. Peter[1]).

d. Mercy, b. before 1627; d.       ; m. Benjamin **Vermayes.**

VIIIb. **Bradford,** Major William[7] (William[6], William[5], William[4], Robert[3], Peter[2], Robert[1]); born Plymouth June 17, 1623-4; died Saturday, Feb. 20, 1703-4; married 1st about Apr., 1650, Alice **Richards**, born 1627, died Dec. 12, 1671, daughter of Thomas **Richards** of Weymouth; married 2nd Mrs. Mary **Wiswell;** married 3rd Mrs. Mary **Holmes,** died Jan. 6, 1714-8; widow of Rev. John **Holmes** of Duxbury, and daughter of John **Atwood** of Plymouth.

Major Bradford lived at Jones River near Kingston, in the same place and in the same house where his father, the Governor, lived 1627-1647. Here he reared his family of 15 children. He was an assistant Deputy Governor and one of Governor Andros' Council in 1687, and was chief military officer of Plymouth Colony.

## CHILDREN BY 1ST WIFE ALICE RICHARDS

a. John, b. Feb. 20, 1651; d. Dec. 8, 1736; m. Mercy **Warren.**
b. William, b. Mar. 11, 1655; d.     1687; m. Rebecca **Bartlett.**
c. Thomas, b.     1657; d. Norwich, Ct., 1708; m. 1st Anna **Smith**; m. 2nd Priscilla **Mason.**
d. Alice, b.     1661; d.     ; m. 1st William **Adams**; m. 2nd James **Fitch.**
e. Mercy, bp. Sept. 2, 1660; d. Hartford, Ct.; m. Samuel **Steele.**
f. Hannah, b. May 9, 1662; d. May 27, 1738; m. Josiah **Ripley.**
g. Melatiah, b.     1667; d. Killingworth, Ct.; m. 1st John **Steele**; m. 2nd Samuel **Stevens.**
h. Samuel, b.     1668; d. Apr. 11, 1714; m. Hannah **Rogers.**
i. Mary, b.     1669; d. Oct. 10, 1720; m. William **Hunt.**
j. Sarah, b.     1671; d.     1704; m. Kenelen **Baker.**

### CHILD BY 2ND WIFE MARY WISWELL, WIDOW

k. Joseph, b.     1674; d. Norwich, Ct.; m. 1st Anna **Fitch**; m. 2nd Mary (**Sherwood**) **Fitch**, wid.

### CHILDREN BY 3RD WIFE MARY HOLMES, WIDOW

l. Israel, b.     1678; d. Mar. 26, 1760; m. Sarah **Bartlett.**
m. Ephraim, b.     1680; d.     ; m. Elizabeth **Brewster.**
n. David, b.     ; d. Mar. 16, 1730; m. Elizabeth **Finney.**
o. Hezekiah, b.     ; d.     ; m. Mary **Chandler.**

IXc. **Bradford,** Joseph[7] (William[6], William[5], William[4], Robert[3], Peter[2], Robert[1]); born Plymouth 1630; died July 10, 1715, at Kingston, age 85; the gravestone is on "Burial Hill"; married Jael **Hobart** May 25, 1664; daughter of Rev. Peter **Hobart**, the first minister of Hingham. She was bapt. Dec. 30, 1643, and died Apr. 14, 1730.

Joseph resided in Kingston (then Plymouth) on the Jones River, half a mile from its mouth at a place called "Flat House Dock." This portion was set off as Kingston in 1726.

### CHILDREN BORN PLYMOUTH

a. Joseph, b. Apr. 18, 1665; d.     ; m.     .
b. Elisha, b.     ; d.     ; m. 1st Hannah **Cole**; m. 2nd Bathsheba **LeBrocke.**

Refs. 544, 289, 291, 213, 212, 123, 234, 235, 248, 233, 232, 9.

# POLITICAL, ECONOMIC AND SOCIAL ENGLAND
## 1580-1620

The older New England Planters, especially of that group who came over on the Mayflower, were, of course, more or less inspired by passing events during the years within their lifetime of personal experience, and, not less so, perhaps, by vivid memories of stories of intrigue and burning at the stake told to them by parents and grandparents who had themselves, in many instances, been active participants in some great moments of history, during the reigns of Henry VIII, Edward VI, Mary and Elizabeth.

The Virginia Company of London, 1606-1624 (?) was a body of determined men, composed for the most part of members and affiliated participants through various commercial companies and "Guilds," such as the companies of Drapers, Clothworkers, Grocers, Goldsmiths, Ironmongers, Merchant Tailors and others.

In June, 1619, soon after Sir Thomas Smith handed over the treasurership of the company to Sir Edwin Sandys, an audit was made, including,

"The Names of the Adventurers with their several summes adventured, paid to Sir Thomas Smith, Knight, late Treasurer of the Company for Virginia."

The list is most illuminating, giving in detail the names of individual share-holders since 1609, and perhaps in some instances, from 1607, also the names of eighteen commercial companies and the number of shares or investment by each company.

The planting of English Colonies in America must be credited largely to the determined enterprise of these individual share-holders, and more especially, to the larger number of unnamed members of the commercial companies. The leading spirits among these English Colonial planters, particularly from 1609-1624, and possibly to 1636, came from the membership of the Virginia Company itself, or from their close friends and relatives.

There were few "yeomen" or farmers among the planters of New England before 1636. They were, for the most part, artisans or small tradesmen, having sufficient funds or credit to finance their passage to the Colonies. Many of these "adventurers" were from the best homes in England, the younger children of successful parents, and had either just about begun an "apprenticeship" or had completed one. These apprenticeships were much sought after by the high and low classes of England for their younger children. It should be remembered that the eldest son received the family estate, while younger brothers and sisters had to shift for themselves. The conditions are about the same in England today, with very slight changes in legal rights.

[ 111 ]

The apprenticeship practice during the reigns of Elizabeth and James explains, to a large extent, the misuse of the word "servant." They do not have the same meaning, although especially in England the word is often used in connection with anyone who has to earn his living by working for someone other than himself. This even applies to government workers.

During the period 1580-1620 the "Commercial Revolution" in England was gaining strength, and the successful merchants were becoming more powerful at Court, especially so, after the defeat of the Spanish Armada in 1588, which must have been a great event in the lives of certain Mayflower Planters, together with that great drama the year before of the trial and execution of Queen Mary.

Naturally, the political atmosphere was charged with attempts of the Court or Crown to stifle some of the growing strength of the Merchants, many of whom were of "Puritan" leanings, even "Separatists" at heart, for they knew that free enterprise and a "State Church" could hardly be expected to exist together without serious friction regarding imposition of taxes and the like.

The close advisors of Elizabeth, such as Burghley, Essex, and Walsingham, were inclined to favor the merchants, and their "Puritan" ideas, although the Queen was rather fearful of their growing power in the Commons.

About this time, or a short while before, laws were passed punishing "vagrancy," which was quite inclusive, by "whipping, jailing, boring the ears and death for a second offense."

Also, it was ordered that "justices and mayors make registers of the impotent poor, and find them habitations at the expense of the inhabitants of their locality."

The rising power of the merchants is shown by this law "compelling every person above seven years of age to wear on Sundays and holidays a cap of wool, knit, made thickened, and dressed in England by some of the trade of cappers, under the forfeiture of three farthings for every day's neglect, certain classes are excepted (i.e., the benefited classes)."

Parliament was not ready in 1580 to grant many of the famous "Four Freedoms," if any, and forthwith sent young Peter Wentworth to the Tower when he protested against the Queen's interference in "freedom of speech."

In 1586 tobacco was introduced into England by Sir Walter Raleigh and Sir Francis Drake (some writers state by Sir John Hawkins, 1565).

However, it was promptly named a "stinking" weed and a proclamation issued against its use.

Constant attempts were being made to murder the Queen, for instance in 1594, Patrick York, an Irish fencing master, is hired by the Spaniards to do the job but failed, and on June 7,

1594, Roderigo, a Jewish royal physician is charged with being bribed to poison the Queen. He was forthwith executed.

Up in Scotland, in 1597, the King orders the prosecution of a whole "assize," for acquitting persons charged with witchcraft.

Between 1590-1600, hair-powder came into use, tea was introduced, and potatoes were generally used in England, while in Scotland in 1598 the first coach was put into use. It caused something of a riot, and was considered quite "effeminate." In fact, in 1601, the English Parliament passed the "anti-effeminacy" act forbidding men to ride in coaches. For hundreds of years real he-men had ridden horseback, and this modern wheeled contraption should only be used sparingly by the weaker sex.

On Dec. 31, 1600, the East India Company is established by charter, and the great commercial docks at Rotherhithe are erected. London is now a city built almost entirely of wood, and having a population of around 300,000. Although Spain had been defeated in 1588, and England seemed well on the road to sea control, absolute confidence was soon qualified by the conviction that the Spaniard would come again. In fact, an atmosphere of uncertainty prevailed throughout the rest of Elizabeth's reign. The fear of attempted invasion was uppermost in the mind of the Queen, and in 1596, Sir Henry Knyvett published a pamphlet on "The Defence of the Realm," which advocated the compulsory military training of all men aged eighteen to fifty. Throughout the nineties there were continual invasion scares.

The offices of Earl Marshal and Master of the Ordnance, temporarily in abeyance, were re-created, and a committee of national defense sat in London, under the presidency of the Earl of Essex, to co-ordinate and systematize the mobilization. Essex was a good friend to Davison, and must have been well known to Brewster, Sandys and other dissenters. His political affiliations were probably the real cause of his execution in 1601. The Liberal party in Parliament was becoming too powerful, even for Elizabeth. Essex was known as the "protector" of the Puritans.

The situation in Ireland was also a constant worry. The Church was still a bitter foe and hoped for the downfall of England through the forces of Spain and Ireland. In 1596 the Earl of Tyrone entered into military relations with Spain. Scotland was none too friendly and not above acts of duplicity.

Church followers were carefully watched, for Elizabeth was in continual fear of the shadowy figure of the assassin. It became difficult for petitioners and even ambassadors to gain access to her presence.

The economic conditions during this period were deplorable. There had been about eleven years of good trade (1576-87), but these were followed by a series of poor years. Industrial and commercial undertakings were lagging, and severe losses were being incurred by the companies trading beyond the seas. There were several reasons for this depression.

(a) Disturbing effects of the war.
(b) Depredations of the Dunkirk "pirates."
(c) Competition of the Dutch as an exporting country.
(d) Bad harvests 1594-8, 1600—corn rose in price.
(e) Plague (sickness) 1592, 1602, 1603—great numbers died.
(f) Distress in the clothing districts.
(g) Sheep farmers could not find a market.
(h) Merchants falling into bankruptcy.
(i) Clothiers could find no market for cloth.
(j) Occasional bread riots.
(k) Heavy taxation due to war—trebled from 1589-1603.
(l) Parliament revolted at constant demand for money.
(m) The Queen sold crown lands to keep solvent.

The last years of Elizabeth must have been very lonely. She had outlived her generation. The men who had served her so ably had all passed away. Leicester had died in 1588, Walsingham 1590, and Burghley in 1598. Her old secretary Davison, however, was still alive.

The epidemic of 1603 began in the parish of Stepney, which then extended from Shoreditch to Blackwall, about the time of Elizabeth's death in March. The great crowds assembling in London for the coronation of James probably caused the spread of the infection. Deaths mounted to a thousand in a week. Funerals, according to Dekker, followed so close that "three thousand mourners went as if trooping together, with rue and wormwood stuffed into their ears and nostrils." On July 18, 1603, the King's coronation progress extended only from the Westminster Bridge (a landing-stage on the river) to the Abbey, instead of passing, in the usual way, from the Tower to Westminister.

The victims of this frightful scourge came mostly from the crowded lanes of the "sinfully polluted suburbs," and "such as do not greatly regard clean and sweet keeping, and where many are pestered together in alleys and houses."

It was near the end of November 1603 that deaths dropped to one hundred a week. The epidemic had taken one-tenth of London's population, about 33,347.

King James granted a license to reopen the Curtain and Boar's Head theatres "as soon as the plague decreases to thirty deaths per week in London." This condition came about the following January.

The Plague bore hardest on the "poor players," because the crowds to see stage plays, bear-fights, dog-fights and the like was a chief means of spreading infection.

[ 114 ]

The playhouses and actors did not stand high in the estimation of preachers. One preacher at Paul's Cross on Nov. 3, 1597, took as his text "Woe to that abominable, filthy, and cruel city." He goes on "Behold the sumptuous theatre-houses, a continual monument of London's prodigal folly! But I understand they are now forbidden because of the plague."

During Shakespeare's time, when he was producing his historical plays and comedies, 1594 to 1603, there were few interruptions because of the plague, but from 1603 to 1610, the stage was greatly hindered by almost continual epidemics. His plays, for the most part, were then given before the Court or in the houses of the nobility, but seldom before the populace in theatres. It is quite probable that Sandys and Brewster, during this period, through their mutual friend, the Earl of Southampton, became acquainted with Shakespeare, who was, himself, a decided dissenter, if not a Puritan.

In 1603 England had lost its more or less liberal Queen, by death from natural causes, and James I is proclaimed King in violation of the will of Henry VIII.

The new King was arrogant, and difficulties for the "Patriot" or "Liberal" party in Parliament began to accumulate. Persecution of the "Puritans" and "Separatists" became intolerable.

A law was passed forcing public attendance on the community parish of the established church. However, one whole section of London, called "Duke's Place," was without a parish church, so that the "Puritan" and "Separatist" merchants and others interested became residents of that place, and held free religious meetings there for some years.

London was without sanitary safeguards. They were substantially unknown at the time. The "plague" prevailed, causing frightful misery and death for thousands. On June 1, 1603, a man is whipped through the streets for going to court when his house was infected with the plague.

In spite of all this social and economic misfortune, our Mayflower Planters were witness to a decided advance in literature, and some scientific attainment. Brewster, at least, kept himself well posted along these lines. In 1588 a first English work on shorthand appeared, by Dr. Timothy Bright, entitled "Characterie, or the arte of shorte, swifte and secrete writing."

Then in 1589 Thomas Nash writes his "Anatomy of absurditie." This same year the famous Marprelate Tracts appear.

In 1590 Thomas Lodge writes "Rosa-Lynde," and about this time Edmund Spencer comes along with his "Faerie Queene."

Sometime in 1590-4 Shakespeare began on his famous collection of plays. Marlowe, Chapman, Jonson, Marston, Stow and Daniel were other writers of the period.

Ben Jonson must have appealed to the Planters in his "The Silent Woman," 1609.

[ 115 ]

In 1594 Shakespeare's Globe Theatre was built in London, he being part owner and proprietor. Some of his plays were produced here. The building was of horse shoe form, partly covered with thatch.

No doubt Brewster, being the "teacher" of the Mayflower Planters, was familiar with the philosophical works of Lord Francis Bacon (1561-1626), especially his "Advancement of Learning," 1604, and perhaps "Novum Organum," 1620. These works set forth the simple need of laborious observation of facts before assuming a general principle. Strange to state, this apparently obvious idea was lost to ancient and medieval thought. Aristotle, for instance, assumed some general principle and tried to "deduce" the consequences.

Whether knowingly or otherwise, our New England forefathers adopted the Baconian idea of inductive reasoning, thereby developing to a high degree the inventive faculty. They were careful observers of existing facts and consequences, and then proceeded to the general principle. The Patent Office holds proof of their clear thinking.

The Mayflower Planters were much better informed on the history of their times than past generations, both through their teachers, or church affiliations, and through printed matter freely circulated.

Somewhere it is written that human civilization depends for progress on reason and emotions, which are expressed in terms of science and art. All great periods in history are marked by advances in art appreciation, sciences and invention. Sometimes one invention can cause something like a world revolution until people and conditions are adjusted to its use. For instance, the airplane has made it necessary to readjust trade centers and routes throughout the world, thereby causing much temporary conflict of interests, and even bloodshed.

There was a great development in the English language and literature during the sixteenth century, which must have affected the actions and thought of the Mayflower Planters. It may be argued that they were uninformed and perhaps illiterate. The facts are otherwise. Both the Leyden and London planters at Plymouth were distinctly cosmopolitan, imaginative, inquisitive, intelligent and well informed. For years they had listened to the great preachers of London and Leyden, most of them independent and instructive. Many of the leading Planters could read and write, and eagerly kept posted on the printed matter freely circulated among them, sometimes to the great disgust of King James.

Of course, Chaucer wrote his "Canterbury Tales" in the fourteenth century, and their archaic words make difficult reading. However, the great stride in England was from the appearance in 1551, almost within the lifetime of the Mayflower group, of the English version of Sir Thomas More's "Utopia," which sets forth an ideal state.

Then followed Granmer's Book of Common Prayer and King James version of the Bible, Edmund Spenser, Shakespeare, Ben Jonson, Marlowe, Francis Bacon, Richard Hooker, Thomas Hobbes, Jeremy Taylor and others.

The Leyden group were fortunate in having access to such outstanding teachers as Brewster and Robinson, and to the many literary advantages of the city. Of course, in Plymouth Brewster's famous collection of books and his house became what might be rightly called the first "Public Library" in America.

Latin was the language of the Middle Ages, but spoken languages were developing among the nations of western Europe, entirely unlike Latin. These were known as the "vernacular languages," mostly in use by the lower classes.

About the time (1480) printing by movable type came into use, scholars were encouraging the study of the "pagan" classics, Virgil, Cicero, Caesar, Tacitus, and the comedies of Plautus and Terence. Petrarch and Erasmus were the great Latin writers. Greek literature was also being revived, yet the masses, of course, did not understand these languages.

During the sixteenth century with its artistic developments, discoveries, religious unrest, national rivalries and social debates, the people, especially the "commercial middle class," clamored to understand, and this demand resulted in introducing the "national literatures" on a large scale, including works in Italian, French, Spanish, Portuguese, German and English. These were the written forms of the "vernacular tongues." Brewster probably could read and write in several of these languages. Elizabeth was a linguist of no mean ability herself, and preferred aides having like attainments.

The sixteenth century, of the "Mayflower Planters," may therefore be considered the cradle of the best known modern languages.

Of course, Italian prose and poetry, sometime before, had been written by Dante, Petrarch and Boccaccio, and later by Machiavelli (1469-1527), who founded the "modern" science of politics and taught the idea, which has been so willingly and completely adopted by politicians, that "a ruler, bent on exercising a benevolent despotism, is justified in employing any means to achieve his purpose."

Italy also gave the world Ariosto (1474-1533), and the "mad" Tasso (1544-1595).

In France, Francis I set up presses, established the College of France and pensioned native writers. However, the only French writer of note in the sixteenth century was the much misunderstood Rabelais (1490-1553).

In Spain, Cervantes (1547-1616), published "Don Quixote," the like of which never appeared before or since. Then there was Lope de Vega (1562-1635), with his many plays. Camoens (1524-1580), a poet of Portugal, sang high praise for Vasco da Gama, the explorer.

Of course, in Germany, Martin Luther had turned from Latin to German, so that he could reach the ears of the common people. His translation of the Bible would have been a tremendous undertaking in any language or age.

The revival of Greek and Roman culture in Europe from the fourteenth to the sixteenth century resulted in ransacking the monasteries for hidden and lost manuscripts.

Art of the Middle Ages had been strictly limited to expressions permitted by the Church. The result is found in Gothic cathedrals, pointing their roofs and lofty spires toward heaven, in the mysterious carvings on stone and wood, in the imaginative portraiture of saints, richly stained glass, spiritual organ music, and the story of the fall and redemption of the human race.

However, classical art became popular again. The painters, sculptors and architects sought models, not alone Christian, but also in the pagan Greek and Roman forms. The union of these two forms brought forth an outburst of artistic energy. The resulting art-expression is the foundation of our present day love of beautiful things.

The rigid straight and plain line of the ancient Greek temples, or the gentle curve of the Roman dome was substituted for the fanciful lofty Gothic. A rounded arch replaced the pointed. The old Greek forms, Doric, Ionic and Corinthian, were dug out of a dim past, and set forth in most beautiful form by the great artists Raphael (1483-1520), Michelangelo (1475-1564), Leonardo da Vinci (1452-1519), and others.

Naturally the first English planters of colonies in America could not clearly define the general movement in which they were such important actors.

They simply knew that for centuries their ancestors had managed to eke out a precarious existence by toiling early and late with the hoe and spade on land belonging to the lord of the manor, with absolutely no hope of owning land themselves.

For no apparent logical reason their ancestors for several hundred years, through this toil and sweat, had paid tribute to the lord of the manor and to the clergy of the established church.

But, after hundreds of years something had really happened. They were, at last, in a new virgin country unfettered by nobles or clergy. Land, to them, was the highest form of personal possession, and here it was, almost for the asking, and in abundance.

More than that they were in the midst of a great "Commercial Revolution," the scope of which even to this day is not clear.

The influence of the nobles and clergy were to steadily decline, and the numbers, ability and importance of traders, promoters, moneyed interests, in fact all those identified with the new wealth being created, such as the lawyers, doctors, professors, engineers and merchants, would, one day, in their own interests, overturn monarchy, nobility and the church. In effect, the great middle-class (bourgeoisie) would then be supreme.

The rival aristocracies of birth and "bourgeoisie," however, are faced with an ever-present danger. The huge mass of "common" people are always in the great majority, a fact which makes any form of government an uncertain experiment. A vote for everyone cannot be conducive to sound government, unless everyone is a thoroughly responsible person adapted to fit into the scheme of things as set up by the original planners, or the government will eventually fall.

---

Refs. 417, 418, 419, 420, 421, 414, 411, 436, 444, 446, 114, 115, 116, 117, 119.

# MORTON

34. **Ring,** Mary[3] (Deborah[2] **Hopkins,** Stephen[1]); married John[3] **Morton** (his 2nd wife); son of John[2] **Morton** (George[1]). He resided in Plymouth.

### CHILDREN BY HIS 1ST WIFE

193. Child, b.     ; d.     ; m.     .
194. Joanna, b. Feb. 1682; d.     ; m.     .
195. Phebe, b. July 7, 1685; d.     ; m.     .

### CHILDREN BY MARY RING

196. Mary, b. Dec. 15, 1689; d.     ; m. Thomas **Thomson.**
197. John, b. June, 1693 d.     ; m.     .
198. Hannah, b. Sept. 1, 1694; d.     ; m. John **Hodges.**
199. Capt. Ebenezer, b. Oct. 19, 1696; d.     ; m. Mercy **Foster.**
200. Deborah, b. Sept. 15, 1698; d.     ; m. Jonathan **Inglee.**
201. Pensis, b. Nov. 27, 1700; d.     ; m.     .

Refs. 85, 182, 183, 185, 170, 184.

# MORTON

2253    I. **Morton,** George[1], born York, England; married Juliana **Carpenter** at Leyden, July 23, 1612; born about 1583; died Plymouth Feb. 19, 1644-45; daughter of Alexander **Carpenter.**

George Morton was a member of the Leyden congregation under Robinson, probably because it was the available English church at that place. Like many of the other members he was a merchant or small trader from York, England.

He came to New England in the ship "Anne" in June, 1623, along with Alice (Carpenter) Southworth, and others.

### CHILDREN

  a. Hon. Nathaniel, b.     1613; d.     ; m. Lydia **Cooper.**
IIb. Patience, b.     1615; d.     1691; m. John **Faunce.**
  c. John, b.     1616; d.     ; m. Lettice (     ).
  d. Sarah, b.     1618; d.     1694; m. George **Bonum.**
  e. Ephraim, b.     1623; d.     ; m. Ann **Cooper.**

Refs. 182, 183.

# FAUNCE

2245

**IIb. Morton,** Patience[2] (George[1]); born 1615; died 1691; married John **Faunce.** - 2244

He came in the "Anne," 1623.

### CHILDREN

a. Priscilla, b.     ; d.     ; m. Joseph **Warren.**
b. Mary, b. July 25, 1658; d.     ; m. William **Harlow.**
c. Patience, b. Nov. 20, 1661; d.     ; m. John **Holmes.**
d. Sarah, b. Feb. 26, 1663; d.     ; m. 1st Edward **Doty**; m. 2nd John **Buck.**
e. Thomas, b.     1647; d.     ; m.     .
f. Elizabeth, b. Mar. 23, 1648; d.     ; m. Isaac **Robinson.**
g. Mercy, b. Apr. 10, 1651; d.     ; m. Nathaniel **Holmes.**
h. Joseph, b. May 14, 1653; d.     ; m.     .
i. John, b.     ; d.     ; m.     .

Refs. 182, 183, 298.

# CARPENTER

The Carpenter Family has been traced back several generations to as follows:

2342 Gen. 1. John **Carpenter,** member of Parliament about 1300.
2340 Gen. 2. Richard, born 1335, buried in St. Martin's.
2338 Gen. 3. John, brother of famous Town Clerk of London.
2336 Gen. 4. John.
2334 Gen. 5. William, born 1440; died 1520.
2332 Gen. 6. James.
2330 Gen. 7. John.
2238 Gen. 8. William.
2259 Gen. 9. Alexander, of Wrington, Somersetshire.

**I. Carpenter,** Alexander[1] (9th Generation from the first John); resided at Wrington, Somersetshire, England, about eight miles from Bristol. He removed to Holland and became, with his wife and five daughters, a member of the church at Leyden.

[ 121 ]

## CHILDREN (KNOWN)

a. Julia Ann, b. Eng. 1583; d. Plymouth Feb. 19, 1664; m. George **Morton.**

b. Agnes, b.    1585; d. Leyden before 1617; m. Samuel **Fuller.**

c. Alice, b.    1590; d. Plymouth Mar. 26, 1670; m. William **Bradford.**

d. Mary, b.    1595; d. Plymouth Mar. 20, 1687; unmarried.

e. Priscilla, b.    1597; d. Duxbury Dec. 29, 1689; m. 1st William **Wright;** m. 2nd John **Cooper.**

The five Carpenter sisters hold an unique and romantic position of honor among the first comers to New England. They were extraordinary; four of these sisters left the impress of sterling characters upon the descendants of Bradford, Morton, Fuller and Wright, many of whom have been men of note and ability.

Even Mary, the unmarried sister, had an interesting life. After the death of her mother in the beautiful English village of Wrington, she became lonesome. William Bradford, her brother-in-law, in far off New England, wrote to her a letter about the year 1645, which is still in existence. It is directed

"To Mary Carpenter at Wrington in Somersetshire x x x x this letter to be left at the house of Joseph Leggatt near the sign of the rose in Ratcliffe Street in Bristol to be conveyed as addressed."

This letter brought her to New England, where she died at Plymouth or Duxbury. The following note, in part, of a church record is quite illuminating:

"Mary Carpenter, a member of the church at Duxbury, died at Plymouth, Mar. 19-20, 1687, being nearly entered into the 91st year of her age. She was a Godly old maid—never married."

Refs. 576, 549.

## ROBINSON

I. **Robinson,** John[2] (Christopher[1]); born about 1550; died Sturton, Notts, Eng., a few miles from Scrooby Manor; married Ann (    ); died Oct. 1616-Jan. 1617.

The Robinsons of Sturton are further described in the article in this volume on Scrooby Manor and vicinity. John[2] had, very likely, taken over the family farm before 1585, and was a prosperous Nottinghamshire yeoman. He was a man of "probity and dependable character." The parish registers of Sturton do not begin until 1638; however, John Jr., was probably taken to the parish church for baptism.

The will of John[2] is recorded in York, dated Mar. 14, 1613, proved Aug. 19, 1614, and mentions sons John, William, and two sons-in-law, Roger Lawson and William Pearte "my lovinge wyfe Anne Robinson my whole and sole executrix."

## CHILDREN BORN STURTON

IIa. Rev. John, b.    1576; d. Leyden Mar. 1, 1625; m. Bridget **White**.
   b. William, b.    ; d.    ; m. Ellen (   ).
   c. Mary, b.    ; d.    ; m. William **Pearte.**
   d. Dau., b.    ; d.    ; m. Roger **Lawson**.

IIa. **Robinson**, Rev. John[3] (John[2], Christopher[1]), born about 1576 in Sturton; died Leyden, Holland, Mar. 1, 1625; buried on Mar. 4th in St. Peter's Church, as clearly shown in the church records. "4 Maart Jan Roelends Predicant van de Engelsche Gemeente by het Kloekuijs begraven in de Pieters Kerk." The translation is: "John Robinson Preacher of the English Congregation by the Belfry—buried in Peter's Church." Under date of Apr. 28, 1625, Roger White of Leyden wrote a touching account of the death and burial to his "loving Friend Mr. William Bradford, Governor of Plymouth in New England," and Edward Winslow states "The University and Ministers of the city accompanies him to his grave with all their accustomed solemnities, bewailing the great loss that not only that particular church had whereof he was pastor, but some of them sadly affirmed that all churches of Christ sustained a loss." However, news of Robinson's death did not reach the Pilgrim Colony in Plymouth for over a year in 1626-7. He married Bridget **White** Feb. 15, 1603-4, at St. Mary-Greasley, Nottinghamshire, daughter of Alexander **White** and Eleanor **Smith**, and it is quite fair to assume that William Brewster of Scrooby Manor a few miles away, friend and another Cambridge man, attended the wedding.

John Robinson spent his boyhood roaming the country around Sturton, and the vicinity which included Retford, Sutton, Scrooby, Gainsboro, and a number of other places. Brewster was older, and must have been something of a hero to the younger men of the surrounding towns, for they were familiar with his history at Cambridge and Court.

Robinson probably was prepared for college at one of the schools in nearby towns, perhaps in the same manner Brewster was ten or twelve years before. No doubt, the vicar of the parish was brought into final consultation on John's general capacity and in due time John Robinson, youthful, and filled with burning aspirations, mounted his horse before his home in Sturton all prepared for the momentous journey. The usual leave takings are completed, and John joins a group of young companions bound in the same direction, all potential scholars. They jog

[ 123 ]

along for hours over the same road that William Brewster traveled twelve years before, and what an exciting group of years. They may have properly discussed the part that Brewster played in the wars of the Low Lands, the trial and execution of Queen Mary, the defeat of the Spanish Armada and many other exciting moments of history.

At last the little cavalcade of ambitious youth came over the hill by Cambridge Castle, and there spread out before their eyes on the far side of the river was the old University town. Oh yes, generations of young men had come down Castle Hill and through Monk's Place over the Great Bridge into Cambridge, but to each generation it was a great and novel adventure. And so John Robinson entered Cambridge, and Corpus Christi College Apr. 9, 1592. Little did he anticipate that it was to be his home as pupil and instructor for the next eleven years. However, opportunities for making an honest living, even for men of the highest type and ability in civil life were very rare. Like most young men in the Universities he had prepared for the ministry, but the "livings" in that status were very small and uncertain at this time. For instance, the city of Norwich, in 1592-5, had forty or more parishes, including many churches. It was getting to be quite an industrial center, but even there the clergy were very poor, as expressed in a petition to Lord Burghley about 1594—

> "the poor and painful ministers of the city of Norwich" x x x x we that serve at the altar live on the basket, and our people that should maintain us cannot agree about our maintenance, the rich will give little, the meaner sort less and the rest nothing at all."
>
> (British Museum Hist. Mss.—Salisbury Papers, Pt. 13, p. 461)

Probably, Robinson thought it desirable, under the circumstances to keep his teaching job in the University, and in that pleasant occupation he led a quiet but useful life for a number of years, perhaps visiting Brewster and other friends in Nottinghamshire from time to time, especially Bridget White of Sturton.

Cambridge was congenial to Robinson because Elizabeth permitted liberal teaching. Cambridge had been a breeder of forceful "dissenters" for many years, but many of the Queen's best supporters were more or less "Puritans," and then she was none too sure of even Burghley, Walsingham and Davison. At times she suspected they had "Puritan" leanings, furthermore, her most consistent tax-payers, the merchants, were mostly of that persuasion, and the Queen had about given up trying to force strict conformity upon such a stubborn group.

However, the Queen died in 1603, and the difficulties of Brewster, Robinson and other "dissenters" of every degree increased several hundred percent immediately.

James commanded an immediate tightening up on "conformity," and the edict extended to Cambridge. He could not tolerate an unchained mind in the University. Rather than give up his intellectual freedom Robinson decided to resign his teaching fellowship in Corpus Christi. There was another reason for resigning which may have, after all, been the real honest-to-goodness reason. Bridget White of Sturton had been waiting back home some time, and married men were not permitted to hold a fellowship. The solution to that problem was simple. John resigned Feb. 10, 1603-4, and was married on the 15th of February. That was fast work, and the most pleasant part of a difficult situation he was facing.

He had to find a "living" as a minister, and Norwich, being more prosperous than ever, he located there as a pastor in 1604. At that time Norwich was the chief manufacturing center of provincial England. The people were becoming industrially minded. Politics and economics were uppermost in the minds of the citizens. Commerce brought the place in contact with Holland and Flanders. Many foreign workmen had settled in the city, some of them religious refugees. The leading townsfolk and the merchants, as in London, were strong for the "Puritan" party, a position which had been encouraged by Rev. John More, Rev. Thomas Roberts and other Cambridge men. Then there was the possible chance of becoming a chaplain to a Society of Merchant Adventurers, in a place like Norwich. The best families in England were now anxious to "apprentice" their sons to the commercial interests which were building up. Everything seemed favorable to Robinson.

However, James, although on the throne but a year, determined on a rule or ruin policy. He showed his teeth by issuing a proclamation July, 1604, requiring all ministers to conform to the new Book of Canons before the end of the following November. The Bishops under pressure from James made life so miserable for Robinson and other "Puritans" that he left Norwich, and took his family back to the old home town of Sturton-le-Steeple in Nottinghamshire. Obviously, his work as a pastor in the established church was over, at least for a time. However, the family could live with the wife's people until the clouds rolled by. They were quite prosperous.

Robinson, of course, was upset about the whole matter. He wanted to carry on his chosen work in the ministry, but apparently his only recourse was to organize his own church and meetings. This was a "Separatist" idea, and he knew that many organizations or meetings of this type had been active in England, especially in London, for a number of years. He also knew that, although merely a harmless religious meeting, they were liable to severe legal restrictive measures at any time, perhaps imprisonment for the leaders, especially now that James reigned.

He visited among his old friends and neighbors where, as he states "I hoped most to fynde satisfaction to my troubled heart." Apparently his fellow Cambridge man, Master William Brewster of Scrooby Manor, was willing to drop the life of a country gentleman which he had been enjoying for some ten years or more after most exciting and dangerous times at Court, and help Robinson organize his church, knowing full well that he would probably get into trouble.

The Manor was just suited for the purpose, and by 1606 the meeting was flourishing. Rev. John Robinson was at last minister to a small but earnest and sincere congregation, made possible, of course, by Brewster.

However, the inevitable happened. Brewster held a government office. He was, in fact, a court official, and when James discovered that a separate church meeting was in full operation at Scrooby Manor, he forced Brewster to resign in 1607.

Robinson was again without a place of meeting, but he still had a loyal following, among them young William Bradford, then a lad of eighteen years, and his brother-in-law John Carver. Many of the congregation expressed a desire to remove to Holland, because of the intolerable attitude of James.

After a number of delays caused by various governmental obstructions, many of the congregation reached Amsterdam. Just when Robinson and Brewster removed to Holland is not known. They did not go with the main group. Brewster may not have gone over for some time.

There is some evidence to show that Robinson had held meetings, not only in the Manor, but at his own house in Sturton. Several relatives of his wife, including her brother-in-law John Carver, accompanied Robinson to Amsterdam from the Sturton district.

In time, the Robinson congregation assembled in Amsterdam, but remained there only a few months when they removed to Leyden where there was more freedom for the exercise of their various crafts. Among the very real reasons why England was so uninviting for a business man or artisan, were the severe restrictions imposed by the "guilds." Conditions in Leyden seemed better, and the group had taken residence there by 1609-10.

The English colony at Leyden was strong, if not large, and the Robinson church prospered. However, a number of its members were much interested in the Virginia Company, and prospects for settling in Virginia, and even Robinson advocated the removal of the congregation to the colony, where the English could establish institutions free from Dutch or other foreign influences.

Having many friends among the Merchant Adventurers, plans were finally made and a "Patent" drawn up May 26, 1619, to transport the Leyden group to Virginia. However, just at this time, William Brewster became involved with King James about printed books distasteful to him, and the first plan had to be abandoned.  Brewster, being a hunted man for some time, a rather complicated scheme was devised by which a number of the Leyden congregation, including Brewster, were, in due course, landed at Plymouth in northern Virginia.  There is sound reason to think that John Robinson intended to join his friends in New England, but circumstances did not permit, and he died in Leyden on Mar. 1, 1625.  The congregation never obtained another pastor, and gradually went out of existence, but the results of his good works will live.

"There is no creature so perfect in wisdom and knowledge but may learn something for time present and to come by times past."

John Robinson.

CHILDREN

a. John, b. Norwich, Eng.; student at Leyden University 1633; no record.
b. Ann, b. Norwich, Eng., married into a Dutch family.
c. Bridget, b. Eng. (?) 1608; d.      ; m. 1st John **Greenwood**; m. 2nd William **Lee.**
IIId. Isaac, b. Holland (?) 1610; d. Barnstable, Mass., 1704; m. 1st Margaret **Handford**; m. 2nd Mary **Faunce.**
e. Mercy, b. Holland (?) 1612; d. 1623 (?).
f. Fear, b. Holland (?) 1614; d.      ; m. John **Jennings.**
g. Jacob, b.      ; d. May 1638.

## SMITH

I. **Smith**, William[1]; married Katherine **Porter**; she m. 2nd Thomas **Disney** of Parliament from Lincolnshire.  William Smith was a substantial person.  He resided at Honington, Lincolnshire, and his tomb may be seen standing on the hill behind the vicarage of St. Wilfrid's Church.  This Smith family was outstanding in a number of directions.  Katherine Porter became the mother of six Smith children, and five Disney youngsters.  One of them

IIa. Smith, Eleanor[2] (William[1]), m. Alexander **White.** (See White Family).

## WHITE

I. **White**, Thomas[1], born Nottinghamshire (?); died in Sturton about 1579.  He was probably well known at Scrooby Manor to the **Wentworths, Sandys** and **Brewsters.**

[ 127 ]

CHILDREN BORN STURTON

IIa. Alexander, b.    ; d.    ; m. Eleanor **Smith.**
 b. John, b.    ; d.    ; m.    .
 c. William, b.    ; d.    ; m.    .
 d. Elizabeth, b.    ; d.    ; m.    .
 e. Mary, b.    ; d.    ; m.    .
 f. John, b.    ; d.    ; m.    .

IIa. **White,** Alexander[2] (Thomas[1]) ; born Sturton (?) ; died Sturton about 1595; his will was proved May 6, 1596; married Eleanor **Smith;** died about 1599; will proved 1599; daughter of William **Smith** and Katherine **Porter.**
Alexander White was prosperous and had numerous properties, some of them at a distance from Sturton. This family was in Sturton before the Robinsons.

CHILDREN BORN STURTON

a. Catherine, b.    ; d. To Leyden; m. 1st George **Leggatt;** m. 2nd John **Carver.**
b. Charles, b.    ; d. 1633; m.    .
c. Bridget, b.    ; d. To Leyden; m. John **Robinson.**
d. Thomas, b.    ; d.    ; m.    .
e. Roger, b.    1589; d. To Leyden; m. Elizabeth **Wales.**
f. Edward, b.    ; d.    ; m.    .
g. Jane, b.    ; d. To Leyden; m. Randall **Thickins.**
h. Frances, b.    ; d. To Leyden; m. Francis **Jessop.**

There is no doubt that the preaching of John Robinson influenced mightily the lives of men like Brewster, Bradford, Allerton, Blossom, Winslow and others, not only from a religious point of view, but also in sound practical ways of life. However, Robinson had been in turn greatly aided in his labors by his family connections, especially the Whites, and by the Brewsters. The relatives of his wife greatly strengthened his aspirations. Several of her brothers and sisters were quite active in church matters. Her brother Charles took up his residence at Beauville Abbey in the parish of Greasley, and his son Charles, Jr., later on took a lively interest in the "Civil War" and in Parliament. Roger White, and at least two sisters, Jane and Frances, were in Leyden very active in several directions. Roger was in Leyden quite early, and started in business as a "grocer," but not until he was thirty-two did the right girl come along. On Feb. 20, 1621, he was betrothed to Elizabeth Wales. Two years later he was admitted to full citizenship on the guarantee of Edmund Chandler and Anthony Clement, and thereafter took a leading part in the English Colony in Leyden, including the church.

Her sister Catherine had first married George Leggatt, a yeoman, of a family long settled at Sturton, but he died within a few years, and she married John Carver, a man skilled in farm management, and interested in trade between Holland and England. Her first husband had left quite an estate, and no doubt Carver managed well, because he seemed on excellent terms with the family, especially with his brother-in-law John Robinson.

Alexander White died, and a few years later his wife Eleanor made her will Apr. 7, 1599, and died a few months later.

This will of Eleanor's is a very interesting document, and clearly shows how anxious people of means in those days were to have their sons (the younger ones especially) apprenticed out as soon as possible. The will states in part:

"I give and bequeath to my three sonnes Thomas, Roger and Edward whereof my will is that as ev'ry of my said sonnes shall accomplish the aige of xiij yeares xxli shalbe bestowed towards the binding of them apprentices at London in sure good places."

The residue of the estate was left to the eldest son Charles, and he was the sole executor.

When this will was made in 1599, neither John Robinson nor John Carver had married into the family. In fact, George Leggatt was still alive.

Carver was well along in years when he married the Widow Leggatt, with children of her own, and it is not thought there are any Carver descendants of the Mayflower Planter and Governor.

IIId. **Robinson**, Isaac (Rev. John[3], John[2], Christopher[1]) ; born Holland (?) 1610; died Barnstable, Mass., 1704; married 1st Margaret **Handford** June 27, 1639; died June, 1649; married 2nd Elizabeth **Faunce**.

He became a freeman in Scituate in 1633, but sold his place there in 1639, and removed to Barnstable. He was disfranchised by Gov. Prence in 1659 for being in sympathy with the Quakers, but was restored to civil rights by Gov. Winslow in 1673. He removed from Barnstable to "Succanessett," and was one of the thirteen who made the first purchase of lands from the aborigines, and began the settlement of Falmouth in 1660, where Isaac built the first house located near "Fresh Pond." He removed to Tisbury, where he was a selectman 1678-84, but he died in Barnstable.

CHILDREN BY 1ST WIFE

a. Sussana, bp. Jan. 21, 1637; d.        ; m.        .
b. John, bp. Apr. 5, 1640; d.        ; m. Elizabeth **Weeks.**
c. Isaac, bp. Aug. 7, 1642; d.    1728; m. Ann (    ).
d. Fear, bp. Jan. 26, 1644; d.        ; m. Samuel **Baker**; no ch.
e. Mercy, bp. July 4, 1647; d.        ; m. William **Weeks.**
f. Child, bp. June 1649; d.        ; m.        .

g. Isreal, bp. Oct. 5, 1651; d.      ; m.      .
h. Jacob, bp. May 15, 1653; d.    1733; m. Experience
  ( ).
i. Peter, bp.      ; d. Norwich, Conn.; m.      .
j. Thomas, bp. Mar. 6, 1666; d. Guilford, Conn.; m.      .

Ref. 339.

# DUNHAM

**2775**   I. **Dunham, John,** born 1588-9, at Scrooby, Nottinghamshire, England. He was the same age as Bradford, and perhaps attended the same primary school around Scrooby, possibly under William Brewster. However, both he and Bradford were too young to have had any leadership in the movement to Holland, although they may have attended the meetings at the Manor between 1604-7, at which time they were about sixteen years old. They may have gone over to Holland more for "trade" purposes than any other reason, for boys of that age were seeking the most likely opportunities for "apprenticeships," and Holland was prosperous. Just when John Dunham went into Holland is not known, but he was married in Leyden, Oct. 17, 1619, to Abigail **Wood,** and his first child, John, was born in Leyden in 1620. He probably was another protege of Brewster's, but apparently did not go over on the Mayflower for family reasons.

However, the Plymouth records show him there as early as 1632, and in 1633 Brewster made him a Deacon of the church, an appointment not at all surprising. By trade he was a "weaver." He was one of the first purschasers of Dartmouth.

### CHILDREN BORN LEYDEN AND PLYMOUTH

a. John, b.    1620; d.    1692; m. Dorothy (    ).
b. Abigail, b.    1623; d.    ; m. Stephen **Wood.**
c. Thomas, b.    1626; d.    ; m. Martha **Knott.**
d. Samuel, b.    1628; d.    ; m. 1st Martha **Fallowell,** wid.; m. 2nd Mary **Watson,** wid.
e. Hannah, b.    1630; d. before May 20, 1662; m. Giles **Rickard.**
f. Jonathan, b.    1632; d. Dec. 18, 1717; m. 1st Mary **Delano;** m. 2nd Mary **Cobb.**
g. Persis, b.    1635; d.    1672; m. 1st Benejah **Pratt;** m. 2nd Jonathan **Shaw.**
h. Benjamin, b.    1637; d.    ; m. Mary **Tilson.**
i. Daniel, b.    1639; d.    ; m. Mehitable **Hayward.**
j. Benejah, b.    1640; d. Piscataway, N. J.; m. Elizabeth **Tilson.**

Refs. 173, 304.

# BROWNE

1. William the Conqueror; m. Matilda.
2. William de Warrenne; m. Gundreda.
3. William de Warrene; b. bef. 1071; died 1138; m. Isabel de Vermandois.
4. William de Warrene; killed 1148; m. Adela de Talvace.
5632   5. Isabel de Warrene; d. 1199; m. Hameline Plantagenent 5631
6. William Plantagenent; m. Maud Mareschall.
7. John Plantagenent; m. Alice le Brun.
8. William Plantagenent; m. Joan de Vere.
5387   9. Alice Plantagenent; m. Edmund Fitz-alan.
5386   10. Richard Fitz-alan; m. Eleanor Plantagenent. 5381
13418   11. John Fitz-alan; m. Eleanor Maltravers. 15917
12. John Fitz-alan; m. Elizabeth le Despencer.
13. Sir Thomas Fitz-alan; m.        .
14. Eleanor Fitz-alan; m. Sir Thomas Browne (see IIIa).
15. Thomas Browne (see IVb).

The above line to Thomas Browne IV is found in the American Historical Society publication of 1929, p. 96.

## BROWNE

I. **Browne,** Sir Anthony; created Knight of the Bath at the coronation of King Richard II. He resided in County Kent, and had at least two sons.

a. Sir Stephen, mayor of London, 1439.
IIb. Sir Robert.

IIb. **Browne,** Sir Robert[2] (Anthony[1]), had a son.
IIIa. Sir Thomas.

IIIa. **Browne,** Sir Thomas[3] (Robert[2], Anthony[1]), was treasurer of the household of King Henry VI, and sheriff of Kent in 1444 and 1460. He married Eleanor **Fitzalan** or **Fitz Alan,** by which marriage he acquired the castle of Beechworth in Surrey.

### CHILDREN

a. Sir George, inherited Beechworth, was beheaded.
IVb. Thomas (see lines of from William the Conqueror).
c. William.
d. Jane.
e. Katherine.
f. Sir Robert.
g. Sir Anthony, standard bearer for King Henry VII.

[ 131 ]

IVb. **Browne,** Thomas[4] (Thomas[3], Robert[2], Anthony[1]).

Va. Peter, b. England      ; d. Plymouth 1633; m. 1st Martha **Ford,** widow; m. 2nd Mary (   ).
   b. John.

Va. **Browne,** Peter[5] (Thomas[4], Sir Thomas[3], Sir Robert[2], Sir Anthony[1]); born England; died at Plymouth between Apr. 4 and Oct. 10, 1633; married 1st 1624-5 at Plymouth a widow, Martha **Ford,** who came in the "Fortune" in 1621, and died between 1627-31; married 2nd Mary (   ) between 1627-31. He was a Mayflower Planter.

During his short life of thirteen years in Plymouth, Peter Browne was a useful citizen, and had business dealings with most everybody in the colony, as his estate inventory clearly shows. A carpenter and builder was in great demand, and his untimely death was a blow to the community.

"An Inventory taken the 10th of October 1633 of the goods & chattels of Peter Browne of New Plymouth deceased as they were prised by Capt. Myles Standish & Mr. Will Brewster of the same & presented upon oath in Court held the 28th of Oct. in the ninth yeare of the Raigne of our Soveraigne Lord Charles, etc."

Among the 91 items of inventory we find the following well known persons listed as creditors or debtors:

| Creditors | Debtors |
|---|---|
| Joh. Jenny | John Browne-Eleaven bushels of corne & a peck. |
| Jonathan Brewster 1. Bush Corn. | Will Palmer |
| Goodman Rowly 1. Bush. Corn. | Mr. Gilson 2/8 in beaver at 6/8. |
| Edw. Bangs | Mr. Heeks 5 bushels of Corne |
| H. Howland 9 oz of shott. | Mr. Weston a bush & ½ of Corne. |
| Expr. Michaell 1 oz of powder. | Tho. Clark 1 bush of Corn & 6d. |
|  | Josiah Wynslow ½ bush Corn. |
|  | Mr. ffog |
|  | Joh. Dunham |
|  | flr. Sprague 5 pecks Corn. |
|  | Joh. Cooke 2 pecks Corn. |
|  | Mr. Collier |
|  | Mrs. ffuller "1 peck malt & purgac." |

[ 132 ]

"to the Surgion for letting her man bloud"
"to Keneln Wynslow for a coffin"
Among the assets were mentioned 130 bushels of corn, 6 "melch goats," 5 young lambs, 2 wether lambs & a Ram, 4 Barrow hoggs, 3 sowes, 2 young sowes & a Bore, 1 heyfer. There were some iron kettles, potts and hangar, brasse candlesticks and skellets," "2 old brasse kettles," 3 old chests, 1 cradle, 2 pr. of Irish stockins. and many other interesting items such as a "Gredyron & a trevet."

"Peter Brown aforesaid dying without will, see how his estate was disposed on by a Court off assistants held the 11th of Nov. An. 1633."

CHILDREN BY 1ST WIFE

VIIa. Mary, b.     (?) 1625; d.     ; m. Ephraim **Tink-ham.**
b. Pricilla, b.     (?) 1627; d.     ; m. William **Allen.**

CHILDREN BY 2ND WIFE

VIIIc.\*Peter, b. (?) 1630; d. Mar. 9, 1691; m. Mary **Gillette.**
IXd. Rebecca, b.     (?) 1632; d.     ; m. William **Snow.**
Xe.\*Isabel, b.     (?) 1634; d. Oct. 2, 1698; m. Anthony **Hoskins.**

and perhaps other children.

———

\* Within recent years several publications of importance have accepted the proposition that Peter and Isabel Browne, brother and sister of Duxbury and Windsor, Conn., are two of the long unidentified children of Peter Browne, the Mayflower Passenger. A rather recent discussion of this complete line from Sir Anthony Browne, and in some detail, may be found in one of the elaborate publications of the American Historical Society, 1928, p. 65, also refer to the following:

Dictionary of English and Welch Surnames.
American Historical Society—American Families 1929, p. 17-20.
Surrey Pedigrees, Vol. I, p. 149-560—Manning and Bray.
Surrey Pedigrees—Berry.
History of Commoners—Burke, Vol. III, p. 382.
Peerage—Collins, Vol. II p. 206, VIII p. 255.
History of Ancient Windsor Com. Stiles, Vol. 2, p. 404.

## TINKHAM

VIIa. **Browne**, Mary[6] (Peter[5], Thomas[4], Sir Thomas[3], Sir Robert[2], Sir Anthony[1]); born Plymouth 1625 (?); married Ephraim **Tinkham.**

## CHILDREN

a. Ephraim, b. Aug. 5, 1649; d.   ; m. Esther **Wright.**
b. Ebenezer, b. Sept. 30, 1651; d.   ; m. Elizabeth **Burrows.**
c. Peter, b. Dec. 25, 1653; d.   ; m. Merry **Mendfall.**
d. Hezekiah, b. Feb. 3, 1655; d.   ; m. Ruth (   ).
e. John, b.   ; d. young; m.——.
f. Mary, b. Aug. 5, 1661; d.   ; m. John **Thomson.**
g. John, b. Nov. 15, 1663; d.   ; m. Sarah (   ).
h. Isaac, b. Apr. 11, 1666; d.   ; m. Sarah **King.**

## BROWNE

VIIIc. **Browne,** Peter[6] (Peter[5], Thomas[4], Sir Thomas[3], Sir Robert[2], Sir Anthony[1]); born Plymouth 1630 (?); died Windsor, Conn., Mar. 9, 1691; age 60; married Mary **Gillette** July 15, 1658, daughter of Jonathan **Gillette.**

He removed from Duxbury to Windsor, and was admitted to the Windsor church June 22, 1662. He had been, among thirty others, a purchaser in Dartmouth in 1652. He was a miller by occupation.

### CHILDREN BORN WINDSOR, CONN.

a. Mary, b. May 2, 1659; d.   ; m.   .
b. Hannah, b. Sept. 29, 1660; d.   ; m.   .
c. Abigail, b. Aug. 8, 1662; d.   ; m. Samuel **Fowler.**
d. Hepzibah, b. Nov. 19, 1664; d.   ; m.   .
e. Peter, b. Mar. 12, 1666; d.   ; m.   .
f. John, b. Jan. 8, 1668; d. Feb. 4, 1728; m. Elizabeth **Loomis.**
g. Jonathan, b. Mar. 30, 1670; d.   ; m.   .
h. Cornelius, b. July 30, 1672; d.   ; m.   .
i. Hester, b. May 22, 1673; d.   ; m.   .
j. Isabel, b. June 1676; d.   ; m.   .
k. Deborah, b. Feb. 12, 1678; d.   ; m. John **Hosford.**
l. Sarah, b. Aug. 20, 1681; d.   ; m. Joseph **Moore.**
m. Dau., b.   ; d.   ; m.   .
n. Dau., b.   ; d.   ; m.   .

## SNOW

IXd. **Browne,** Rebecca[6] (Peter[5], Thomas[4], Sir Thomas[3], Sir Robert[2], Sir Anthony[1]); born Plymouth 1632 (?); married William **Snow;** born in England 1624 (?); died 1708; age 84 years.

William Snow was brought to New England in 1635 by Richard Derby, to whom he had been apprenticed according to the custom of the times, and assigned to Edward Doten of Plymouth in 1638 to serve him seven years. He was able to bear arms in 1643, and removed to Duxbury as early as 1645, and was among the first settlers of West Bridgewater. His will is dated Mar. 9, 1698-9, and proved 1708. It mentions wife, sons Joseph, Benjamin and William, daughters Mary, Lydia, Hannah and Rebecca. Witnesses—Thomas Hayward, Nathaniel Ames and Thomas Wade.

CHILDREN BORN BRIDGEWATER

a. William, b.      ; d.      ; m. Naomi **Whitman.**
b. James, b.      ; d. Canada Expedition 1690; m.——.
c. Joseph, b.      ; d.      1753; m. Hopestill **Alden.**
d. Benjamin, b.      ; d.      ; m. 1st Elizabeth **Alden;** m. 2nd Sarah (**Allen**) **Cary.**
e. Mary, b.      ; d.      ; m.      .
f. Lydia, b.      ; d.      ; m.      .
g. Hannah, b.      ; d.      ; m. 1st Giles **Rickard;** m. 2nd John **Hawks.**
h. Rebecca, b.      ; d.      ; m. Samuel **Rickard.**

## HOSKINS

I. Hoskins, John[1], born England; died Windsor, Conn., May 3, 1648; married Ann (**Filer?**). She died Windsor Mar. 6, 1662-63.

He came to New England in the ship "Mary and John" in 1630, and was among the original settlers of Boston, where he was made freeman 1631. He was of the company which founded Windsor, Conn., and in 1637 was a delegate to the General Court of Conn. He received land grants in 1640.

CHILDREN

a. Thomas, b. Eng.      ; d. Apr. 13, 1666; m.      .
b. John, b. Eng.      ; d. Dorchester, Mass.; m.      .
IIc. Anthony, b. Mass. 1632; d. Jan. 4, 1706-7; m. Isabel **Browne.**
d. Rebecca, b. Conn., 1634; d.      1683; m. Mark **Kelsey.**

IIc. (See Isabel Browne Xe).

## HOSKINS

Xe. **Browne,** Isabel[6] (Peter[5], Thomas[4], Sir Thomas[3], Sir Robert[2], Sir Anthony[1]); born Plymouth, Mass., 1633 (?); died Windsor, Conn., Oct. 2, 1698; married Anthony[2] **Hoskins** (John[1]); born Boston (?) 1632; died Windsor, Conn., Jan. 4, 1706-7. They were married on July 16, 1656.

Anthony was a prosperous citizen of Windsor, and accumulated quite an estate.

[ 135 ]

CHILDREN BORN WINDSOR

a. Isabel, b. May 16, 1657; d.     ; m.     .
b. John, b. Oct. 14, 1659; d.      ; m.     .
c. Robert, b. June 6, 1662; d.     ; m. Mary **Gillette.**
Gen. 7d. Anthony, b. Mar. 6, 1664; d. July 9, 1747; m.     .
e. Grace, b. July 26, 1666; d.     ; m. Thomas **Eggleston.**
f. Rebecca, b. Dec. 3, 1668; d.     ; m.     .
g. Jane, b. Apr. 30, 1671; d.     ; m. (     ) **Alvord.**
h. Thomas, b. Mar. 14, 1672; d.     ; m.     .
i. Joseph, b. Feb. 28, 1674; d.     ; m.     .

Gen. 8. Alexander[4] Hoskins (Anthony[3], Anthony[2], John[1]).
Gen. 9. Hannah Hoskins, m. 1778 Hosea[4] Clark (Capt. Solomon[3], John[2], Hon. Daniel[1]).
Gen. 10. Joel Clark, m. 1808 Candace[2] Bowns (Joseph[1] of L.I.).
Gen. 11. Mary A. Clark, m. 1836 Oliver[7] S. Hills (Oliver[6], Joseph[5], John[4], John[3], William[2], William[1]).
Gen. 12. Franklin B. Hills, m. 1876 Frances[7] M. Coons (see Koon-Coons Gen. 1937 p. 269-354.
Gen. 13. Leon C. Hills, m. 1908 Ina[5] S. King (Jerome[4], Ebenezer[3], Elijah[2], Hezekiah[1]).
Gen. 14. (Norma E. Hills, b. 1915 Newark, N. J.
(Robert J. Hills, b. 1918 Washington, D. C.

## CLARK

I. **Clark,** Hon. Daniel, born Chester, England, 1622; died Windsor, Conn., Aug. 12, 1710; married 1st Mary **Newberry** June 13, 1644; daughter of Thomas **Newberry** and Jane (     ), of Mypern, Devonshire, England; died Aug. 29, 1688; married 2nd Martha (**Pitkins**) **Wolcott,** widow of Simon **Wolcott,** and sister of William **Pitkins,** Esq., of Hartford. She died Dec. 13, 1719.

This family is old in England. Daniel came from Weaxil, near Kenilworth, England, at the age of seventeen, with his uncle Rev. Ephraim **Hait,** who became pastor of the old Windsor Congregational Society, as a colleague of Rev. John Wareham.

Daniel became one of the first settlers of Windsor, and a man of influence. He was an attorney, and held many public offices such as Secretary of the Colony 1658-64, 1665-66, and was in the land directory at Hartford 1639-40. He was admitted to the Windsor church June 18, 1643, and "Captain Clark's wife" was admitted Apr. 16, 1658.

[ 136 ]

# CHILDREN BORN WINDSOR

a. Mary, b. Apr. 24, 1645; d. young; m.———.
b. Josiah, b. Jan. 21, 1648; d.      ; m. Mary (Burr) Crow, wid.
c. Elizabeth, b. Oct. 28, 1651; d.      ; m. 1st Moses Cooke; m. 2nd Lt. Job Drake.
d. Daniel, b. Apr. 4, 1654; d.      ; m. Hannah Pratt.
c. John, b. Apr. 10, 1656; d.      ; m. Mary Crow.
f. Mary, b. Sept. 22, 1658; d.      ; m. 1st John Gaylord; m. 2nd Jedidiah Watson.
g. Samuel, b. July 6, 1661; d.      ; m. Mehitable Thrall.
h. Sarah, b. Aug. 7, 1663; d.      ; m. 1st Isaac Kinney; m. 2nd (      ) Marsh (?).
i. Hannah, b. Aug. 29, 1668; d. young; m.———.
j. Nathaniel, b. Sept. 9, 1666; d. killed by Indians 1690; m.———.

Ref. 540.

[ 137 ]

# DOTY

39. **Cooke**, Elizabeth[3] (Darmaris[2] **Hopkins**, Stephen[1]) ; born Plymouth Jan. 18, 1648-9; died Nov. 21, 1692; married John[2] **Doty**; born Plymouth 1639-40; died May 8, 1701, in Plymouth, son of Edward[1] **Doty**. He married 2nd Sarah **Rickard** about 1694; daughter of Giles **Rickard**; Sarah married 2nd 1704, Joseph **Peterson**.

John Doty was a farmer and probably the only one of Edward's children to remain in Plymouth at that occupation. Many of his descendants remained in Plymouth for generations. Others settled at Plympton, Carver and Kingston, and along the coast of Maine. This particular line seems to like the spelling of the name "Doten."

### CHILDREN BY ELIZABETH COOKE

202. John, b. Aug. 27, 1668; d.      ; m. 1st Mehitable **Nelson**; m. 2nd Hannah **Sherman**.
203. Edward, b. June 28, 1671; d. young; m.——.
204. Jacob, b. May 27, 1673; d. young; m.——.
205. Elizabeth, b. Feb. 10, 1675; d.      ; m. Joshua **Morse**.
206. Isaac, b. Oct. 25, 1678; d.      1724; m. Martha **Faunce**.
207. Samuel, b. Jan. 31, 1682; d.      1740; m. Mercy **Cobb**.
208. Elisha, b. July 13, 1686; d. before 1756; m. Hannah **Horton**.
209. Josiah, b. Oct. 1689; d.      ; m. Abigail (      ).
210. Martha, b. Oct. 1692; d.      ; m. Ebenezer **Curtice**.

### CHILDREN BY SARAH RICKARD

211. Sarah, b. Feb. 19, 1695; d.      ; m.            .
212. Patience, b. July 3, 1697; d.      ; m. Kenelen **Baker**.
213. Desire, b. Apr. 19, 1699; d.      ; m. George **Barrows**, Jr.

Refs. 157, 167, 169, 182, 183, 186.

# DOTY

I. **Doty**, Edward[1], born England (London?) 1600 (?) ; died Yarmouth Aug. 23, 1655; married 1st (?) ; married 2nd Faithe[2] **Clarke**, Plymouth, Jan. 6, 1635; born 1619 England; died Dec. 21, 1675; daughter of Tristam **Clarke**, who came in the "Francis" 1634 with his wife and children. She married 2nd Mar. 14, 1667. John **Phillips** of Marshfield, Mass.

Edward Doty, a very promising and sturdy young man, was probably residing in or near London in 1619, and well acquainted with some of the Merchant Adventurers, active in the affairs of the Virginia Company under Sir Edwin Sandys. It was the growing custom for the best of families to "apprentice" their sons as soon as possible to a seven-year period with some London merchant, and no doubt his family was of good standing. The use of the word "servant" in the early centuries, especially the sixteenth and seventeenth, should not be taken too seriously. Every individual not a member of the "nobility," or of the "clergy," in order to exist in the country at all, had to exhibit by word and action the appearance of humility. History has proved that much of this apparent humbleness of spirit disclosed by Bradford and other early writers of history, was merely the current form of expression, and that underneath all of the demanded humility was a seething and militant individualism.

The Will and Inventory of Edward Doty is recorded in Ply. Col. Wills, Vol. II, Pt. I, p. 14-16.

He died at Plymouth, Thursday, Aug. 23 to Sept. 2, 1655, and his widow, Faith (Clark) Doty, married second, at Plymouth, on Thursday, Mar. 14-24, 1666-7, John Phillips of Marshfield. She was buried at Marshfield on Tuesday, Dec. 21-31, 1675, and had disposed of the house and land at High Cliff, Plymouth, left her in Edward Doty's will, by deed of gift to her son John Doty, made May 9-19, 1671. Her will is recorded Ply. Col. Wills, Vol. III, Pt. II, p. 12.

(p. 14) May 20, 1655

In the Name of God Amen.

Know all men to Whom It may concerne that I Edward Dotten seni<sup>r</sup>; of the Towne of New Plymouth in New England being sicke and yett by the mercye of God in prfect memory and upon matture Consideration Doe by this my last Will and Testament leave and bequeath my purchase land lying att Coaksett unto my sons; my son Edward I give a Double portion and to the rest of my sonnes equal alike if they live to the age of one and twenty if they Die before then to bee prted among the rest onely. To my wife I leave a third During her life then after to returne to my sonnes, And unto my loveing wife I give and bequeath my house and lands and meddows within the precincts of New Plymouth together with all chattles and moveables that are my proper goods onely Debts and engagements to be paid; as for my Share of land att Punckquetest if it come to anything I give it unto my son Edward; this being my last will and Testament; I Edward Dotten Doe owne it for my act and Deed before these my loveing ffrinds whose are

[ 139 ]

Witnesses; and Doe sett my hand to the same; the Day and yeare above written.

Witnesse  
John Howland  
James Hurst  
John Cooke  
William Hoskins

Edward Dotten  
his marke  
Ther being many names besides  
Coaksett I mean all my purchase  
land According to Deed.

CHILDREN BORN PLYMOUTH

IIa. Edward, b. 1637; d. drowned Feb. 8, 1689; m. Sarah **Faunce.**  
IIIb. John, b. 1639-40; d. May 8, 1701; m. 1st Elizabeth **Cooke;** m. 2nd Sarah **Rickard.**  
IVc. Thomas, b. 1641; d. 1679; m. Mary **Churchill,** widow.  
Vd. Samuel, b. 1643; d. Oct., 1715; m. Jeane **Harmon.**  
VIe. Desire, b. 1645; d. 1731; m. 1st. William **Sherman;** m. 2d Isreal **Holmes;** m. 3rd Alexander **Standish.**  
VIIf. Elizabeth, b. 1647; d. 1717; m. John **Rouse.**  
VIIIg. Isaac, b. Feb. 8, 1648; d. 1728; m. Elizabeth **England.**  
IXh. Joseph, b. Apr. 30, 1651; d. ; m. 1st Elizabeth **Warren;** m. 2nd Deborah **Hatch;** m. 3rd Sarah **Edwards.**  
Xi. Mary, b. 1653; d. ; m. Samuel **Hatch.**

IIa. **Doty,** Edward[2] (Edward[1]), born Plymouth 1637; drowned Feb. 8, 1689-9; married Sarah **Faunce,** Feb. 25, 1662; born Plymouth 1645; died Scituate June 27, 1695; daughter of John **Faunce.** She married 2nd John **Buck** Apr. 26, 1693. He was a seaman, and with his son John was drowned in a storm in Plymouth Harbor.

CHILDREN BORN PLYMOUTH

a. Sarah, b. May 20, 1664; d. ; m.——.  
b. Sarah, b. June 9, 1666; d. ; m. James **Warren.**  
c. John, b. Aug. 4, 1668; d. Feb. 8, 1689; m.——.  
d. Mary, b. July 9, 1671; d. ; m. Joseph **Allyn.**  
e. Martha, b. July 9, 1671; d. ; m. Thomas **Morton.**  
f. Elizabeth, b. Dec. 22, 1673; d. ; m. Tobias **Oakman.**  
g. Patience, b. July 7, 1676; d. Feb. 26, 1690; m.——.  
h. Mercy, b. Feb. 6, 1678; d. Nov. 30, 1682; m.——.  
i. Samuel, b. May 17, 1681; d. Jan. 26, 1750; m. Anne **Buckingham.**  
j. Mercy, b. Sept. 23, 1684; d. ; m. Daniel **Pratt.**  
k. Benjamin, b. May 30, 1689; d. ; m. Hester **Beaman.**

IIIb. **Doty,** John[2] (Edward[1]), married 1st Elizabeth **Cooke;** married 2nd Sarah **Rickard.** (See Fam. No. 39).

IVc. **Doty,** Thomas[2], (Edward[1]), born Plymouth 1641; died 1679; married Mary **Churchill,** widow.
He was a seaman.

### CHILDREN

a. Hannah, b. Dec. 1675; d. Apr. 12, 1764; m. Jonathan **Delano.**
b. Thomas, b. July 22, 1679; d. Jan. 1722; m. Elizabeth **Harlow.**

Vd. **Doty,** Samuel[2] (Edward[1]), born Plymouth 1643; died Oct. 1715; married Jeane **Harmon,** Nov. 10, 1678.

### CHILDREN BORN PISCATAWAY, N. J.

a. Samuel, b. Aug. 27, 1679; d.      ; m. Elizabeth **Hull.**
b. Sarah, b.      ; d.      ; m.      .
c. Isaac, b. Aug. 12, 1683; d.      ; m. Frances (      ).
d. Edward, b. May 14, 1685; d.      ; m.      .
e. James, b. Sept. 17, 1686; d.      ; m. Phebe **Slater.**
f. Jonathan, b. Feb. 24, 1687; d.      ; m. Mary (      ).
g. Benjamin, b. May 14, 1691; d.      ; m. Abigail **Whitehead.**
h. Elizabeth, b. Feb. 26, 1694; d.      ; m. David **Martin.**
i. Joseph, b. Oct. 30, 1696; d.      ; m.      .
j. Daniel, b.      ; d.      ; m.      .
k. Margaret, b.      ; d.      ; m.      .
l. (?) John, b.    (?) 1680-85; d.      ; m.      .
m. (?) Nathaniel, b.    (?) 1707; d.      ; m.      .

## SHERMAN—HOLMES—STANDISH

VIe. **Doty,** Desire[2] (Edward[1]), born Plymouth 1645; died 1731; married 1st William[2] **Sherman** Dec. 25, 1617; born 1644; died Oct. 25, 1679; son of William[1] **Sherman;** married 2nd Isreal **Holmes** of Marshfield Nov. 24, 1681; died Feb. 24, 1684-5; married Alexander **Standish** Feb. 24, 1684-5.

### CHILDREN (SHERMAN)

a. Hannah, b. Feb. 21, 1668; d.      ; m. William **Ring.**
b. Elizabeth, b. Mar. 17, 1670; d.      ; m.      .
c. William, b. Apr. 19, 1672; d.      ; m. Mary **White.**
d. Patience, b. Aug. 3, 1674; d.      ; m.      .
e. Experience, b. Sept. 22, 1678; d.      ; m. Miles **Standish.**
f. Ebenezer, b. Apr. 21, 1680; d.      ; m. 1st Margaret **Decrow;** m. 2nd Bathsheba **Ford.**

[ 141 ]

CHILDREN (HOLMES)

g. Isreal, b. Feb. 17, 1682-8; d.         ; m. Elizabeth **Turner.**
h. John, b. Jan. 15, 1684-5; d.          ; m. 1st Joanna **Sprague;**
   m. 2nd Sarah **Thomas.**

CHILDREN (STANDISH)

i. Desire, b. May 5, 1689; d.        ; m. Nathan **Weston.**
j. Thomas, b. Jan. 29, 1690; d.      ; m. Mary **Carver.**
k. Ichabod, b. June 10, 1693; d.     ; m. Phebe **Ring.**

## ROUSE

VIIf. **Doty,** Elizabeth² (Edward¹), born Plymouth 1647; died 1717; married John **Rouse** Jan 13, 1674; born Duxbury Sept. 28, 1643; son of John **Rouse** and Annis **Peabody.**

   a. John, b.     1678; d. May 26, 1704; m.

## DOTY

VIIIg. **Doty,** Isaac² (Edward¹), born Plymouth Feb. 8, 1648-9; married Elizabeth **England,** about 1673 at Oyster Bay, L. I., she was possibly born 1651-5 at Portsmouth.

When his father died Isaac was about six years old, but continued to live with his mother until her marriage to John **Phillips** in 1667. He seems to have gone to Oyster Bay soon after, because at a town meeting in 1672 he was allowed a piece of land for a house. It was a beautiful location. He probably married about this time.

CHILDREN BORN OYSTER BAY, L. I.

   a. Isaac, b.     1673; d.       ; m. Elizabeth **Jackson.**
   b. Joseph, b.    1680; d.    1716; m. Sarah      .
   c. Jacob, b.     1682; d.       ; m. Penelope **Alberton.**
   d. Solomon, b.      1691; d.    1761; m. Rachel **Seaman.**
   e. James, b.     1693; d. Feb. 4, 1773; m. Catherine **Latting.**
   f. Samuel, b.    1695; d.       ; m. Charity **Mudge.**

IXh. **Doty,** Joseph² (Edward¹), born Plymouth Apr. 30, 1651; died Rochester, Mass., 1732-5; married 1st Elizabeth **Warren** at Plymouth about 1674; born Plymouth Sept. 5, 1654; died Sandwich about 1679; daughter of Nathaniel **Warren** and Sarah **Walker;** married 2nd Deborah **Hatch** at Sandwich about 1680; born Scituate about 1662; died Rochester June 21, 1711; daughter of Walter **Hatch** and Elizabeth **Holbrook;** married 3rd Sarah **Edwards** at Rochester Mar. 9, 1711-2.

[ 142 ]

He was four years old at his father's death. He was living in Plymouth 1672, and resided in Sandwich for a time, but before 1683 he had settled in Rochester, Mass., where he died.

### CHILDREN BY ELIZABETH WARREN

a. Theophilus, b. 1674; d.     ; m. Ruth (     ).
b. Elizabeth, b. 1678-9; d.     ; m.     .

### CHILDREN BY DEBORAH HATCH

c. Ellis, b. 1681; d.     ; m. Ellinor (     ).
d. Joseph, b. Mar. 31, 1683; d.     ; m. Hannah **Edwards.**
e. Deborah, b. Mar. 30, 1685; d.     ; m.     .
f. John, b. Mar. 1, 1688; d.     ; m. Elizabeth (     ).
g. Mercy, b. Jan. 12, 1691-2; d.     ; m.     .
h. Faith, b. Jan. 18, 1696-7; d.     ; m. James **Shaw.**
i. Mary, b. July 28, 1699; d.     ; m. Samuel **Waterman.**

### HATCH

Xi. **Doty,** Mary[2] (Edward[1]), born Plymouth 1653; died     ; married Samuel[2] **Hatch** 1676 (?); born Dec. 22, 1653; son of Walter[1] **Hatch** and Elizabeth **Holbrook** of Scituate.

### CHILDREN

a. Samuel, b. Nov. 10, 1678; d.     ; m. Elizabeth **Oldham.**
b. Josiah, b. May 30, 1680; d.     ; m. Desire **Hawes.**
c. Hannah, b. Feb. 15, 1681; d.     ; m. Japhet **Turner.**
d. Ebenezer, b. Apr. 6, 1684; d.     ; m.     .
e. Isaac, b. Dec. 20, 1687; d.     ; m. Penelope **Ewell.**
f. Elizabeth, b. June 16, 1690; d.     ; m. John **Bonney.**
g. Elisha, b. Nov. 7, 1692; d.     ; m. Patience **Keen.**
h. Ezekiel, b. May 14, 1695; d.     ; m. Ruth **Church.**
i. Desire, b. Sept. 25, 1698; d.     ; m.     .

### HATCH

I. **Hatch,** Walter[1]; born England; married Elizabeth **Holbrook** May 6, 1650; daughter of Thomas **Holbrook.**
He resided at Scituate, Mass.

[ 143 ]

CHILDREN BORN SCITUATE

a. Hannah, b. Mar. 3, 1651; d.      ; m.      .
IIb. Samuel, b. Dec. 22, 1653; d.  .  ; m. Mary **Doty.**
  c. Jane, b. Mar. 7, 1655; d.      ; m.      .
  d. Antipas, b. Oct. 26, 1658; d. Dec. 7, 1705; m.      .
  e. Bethia, b. Mar. 31, 1661; d.      ; m.      .
  f. John, b. July 8, 1664; d. July 20, 1737; m.      .
  g. Isreal, b. Mar. 25, 1667; d.      ; m. Elizabeth (    ).
  h. Joseph, b. Dec. 9, 1669; d.      ; m.      .

IIb. (See **Doty²** Mary Xi).

Ref. 169.

## HOLMES

I. **Holmes,** William¹, born England 1592; died Marshfield
Nov. 9, 1678, age 86; married Elizabeth (    ); she died Marshfield Feb. 17, 1688-9, age 86.

He was in Scituate about 1641, but by 1661 had crossed the
river into Marshfield, where he settled next to Goodman **Carver**
and **Dingley.**

His will is dated Mar. 4, 1677-8, proved Feb. 25, 1678-9.  (Old
Col. Recs., Vol. IV, p. 2).

CHILDREN BORN MARSHFIELD

IIa. Rev. Jóhn, b. England; d. Dec. 24, 1675; m. Mary **Wood.**
  b. Josiah, b. England; d.      ; m. Hannah **Sampson.**
  c. Abraham, bp.   1641; d.      ; m. 1st Elizabeth **Ar-
    nold;** m. 2nd Abigail **Nichols.**
IIId. Isreal, bp.    ; 1642; d.      ; m. Desire (**Doty**) **Sher-
    man.**
  e. Capt. Isaac, bp.    1644; d. about 1724; m. Anna **Rouse.**
  f. Sarah, bp.    1646; d.      ; m.      .
  g. Rebecca, bp.    1648; d.      ; m.      .
  h. Mary, bp.    1655; d.      ; m. (    ) **Cheney.**
  i. Elizabeth, bp.    1661; d.      ; m. Thomas **Bourne.**

IIa. **Holmes,** Rev. John² (William¹), born England; died Dec.
24, 1675; married Mary **Wood** Dec. 11, 1661; daughter of John
**Wood** of Plymouth.

He was a minister.

CHILDREN

a. Joseph, b. July 9, 1665; d.      ; m. 1st Sarah **Sprague;**
  m. 2nd Mary **Brewster.**
b. Mary, b.    ; d.    ; m.      .
c. Isaac, b.    1674; d.      ; m. Mary **Allerton.**

[ 144 ]

IIId. **Holmes,** Isreal[2] (William[1]), bapt. Marshfield 1642; married Nov. 24, 1681; Desire **(Doty) Sherman,** daughter of Edward **Doty** and widow of William **Sherman.** She married 3rd Alexander[2] **Standish** (Myles[1]).

CHILDREN

a. Isreal, b. Feb. 4, 1682-3.
b. John, b. Jan. 15, 1684-5.

## CHURCHILL

I. **Churchill,** John[1], born England; died Plymouth Jan. 1, 1662-3; married Hannah **Pontus** Dec. 18, 1644; born Holland or England in 1623; died Hobb's Hole, Mass., Dec. 22, 1690; daughter of William **Pontus.** She married 2nd Giles **Rickard** June 25, 1669.

He appeared first in Plymouth 1643, and purchased a farm of Richard Higgins in 1645. He was propounded a freeman 1650, and admitted 1651. A nuncupative will was made and exhibited before court held at Plymouth, Mar. 3, 1662. Book of Wills, 2nd Part, Vol. 2nd, page 83.

CHILDREN BORN PLYMOUTH

a. Joseph, b.     1647; d.     ; m. Sarah **Hicks.**
b. Hannah, b. Nov. 12, 1649; d.     ; m. John **Drew.**
c. Eleazer, b. Apr. 20, 1652; d.     ; m. 1st Mary (   );
   m. 2nd Mary **Doty.**
d. Mary, b. Aug. 1, 1654; d.     ; m. Thomas **Doty.**.
e. William, b.     1656; d. Oct. 5, 1722; m. Lydia **Bryant.**
f. John, b.     1657; d. June 13, 1723; m. Rebecca **Delano.**

Ref. 150.

## COOKE

40. **Cooke,** Caleb[3] (Damaris[2] **Hopkins,** Stephen[1]), born Plymouth, Mass., Mar. 29, 1651; died of small-pox Feb. 13, 1721-2; married Jane (   ) before 1682.

He resided at Rocky Nook, that part of Plymouth set off in 1707 as Plympton. He was a soldier under Captain Benjamin Church in the King Phillip's War, and had much to do with the disposal of the "King" in death on Saturday morning, Aug. 12, 1676. So much so that he received a special grant of land for the services, located in "Narragansett Number Four," now Greenwich, Mass. A part of the gun that killed Phillip is now in the Pilgrim Memorial Hall in Plymouth.

In 1686 Caleb was Governor's assistant.

214. John, b. Feb. 5, 1682; d. May 6-July 6, 1741; m. 1st Elizabeth **Sears**; m. 2nd Hannah **Morton**, wid.
215. Mary, b. Feb. 21, 1683; d. Feb. 11, 1713-4; m.——.
216. Anne, b. Aug. 21, 1686; d. Middletown, Conn.; m. James **Johnson.**
217 Jane, b. Mar. 16, 1689; d. Feb. 8, 1716-7; m. Isaac **Harris.**
218. Elizabeth, b. Nov. 30, 1691; d. N. Yarmouth, Me.; m. Robert **Johnson.**
219. Mary, b. Aug. 20, 1694; d.     ; m. Robert **Carver.**
220. Caleb, b. Apr. 17, 1697; d. Mar. 15, 1724; m. Abigail **Howland.**
221. James, b. Aug. 19, 1700; d.     1757; m. Abigail **Hodges.**
222. Joseph, b. Nov. 28, 1703; d. Middletown, Conn.; m. Experience **Hodges.**

Refs. 143, 182, 183, 262, 172, 170, 295.

# CARVER

I. **Carver,** James[1], of Doncaster, Yorkshire yeoman, and his wife Catherine had two sons who became merchants. Many Yorkshire and north country men were entering commerce and industry.

## CHILDREN

IIa. Isaac, b.    1563 (?); d. probably Leyden; m.——.
IIIb. Gov. John, bp. Sept. 9, 1565; d. New Eng. April, 1621; m. Catherine (**White**) **Leggatt.**

IIa. **Carver,** Isaac[2] (James[1]), born Doncaster about 1563, and became a merchant doing business in England and Holland. He finally located in Leyden, perhaps dying there, and had a son, among others.

## CHILD

IVa. Robert, b. Eng. 1594 (?); d. Marshfield, Mass., April 1680; m.    .

IVa. **Carver,** Robert[3] (Isaac[2], James[1]), born England about 1594; buried Marshfield, Mass., Apr. 1680; had a son.

## CHILD

Va. John, b. 6, 1637 (?) Duxbury; d. June 22, 1679; m. Millicent **Ford.**

Va. **Carver,** John[4] (Robert[3], Isaac[2], James[1]), born Duxbury 1637 (?); died June 22, 1679; married Millicent **Ford,** about 1657?

## CHILDREN BORN MARSHFIELD

a. William, b. Sept. 6, 1659; d. Oct. 2, 1760; m. 1st Elizabeth **Foster;** m. 2nd Elizabeth **Rouse,** wid.
b. John, b.    1661; d.    1747; m. Mary **Barnes.**
c. Elizabeth, b. Mar. 4, 1662; d. Apr. 4, 1694; m.    .
d. Robert, b.    ; d.    ; m.    .
e. Eleazer, b.    1668; d. Jan. 25, 1744; m. Experience (**Blake**) **Sumner.**
f. David, b.    1669; d. Sept. 17, 1727; m. 1st Ruth **Whitmarsh;** m. 2nd Hannah **Dyer;** m. 3rd Sarah **Butterfield.**
g. Mercy, b. Feb. 11, 1672; d.    .
h. Anna, b. Feb. 20, 1675; d. Mar. 21, 1766; m. 1st Joseph **Richards;** m. 2nd Joseph **Pratt.**
i. Mehitable, b.    ; d.    1679; m.    .
j. Rebecca, b. Feb. 20, 1670; d.    ; m.    .

IIIb. **Carver,** John[2] (James[1]), bapt. Doncaster, Yorkshire, Eng., Sept. 9, 1565; died Plymouth, Mass., Apr. 12-May 10, 1621; married Catherine (**White**) **Leggatt** of Sturton-le-Steeple, Eng. She died Plymouth May, 1621.

During the last years of Elizabeth she encouraged the spirit of commerce, trade, and industry among her people. The shackles of royal rule and state church had been greatly softened. The fear of unjust taxation by an arrogant and selfish nobility and a powerful, hungry state church had been greatly lessened, and this very real fear had been the main reason for lack of enterprise in the realm for centuries. Naturally, most of the merchants, for these reasons, cultivated a "Puritan" leaning, many of them even being for an independent church. They felt about as John Robinson expressed it, "A man hath, in truth, so much of religion as he hath between the Lord and himself in secret, and no more." To them the crushing cost of a formal state church was entirely unnecessary.

Many north country men of Yorkshire, Nottinghamshire and east coast counties had given up the century old occupation of "yeoman" or farmer, and had become some kind of a merchant or trader between England and the continent, especially with Holland, through the growing commerce center of Norwich. Parents of high or low degree were anxious to apprentice their sons as soon as possible to some successful merchant, and, for a seven year period.

Isaac Carver and his brother John inherited some property from their father James, and both of them were merchants with interests in Holland. Some of their lands were in Yorkshire and Lincolnshire. Doncaster is but a few miles from Austerfield, Scrooby and Sturton, where the Bradfords, Brewsters and Robinsons lived.

The Carvers were business men, and interested in religion and forms of worship only as good citizens and laymen. They were, probably, never very active in the "separatist" movement. They had been in Holland long before Robinson ever thought of organizing a church there, and while in Leyden, they would, of course, join the English church in that place. Anyway, John Carver was a brother-in-law of Robinson's, and perhaps aided the good pastor to meet some of the expenses. He must have been a welcome addition to the congregation. Brewster, o course, having marked teaching capacity was the ruling elder for a time in Leyden, but Carver was made a Deacon.

Under the Robinson family in this volume will be found mor extended comments on the relationship between Carver an the pastor.

John Carver was about the same age as Brewster, but withou his training, education and ability. He had been a land owne and merchant for many years. In fact he removed from Nor wich, England, to Middleburgh, Holland, in 1591, to Naarde

1592, to Amsterdam in 1596, and to Leyden in 1596, where some years later his brother-in-law organized a congregation which he joined.

About this time, 1608, he married Mrs. Catherine (White) Leggatt, widow of George Leggatt and daughter of Alexander White of Sturton-le-Steeple on the River Trent of North Nottinghamshire. This union brought him the additional burden of managing his wife's property in England, which must have taken some considerable portion of his time. However, he was living in Leyden in 1609, for he buried a child there in July, 1609, and was in Leyden residing on "Middelgracet" 1617. About this time Robert Carver, his nephew, came to Leyden. His father, Isaac, had probably died there.

In 1617 Brewster, Carver and Cushman were in active negotiation with Sir Edwin Sandys of the Virginia Company, regarding plans for transporting a portion of Robinson's congregation to the Colonies. The Company sent out six vessels 1619-20, one of them, the Mayflower, transported the Leyden group and others to Cape Cod, where the Plymouth Plantation was founded. A few weeks after reaching the Cape, on Jan. 18, 1621, Christopher Martin, the Governor, died. John Carver was elected in his place, but died soon after between Apr. 12-May 10, 1621. Being a plain business man Carver left no writings of any kind. His only known signature is on the will of William Mullins Mar. 3, 1621. He left no descendants.

## HOOKE

I. **Hooke, John**[1], born England; died Plymouth Plantation early 1621, after Jan. 11, 1621. He was a Mayflower Planter.

This name is found in the parish of St. Giles, Cripplegate in 1600, and also in the parish of St. Bartholomew the Great in 1620 or the year before. The Martin and Rogers families are of this parish sometime before 1620.

# WARREN

I. **Warren,** Richard[1], born England; died Plymouth, Mass., 1628; married before 1611, Elizabeth **March,** widow of Juat **Pratt;** born England 1583 (?); died Plymouth Oct. 12, 1673. (See Warren Family, by Prof. J. C. Warren, 1854).

He was closely affiliated with the Merchant Adventurers of London, but the details of his life in England are not now available, and will be commented upon in future volumes of this work as they are found. His life in Plymouth was short. Bradford states "Mr. Richard Warren, but his wife and children were left behind and came afterwards."

Mrs. Warren and her five daughters came to Plymouth in 1623. After the death of her husband in 1628, she demonstrated a high efficiency, especially in property transactions.

There is no account of the settlement of his estate in Plymouth, and the papers are probably carefully preserved somewhere in England.

During the landing operations, Warren went out with the 3rd exploring party from the Mayflower as it lay at anchor in Cape Cod Harbor. The party set out in the Shallop on Wednesday, Dec. 6, 1620, and after numerous adventures, including a fight with the Indians early Friday morning, landed at Plymouth on the following Monday, Dec. 11, 1620. A few weeks after the arrival of his wife and daughters in the "Anne," he received lots on "the north side of the eele-river."

He was among the "Purchasers" of 1627 to buy from the London Adventurers all their rights in the Colony. In the division, the 9th lot fell to Richard Warren, naming his family.

In "New England's Memorial—Morton—1667," p. 68 is this statement about Warren:

"This year (1628) died Mr. Richard Warren, who hath been mentioned before in this Book and was an useful Instrument, and during his life bore a deep share in the Difficulties and Troubles of the first Settlement of the Plantation of New Plimouth."

### CHILDREN

IIa. Mary, b. Eng.      ; d.      ; m. Robert **Bartlett.**
IIIb. Anna, b. Eng.   (?) 1612; d.      ; m. Thomas **Little.**
IVc. Sarah, b. Eng.    ; d. after July 15, 1676; m. John **Cooke.**
Vd. Elizabeth, b. Eng.    ; d. Mar. 9, 1669; m. Richard **Church.**
VIe. Abigail, b. Eng.    ; d.      ; m. Anthony **Snow.**
VIIf. Nathaniel, b. Ply.   1624 (?); d.   1667; m. Sarah **Walker.**
VIIIg. Joseph, b. Ply.   1626 (?); d.      ; m. Priscilla **Faunce.**

# BARTLETT

**IIa. Warren**, Mary[2] (Richard[1]), married Robert **Bartlett**. (See Brewster I).

## LITTLE

**IIIb. Warren**, Anna[2] (Richard[1]), born England; married Thomas **Little** after 1633; died Marshfield Mar., 1672. His will is dated May 17, 1671, probated July 1, 1672. Thomas Little was in Plymouth after 1633, where he married Anna **Warren**. In 1650 he removed to Marshfield, where he assumed the functions of a legal advisor or "Lawyer."

### CHILDREN

a. Lt. Isaac, b.     ; d.     ; m. Bethia (    ).
b. Ephraim, b.     ; d.     ; m. Mary **Sturtevant**.
c. Thomas, b.     ; d. Mar. 26, 1676; m.——.
d. Samuel, b.     ; d.     ; m. Sarah **Grey**.
e. Ruth, b.     ; d.     ; m. .
f. Hannah, b.     ; d.     ; m. Stephen **Tilden**.
g. Patience, b.     ; d.     ; m. .
h. Mercy, b.     ; d.     ; m. John **Sawyer**.

Ref. 291.

## COOKE

**IVc. Warren**, Sarah[2] (Richard[1]), married John **Cooke**. (See Vol. I, p. 158, for family record).
Rev. John[2] **Cooke** (Francis[1]), removed to Dartmouth, Mass., as one of the original proprietors, and became a Baptist minister. He died Dartmouth Nov. 23, 1695 (N. S.). His will and inventory are in Bristol Co., Mass., Probate Records, Vol. I, p. 139-140.

## CHURCH

**Vd. Warren**, Elizabeth[2] (Richard[1]), born England; died Hingham, Mass., Mar. 9, 1669; married Richard **Church** 1636 7; born 1608 (?); died Dedham, Mass., Dec. 27, 1668, and was buried at Hingham. His will is recorded in Suffolk Co. at Boston, Vol. 6, p. 26, Inventory Vol. V, p. 116.
Richard[1] Church came to New England about 1630. He may have come over with Winthrop's fleet, but was in Plymouth as a freeman Oct. 4, 1632. He seems to have paid his own way over, and was free to do as he chose. He was a carpenter and builder, and, together with John Thomson, built the first church in the

Colony, but he had to sue the Pilgrim Fathers for his pay. At various times he resided at Plymouth, Duxbury, Eastham and Charlestown, 1653, and last at Hingham, 1668, residing there for the rest of his life.

He is mentioned in an interesting deposition taken at Sandwich Aug. 25, 1664. "Richard **Church** aged about 56 yeares this Deponant saith that hee being att worke about the mill the 19th of August hearing of a Cry that the man was killed; hasted p'sently and healped to remove the earth from Thomas **ffisk** whoe being much bruised thereby was gott to bedd and in four Dayes and a halfe Dyed: and further saith not."

Richard **Church** died in Dedham, where he was on a visit, his death taking place "Sabbath day erly in the morning."

Eleven of his children reached maturity.

### CHILDREN

a. Elizabeth, b.      ; died young.
b. Joseph, b.      1637-8; d. Mar. 5, 1711; m. Mary **Tucker.**
c. Col. Benjamin, b.      1639; d. Jan. 17, 1718; m. Alice **Southworth.**
d. Elizabeth, b.      ; d. Feb. 3, 1658-9; m. Caleb **Hobart.**
c. Nathaniel, b.      ; d.      1688-9; m. Sarah **Barstow.**
f. Caleb, b.      1642; d.      1722; m. 1st Joanna **Sprague;** m. 2nd Deborah (      ); m. 3rd Rebecca **Scotto.**
g. Charles, killed Oct. 30, 1659; cart overturned.
h. Richard, died young.
i. Abigail, b. June 22, 1647; d. Dec. 25, 1677; m. Samuel **Thaxter.**
j. Hannah, bp. Aug. 8, 1647; m. Josiah **Sturtevant.**
k. Mary, died Duxbury 1662.
l. Sarah, bp. Dec. 8, 1674; m. James **Burroughs.**
m. Lydia, married a Frenchman; resided in France.
n. Priscilla, b. 1645.
o. Deborah, b. Jan. 27, 1657 (?); d. Jan. 17, 1690.

Ref. 311.

## SNOW

VIe. **Warren,** Abigail[2] (Richard)[1]), born England; married Anthony **Snow;** died Marshfield, Mass., Aug., 1692. His original will is in possession of the Conn. Hist. Soc. at Hartford; however, it is recorded in Plymouth Co., Mass., Vol. I, p. 156-8. The original will carries his signature.

He was at Plymouth 1638, and an early settler at Green Harbor, Marshfield. He gave the town land near the meeting house for a burial ground, later called Cedar Grove Cemetery.

a. Josiah, b. Mar. 25, 1655; d. Aug. 1692; m. Rebecca **Baker.**

b. Alice, b. Jan. 18, 1657; d.      ; m.      .

c. Sarah, b.      ; d.      ; m. Joseph **Waterman.**

d. Abigail, b.      ; d.      ; m. Michael **Ford.**

e. Lydia, b.      ; d.      ; m.      .

## WATERMAN

I. **Waterman,** Robert[1], arrived in New England from Norwich, England, in 1636. The most valuable sites around Plymouth had already been taken up, so that the new comers had to push out in boats along the shores of Massachusetts Bay to find suitable places to settle.

Although a living was made by hunting and fishing, land was the great desire of the colonists, partly because it was the natural way of obtaining a living in those pioneer days in any country, and also because the owner of real estate was held in such high regard in the mother country.

Robert finally located a pleasant place near Green's Harbor in what is now Marshfield. Here he resided until his death in Dec. 12, 1652, and served efficiently in numerous town offices, such as selectman, and deputy to the legislature from 1644 to 1649. He married Elizabeth **Bourne** of Plymouth, Dec. 11, 1638, daughter of Thomas **Bourne.**

### CHILDREN BORN MARSHFIELD

a. Dea. John, b. Apr. 19, 1642; d. Sept. 14, 1718; m. Ann **Sturtevant.**

IIb. Joseph, b.      1643; d. Jan. 1, 1712; m. Sarah **Snow.**

c. Thomas, b.      1644; d.      1708; m. Marian **Tracy.**

d. Robert, b.      1652; d. May 18, 1741; m. 1st Sussana **Lincoln;** m. 2nd Sarah **Lincoln.**

e. (?) Elizabeth, b.      ; d.      ; m.      **Rider.**

IIb. **Waterman,** Joseph[2] (Robert[1]), born Marshfield 1643; died there Jan. 1, 1712; married Sarah **Snow,** daughter of Anthony **Snow** and Abigail[2] **Warren** (Richard[1]), a Mayflower Passenger.

Joseph had succeeded to his home in Marshfield.

CHILDREN BORN MARSHFIELD

a. Sarah, b. May 4, 1674; d.      ; m. Solomon **Hurst.**
b. Joseph, b. June 20, 1676; d. Nov. 23, 1715; m. Susanna **Snow.**
c. Elizabeth, b. Sept. 7, 1679; d.      ; m. Ichabod **Bartlett.**
d. Abigail, b. Dec. 31, 1681; d.      ; m. Kendall **Winslow,** Jr.
e. Anthony, b. June 4, 1684; d. Apr. 3, 1715; m. Elizabeth **Arnold.**
f. Bethia, b. Aug. 20, 1687; d.      ; m. Samuel **Daggitt.**
g. Lydia, b. Feb. 20, 1689; d.      ; m. John **Thomas.**

Ref. 210.

## WARREN

VIIf. **Warren,** Nathaniel[2] (Richard[1]), born Plymouth 1624 (?); died Plymouth 1667; married Sarah **Walker.**
His will is dated June 29, 1667, codicil July 16, 1667, and the inventory is Oct. 30, 1667, on the oath of Sarah Warren, widow. Plymouth Colony Wills and Inventories, Vol. II, Pt. II, folios 46 and 47.

CHILDREN BORN PLYMOUTH

a. Richard; b.      ; d.      1696; m. Sarah (      ).
b. Jabez; b.      ; d. young; m.———.
c. Sarah; b. Aug. 29, 1649; d.      ; m. John **Blackwell.**
d. Hope; b. Mar. 7, 1651; d.      ; m.      .
e. Jane; b. Dec. 31, 1652; d.      ; m. Benjamin **Lombard.**
f. Elizabeth, b. Sept. 5, 1654; d.      ; m. William **Green.**
g. Alice; b. Aug. 2, 1656; d.      ; m. Thomas **Gibbs.**
h. Mercy; b. Feb. 20, 1658; d.      ; m. Jonathan **Delano.**
i. Mary; b. Mar. 9, 1660; d.      ; m.      .
j. John; b. Oct. 23, 1663; d. young; m.———.
k. James; b. Nov. 7, 1665; d.      ; m. Sarah **Doty.**
l. Nathaniel; b.      ; d.      1707; m. Phebe **Murdock.**

VIIIg. **Warren,** Joseph[2] (Richard[1]), born Plymouth 1626 (?); died Plymouth May 4, 1689; married Precilla **Faunce** 1651; died May 15, 1707, age 74 (?). His will and inventory are in Plymouth County Records, Vol. I, p. 38-39.
He was a highly esteemed citizen.

CHILDREN BORN PLYMOUTH

a. Mercy, b. Sept. 23, 1653; d. Mar. 1747; m. John **Bradford.**
b. Abigail, b. Mar. 15, 1655; d. young; m.———.
c. Joseph, b. Jan. 8, 1657; d.      1696; m. Mehitable **Wilder.**
d. Patience, b. Mar. 15, 1660; d.      ; m. Samuel **Lewis.**
e. Elizabeth, b. Aug. 15, 1662; d.      ; m. Josiah **Phinney.**
f. Benjamin, b. Jan. 8, 1670; d.      ; m.      .

# FIVE SISTER SHIPS OF THE MAYFLOWER
## 1620

Sir Edwin Sandys, immediately on assuming the office of treasurer of the Virginia Company, under the Earle of Southampton, friend of Shakespeare, and dissenters in general, made plans to send another expedition of planters to America or "Virginia."

The Jamestown Colony after twelve years was almost an accepted failure, in fact, was so classed by King James, who had lost all interest in the matter, since "gold" was not forthcoming.

However, the Merchant Adventurers had invested real funds in the colonization enterprise, and could not be so easily dis‧couraged. Many of them felt that South Virginia (Jamestown), with its single crop of "tobacco," questionable geographic position, and climate, was not the best location along the Atlantic seaboard for a successful settlement. How and where to plant another colony was a problem. The French, Dutch and Spanish were pressing them hard, and something must be done without delay, or the English would be without a colony in America. James had also lost interest in the Northern Virginia patent, and it was dormant, although the fishing business in that section had been more or less active for many years.

Naturally, all angles of the situation were discussed at the Company meetings in London. The King and his Court had dropped the matter, and the Company had full power of decision and action. In fact, the Company had been in control since 1609. It was decided to proceed with the organization of an expedition, and the question of planting a new colony could be determined on its merits by agents of the Company at the proper time, wherever they might be.

After some searching six ships were found and engaged to transport the expeditions, according to a record No. 152 in the Public Record Office, London.

"a note of the shipping, men and Provisions sent and provided for Virginia by the Right Honorable, the Earle of Southampton, and the Company, the yeare 1620."

### Ships

1. The Bona Nova, 200 tons, sent in Aug. 1620; 120 persons.
2. Elizabeth, 40 tons, sent in Aug. 1620; 20 persons.
3. Mayflower, 140 tons, sent in Aug. 1620, 100 persons.
4. The Supply of Bristol, 80 tons, sent in Sept. 1620, 45 persons.
5. Margaret and John, 150 tons, sent in Dec. 1620, 85 persons.
6. Abigail, 350 tons, sent in Feb. 1620, 230 persons.

Some instructions were issued to raise the personnel of the expedition, such as,

"So we now also declare that the persons to be admitted to goe, x x x x shall be no other than good men, that is to say, of good trades, of skill in husbandry or industrious laboures, and such of those as shall be commended for their honest conversation, which persons repairing to the citie of London, to Mr. Ferrar, Deputy to the Company, his house in St. Sithes' Lane, in the beginning of August (1620) x x x x according to the several numbers at those times to be sent, shall from thence-forward be entertained at the Companies charges till such time as they be shipped for Virginia, there being especiall care likewise taken for providing of good commanders and Directors of their workes."

"We have thought fit, to make it publikely kowne, that besides the great store of particular Plantations now in providing, and like very shortly in large proportion to augment, the Company have resolved in a late general meeting, by the blessing of God x x x to fit out this yeare x x x x and to send to Virginia, eight hundred choice persons."

A number of the "Mayflower Planters," and close friends such as Brewster, Hopkins, Rogers, Southworth, Mullins,‑ Martin, Carver, Cushman, Robinson, Bradford, Allerton and others were frequent visitors in 1619 at Sir Thomas Smith's house in Philpott Lane, and at Sir Edwin Sandy's house near "Aldersgate." This was in or near the famous "Duke Place," and, of course, during the final decision in 1620, they were callers at Mr. Ferrar's in St. Sithe's Lane.

It may be noted that among the instructions is a rather suggestive statement:

"Plantations now in providing, and like very shortly in large proportion to augment."

They may have had in mind the planting of a colony in Northern Virginia, perhaps on Cape Cod, especially, when it is remembered that the "Mayflower" had as its Governor, Christopher Martin, a direct agent of the Company, and one who was thoroughly familiar with the Jamestown Plantation, in fact, had lived there. Brewster, Hopkins and other passengers were also quite familiar with the whole situation.

At last the expedition of 1620 was ready to depart. The **Bona Nova,** Elizabeth and Mayflower managed, after various delays, to sail from England between August-November, 1620.

In a letter from Sir Edwin Sandys to John Ferrar dated Sept. 18, 1620, he states

> "On Thursday, the 7th of this instant, the Bona Nova w[th] her Pinnace set saile from the Downs w[th] a prosperous wynd, & was met that evening beyond the Nosse. That day we spent here amongest o[r] frends in great joy."
>
> Edwin Sandys.

The ship **Elizabeth** was small, and with 20 persons on board left England not long before the Mayflower, and seems to have gone to the vicinity of "NewFoundland," and Cape Cod.

The first three ships appear to have tarried around Northern Vrginian waters for some time. Finally the Bona Nova left for Jamestown where she arrived safely, while the Elizabeth remained somewhere near the Mayflower until the spring of 1621, when she sailed for Southern Virginia, taking, it is thought, at least one Mayflower passenger with her, the young man, Edward Leister, who had recently fought a duel with Edward Doty, the first one in the Colony.

Edward Leister was murdered by Indians at Capt. Samuel Maycock's dividend near Flowerdien Hundred, Friday morning, Mar. 22, 1622, in the vicinity of Jamestown.

The **Mayflower** ship was described in Volume I of this Series, page 23. Her "Pinnace," the Speedwell, was abandoned.

The **Supply of Bristol** and its passenger list are of record, and quite complete, similar to that of the sister ship "Mayflower." It sailed, apparently, direct for Jamestown, where many of the planters were murdered by Indians in 1622. The details in connection with this ship are substantially as follows:

"Thomas Parker, mayor of Bristol, Certificate for sailing of the ship "Supply," Sept. 18, 1620.

To the Treasurer Counsell and Company of adventurers and planters of the City of London for the first colony in Virginia.

Theis are to certify that in the good ship called the Supply this present xviij[th] day of September 1620, were shipped from our port of Bristoll for plantacon in Virginia at the charge of Richard Berkeley, George Thorpe, Willm Tracy and John Smyth, Esqs., under the conduct of the said Willm Tracy appoynted Captayne and Governor over them theis fifty six psons whose names ensue, who forthwith proceeded in their voyage accordingly."

Willm Tracy, Esq.
Mary Tracy, his wife.
Thomas Tracy, their sonne.
Joyce Tracy, their daughter.
ffrancis Grevill.
Joane Green.
Elizabeth Webb.
Isabell Gifford.
Gyles Carter.
George Hale.
John Bayly.
Thomas Baugh.
Gabriell Holland.
Richard Holland.
Giles Wilkins.
John Page.
ffrancis, his wife.
Willm Piffe.
John Linsey.
Richard Hopkins.
Richard Smyth.
Joane, his wife.
Anthony, their sonne.
William, their other sonne.
Robert Bysaker.
ffayth, his wife.
Gyles Brodway.
Richard Dutton.
Richard Milton.

Arnold Oldsworth, Esq.
Robt. Pawlet, divine.
Thomas Kemis, gent.
Arthur Kemis, gent.
Robert Longe, gent.
John Holmeden, gent.
Richard ffereby, gent.
Thomas Shepy, gent.
George Keene, gent.
Nicholas Carne, gent.
Willm ffinch.
Elizabeth, his wife.
ffrancis, their sonne.
Willm Peirs, the elder.
Richard Peirs.
John Gibbes.
Robert Baker.
John Howlet, the elder.
John, his sonne.
Roger Linsey.
Walter Prosser.
Willm Howlet.
James Jelfe.
Richard Rowles.
Jane, his wife.
Benedict Rowles.
Alexander Brodway.
Joane Coopy.
Anthony & Elizabeth, her children.

Signed: Thomas Parker, Mayor.

The **Margaret and John** was in service quite frequently, and either a few months before or after the arrival of the Mayflower at Plymouth was in a sea battle. The report of it is headed,

"A true relation of a sea fight between two great well appointed Spanish men of war and the Margaret and John, Mar. 30, 1620-21."

Sections of the report with comments follow: "The Margaret and John of 150 tons left England early in January with 85 persons. At Guadeloupe, she took on 6 Frenchmen" and then there were in all, including the crew, 103 persons, men, women and children.

When off "Mevis," they desired to take on water, "being the common trade way both for English and Dutch." On Mar. 30, 1620-1, they fell in with two large ships "pretending to be Hollanders," but as soon as these ships had gained a fair position, and after some parley, they took in their Holland flag, advanced the Spanish colors, and opened fire on the "small and not well provided English shipp, who, parforce was constreyned to enter into the conflict, which continued 5 or 6 houres most desperate."

The English finally beat off both Spanish ships, after killing their captains and making the "Skuppers run with blood," and "coulering the sea in their quarter."

The burden of the largest Spanish ship was 300 tons, with 22 pieces of brass, of the other, 200 tons, having 16 pieces of brass.

The English ship had eight cast iron pieces and one small "faulcon," and lost eight men.

This sea fight became more or less famous, and an account of it appeared in London in 1621.

The ship **Abigail** probably left England in February, 1620, and very likely arrived at Jamestown in June, being delayed for various reasons.

Although the passenger list is not available, there is a record of certain items which were taken along, and price paid for them.

"Payd for white and blue beads 2$^l$ 1$^s$ 3$^d$, and for .36 bed cords at 6$^l$ 7$^s$ 8$^d$ and 9$^{d·}$, the pound peece .22$^s$, and for a rope for the fishing net at .3$^d$ the pound, vj$^s$, iij$^d$, and for booke vizt Babingtons work 10$^s$, ffrench surgeon V$^s$, Euchiredion medicn 18$^d$, Smyth of doctrines Vj$^{d·}$ Toto 17$^s$. The barrel to put the "pimisses" in 2$^s$6$^d$, porter & packinge 6$^d$.

In all sent by the Abigaill .18. Januar 1620."

Refs. 409, 410, 476, 473, 472, 474, 480, 481.

# HOWLAND

The surname, since its appearance in England in the 14th century, has undergone several ways of spelling, such as Howlande, Houland, Holan, Hollan, Hoyland and others. The English ancestry has been the subject of considerable investigation.

Eighty-seven years ago on May 21, 1855, Mr. John B. Howland of Providence, R. I., wrote to "Notes and Queries" in London, requesting information about John Howland, "salter," and his twelve children.

Sometime before 1880, Col. Chester in England, a very thorough searcher, made some investigations, and without doubt accumulated much valuable material that does not now seem readily available.

Mr. L. M. Howland, of New York, communicated some extracts, apparently received from Col. Chester, under date of April, 1880, to the New England Historical and Genealogical Register (Vol. 34, p. 192). Unfortunately, the details of essential family records were omitted from this article, although it appears that the family records in question were probably known, at least, to Col. Chester.

For instance, John, the "Salter" and brother, Ralph, are mentioned, with the remark that John "had eleven sons and one daughter, who died an infant."

Then a little later, it is stated that John Howland and Blanche Nightingale "Had four sons and three daughters."

In the last paragraph of the article, Mr. Howland states: "The history which Mr. Chester will prepare will serve as a most suitable preface to a work one day to be compiled as a record of the descendants of Arthur, John and Henry Howland."

Such a work has appeared, in 1885, but, for some reason, without the vital records above mentioned, and they are quite important. Col. Chester's notes must be preserved among some of the London archives on this family.

Brig. Gen. Charles R. Howland, U.S.A. Ret., is now making efforts to collect the early English records pertaining to Howland, which are all within a radius of fifteen or twenty miles of Cambridge, England, including Newporte, Wicken, Debden, Fen Stanton and Ely. These early Howlands were all closely related, no doubt.

I. **Howland,** Arthur, born England; died Marshfield, Mass., 1675; married Margaret **Reed,** widow; died 1683.

It is not known just when he arrived in Plymouth, but after a few years he became a landowner and resident of Marshfield, where he died. He was a member of the Society of Friends, and his house was a headquarters for the sect. He was fined and persecuted at various times for permitting Quaker meetings at his house. He was even committed to jail. He was before one court on June 1, 1658, and one of the members of this particular court was his brother John Howland, the Mayflower Planter.

## CHILDREN

a. Arthur, b.   ; d.   ; m. Elizabeth **Prence.**
b. Deborah, b.   ; d.   ; m. John **Smith,** Jr.
c. Mary, b.   ; d.   ; m. 1st Timothy **Williamson**; m. 2nd Robert **Sanford.**
d. Martha, b.   ; d.   ; m. John **Damon.**
e. Elizabeth, b.   ; d.   ; m. John **Low.**

I. **Howland,** Henry, born England; died Duxbury, Mass., Jan. 17, 1671; married Mary **Newland;** died Duxbury, June 16, 1674. She was a sister of William Newland who came from Lynn in 1637 and settled in Sandwich. She and her brother were Quakers.

Henry resided for a while in Plymouth, but became an early settler in Duxbury "by the bayside, near Love Brewster." He was a surveyor of highways, and able to bear arms in 1643. As a Quaker he suffered the persecutions of the times. On April 2, 1659, Henry with 26 others bought of the Indians what is now Freetown, for a few old coats, rugs, iron pots, etc., including "one little kittle." In 1664 he purchased a large portion of land in Mattapoisett (Swansea). Henry was owner of the sixth lot in Freetown. However, his sons, John and Samuel, really became the actual settlers.

## CHILDREN BORN DUXBURY

a. Joseph, b.   ; d. June 15, 1692; m. Rebecca **Huzzey.**
b. Zoeth, b.   1636 (?); d. Jan. 31, 1676; m. Abigail (  ).
c. John, b.   ; d.   1687; m.   .
IId. Samuel, b.   ; d.   1716; m. Mary (  ).
e. Sarah, b.   ; d.   ; m. Robert **Dennis.**
f. Elizabeth, b.   ; d.   ; m. Jedidiah **Allen.**
g. Mary, b.   ; d.   ; m. James **Cudworth.**
h. Abigail, b.   ; d.   ; m. John **Young.**

IId. **Howland,** Samuel[2] (Henry[1]), born Duxbury; died Freetown, Bristol County, Mass., 1716.

CHILDREN PROBABLY BORN FREETOWN

a. Content, b.    ; d. Swansea; m. (    ) **Sanford** of Swansea.
*b. Samuel, b.    ; d.    ; m.    .
c. Isaac, b.    ; d.    ; m. Alice **Sherman** of Dartmouth.
d. Abraham, b. May 9, 1675; d.    ; m. 1st Ann **Colson**; m. 2nd Ann **Rouse**.
e. John, b.    ; d.    ; m.    .
f. Joshua, b.    ; d.    ; m. 1st Elizabeth **Holloway**; m. 2nd Dorothy **Lee**.
*g. Gersham, b.    ; d.    ; m.    .
h. Alice, b.    ; d. Swansea; m. Job **Mason** of Swansea.
i. Mary, b.    1673; d. May 8, 1744; m. Phillip **Roundsville**.

* Although Samuel and Gersham were living in 1716, the Howland Genealogy (1885) fails to clearly give their family records. At the death of their father in 1716, they apparently were residing in Freetown or vicinity.

I. **Howland**, John, born England; died Plymouth Mar. 5, 1675 (N. S.); married Elizabeth[2] **Tilley** at Plymouth before 1624; born England about 1607; died Swansea, Mass., Dec. 31, 1687 (N. S.), age 80; daughter of John **Tilley**, the Mayflower Passenger, brother of Edward **Tilley**.

John Howland resided in Plymouth until 1638, when he removed to Rocky Nook, now a part of Kingston. He was a respected and useful citizen, holding various town offices, and active in support of the church, although his two brothers, Henry of Duxbury, and Arthur of Marshfield, were Quakers.

Apparently Elizabeth Tilley was married at about the age of sixteen, and John was probably somewhere near the same age as several other of the unattached persons on the Mayflower, twenty in all, mentioned on pages 47-50, Vol. I of this series.

Of these unattached persons, who were probably "put" in the family groups according to agreement (see page 31, Vol. 1), only four, John Howland, Richard More, Edward Doty and George Soule, married and brought up families in the Colony.

It appears certain that this group of twenty were of substantial families in England. Only eight survived the first winter, and, strange to relate, three of these, Desire Minter, Edward Litster, and William Latham left the Colony within a short time after landing.

Six had been placed in Carver's family, two young ladies, one unidentified, and four young men, two of them mere boys. John Howland was the only one to bring up a family, so far as known.

The brothers, John, Arthur and Henry Howland, apparently came to the Colony through the powerful influence of the Company of Drapers in London, with whom their brother Humphrey was associated. This Company of Merchants held a large block of stock in the Virginia Company, and were anxious to send a high type of settler to the colonies. Members of the Brewster family were also associated with the Draper's Company of London.

CHILDREN BORN PLYMOUTH

(Order of birth uncertain.)

IIa. Desire, b. 1623; d. Oct. 13, 1683; m. John **Gorham.**

IIIb. John, b. Feb. 24, 1627; d. ; m. Mary **Lee.**

IVc. Jabez, b. 1628; d. 1712; m. Bethia **Thatcher.**

Vd. Hope, b. Aug. 30, 1629; d. Jan. 8, 1683-4; m. John **Chipman.**

VIe. Lydia, b. ; d. ; m. James **Brown.**

VIIf. Ruth, b. ; d. 1672-9; m. Thomas **Cushman.**

VIIIg. Hannah, b. ; d. ; m. Jonathan **Bosworth.**

IXh. Joseph, b. 1644; d. Jan. 1703-4; m. Elizabeth **Southworth.**

Xi. Isaac, b. Nov. 15, 1649; d. Mar. 9, 1723-4; m. Elizabeth **Vaughn.**

XIj. Elizabeth, b. ; d. ; m. 1st Ephraim **Hicks;** m. 2nd John **Dickinson.**

## GORHAM

IIa. **Howland,** Desire[2] (John[1]), born Plymouth 1624; died Barnstable, Mass., Oct. 13, 1683; married Capt. John[2] **Gorham** 1643; bapt. Benefield, Northamptonshire, Eng., Jan. 28, 1621; died Swansea Feb. 5, 1675, son of Ralph[1] **Gorham** of Duxbury.

This family has a line to the De Gorrams of La Tanniere, near Gorram, in Maine, on the borders of Brittany, where they lived in a castle. Members of the family came to England with William the Conqueror.

Many of the name in England became men of learning, wealth and influence. His father, Ralph, and grandfather, James, resided at Benefield. Ralph was born 1575 and came to New England with his family, being in Plymouth 1637.

Captain John Gorham became a very useful citizen, residing at times in Plymouth, Marshfield, Yarmouth and Barnstable.

During King Philip's War he was in command of a company.

CHILDREN

a. Desire, b. May 20, 1644; d. June 30, 1700; m. John **Hawes.**
b. Temperance, b. May 5, 1646; d. Mar. 12, 1714-5; m. 1st
   Edward **Sturgis;** m. 2nd Thomas **Baxter.**
c. Elizabeth, b. Apr. 2, 1648; d.          ; m. Joseph **Hallett.**
d. James, b. Apr. 28, 1650; d.      1707; m. Hannah **Huckins.**
e. Lt. Col. John, b. Feb. 20, 1652; d. Dec. 9, 1716; m. Mary
   **Otis.**
f. Ens. Joseph, b. Feb. 16, 1654; d. July 9, 1726; m. Sarah
   **Sturgis.**
g. Jabez, b. Aug. 3, 1656; d.          ; m. (      ) **Sturgis.**
h. Mercy, b. Jan. 20, 1658; d.      ! m. George **Denison.**
i. Lydia, b. Nov. 16, 1661; d. Aug. 2, 1744; m. Col. John
   **Thatcher.**
j. Hannah, b. Nov. 28, 1663; d. Cape May, N. J., 1728; m.
   Joseph **Whilldin.**
k. Shubel, b. Oct. 21, 1667; d.          ; m. Puella **Hussey.**

## HOWLAND

IIIb. **Howland,** John² (John¹), born Plymouth Feb. 24, 1627;
died Barnstable Oct. 26, 1651; married Mary **Lee** Dec. 26, 1651;
daughter of Robert **Lee** of Barnstable.
   He resided in Barnstable. In 1674 he was appointed "En-
signe of the Milletary companie of Barnstable" and became in
1689 a selectman. Later on he attained the rank of Lieut. in the
militia.

CHILDREN BORN BARNSTABLE

a. Mary, b.      1652; d.      ; m. John **Allyn.**
b. Elizabeth, b. May 17, 1655; d.      ; m. 1st John **Bursley;**
   m. 2nd Isaac **Hamblin.**
c. Isaac, b. Nov. 25, 1659; d.      ; m. Ann **Taylor.**
d. Hannah, b. May 15, 1661; d.      ; m. Jonathan **Crocker.**
e. Mercy, b. Jan. 21, 1663; d. before 5 mo. 1717; m. Joseph
   **Hamblin.**
f. Lydia, b. Jan. 9, 1665; d.      ; m. Joseph **Jenkins.**
g. Experience, b. July 28, 1668; d.      ; m. James **Bearse** (?).
h. Anne, b. Sept. 9, 1670; d.      ; m. Joseph **Crocker.**
i. Shubel, b. Sept. 30, 1672; d.      1737; m. Mercy **Blossom.**
j. John, b. Dec. 31, 1674; d.      1738; m. 1st Abigail
   **Crocker;** m. 2nd Mary **Crocker.**

IVc. **Howland,** Jabez² (John¹), born Plymouth; died Bristol,
R. I., 1711-2; married Bethia **Thatcher;** born Yarmouth 1640-5;
died Bristol, R. I., Dec. 19, 1725; daughter of Anthony **Thatcher**
from Salisbury, England.

[ 164 ]

In 1667 Jabez bought what is now known as the old Howland House. He resided at Duxbury and Plymouth, but in 1680 or about that time, removed to Bristol, R. I., where he built up a large business as blacksmith and cooper. He also ran the inn. He was representative to the General Courts at Plymouth, and Bristol, also an assessor. At the first town meeting in Bristol, Nov. 10, 1681, he was chosen town clerk.

He was also, at one time, a Lieut. under Capt. Benjamin Church in the Indian Wars, and was present at the battle in which King Phillip was killed.

His first five children were born in Plymouth, the others in Bristol.

### CHILDREN

a. Jabez, b. Nov. 15, 1669; d. Oct. 17, 1732; m. Patience **Stafford.**

b. John, b. Jan. 15, 1673; d. 1st mo. 1673; m.——.

c. Bethia, b. June 3, 1674; d.    1676; m.——.

d. Josiah, b. Aug. 6, 1676; d. Feb. 8, 1717; m. Yetmercy **Shove.**

e. John, b. July 26, 1679; d.    ; m.    .

f. Judah, b. May 5, 1683; d. Nov. 1683; m.——.

g. Seth, b. Jan. 5, 1685; d. 4th mo. 1685; m.——.

h. Dea. Samuel, b. May 24, 1686; d. May 15, 1748; m. 1st Abigail **Cary;** m. 2nd Rachel **Allen,** wid.; m. 3rd Dorothy **Hunt,** wid.

i. Experience, b. May 19, 1687; d. infancy; m.——.

j. Joseph, b. Oct. 14, 1692; d. Aug. 16, 1737; m. Bathsheba **Cary.**

k. Elizabeth, b.    ; d.    ; m. Nathan **Townsend.**

## CHIPMAN

Vd. **Howland,** Hope[2] (John[1]), born Plymouth Aug. 30, 1629; died Jan. 8, 1683-4; married John **Chipman** 1646, his 1st wife. He married 2nd Ruth **Sargent,** widow of Jonathan **Winslow,** and the Rev. Richard **Bourne.** He was probably born at Bryan's Piddle, near Dorchester, Eng., 1614, and died at Barnstable Apr. 7, 1708. His will is dated Nov. 12, 1702, proved May 17, 1708.

John Chipman resided in Yarmouth where his first child was born, then in Barnstable Marshes (West Barnstable) where his ten other children were born. He was a prominent man in Barnstable, holding the offices of selectman, deputy and the like, besides being a Ruling Elder in the church.

[ 165 ]

CHILDREN

a. Elizabeth, b. June 24, 1647; d. after 1712; m. Hosea Joyce.
b. Hope, b. Aug. 31, 1652; d. July 26, 1728; m. 1st John Huckins; m. 2nd Jonathan Cobb.
c. Lydia, b. Dec. 25, 1654; d. Mar. 2, 1730; m. John Sargent.
d. John, b. Mar. 2, 1656; d. May 29, 1657; m.——.
e. Hannah, b. Jan. 14, 1658; d. Nov. 4, 1696; m. Thomas Huckins.
f. Samuel, b. Apr. 15, 1661; d.    1723; m. Sarah Cobb.
g. Ruth, b. Dec. 31, 1663; d. April 8, 1698; m. Eleazer Crocker.
h. Bethia, b. July 1, 1666; d. before 1699; m. Shubel Dimock.
i. Mercy, b. Feb. 6, 1668; d. June 12, 1724; m. Nathan Skiff.
i. John, b. Mar. 3, 1669; d. Jan. 4, 1756; m. 1st Mary Skiff; m. 2nd Elizabeth Handley.
k. Desire, b. Feb. 26, 1673; d. Mar. 28, 1705; m. Col. Melatiah Bourne.

## BROWN

VIe. Howland, Lydia² (John¹), born Plymouth; married Major James Browne, son of John Browne. He died Oct. 29, 1710, near Swansea, where some of his children are recorded, and he resided.

Lydia received by will from her mother "my best feather bed & Boulster," which was no mean gift in those days.

Maj. James Browne was a brother of Capt. Thomas Willett's wife. He and Willett were the first trustees of Swansea.

CHILDREN RECORDED

a. James, b. May 4, 1655; d. Apr. 15, 1718; m. Margaret Denison.
b. Dorothy, b. Aug. 29, 1666; d. Nov. 12, 1727; m. Joseph Kent, Jr.
c. Jabez, b. July 9, 1668; d. before July 7, 1747; m. Jane (    ).

## BROWN

I. Brown, John, born England; died 1662 at Mattapoisett. He was an English shipbuilder, who knew the Pilgrims at Leyden, but did not join them there. In 1633 4, when about fifty years old, he came to Plymouth, with his wife Dorothy (    ), and at least three children. He brought a fair property, and in 1635 became a citizen and the next year began eighteen years on the board of assistants. In 1637 he was an original purchaser of Taunton, and in 1645 removed to Rehoboth, settling at Mattapoisett, now Swansea, on land bought from Massasoit. He was colonial commissioner for twelve years.

## CHILDREN

a. John, b.　　; d. before 1662.
IIb. James; b.　　; d.　　; m. Lydia **Howland.**
c. Mary; b.　　; d.　　; m. Thomas **Willet.**
IIb. (See VIe. Howland, Lydia).

## CUSHMAN

VIIf. **Howland,** Ruth² (John¹), married Thomas Cushman (see Cushman IIIa).

## BOSWORTH

VIIIg. **Howland,** Hannah² (John¹), born Plymouth; married Jonathan **Bosworth** of Swansea July 6, 1661.

He resided in Swansea, holding various town offices, and was highly respected. On Mar. 28, 1697, the Selectmen "confirmed the agreement made by the Selectmen with Mr. Jonathan Bosworth to be school-master to the town of Swansea the year ensuing, and to teach school in the several places in the town by course, and to have for his salary 18 pounds per year, one quarter in money, and the other three quarters in provisions, at money price."

## CHILDREN BORN SWANSEA

a. Mercy, b. May 30, 1662; d.　　; m.　　.
b. Hannah, b. Nov. 5, 1663; d.　　; m. Nathaniel **Jencks.**
c. Elizabeth, b. June 6, 1665; d. July 31, 1676; m.——.
d. Jonathan, b. Dec. 24, 1666; d. July 16, 1676; m.——.
e. David, b. Sept. 15, 1670; d.　　; m. Mercy **Sturdevant.**
f. John, b. Apr. 6, 1671; d.　　; m. Elizabeth **Toogood.**
g. Jabez, b. Feb. 14, 1673; d.　　; m. Sussanah (　　).
h. (?) Ickabod, b. Mar. 18, 1676; d.　　; m.　　.
i. Jonathan, b. Sept. 22, 1680; d.　　; m. Sarah **Rounds.**

## HOWLAND

IXh. **Howland,** Joseph² (John¹), born Plymouth 1644 (?); died Plymouth Jan. 1703-4; married Elizabeth³ **Southworth** Dec. 7, 1664, daughter of Thomas² **Southworth** (Edward¹).

He always resided in Plymouth, where he was a large owner of land near Pilgrim Hall. For many years he was a Lieut. of Militia.

CHILDREN BORN PLYMOUTH

    a. Lydia, b.     1665; d. June 7, 1717; m. Jeremiah **Thomas.**

    b. Elizabeth, b.  ; d.  ; m. Joseph **Hamblin.**

    c. Mary, b.  ; d.  ; m. George **Conant.**

    d. Thomas, b.  ; d. Dec. 7, 1739; m. Joanna **Cole.**

    e. James, b.  ; d.  ; m. Mary **Lothrop.**

    f. Nathaniel, b.  ; d. Dec. 29, 1746; m. Martha **Cole.**

    g. Sarah, b.    1687; d. before 1703; m.  .

    h. Benjamin, b.    1689; d. Sept. 7, 1689; m.——.

    i. Joseph, b.  ; d. July 8, 1689; m.——.

Xi. **Howland,** Isaac[2] (John[1]), born Plymouth Nov. 15, 1649; died Middleboro Mar. 9, 1723-4; married Elizabeth **Vaughn,** daughter of George **Vaughn** of Middleboro; born 1652; died Oct. 29, 1727, age 75.

He resided in Middleboro on land willed to him by his father. In August, 1676, he was a Lieut. under Col. Benjamin Church in his raids on the Indians, and held various town offices.

CHILDREN BORN MIDDLEBORO

    a. Seth, b. Nov. 26, 1677; d. Oct. 26, 1729; m. Elizabeth **Delano.**

    b. Isaac, b. Mar. 6, 1679; d.  ; m. Sarah **Thomas.**

    c. Pricilla, b. Aug. 22, 1681; d.  ; m. Peter **Bennett** (?).

    d. Elizabeth, b. Dec. 2, 1682; d. Apr. 1, 1685; m.——.

    e. Nathan, b. Oct. 13, 1687; d.  ; m. Frances **Coombs.**

    f. Jael, b. Oct. 13, 1688; d. Nov. 1743; m. Nathaniel **Southworth.**

    g. Sussanah, b. Oct. 14, 1690; d. Nov. 1743; m. Ephraim **Wood.**

    h. Hannah, b. Oct. 16, 1694; d. Mar. 25, 1792; m. John **Tinkham.**

**HICKS-DICKINSON**

XIj. **Howland,** Elizabeth[2] (John[1]), born Plymouth; married 1st Ephraim **Hicks** Sept. 13, 1649; he died three months later on Dec. 2, 1649, at Plymouth; married 2nd Capt. John **Dickinson** July 10, 1651, of Plymouth, who had married as his 1st wife Elizabeth **Hicks,** sister of Ephraim.

Capt. **Dickinson** (Dickarson) removed to Oyster Bay, L. I.

a. Elizabeth, b. Oct. 11, 1652; d.    ; m. Caleb **Wright.**
b. Joseph, b. Dec. 24, 1654; d.    ; m. Rose **Townsend.**
c. Mercy, b. Feb. 23, 1657; d.    ; m.   .
d. Jabez, b. July 1660; d.    ; m.   .
e. Lydia, b. Aug. 5, 1662; d.    ; m.   .
f. Samuel, b. Jan. 26, 1665; d.    ; m.   .
g. Mehetabell, b. Feb. 1667; d.    ; m.   .
h. Hannah, b. Jan. 6, 1671; d.    ; m.   .
i. James, b. May 27, 1675; d.    ; m.   .

# THATCHER

I. **Thatcher,** Rev. Peter[1], born 1545-49 at Queen Camel, Somersetshire, England. He married and brought up his family during the stirring times of Queen Elizabeth, and, for a minister who was more or less liberal in his views, there were many uncertain moments.

### CHILDREN (KNOWN)

a. Rev. Peter, b.    1587-8; d. Eng. 1640; m.   .
IIb. Anthony, b.    ; d.    ; m. Mary (   ).
c. John, b.    ; d. Eng. 1653; m.   .
d. Giles, b.    ; d. Eng. 1602; m.   .
e. Thomas, b.    ; d. Eng. 1650; m.   .

IIb. **Thatcher,** Anthony (Rev. Peter[1]), born England 1587-8; died Yarmouth 1667; married 1st Mary (   ) in England; died 1634; married 2nd, six weeks before sailing for New England, Elizabeth **Jones.** Before embarking he had to enter himself as some sort of a craftsman, and was listed as a "Taylor." The ship "James" arrived in New England June, 1635. After an attempt to settle at Marblehead, during which he lost his children by drowning, he removed to Yarmouth, prospered and accumulated a large estate.

### CHILDREN 1ST WIFE

a. William, b. Eng. 1620 (?); drowned Marblehead, Mass., 1635.
b. Edith, b. Eng.    ; drowned 1635.
c. Mary, b. Eng.    ; drowned 1635.
d. Peter, b. Eng.    ; drowned 1635.
e. Benjamin, b. Eng. April 13, 1634; d. Eng. Sept. 1, 1634.

CHILDREN 2ND WIFE

f. Col. John, b. Marblehead, Mar. 17, 1638; d. May 8, 1713; m. 1st Rebecca **Winslow**, wid.; m. 2nd Lydia **Gorham**.
g. Judah, b.    ; d. Nov. 4, 1676; m. Mary **Thornton**.
IIIh. Bethia, b.    ; d.    ; m. Jabez **Howland**.

IIIh. Bethia (see Howland IVc.).

Refs. 289, 172, 176, 290.

## COOKE

41. **Cooke,** Jacob[3] (Damaris[2] **Hopkins,** Stephen[1]), born Plymouth March 29, 1653; died 1747; married Lydia[3] **Miller** Dec. 29, 1681.

CHILDREN BORN PLYMOUTH

He resided near the river on the north side.
223. William, b. Oct. 5, 1683; d.    ; m. Tabitha **Hall**.
224. Lydia, b. May 18, 1685; d.    ; m. John **Faunce**.
225. Rebecca, b. Nov. 19, 1688; d.    ; m. Benjamin **Sampson**.
226. Jacob, b. June 16, 1691; d.    ; m. 1st Phebe **Hall**; m. 2nd Mary **Hercy**.
227. Margaret, b. Nov. 3, 1695; d.    ; m. Simon **Lazell**.
228. Josiah, b. May 14, 1699; d.    ; m.    .
229. John,    b. May 23, 1703; d.    ; m. Phebe **Crossman**.
230. Damaris,   b. May 23, 1703; d.    ; m.    .

Refs. 179, 182, 183, 190, 189.

## RICKARD

42. **Cooke,** Mary[3] (Damaris[2] **Hopkins,** Stephen[1]), born Plymouth Jan. 12, 1658; married John[3] **Rickard** (Giles[2], Giles[1]).

CHILDREN BORN PLYMOUTH

231. Marcy, b. Oct. 27, 1677; d. young; m.——.
232. Lydia, b. Dec. 12, 1680; d.    ; m. John **Tilson**.
233. John, b. Dec. 29, 1681; d.    ; m.    .
234. Joseph, b. Feb. 7, 1683; d.    ; m. Deborah **Miller**.
235. Marcy, b. May 14, 1687; d.    ; m. Ephraim **Tilson**.
236. Joanna, b. Sept. 22, 1691; d.    ; m. 1st Isreal **Dunham**; m. 2nd Elisha **Whiting**.
237. Abigail, b. May 22, 1694; d.    ; m. Samuel **Ransom**.
238. Rebecca, b. Jan. 3, 1699; d.    ; m. Thomas **Pratt**.

Refs. 173, 191, 292, 173.

# CUSHMAN

43. **Cooke, Martha³** (Damaris² **Hopkins, Stephen¹**), born Plymouth Mar. 16, 1659; died Plympton Sept. 17, 1722; married Elkanah³ **Cushman** Mar. 2, 1682 (his 2nd wife); born June 1, 1651; died Sept. 4, 1727. He married 1st Elizabeth **Cole** Feb. 10, 1676-7; she died Sept. 4, 1727; daughter of James **Cole,** Jr. Elkanah was a deacon in the Plympton Church for nine years, of which his brother was pastor (see Cushman Family), and an Ensign in the militia.

He served on important jury trials, and as Representative to the General Court of Massachusetts three sessions. His house stood on the highway leading eastward from Plympton Green to Kingston.

### CHILDREN BY ELIZABETH COLE

239. Elkanah, b. Sept. 15, 1678; d. Jan. 9, 1714-15; m. Hester **Barnes.**

240. James, b. Oct. 20, 1679; d. young; m.——.

241. Jabez, b. Dec. 28, 1681; d. May 1682; m.——.

### CHILDREN BY MARTHA COOKE

242. Allerton, b. Nov. 21, 1683; d. Jan. 9, 1730-1; m. 1st Mary **Buck;** m. 2nd Elizabeth **Sampson.**

243. Elizabeth, b. Jan. 16, 1685; d. Mar. 1724; m. Robert **Waterman.**

244. Lt. Josiah, b. Mar. 21, 1687; d. Apr. 13, 1750; m. Sussanah **Shurtleff.**

245. Martha, b.     1691; d.     ; m. Nathaniel **Holmes.**

246. Mehitable, b. Oct. 8, 1693; d.     ; m. unmarried.

Refs. 174, 177.

# SHURTLEFF

I. **Shurtleff, William¹**, born England May 16, 1624; killed by lightning June 23, 1666, in Marshfield, Mass. Soon after landing in Plymouth he became apprenticed to Thomas **Clark,** a builder and carpenter, of Plymouth; married Oct. 18, 1655, Elizabeth Lettice; born 1636; died Oct. 31, 1693; daughter of Thomas **Lettice** and Ann (     ). She married 2nd Jacob **Cooke,** and 3rd Hugh **Cole** Jan. 1, 1689. William was chosen surveyor of Plymouth June 3, 1656, and constable June 7, 1659.

CHILDREN

a. William, b.     1657; d. Feb. 4, 1729-30; m. Sussana
   **Lothrop.**
b. Abiel, b. June 1666; d. Oct. 28, 1732; m. Lydia **Barnes.**
c. Thomas, b.     1658-63; d.     ; m. Sarah **Kimball.**

Ref. 177.

# ALLERTON

I. **Allerton, Isaac**[1], born England about 1586; died New Haven, Conn., between Feb. 1-12, 1658; married 1st at Leyden Nov. 4, 1611, Mary **Norris** of Berkshire Co., Eng.; died Plymouth, Mass., Mar. 7, 1621; married 2nd Plymouth between July, 1623, and June 1, 1627; Fear[2] **Brewster**, daughter of William[1] **Brewster**; she died Dec. 12, 1634; married 3rd Joanna (    ) prior to 1644; she died in New Haven, 1659.

He may have been with the Pilgrims in Amsterdam about 1610, and earlier as a merchant in Holland, but most likely he joined the Robinson church with others from London. It is known he was of London before 1609, and that he was admitted as burgess of Leyden, Holland, in 1614. A Robert Allerton was residing there at the same time.

His son Bartholomew returned to England, married and became a preacher. No doubt much of his education was obtained through the teaching of William Brewster, who also later on, brought up and prepared his brother Isaac, Jr., for Harvard.

He appears to have been a merchant tailor. His name is first recorded in Leyden with that of a widowed sister Sarah (Allerton) Vincent, also of London, who married Degory Priest Nov. 4, 1611. His own marriage to Mary Norris took place at the same time.

The Allerton family is old and honorable in England, a mixture of Saxon and Danish. There is a fine coat of arms in the Heraldic College at London. "Allerton" is the name of a parish in north Yorkshire.

While in Leyden, Isaac Allerton seems to have carried on his business of tailor. When admitted to citizenship in 1614, he was guaranteed by Roger Wilson and Henry Wood, and in 1615 "guaranteed" his brother-in-law Priest. He and his wife witnessed the betrothal Apr. 27, 1618, of Edward Winslow to Elizabeth Barker of Chester, England. His residence was in the famous "Pieterskerkhof," among a little group of houses built upon the grounds of the Robinson place. It was sometimes called "Groenepoort."

Like most of the Mayflower group born in the sixteenth century Allerton was an ambitious man striving to succeed in a business way, and his associates had a profound respect for his sound judgment. During the preparations for removal from Leyden in 1620, and the negotiations with the Virginia Company in London for transportation to the Colonies, he cooperated actively with Cushman, Carver, Winslow, Fuller and others in that rather complicated affair. Although the London and Leyden groups of merchants connected with the Virginia Company were good friends, most of them Puritans and Separatists, yet the financial arrangements for transportation were the cause of some misunderstandings and considerable controversy. They sent Cushman and Carver, two good business men, to talk "ways and means" with their London friends, but the deal obtained did not seem to satisfy Allerton and others in Leyden. This is quite evident from a letter written by Allerton, Fuller and Winslow to Cushman and Carver dated Leyden June 10, 1620, in part as follows:

"ye new conditions x x x x which all men are against x x x x whereas Robart Cushman desires reasons for our dislike, promising therupon to alter ye same or els saing we should think he hath no brains, we desire him to exercise them therein."

Here we have a pretty good glimpse of the solid character of the Mayflower Planters, and the real reason why New England flourished from the beginning. Isaac Allerton, no doubt, had much to do with the wording of this remarkable letter, and, perhaps, it is not so strange, therefore, that he became, in truth, the "Father of American Commerce."

The Speedwell finally left Delfshaven, Holland, with Allerton and family on board. The family including himself consisting of wife, Mary, children Bartholomew. Remember and Mary were transferred to the Mayflower, in which they made the voyage to New England. Every member of his family appears in the list of cattle distribution by the Court at Plymouth under date of May 22, 1627. He called himself "merchant," but was mentioned in papers as "Mr." or "Gentlemen." During his last years in Connecticut he was designated "Captain" or "Master."

Among several outstanding characters associated with the Mayflower Planters, Isaac Allerton holds a very unique position. His vision was somewhat broader than any of the others, especially in the matter of commerce, and his immediate contemporaries were quick to take advantage of his exceptional abilities.

He was one of the mainstays in Holland, and from the beginning in Plymouth served almost continuously until 1633-4 as assistant to the Governor. After the death of Robert Cushman, the Plymouth Agent in London, in 1625, Allerton was chosen to take his place. He made several trips between England and America which brought him very little except unfriendly criticism, yet the supplies that he brought over during the period of adjustment with the Merchant Adventurers saved much distress, although Bradford claimed they were "on his owne perticuler."

Later, when he was free to follow personal inclinations, he visited, in his ship, every known port on the Atlantic coast, besides Barbadoes, the Dutch West Indies, Spain, Portugal and England.

He carried valuable cargoes of his own, and built up a flourishing general shipping business, the very first of its kind in America. The true value of his services to the early colonists was greatly underrated by the unfair and restrictive writings of certain religious historians, and, unfortunately, the Bradford Manuscript is not free from some petty insinuations along this direction.

Allerton was the only Mayflower Planter to become a resident of New York. A tablet to his memory may be seen at No. 8 Peck Slip. It reads, in part, as follows:

"From 1647 until 1659 this ground was occupied by the warehouse and residence of Isaac Allerton, a passenger on the ship Mayflower in 1620. Assistant Governor of Plymouth Colony, the Father of New England Commerce, one of the eight men at New Netherlands in 1643, and for twenty years a leading merchant of New Amsterdam."

For some years he was about the only English trader at New Amsterdam. They were mostly Swedes, Dutch and Indians.

He was tolerant toward various forms of worship, and was frequently interpreter, referee or arbitrator. His tolerant attitude regarding the Quakers probably hastened his departure from Plymouth. He was censured by the Plymouth Church and Colony, for various acts, and later on when residing in Marblehead he was invited to leave that place because of kindness extended to Roger Williams.

It is supposed that Isaac Allerton was buried in New Haven on a plot of land which is now a part of the beautiful "Green" in the center of the city adjacent Yale College.

His residence in New Haven from 1646 to 1659 was on Fair Street, and is marked by a tablet, stating:

"Isaac Allerton, a pilgrim of the Mayflower and the father of New England Commerce lived on this ground 1646 till 1659."

After his death, it is related that the widow, Joanna, following the practice of her departed husband, gave temporary shelter and concealment in the summer of 1661 to the regicide judges, Col. Whalley and Col. Goffe.

In spite of a proclamation "that whosoever shall be found to have a hand in concealing the said colonels, or either of them, shall answer for the same as an offence of the highest nature." Joanna secretly harbored them from June 11 to June 22, 1661, and perhaps longer.

There is reason to suppose that Isaac Allerton was connected with the Allertons of Suffolk, England, and was born in 1585-6. From a deposition made Sept. 26, 1639, he is described as "Isaacke

[ 175 ]

Allerton of New Plimmouth in New England, Merchant, aged about 53 years."

The will and inventory of Isaac Allerton are recorded in New Haven, Conn., where he died between Feb. 1, 1658-9, when he appeared in court as defendant in a suit brought to compel the payment of of an old debt, and the 12th of the same month, the date on which his inventory was taken. New Haven Probate Records, Vol. I, Pt. I, p. 82-83.

(p. 82). At a Court of Magistrates Octob. 19, 59.

A writeing presented as the last Will & Testament of Isaac Alerton, late of Newhaven deceased, w$^{th}$ an account of certaine debts, dew to him: & from him;

An account of Debts at the Duch

first, 700 & odd gilders from Tho: Hall by Arbitration of Captaine Willet, & Augustine Harman; about Captaine Scarlet w$^{ch}$ I paid out,

and there is 900 gilders owing by John Peterson the Bore as by Georg Woolseyes booke will appeare; & several obligations thereto,

ffrom Richard Cloufe owes, as Georg: Woolseyes Booke will make appeare: I thinke 900 gilders, but his Estate being broken. I Desire that what may be gotten may be layd hold on for mee.

Due from William Goulder 270, od gilders, by his Bill appeares:

Due from John Snedecare a shoo maker 150, od gilders as by his acc. appeares.

from the weddow of the Hanc Hancson due as by severall Bills & accounts;

Peter Cornelioussen 120. od guilders as by ye account will appeare.

Due from Henry Brasser for rent for 18 months, from the first October 1656 to the last of May, 58; for three roomes at 3 gilders a week. I am in his Debt for worke of the old acc. w$^{ch}$ must be Deducted;

there is 20li in Georg. Woolseyes hand, that came from Mr. Tho. Mayhue for mee

There is 400. od. gilders that I owe to Nicholas, the ffrenchman, & a Cooper. I owe something to, w$^{ch}$ I would have that 20li in Georg. Woolseyes hand, & the rest of that in Henry Brassers hand to them two;

And now I leave my son Isaac Allerton, and my wife, as Trustees to receive in my debts, & to pay what I owe, as farr as it will goe & what is overpluss I leave to my wife and my sonne Isaac, as far as they receive the Debts to pay what I owe;

[ 176 ]

In Captaine Willetts hand, a pcell of booke lace 1300 & odd guilders w<sup>ch</sup> I left in trust with Captaine Willett to take care of:

(Seale)

My brother Bruster owes mee foure score pounds & odd, as the obligations will appeare.

Besides all my Debts in Delloware Bay & in Virgenia w<sup>ch</sup> in my booke will appeare, & in Barbadoes, what can be gott;

Isaac Allerton Senio<sup>r</sup>

Witness
Edward Preston.
John Harriman.

The inventory of Allerton's estate seems to indicate that he cared little for religion or books. Not a book is listed, not even the usual Bible. Both the will and inventory are short and extremely of a "business type."

The main item of the inventory is "Imp<sup>r</sup> the Dwelling house, Orchard & Barne w<sup>th</sup> two acres of meadow." There are other items, such as "a pcell of Tubbs," "8 Jarrs," "1 pre of Ondirons," "3 Iron potts," "a pcell of wearing cloaths," "2 sowes," "4 piggs," "a bedstead," "a pre spectacles" and a few other articles.

The general opinion that Isaac Allerton was a hard driving business man, seems to be amply proved by a study of his will. The extensive ramifications of his business interests are also apparent. He was a "Merchant Adventurer," and probably a close follower of the Virginia Company, especially during the Sandys administration in 1618, 1619, and 1620. In fact, he was a real builder and leader, with plenty of initiative, sound judgment and practical imagination, traits which were quite common among the early planters in New England, and which have been handed down through the generations.

### CHILDREN BY 1ST WIFE MARY NORRIS

\*a. Bartholomew, b. Leyden (?) 1612; d. England      ; m. had issue in Eng.

IIb. Remember, b. Leyden (?) 1614; d. Salem, 1652-56; m. Moses **Maverick.**

IIIc. Mary, b. Leyden (?) 1616; d. Nov. 28, 1699; m. Thomas **Cushman.**

d. Sarah, b. Leyden (?) 1618; d. before 1651; m.——.

e. Child, b. Leyden, buried Pieterskerk, Leyden, Feb. 5, 1620.

f. Son, b. Cape Cod; d. infancy, Provincetown Harbor.

### CHILD BY 2ND WIFE FEAR BREWSTER

IVg. Isaac, b. Plymouth (?) 1630; d. Virginia 1702; m. 1st Elizabeth (     ); m. 2nd Elizabeth **Colclough,** wid.

\* Bartholomew came to Plymouth with his parents on the Mayflower, and was in Plymouth as late as 1627. William Brewster was, no doubt, his early teacher in the classics. Just when he returned to England is not known, but according to various writers he became a preacher in England, married and brought up a family there. His history and family record would be interesting. Bradford states "Bartle is married in England, but I know not how many children he hath."

IIb. **Allerton**, Remember[2] (Isaac[1]).
        (See Maverick Family IId)

IIIc. **Allerton**, Mary[2] (Isaac[1]).
        (See Cushman Family)

## MAVERICK

I. **Maverick**, Rev. John[1], born 1577, in County Devon, England; died Boston, Mass., Feb. 3, 1636-7, at age of about 60. He was buried in the "old Burying-Ground" at Dorchester. His widow was still living in 1668.

He was ordained a deacon at Exeter, England, July 26, 1597, and later by a bishop of the Episcopal Church, as a minister of the Church of England. In 1615, he was rector of Beaworthy, County Devon, and became acquainted with the Rev. John Warham of Exeter, also a minister of the Church of England. These "West Country ministers became imbued with the spirit of the 'dissenter,'" and forthwith joined a group of Puritans of Devonshire, Dorsetshire and Somersetshire about to sail for New England. The company of 110, set sail on Mar. 30, 1629-30, in the "Mary and John," 400 tons, Captain Squeb, Master, and "on Lord's day May 30 (?), 1629-30, arrived at Nantasket, where the Captain put them ashore, notwithstanding, his engagement was to bring them up the Charler River." They succeeded in "planting" Dorchester, a month before the arrival of Gov. Winthrop with his famous fleet at Charlestown.

### CHILDREN BORN ENGLAND

    a. Samuel, b.   1602 (?); d.    ; m. Amias **(Cole)** Thomson.
    b. Elias, b.   1604 (?); d. Sept. 8, 1681; m. Ann **Harris**.
    c. Antipas, b.   ; d.   ; m.   .
  IId. Moses, b.   1610 (?); d. Jan. 28, 1685 6; m. 1st Remember **Allerton**; m. 2nd Eunice **(Cole)** Roberts.
    e. Abigail, b.   ; d.   ; m.   .

IId. **Maverick**, Moses[2] (Rev. John[1]), born 1610 (?); died Marblehead, Mass., Jan. 28, 1685-6; married 1st Remember[2] **Allerton**

[ 178 ]

before May 6, 1635; born Leyden, Holland, 1614 (?); died Salem, Mass., 1652-1656; daughter of Isaac[1] **Allerton**; married 2nd at Boston by Gov. **Endicott**, Eunice (Cole) **Roberts**, Oct. 22, 1656, widow of Thomas[2] **Roberts** (John[1]).

He was probably a member of the first church at Dorchester, of which his father was pastor before its reconstruction. He was admitted a freeman of the Bay Colony on Sept. 3, 1634, as a citizen of Dorchester, and no one was made a freeman unless a church member.

Moses Maverick arrived at Marblehead with Isaac Allerton in 1631 in the "White Angel." They first settled at Peach Point, near Little Harbor, where Moses lived as early as 1634. He and Allerton engaged in fishing as a business, and had a number of employees. On May 6, 1635, Moses took over all houses, fish-stages and the like on a point of land called Maverick's Island. He became a member of the first church at Salem in 1638, and thereafter was active in church and town affairs for over fifty years. The last service of Moses Maverick was as town clerk, and he had probably been doing much of the clerical work even in the early settlement.

CHILDREN BY REMEMBER ALLERTON

a. Rebecca, bp. Aug. 7, 1639; d. Nov. 4, 1659; m. John **Hawkes.**
b. Mary, bp. Feb. 14, 1640-1; d. Feb. 24, 1655; m.      .
c. Abigail, bp. Jan. 12, 1645; d.      ; m. Samuel **Ward.**
d. Elizabeth, bp. Dec. 3, 1646; d. before Sept. 1649; m.      .
e. Samuel, bp. Dec. 19, 1647; d.      ; m.      .
f. Elizabeth, bp. Sept. 30, 1649; d.      ; m. 1st Nathaniel **Grafton**; m. 2nd Thomas **Skinner.**
g. Remember, bap. Sept. 12, 1652; d.      ; m. 1st Edward **Woodman**, Sr.; m. 2nd Thomas **Perkins.**

CHILDREN BY EUNICE (COLE) ROBERTS

h. Mary, b.      ; d.      ; m. Archibald **Ferguson.**
i. Moses, b.      ; d.      ; m.      .
j. Son, b.      ; d.      ; m.      .
k. Sarah, b.      ; d.      ; m.      .

Refs. 194, 149, 292.

## CUSHMAN

I. **Cushman**, Robert[2] (Thomas[1]), baptized at Rolvenden, County Kent, England, Feb. 9, 1577-8; died England, 1624-25; married 1st Sara **Reder** July 31, 1606, at Canterbury; died at Leyden, Oct. 11, 1616; married 2nd Mary (**Clarke**) **Singleton** at Leyden, Holland, June 5, 1617.

[ 179 ]

Robert was the son of Thomas[1] **Couchman** "Husbandman," of the Parish of Rolvenden, Kent, who left a will dated Feb. 10, 1585 6, on file at the archdeaconry of Canterbury. It mentions sons Richard, Robarte, daughter Sylvestra, godchildren Thomas **Bredman**, Thomas **Coyle**, Thomas **Gabriell**, Marion **Hosleman**, and Jane **Couchman**, also wife Ellen. His wife was Elinor Hubbard.

Robert had received an education common to the other boys in his neighborhood of equal financial and social standing, perhaps at some of the numerous schools in Kent. Industry and business was taking the best young men from agriculture and the country. Towns were beginning to flourish. Parents of all classes were anxious to "apprentice" their sons, as soon as possible, in some promising enterprise. In due time Robert was apprenticed as a "grosser" to George Masters. Obviously, he was interested in the wool or cloth trade, and, gradually, became acquainted with certain Merchant Adventurers, and guilds in London, who were quite busy organizing the Virginia Company for planting colonies and trade beyond the seas.

At the same time he was a "Puritan" at heart, like most of the merchants. This was tolerated to some extent by Queen Elizabeth, but she died in 1603, and then bedlam broke loose. James I began, immediately, to persecute the "Puritans," and in 1604 Robert was presented by the church wardens of St. Andrew's Parish, Canterbury, "for that he doth say he will not come to his parish church because he cannot be edified and saith he can and will defend it by the word of God." Now, this was real fighting language. Failing to do penance he was excommunicated on Nov. 12, 1604. This was about the time Rev. John Robinson had to give up his pastorate at Norwich, in another section of England, and returned to his old home in Notts where Brewster soon became involved in the complicated affair.

However, in Rolvenden or Canterbury, Robert had a business and he wanted to save it, so on June 28, 1605, he appeared in Court and asked for absolution. It was granted and he again was received into the established Church of England. This was possible, probably, because he was still apprenticed to Masters.

The truce did not last for long. The spirit of freedom through commercial contacts had taken a firm hold of Cushman, and with many other dissenters from London and vicinity he went over into Holland to obtain a little desired liberty in the form of worship, and some freedom in business enterprise.

In Leyden he was listed as from Canterbury, Wool Comber, and bought a house Nov. 4, 1611, from Cornelius Ghysberts van Groenendael, and bought another one Apr. 19, 1612. He sold one house on Sept. 19, 1619. Together with Brewster and Carver he acted as agent of the Leyden group in London with the Virginia Company 1617-20. Although he probably intended to go with the Mayflower to the colonies, for some reason he turned back at Plymouth, England, and returned to London, where he represented the Plymouth Plantation in negotiations with the Merchant Adventurers. In 1621 he visited the Plymouth Colony with his young son, but immediately returned to England, leaving his son Thomas in New England with friends. His last letter to the Plymouth Plantation is dated Dec. 22, 1624, and he died suddenly within the year.

## CHILDREN BORN

IIa. Thomas, b. Feb. 1608; d. Dec. 21, 1691; m. Mary **Allerton.**
 b. Child, buried in Leyden Mar. 11, 1616; m.      .
 c. Child, buried in Leyden Oct. 24, 1616; m.——.
 d. Sara, b.      ; d.      ; m. William **Hodgekins.**

IIa. **Cushman,** Thomas$^3$ (Robert$^2$, Thomas$^1$), born Feb., 1608, Leyden; died Plymouth, Mass., Dec. 21, 1691; buried on Burial Hill; married Mary **Allerton** at Plymouth 1635-6; born June, 1616, Leyden; died Nov. 28, 1699, at Plymouth. She was the last Mayflower Survivor, daughter of Isaac **Allerton** and Mary **Norris.**
 Thomas sailed for New England with his father on the "Fortune," arriving at New Plymouth Nov. 10, 1621. His father, Robert, was delegated to represent the Plymouth Planters in England, and returned to London on the same ship, leaving Thomas in the care of William Bradford, who treated him as a son. No doubt Master William Brewster tutored him as he had done many another including Bradford himself.
 Anyway, the education was so thorough that Thomas Cushman succeeded Brewster as Elder in 1649, he having died in 1644. Thomas was Elder for 42 years until his death, a most exceptional record. He held various town offices, and was an extremely useful citizen.

## CHILDREN BORN PLYMOUTH

IIIa. Thomas, b. Sept. 16, 1637; d. Aug. 23, 1726; m. 1st Ruth **Howland;** m. 2nd Abigail **Fuller.**
 b. Sarah, b.      (?) 1641; d. living 1695; m. John **Hawkes.**
 c. Lydia, b.      ; d.      ; m. William **Harlow.**
 d. Rev. Isaac, b. Feb. 8, 1647; d. Oct. 21, 1732; m. Rebecca **Rickard.**
IVe. Elkanah, b. June 1, 1651; d. Sept. 4, 1727; m. 1st Elizabeth **Cole;** m. 2nd Martha **Cooke.**
 f. Fear, b. June 20, 1653; d. young; m.——.
 g. Eleazer, b. Feb. 20, 1656; d.      ; m. Elizabeth **Coombs.**
 h. Mary, b.      (?) 1659; d. before 1690; m. Francis **Hutchinson.**

**IIIa. Cushman, Thomas⁴** (Thomas⁸, Robert², Thomas¹), born Plymouth Sept. 16, 1637; died Plympton Aug. 23, 1726; married Nov. 17, 1664, Ruth **Howland**; died 1672-79; daughter of John¹ **Howland**; married 2nd Oct. 16, 1679, Abigail **Fuller** of Rehoboth. Thomas **Cushman** and his wife were members of the church at Plympton. He resided on the west side of the highway that leads from Plympton meeting house to the north part of the town. The "Colechester Brook" ran through his farm.

CHILDREN BORN PLYMPTON

a. Robert, b. Oct. 4, 1664-5; d. Sept. 7, 1757; m. 1st Persis ( ); m. 2nd Prudence **Sherman.**
b. Desire, b. 1668; d. Feb. 8, 1763; m. Samuel **Kent.**
IVe. Elkanah (see Fam. No. 43).

Ref. 174.

## HAWKES

I. **Hawkes, Adam¹**, came to New England in Winthrop's fleet, and landed in June, 1630, at Salem. He was admitted as freeman at Charlestown 1634, and married 1st Anne ( ) **Hutchinson**, widow, who was admitted to the 1st church at Charlestown Nov. 21, 1634. She died Dec. 4, 1669, in Lynn, and her husband married 2nd in June, 1670, Sarah **Hooper**. Before 1638 Adam Hawkes removed to Lynn, where he received one hundred acres as a grant on the banks of the Saugus River where he built his home. He died April 13, 1671-2, in Lynn, aged 64, leaving a widow, Sarah. His son, John, was appointed executor of the estate. Adam Hawkes also brought up the Hutchinson children.

CHILDREN BY ANN **HUTCHINSON**

a. Adam, died before 1671.
b. John (twin), b. 1633; d. Aug. 15, 1694; m. 1st Rebecca **Maverick**; m. 2nd Sarah **Cushman.**
c. Sussana (twin), b. 1633; d. ; m. William **Cogswell.**
d. Moses, died before 1671.
e. Benjamin, died before 1671.
f. Thomas, died before 1671.

CHILDREN BY SARAH **HOOPER**

g. Sarah, b. June 1, 1671.

Ref. 194, 149.

[182]

# HUTCHINSON

I. **Hutchinson, Anne,** a widow with five young children was early of Lynn. Her husband, not clearly placed, was dead before 1630. She was fortunate in her 2nd husband Adam **Hawkes,** who married her before Nov. 21, 1634, at which time she was admitted to the church at Charlestown as his wife. He accepted the responsibility of bringing up the five Hutchinson children, in addition to six of his own which she became the mother of before her death in Lynn on Dec. 4, 1669. The children by her first husband were:

### CHILDREN (HUTCHINSON)

a. Samuel, b. 1617-8; d. Andover 1740-1; m. Hannah ( ).

b. Elizabeth, b. 1622; d. Nov. 28, 1700; m. Isaac **Hart.**

c. Edward, b. ; d. Dec. 8, 1694; m. 1st ( ); m. 2nd Mary ( ).

d. Thomas, b. ; d. Long Island.

e. Francis, b. 1630; d. ; m. 1st ( ); m. 2nd Mary **Cushman.**

Ref. 194, 149.

## ALLERTON

IVg. **Allerton,** Col. Isaac[2] (Isaac[1]), born Plymouth about 1630; died Westmoreland Co., Va., 1702; married 1st Elizabeth ( ); died, probably, before 1660; married 2nd about 1663 Elizabeth (**Willoughby**) (**Overzee**) Colclough, daughter of Captain Thomas **Willoughby,** and widow of Simon **Overzee,** a Hollander, and of Major George **Colclough.**

His father removed to New Amsterdam (New York) in 1638, while he remained at Plymouth with his grandfather, William Brewster, by whom he was prepared for Harvard where he graduated in 1650. It was fortunate for young Isaac that he had such a grandfather with a glorious background of teaching experience in England and Holland. Apparently he was the only son and grandson of a Mayflower Planter to attend Harvard, and it must be considered another link in a chain of circumstances proving Master William Brewster to have been a very exceptional person. After graduation Isaac joined his father in business in New York, New Haven, Virginia and elsewhere.

Soon after the death of his father in New Haven in 1659, young Isaac removed to Virginia where land had been acquired about ten years before on the Machcatick River in Westmoreland County. He resided there until his death in 1702.

[ 183 ]

It may be recalled that several Mayflower Planters had been in southern Virginia (around Jamestown) before 1620, among them Hopkins, Martin, Brewster, and probably Allerton, Standish and others, so that possession of land there by young Isaac Allerton may not be surprising.

CHILDREN BY 1ST WIFE BORN NEW HAVEN

Va. Elizabeth, b. Sept. 27, 1653; d. Nov. 17, 1740; m. 1st Benjamin **Starr**; m. 2nd Simon **Eyres.**
VIb. Isaac, b. June 11, 1655; d.      ; m. Elizabeth (      ).

CHILDREN BY 2ND WIFE BORN VIRGINIA

VIIc. Willoughby, b.      (?) 1665; d.      1723-25; m. Hannah (**Keene**) **Bushrod.**
VIIId. Sarah, b. about 1670; d. May 17, 1731; m. 1st (      ) **Newton**; m. 2nd Hancock **Lee.**
IXe. Frances, b.      ; d.      ; m. Captain Samuel **Travers.**

## STARR-EYRES

Va. **Allerton**, Elizabeth[3] (Isaac[2], Isaac[1]), born New Haven, Conn., Sept. 27, 1653; died Nov. 17, 1740; married 1st Benjamin **Starr** of New Haven Dec. 23, 1675; died 1678, age 31; married 2nd Simon **Eyres**, July 22, 1679—a sea captain, born Boston Aug. 6, 1652; died 1695, and her first husband's cousin.

CHILDREN (STARR) BORN NEW HAVEN

a. Allerton, b. Jan. 6, 1677; d.      ; m.      .

CHILDREN (EYRES) BORN NEW HAVEN

b. Simon, b. Sept. 1682; d.      ; m.      .
c. Isaac, b. Feb. 23, 1683-4; d.      ; m.      ; and possibly others.

Refs. 149, 194.

## ALLERTON

VIb. **Allerton**, Isaac[3] (Isaac[2], Isaac[1]), born New Haven June 11, 1655; married Elizabeth (      ).

He did not remain in Virginia, but returned to New Haven about 1683, residing there and at Norwich, Conn., the rest of his life.

a. John, b.  1685; d. Coventry, R. I., 1750; m. Elizabeth
   (    ).
b. Jesse, b.  1686-7; d. New Jersey; m.        .
c. Isaac, b.   ; d. young; m.———.

VIIc. **Allerton**, Willoughby[3] (Isaac[2], Isaac[1]), born Virginia; married about 1719 Hannah (**Keene**) Bushrod of Nominy, widow of Captain John **Bushrod**, and daughter of William **Keene.** His will is dated Jan. 16, 1723 4, proved Mar. 25, 1724.

Willoughby Allerton was a large land owner residing on the west side of Machoatick Creek, and had a number of slaves. He held offices in civil and military life. In 1711 he was a Deputy Collector of Customs for York River, an occupation for which he was well qualified. This section of the Atlantic seaboard was still a one-crop farming district, mostly tobacco. These farms, small and large, were scattered along the tide-water shores, the labor on them being performed by slaves. Most of the real planters of the colony at Jamestown and vicinity, up to 1619-22, either returned to England discouraged, some of them later on settling in New England, or were murdered by the Indians. In 1711 there were few descendants of the planters in tide-water Virginia. Most of the inhabitants were, more or less, recent comers, and could not be termed planters in its original true sense.

A glance at the map in this volume will show why the original planters, the leaders of whom were business men and merchants, failed to appreciate that section of the coast line. Furthermore, from the first, severe restrictions on freedom of enterprise and forms of worship were imposed which did not appeal to the independent spirit of the times. Isaac Allerton, Sr., would never have become the "Father of American Commerce" if he had settled in Southern Virginia.

CHILDREN

*a. Elizabeth, b.   ; d.    ; m. (    ) **Quills.**
*b. Isaac, b.    ; d.    1739; m. Ann **Corbin.**

---

*a. Two children—Sarah and Margaret Quills.
*b. Three children—Willoughby, Isaac and Gawin Allerton.

NEWTON-LEE

VIIId. **Allerton**, Sarah[3] (Isaac[2], Isaac[1]), born Virginia about 1670; died 1731; buried on the estate, married 1st (    ) **Newton**; married 2nd Hancock[2] **Lee** (his 2nd wife); died 1709; buried on the estate, son of Col. Richard[1] **Lee.**

The 1st wife of Hancock **Lee** was Mary **Kendall,** daughter of Col. William **Kendall.**

Hancock Lee was Justice of Northampton County, Va., in 1677. He removed to Wycomico Parish in Northumberland County in 1688, where he was Justice 1689, 1699, 1702, Burgess 1688 and Naval Officer 1699. He and his wife were buried on the estate. The inscription on the tombstone reads "and Sarah his last wife, daughter of Isaac Allerton, Esq., who departed this life the 17th May Anno Domi 1731."

### CHILD (NEWTON)

a. Allerton, b.   ; d.   ; m.   .

### CHILDREN (LEE)

b. Isaac, b.   ; d. England 1727; m.   .
Xc. Hancock, b.   ; d.   ; m. Mary **Willis.**
d. Elizabeth, b.   ; d.   ; m.   .
e. John, b.   ; d. Aug. 11, 1789; m.———.

## TRAVERS

IXe. **Allerton,** Frances[3] (Isaac[2], Isaac[1]), born Virginia; married Captain Samuel **Travers,** son of William, born about 1660.

He resided at Fairham Creek, north of Fairham Parish, Richmond County, Va. In 1690 he was Justice of the County of Rappahanock. Captain of militia 1685, 1690 and 1693.

### CHILDREN

a. Elizabeth, b.   (?) 1688; d.   ; m. John **Tarpley.**
b. Rebecca, b. Oct. 15, 1692; d.   ; m. Charles **Colston.**
c. Winifred, b.   (?) 1693; d. Aug. 10, 1749; m. Daniel **Hornby.**

---

Refs. 194, 149.

## LEE

Xc. **Lee**[4], Hancock, Jr. (Sarah[3] Allerton, Isaac[2], Isaac[1]), born Virginia; married Mary **Willis,** daughter of Col. Henry **Willis** of Fredericksburg, Va.

## CHILDREN (LEE)

a. Willis, b.       ; d.       ; m.       .
b. Hancock, b.      1736; d.      1815; m. Winifred **Beale.**
c. John, b.       ; d.      1802; m. Elizabeth **Bell.**
d. Henry, b.       ; d.       ; m.       .
e. Richard, b.       ; d. unmarried; m.——.
f. Sarah, b.       ; d.       ; m. Col. John **Gillison.**
g. Mary, b.       ; d.       ; m. Capt. Ambrose **Madison.**
h. (?) Elizabeth, b.       ; d.       ; m.

# MORE

I. **More,** Samuel[1], born England, perhaps Shropshire; married Katharine (      ) of Larden, England, Feb. 4, 1610.

The **More** Family is old and honorable in England, and will be more fully described in a later volume of this series.

The following family is recorded in the Parish Register of Shipton, Shropshire, England, as "Generosus," meaning of "genteel birth."

### CHILDREN BORN SHIPTON, ENGLAND

   a. Ellinora, b. May 24, 1612; d. Early in 1621; m. ——.
   b. Jasper, b. Aug. 8, 1613; d. Dec. 16, 1620; m. ——.
IIc. Richard, b. Nov. 13, 1614; d.      ; m. 1st Christine **Hunt;**
     m. 2nd Jane **Hollingsworth.**
   d. Maria, b. Apr. 16, 1616; d.      ; m.      .

IIc. **More,** Richard[2] (Samuel[1]), born Shipton, England, Nov. 13, 1614; died Salem, Mass., after Mar. 29, 1693 (N. S.); married 1st Christine **Hunt,** born 1616, died Salem Dec. 28, 1676 (N. S.), age 60; married 2nd Jane[2] **Hollingsworth,** born 1631, died Oct. 18, 1686 (N. S.), age 55, daughter of Richard[1] **Hollingsworth.**

The four More children, including Richard age 6 years, were living in the home of Thomas Weston, Merchant Adventurer, and friend of the Mayflower Planters, in 1620, and he arranged personally, for their passage to the Colonies on the Mayflower. They may have been related to him.

### CHILDREN

   a. Caleb, b.      1644; d. Jan. 1678-9; unmarried.
   b.Richard, b.      ; d.      ; m. Sarah (      ).
   c. Sussanah, b.      1650; d.      ; m. 1st Samuel **Dutch;** m. 2nd Richard **Hutton;** m. 3rd John **Knowlton.**
   d. Christine, b.      1652; d. May 30, 1680; m. Joshua **Conant.**

# CONANT

I. **Conant,** Roger[3] (Richard[2], John[1]), baptized Apr. 9, 1592, East Budleigh, Devon County, England; died November 19, 1679, at Beverly, Mass.; married Nov. 11, 1618, Sarah **Horton** at St. Ann's Blackfriars, London; died June 1667-Sept. 20, 1667.

In 1619 and 1620 he was a resident of the Parish of St. Lawrence, Jewry, London, carrying on the business of a "Salter." The business required an apprenticeship of seven years.

He came to New England 1622-3, probably with his wife and oldest son. Perhaps he arrived in the "Ann" like his brother Christopher. After about a year at Plymouth, he removed to Nantasket, and within a few months thereafter he was invited by the Dorchester Company of England, a group of Merchant Adventurers or investors and liberty-minded people, who had been maintaining a fishing settlement at Cape Ann (Gloucester) to go there and be their "governor," having charge of both fishing and the colony. His training as a "Salter," of course, was right along this line of wholesale fish or meats. In 1626 the settlement was abandoned, and the colony removed to Naumkeog (Salem) where Conant built the first house. In 1628 Endicott arrived and superseded him as Governor. He was a delegate to the first General Court 1634, and was granted 400 acres of land.

His will is dated Jan. 1, 1677, and proved Sept. 25, 1679. It disposed of quite a large estate.

### CHILDREN

   a. Sarah, bp. Sept. 16, 1619; d. Oct. 30, 1620; m. ——.
   b. Caleb, bp. May 27, 1622; d. before 1633 in England.
   c. Lot, b.    (?) 1624; d. Sept. 29, 1674; m. Elizabeth **Walton.**
IId. Roger, b.    (?) 1626; d. June 15, 1672; m. Elizabeth **Weston.**
   e. Sarah, b.    (?) 1628; d. June 1662; m. John **Leach.**
IIIf. Joshua, b.    (?) 1630; d.    1659; m. Seeth **Gardner.**
   g. Mary, b.    (?) 1632; d. before 1685; m. 1st John **Balch;** m. 2nd William **Dodge.**
   h. Elizabeth, b.   ; d.   ; m.   .
   j. Exercise, bp. Dec. 24, 1637; d. April 28, 1722; m. Sarah (   ).

IId. **Conant**, Roger[4] (Roger[3], Richard[2], John[1]), born 1626 (?); died June 15, 1672; married Elizabeth **Weston,** daughter of Thomas **Weston,** the Merchant Adventurer, and "Iron Monger" of London who greatly aided the "Leyden" group in their exodus to New England on the Mayflower.

IIIf. **Conant**, Joshua[4] (Roger[3], Richard[2], John[1]), born 1630 (?); died 1659; married Seeth **Gardner;** bapt. Dec. 25, 1636; daughter of Thomas **Gardner.** She married 2nd Joseph **Grafton** (?).

### CHILD (KNOWN)

   a. Joshua, b. June 4, 1657; d.   ; m. 1st Christine **More;** m. 2nd Sarah **Newcomb.**

Ref. 574.

# THE EARLY BRITAIN OF OUR FOREFATHERS

By whom and when Britain was first peopled is unknown. No doubt man was living there during the "Neolithic" age, the third millenium before Christ, following an agricultural existence, amassing some wealth, enjoying a political organization, and some form of religion.

Then came the Bronze Age during which period the "Beaker" people arrived in Britain. This name has been given them because of the bronze drinking cups found in their graves.

These two civilizations amalgamated and formed a race of people who for hundreds of years inhabited the chalk plains of Britain.

Apparently, for over two thousand years before the coming of the Romans, Salisbury Plain had been the locality which appealed to newcomers. This plain is a large plateau of chalk, and the early civilizations found the soil fairly fertile, and, at the same time, easily drained. They discovered that the heavy moisture of Britain readily absorbed in the porous sub-soil.

During the late Bronze Age, especially in southern Britain, about 1,000 to 400 B. C., living conditions were backward in comparison with the continent. The people were very primitive, stagnant and passive, receiving whatever progress they enjoyed through invasion or importation.

They either lived on isolated farms or in hut villages, located usually on the gravel of river banks of the light upland soils, such as the chalk downs.

Each settlement was surrounded by small fields tilled, either with a foot-plough of a type still in use not long ago, or sometimes by a light ox drawn plow which merely scratched the soil without turning the sod.

The dead were cremated and the ashes preserved in urns, to be buried in regular cemeteries.

There is really little known about the inhabitants of Britain until the two Celtic invasions, the "Goidels" in the later part of the Bronze Age, and the "Brythons" and "Belgae" in the Iron Age.

These people invaded the island, bringing a Celtic civilization and dialects. They were, probably, of the same race as the Celtic speaking peoples of the continent, and numerous enough to obliterate the races found on the island, because Julius Caesar, in his time, stated that all Britains were Celts except a few tribes in the north.

They were formed in separate tribes and quite warlike, each tribe was headed by a prince. Their dwellings were usually round huts sunk in the ground, or subterranean chambered houses, or pile-abodes constructed among the marshes.

[ 190 ]

It was a fairly industrious peasant population, living by agriculture, raising livestock, also hunting and fishing. They made rude pottery without a wheel, and used flint for arrowheads.

Apparently, they were visited by itinerant bronze-founders able to make swords, spears, socketed axes, sickles, carpenter tools, metal parts of wheeled vehicles, buckets, cauldrons and numerous other utensils.

There were no large towns and no fortifications. These people were not expecting warfare on a large scale. The political life was simple, but there was some distinction between rich and poor.

The Iron Age gradually overlapped from the Bronze Age, and for several hundred years previous to the interference of Caesar in the affairs of Britain there were a number of minor political, economical, and social changes.

Meanwhile they had developed into good fighters, this being more Germanic than Celtic in nature, and all the tribes had adopted the Celtic language, which must have been introduced about 600 B. C.

During the years 100 B. C., the Belgae invaded Britain. They came from "Belgic Gaul," first to plunder, and then to settle in large numbers along the straits of Dover, where they tilled the soil. They brought, probably the Germanic element, an improved technic into the primitive way of British agriculture. It was a plow that would really turn the sod for the first time in the history of Britain. They began to clear the forests, and work the heaviest soils, they covered the country with isolated farm houses and stocked them with cattle.

They also made a good pottery, but defective in artistic qualities to earlier specimens.

The Belgae brought coins into Britain, the earliest coins found in Britain apart from stray specimens of Mediterranean Gaulish Bellovaci, struck early in the 100 B. C. These were brought in by the invaders. After the Belgae settlements, coins began to be struck in Britain itself, although the main development of British coinage belongs to a later date.

Caesar found market centers among the southern tribes, also a gold coinage and a currency of iron ingots weighing about a pound. Some of this currency, not used by the Belgae but by some southwestern tribes, were objects resembling a half finished sword with a roughly formed handle.

The principal feature of their religion was the Druid priesthood, practicing magical arts, and barbarous rites. They taught a secret lore, but took no part in politics.

Their skill in certain arts was considerable, depicting wonderful but rather weird and fantastic forms of plants and animals, although never the human form. The art involved a more or less free use of the geometrical figure called the "returning spiral." The works were produced in bronze, wood and pottery.

Around the mouth of the Thames, and in east Kent, a large population of vigorous Belgie settled, scattering their farms over the countryside, clearing forest, breaking up new land with the heavy plows and reaping rich crops of wheat off the virgin soil.

They were divided into small tribes and often engaged in petty warfare. There was no capital or large town. They mainly pushed on north and north-east. They were hedged in on the south by the forest of the Weald, and by an older civilization extending from the Belgie area to the Wash, the forests of the Midlands, and the uplands of Wiltshire. It was a mixture of primitive Bronze Age and other civilizations.

The tribes in Somerset, Dorset, Lincolnshire and Yorkshire were progressive and warlike. Cornwall had a tin trade. Devonshire and Wales were backward.

Before the rise of the Roman system of society in Britain social distinctions were those between tribesmen and villagers. It was a period before the birth of Christ. The tribesman ruled with all his pride of race. The villager, who could boast of no ancestry, served or paid tribute.

The tribe was a community of free heads of families united together for purposes of defense, of law, and of tillage.

The homesteads are scattered along the borders of the woods, between the pasture lands, and the hunting grounds. Each homestead is large enough to accommodate a whole family in its one room.

It is a square or a round edifice, built of unhewn or roughly hewn trees placed on end, with a roof of interlaced boughs, covered with rushes or turf.

In the middle of the floor the family fire burns, and the members of the family sit around it, along the side of the room, upon a bed made of rushes and covered with hides or coarse cloth.

Upon this bed, around the fire, which continued to burn by night as well as by day, the members of the family had the right to sit at meal-times and to lie at night.

At meal times large platters containing meal cakes, meat and broth, would be placed on the rushes or green grass between the family bed and the family fire.

At dusk the fire would be renewed, and the privileged circle, from grandfather to grandson, lay with their feet towards it. The land belonged to the family, which assured the right of reposing in the family bed. The family remained united to the third generation, at least. Then the old family was regarded as having broken up into new families—all anxious, however, to remember the common descent.

The "villagers" were subject to the free tribal communities. They are called "villeins" in the 13th century laws. They were "communists" and subjective.

[ 192 ]

Land belonged equally to all, son and stranger alike. No heir among the "villagers" was recognized, except the whole community. The land was tilled in common, and its produce was common property. These bond communities, were no doubt, non-Aryan.

Gradually, the conditions of tribesman and villager became assimilated, resulting in the rise in power of the tribal King. The governing of the subject people was the tribal chief's source of strength. By them his dwelling place was built or repaired, his table was furnished, his dogs and slaves were maintained.

The two communities, family and communistic, were finally united in one political society under the jurisdiction of a lord and his officers.

When the Romans invaded Britain in 54 B. C., and 43 A. D., they found a great tribal king trying to subdue other tribes.

The Romans destroyed for the time the power of tribal chiefs, and united the southern part of Britain under their own rule. The later history of the British Isles is really a struggle between the tribal independence and the traditions of Roman unity.

For centuries before, and sometime after the Roman occupation the social condition of Britain was its political history. The lowest class subjected to all invaders were the first inhabitants of Britain, then the Celtic tribesmen united in families and tribes, and jealous of their privileges. Above the Celtic tribesmen were the kings, and then even they were subjected to the Romans, whose "red tunic" was a token of nobility long after their departure. When these classes had once been formed, Druidism forged chains of iron for each subject class. In the world to come, as in Britain, the slave was never to be entirely free of his master. New invasions and higher classes came, old social history repeated itself with weary monotony until the two leveling agencies, religion and military invention, brought in a new social order.

The Roman conquest of northern Gaul (57-50 B. C.), brought Britain into definite relation with the Mediterranean, and when Roman civilization and its products invaded Gallia Belgica, they extended over into Britain, where the coinage began to bear Roman signs.

After the two raids of Caesar, 55, 54 B. C., the south Britain tribes were regarded as vassals, although the real conquest had not been accomplished, and the tribes of Britain were far from subdued.

The conquest was undertaken by Claudius in 43 A. D., under the plans of Augustus and others formulated several years before. It, apparently, was quite an expedition, for Aulus Plautius landed in Kent with a well equipped army of 40,000 men and advanced on London. The foe he met was much stronger than expected, and fighting was, apparently, more or less continuous for the next 300 years.

[ 193 ]

In fact, the Romans had very little peace in Britain until about 208 A. D., when the conquest was considered complete in the main features. For 200 years the Romans ruled the country with some efficiency. They built fine streets, roads, buildings and "villas." It is well established that the fourth century was a prosperous period for Britain, although no details of trade are extant. Wool and wheat were exported in large quantities, and mines of lead and iron were being worked to advantage.

The Roman rule in Britain had been continually contested by the tribes of the island for 300 years; especially warlike were the northern tribes, and early in the fourth century it seemed wise to construct a long coast defence "reaching from the Wash to Spithead" against the Saxon "pirates"; various forts were also built.

However, "barbarian" assaults, not only of the Saxons, but of the Irish (Scoti) and Picts became more common and terrible.

There is no clear date for the fall of the Roman rule in Britain. Early in the fourth century the end became certain. After over 300 vicious assaults by Saxons, Scoti and Picts, the power of the Roman troops was hopelessly weakened. Near the end of the century it is apparent that many Roman troops withdrew from the island.

In the forepart of the fifth century the Teutons conquered Gaul, thereby cutting the island off from Rome.

However, it is not thought many of the people living under the Roman rule in Britain left the island. The central government, apparently, merely evacuated, while the "Romano-British were driven from the "walled cities" and "civilized houses" into the hills of Wales and the northwest, where the old Celtic element, together with the people of Ireland, gradually absorbed their identity, and revived the Celtic language and art.

After the fall of the Roman government in Britain, the morale of the people decayed, and gradually fell to a very low level. The remarkable works of engineering, walls, fine roads, and beautiful villas were permitted to disintegrate. History is obscure for many years concerning this period.

However, some writers claim that the vicious raids of Scoti and Picts, finally caused the "Britons" to ask aid of the Saxons. They came, and were victorious over the northern tribes, but, in the end, turned against the Britons, claiming they were not paid for services.

By the end of the fifth century the Saxons had control of the eastern portion of Britain to the Humber. The siege of "Mons Badonicus" took place in 517 A. D. As time passed one "kingdom" after another was established, each having a king of its own. Up to about 600 A. D. English history was that of Britain.

Augustine and others converted England to Christianity about A. D. 597 to 686.

Toward the end of the fifth century the "English" took over Britain, or the most civilized part of it. Village and agriculture was given a new "way of life." The average Old English village with its classes would appear something like this table for several hundred years.

| | | |
|---|---|---|
| a. Gentry | Thane or Thegen (squire, landlord) | Living on his own land, but owing special duties to the king to whose "comitatus" he has belonged. Of gentle blood or rank. |
| | Priest (parson) | Living on the "glebe" with which the lord (his patron) has endowed the village church. He receives and administers the tithes and other church dues. Of gentle birth. |
| b. Farmer | Yeoman or "Geneat" (tenant-farmer) | A freeman farming his own land, or farming his lord's and then working for, as well as paying rent to, the landlord. |
| c. Peasants | Cottager (cotsetla) | A labourer with five acres in lieu of wages. Unfree. |
| | Copyholder (gebur) | A copyholder, with no stock of his own and bound to heavy task work. Unfree. |
| d. Labourers | Bee-keepers, cheese-wrights, barn-keepers, swine-herds, ox-herds, shepherds, beadle, woodward, hayward. | Serfs, who were paid partly in food and clothes, partly in the case of the village officials, in perquisites and dues. |
| e. Village tradesmen | Fisher, hunter, fowler, craftsmen (smiths, carpenters) merchant-peddler, potter, traveling tradesman | Freemen—who either took services or pursued some trade or occupation. The traveling "tradesman" sometimes had their houses in the towns. |

It is probable that the thanes, yeomen and tradesmen were mostly of English blood, although soon mixing with the British women.

About the same kind of class division in the English village exists today, except for certain slight changes in legal rights. Thus in early times the women-servants and menials about the yeoman's or gentlemen's house were absolute slaves, and were bought and sold as cattle. The regular laborers, though serfs, had some protection in the "custom" of the place, which limited their lord's right over them, and they lived in their little cottages and not at their master's houses.

Pestilence on a large scale afflicted the life of the English in the Middle Ages. Many of these scourges were due to the failure of crops and loss of cattle in bad seasons.

London was the only town on the Thames till the tenth century, and all of the towns in Britain were small. The Domesday Book shows eighty towns having a total population of about 200,000.

An Old English borough was little more than a collection of wooden thatched huts with two or three small churches, some having towers.

The basis of Old English social life must be sought in the primitive institutions common to the whole Teutonic race.

The general impression derived from the "Germania" is that of a community of freemen loosely bound together for common enterprise on a large scale, such as warlike expeditions, but otherwise united only by the tie of kindred.

The origin of the name Britain is obscure. Among the Belgie tribes along the straits of Dover was one called "Britanie," which Caesar called "Britain." However, long before this period Britain was called the "Bretanic Isles."

English history may be considered as beginning with the reign of Egbert of Wessex, 827 836. He was not the first King of England, but was quite an able man according to the times, which were certainly cruel and crude to the highest degree.

Although England was well suited for maritime trade, early history is almost a total blank regarding commerce and industry. Except for a few scattered allusions, it might be assumed to have had no commerce until sometime after the Norman Conquest, and no exports, save of raw products, until much later.

It is strange that the Saxons and Angles, who in their old homes were great boat builders and daring seafarers, should have lost these traits after a few generations in England. They built no more ships, and made no more adventurous voyages for traffic or for spoil.

However, there was a very large trade in human slavery, dating back, at least, to the sixth century. To judge by the evidence it was quite the chief business.

The story of those fair haired English boys being sold in the market place of Rome is no fable.

Warfare, debt and crime were the mediums through which men and women became slaves in early England. The invaders of Britain brought their bondservants with them, and the gradual progress westward must have produced a constant supply of slaves from the conquered Welsh and others.

Medieval Christianity partly condoned the traffic, although the church from time to time issued wordy tirades against it. The church seemed concerned, more especially, about where the slave was to be sold, suggesting, for instance, "that Christian men and uncondemned be not sold out of the country, especially into a heathen nation."

The contemporary biographer of Bishop Wulfstan in the eleventh century relates the efforts of the good bishop to turn the traders of Bristol from their evil ways. One rather extraordinary passage reads as follows: "The people of Bristol had an odious and inveterate custom of buying men and women in all parts of England, and exporting them to Ireland for gain. The young women they carried to market in their pregnancy, that they might get a better price x x x x nor were these men ashamed to sell into slavery their nearest relatives, nay, even their own children."

This practice was continued through the eighteenth, and into the nineteenth centuries, with only a slight change in the permissable race and relationship of the slave, and slavery exists today in some parts of the world.

Historians have been very slovenly when treating the subject of trade and commerce in England during the medieval period about 375-1492 A. D., and they are extremely important in the life of a people. Of course, they are separate processes, and may be carried on, one without the other. A huckster with his cart carries on trade, while commerce requires an exchange of goods between nations.

Trade brushes off the rust of barbarism, supersedes the rude customs of seclusion, and above all, industry and trade breaks down the benumbing chains of feudalism.

England owes her civil and religious liberty, and her independence as a nation, together with her enjoyments, or most of them, to the commercial and industrial advances of the sixteenth and seventeenth centuries.

There appears to have been little change in the social, economic and religious life of the English for several generations before William the Conqueror took over affairs in 1066. If anything, perhaps, the shift was still farther away from the old tribal independence to slavery, serfdom and feudalism. Very little of the old fierce individualism remained.

William the First, was born at Falaise, and became the Duke of Normandy 1035. On Oct. 14, 1066, he won a battle over Harold at Hastings, and was forthwith crowned King of England, after which the collection of taxes and rewarding his followers by grants of land taken from the conquered seemed to be his main object in life.

The "Domesday" is the record of the great survey of England executed for William the Conqueror. The scheme for the work was considered at the Xmas assembly of 1085, and the work was completed in 1086. It is not certain, however, that the Book was made at this date, although it was finally compiled from these returns.

The original MS. of the Domesday Book consists of two volumes. Vol. 2 is devoted to the three eastern counties. Vol. 1 the rest of England. The northwestern portion, under Carlisle, had not yet been conquered, and was not for some years after the survey. The omission of Northumberland and Durham has never been explained satisfactorily. Several towns, such as Winchester and London, were not surveyed.

The primary object of the survey was to ascertain
    (a) The national land-tax (geldum) paid on a fixed assessment;
    (b) Certain other dues;
    (c) Proceeds of crown lands.

There had been a great political change, and William wanted to make sure that his "rights" to taxes were thoroughly understood. He did not trust his Norman followers, to whom he had recently granted the lands of the vanquished. They seemed disposed to evade the liabilities of their English predecessors. He directed that Domesday record the names of the new holders of lands and the assessments on which their tax was to be paid. He attempted, also, to form a national valuation list, estimating the annual value all land, and reckoned also that rather foggy item, called "potential" value. In this connection it may be well to remember that kings, nobles, "governments" and "rulers" in general are penniless, depending on "taxes" for their upkeep, and that the collecting of these taxes is, as a rule, their main occupation. It has ever been thus, and the present is no exception. This is a problem for future solution.

Domesday records the "Christian" name of many "undertenants," but genealogists do not find it very useful because the surnames are omitted. In some cases they have been identified. The great bulk of these "Christian" names are not English.

The original Domesday may be seen in a glass case in the Public Record Office, London.

During the Middle Ages and sometime after, "ale" was the common drink, and the addition of hops forming a beer was not in favor until the reign of Henry VIII. Another drink was "mead," a compound of ginger, sugar and honey. Then there was "metheglin," made of herbs and honey. Also "braggot," a concoction of spices. "Posset" was a drink of hot milk poured on ale or sack, and flavored with sugar, eggs, grated biscuit, and other ingredients.

The wines in use were numerous, and came from Gascony, Spain, Italy, Greece, Cyprus and the Archipelago. The most familiar are "muscadel" and "malmsey." Many of these wines were highly acid, and used in mixing drinks such as "pymont," "clarry" and "hippocras." The two former were preparations with honey. The compounding of "hippocras" included all the choicest spices.

It may be stated that during the first half of the fourteenth century definite steps were taken toward the extinction of "serfdom" in agriculture and among the peasantry. A new class of laborers were permitted who worked for wages, and, who, though not entirely free, were their own masters so far that they could seek work wherever they could find it.

This was a great advance, for the old tribal independence had long since passed, and the peasants, comprising nearly all the population had been in serfdom for several hundred years, very much so, since the Norman Conquest. On the Continent even this little advance did not take place for some centuries.

However, a pestilence killed off so many people, that the laborer became scarce and, therefore, demanded what was considered by the landlords excessive wages. The nobility forthwith put everybody back into serfdom by the following proclamation, in part, issued by the King June 18th, 1349:

"Because a great part of the people, and, especially of workmen and servants, late died of the pestilence, many, seeking the necessity of Masters and great scarcity of servants, will not serve unless they may receive excessive wages, and some are rather willing to beg in idleness than by labour to get their living."

There were eight chapters along this line, and much of the matter, although six hundred years old, could easily pass for modern comments on the same subjects. This general problem has been a nightmare to the human race ever since the dawn of man.

Careful note should be taken of the chief remedy provided in this document, in part,

"That every man or woman, bond or free, able in body and within the age of three score years, not having his own whereof he might live, nor land of his own about which he might occupy himself, and not serving any other, should be bound to serve the employer, who should require him to do so, provided that the lords of any bondman or landservant should be preferred before others for his services. That such servants should take only the wages which were accustomed to be given in the places where they ought to serve in the twentieth year of the King's reign, that is in 1347, or the year before the plague x x x x x neglect so to serve should be committed to gaol x x x any reaper, mower or other workman, who should leave his service should be imprisoned x x x x finally; that no one should give anything, even under colour of alms, to valiant beggars, upon pain of imprisonment."

And so, what little liberty of contract was sparingly granted by the lords, was taken away, and the peasants found themselves again tied to the soil, and were forbidden to travel without letters of authorization. Runaway workers were outlawed and branded with an "F" for their "falsity."

During the reign of the Plantagenets (1135-1400), it cannot be claimed there was any industrial progress or commercial enterprise to amount to anything. The whole system of trade was provincial and archaic.

Agriculture was still the main business. The manors were cultivated in one of two ways:

1. Customary and unpaid labor of "villeins," who in return had living holdings for nothing.
2. Paid services of "free" laborers, who if they had living holdings paid rent to the lord for them.

An act was passed in 1389 ensuring an undiminished supply of "villeins" to serve the lords of the manor, so that for many generations history is almost silent about the "man with the hoe" in England, although agriculture was the support of about everybody on the island, including the nobility and clergy, who lived on the sweat and toil of the "villein."

The condition of the agriculturer laborer as late as the sixteenth century led Sir Thomas More to declare "the state of and condition of labouring beasts were much better."

From 1066 to 1500, the approximate beginning of the great "Commercial Revolution," England remained a stagnant people. It was just one king after another. The House of Normandy (1066-1135) included William the Conqueror, William the Second, his brother Henry I, and Stephen. Then came the House of Plantagenet (1135-1400), including Henry II, Richard the First, famous soldier of the cross, surnamed Coeur de Lion, John, Henry III, Edward I, Edward II, Edward III and Richard II. There followed the House of Lancaster (1400 1461) with Henry IV, Henry V, and Henry VI. These were the famous three of the "Red Rose." After these, the House of York, 1400-1485, Edward IV, Edward V, Richard III, all three of the "White Rose" clan.

Then came the House of Tudor (1485-1603), comprising Henry VII (1485-1509), Henry VIII (1509-1547), Edward VI (1547-1553). Mary I married Philip II, king of Spain, July 25, 1554. She reigned 1553-1558. Then came Elizabeth (1558-1603).

MAP No 4

ATLANTIC OCEAN

NORWAY

SWEDEN

BALTIC SEA

NORTH SEA

Scotland

Ireland

England

DENMARK

TEUTONIC ORDER

MUSCOVY

LITHUANIA

HOLY ROMAN EMPIRE

Bohemia

POLAND

Austria

HUNGARY

FRANCE

Swiss

Savoy

Milan

Venice

Moldavia

Wallachia

OTTOMAN EMPIRE

NAVARRE

PORTUGAL

CASTILE

ARAGON

GRANADA

Corsica

Sardinia

Naples

MEDITERRANEAN SEA.

Sicily

AFRICA

Crete

L.C.H.
1941

WESTERN EUROPE · 1500

It is the period of the Tudors that the Mayflower Planters were so interested in. Along about 1456 movable type had been perfected, and during the later portion of Elizabeth's reign printed matter was circulated quite freely so that citizens were better posted on passing events than ever before.

At the end of the fifteenth century, and beginning of the sixteenth, the process of filling the ranks of the nobility with new men was begun. The gap was caused by wars, confiscations, and attainders.

The new nobles came from the upper rural class. During the past years they had been in agriculture and wool selling, and had accumulated some means, a qualification which greatly appealed to the King. The new peerage was distinctly based on the new wealth, and entirely ignorant of the traditions or history of earlier nobility.

In fact, the Tudors, with Henry VII brought in a sort of new monarchy, based on the budding era of commerce which replaced, in time, feudalism, and a new individualism which replaced the old ecclesiastical system. There was a change in balance between Church and State, and between the Crown and the Estates.

In the sixteenth century, the Commons assumed, to a large extent, the leading position they were created for.

It cannot be claimed that the "arts of life," personal habits, refinement of manners and the like had improved very much for centuries before 1600. Such laudable objectives can only be attained through science and invention, and politicians, for reasons best known to themselves, have always been fearful of "innovations," probably, in most instances, being afraid of the adverse effects on their personal position in life. For centuries individuals kept themselves in power by the simple process of refusing to encourage anything but ignorance, debt and misery among their subjects. This was a crude negative method but very effective. The great and the near great never seemed to appreciate that failure to reward initiative, especially along inventive lines, seriously limited their own pleasures in life.

In fact, from the distant past to comparatively recent times, there were no real "luxuries" for anybody, high or low.

Oh yes, great nobles and the clergy lived in huge castles. They had a host of personal attendants to wait on them. There was an excessive extravagance in dress. However, a prince or a peer might wear velvet or ermine on his back, but he had rushes under his feet, the great hall of the cold barn-like castle might be grand in proportion and rich in decoration, but without illumination worthy of the name. His meal might be brought to him on costly dishes, but he fed himself with his fingers.

---

Refs. 99, 100, 103, 111, 112, 437, 497, 498, 499, 595, 596.

# ALDEN

I. **Alden**, John[1], born England about 1599; died Duxbury Sept. 22, 1687 (N. S.), age 84; married before 1624 at Plymouth; Pricilla[2] **Mullins**, daughter of William[1] **Mullins**, Mayflower Planter, and Merchant Adventurer. She died after 1650.

During the early portion of the 17th century the Aldens were quite numerous in Essex Co., England, especially around Harwich. These Aldens were related by marriage to Captain Christopher Jones of the Mayflower.

The story of John Alden is too familiar for much comment here. He lived a long and useful life of unselfish devotion to the public interest, and died, full of honors, but poor in its service. John Alden left no will. He died at Duxbury Sept. 12, 1687 (O. S.), and on Oct. 31st, the inventory of his estate was taken by his son Jonathan, who was appointed administrator Nov. 8th. During lifetime he had deeded land portions to his children, and since the inventory mentions no real estate, it must have all been disposed of before his death.

The estate was very small, amounting to only £49 17s.6d.

The papers relating to the settlement of this estate are found in Ply. Co. Probate Recs., Vol. I, p. 10, 16.

p. 10. The Eighth day of November 1687 Administration was Granted unto Leutt Jonathan Alden to administer upon the Estate of his father Mr. John Alden late of Duxbury deceased.

The Inventory of the Estate of the late deceased Mr. John Alden Oct. 31 day 1687.

The assets were few, probably, having been distributed among his children previously. There were, however, some "Neate Cattell sheepe swine & one horse," "andirons pot hookes and hangers," "augurs and chisells," "2 old guns," "one Spitt 1ˢ 6ᵈ & baggs 2ˢ," "one horse bridle and Saddle liberary and Cash and wearing clothes," "table linen & other linen" and some other small items.

## CHILDREN

IIa. **Elizabeth**, b. 1623; d. May 31, 1717; m. William **Pabodie.**

IIIb. **John**, b. 1626; d. Mar. 14, 1701; m. 1st Elizabeth (  ); m. 2nd Elizabeth (**Phillips**) **Everett.**

IVc. **Joseph**, b. 1627; d. Feb. 8, 1697; m. Mary **Simons.**

Vd. **Sarah**, b. 1629; d.  ; m. Alexander **Standish.**

VIe. **Jonathan**, b. 1632; d. Feb. 14, 1697 (?); m. Abigail **Hallett.**

VIIf. Ruth, b.     1634; d.     ; m. John **Bass.**
  g. Rebecca, b.     (?) 1637; d.     ; m.    .
  h. Precilla, b.     ; d. alive 1688; m.    .
VIIIi. Mary, b.     1643; d. before Sept. 12, 1688; m. Thomas
     **Delano.**
IXj. David, b.     ; d.     ; m. Marie **Southworth.**
  k. Child, b.     ; d.     ; m.    .

## PABODIE

IIa. **Alden,** Elizabeth[2] (John[1]), married William **Pabodie.**
(See Pabodie IIIc.).

## PEABODY

I. **Pabodie** (Peabody), John[1], born England; arrived in Plymouth as early as 1636, and was a freeman there in 1637. His grant of land in Jan., 1636, was for 10 acres on the Duxbury side, lying between the lands of William Tubs and Experience Mitchell, and from "Blew Fish River in the caste." He received other lands, and served on juries, but, apparently, led a quiet life. He made a will dated July 16, 1649, at Duxbury, which seems to have been recorded in April 27, 1667, by one John "ffernesyde," the witness to the will. He mentions Thomas, eldest son, Francis, second son, and William, youngest son, also Annis Rouse, daughter, wife of John Rouse.

### CHILDREN

  a. Thomas, b.     ; d.     ; m.    .
IIb. Francis, b. Eng. 1612-14; d. Feb. 19, 1697-8; m. 1st
     Lydia     ; m. 2nd Mary    .
IIIc. William, b.     1619 (?); d. Dec. 13, 1707; m. Elizabeth
     **Alden.**
IVd. Annis, b.     ; d.     1688 (?); m. John **Rouse.**

IIb. **Peabody,** Francis[2] (John[1]), born England 1612-14; probably came to New England in the spring of 1635, and located in Ipswich. By 1640 he was an inhabitant of Hampton, where he became a freeman in 1645, married after 1649 Mary **Foster,** daughter of Reginald. His first wife may have been Lydia ( (?) ). Apparently, he spent almost a half century of his life in Topsfield, where he was a selectman, a militia Lt., and an honored member of the church. He died Feb. 19, 1697-8, leaving a most interesting will dated Topsfield, Essex Co., Mass., Jan. 20, 1695-6, proved Aug. 7, 1698. Witnesses were Joseph Capen and Thomas Baker.

CHILDREN

a. Lydia, bp. Aug. 30, 1640; d.        ; m. Thomas **Perley.**
b. John, b.     1642; d. July 5, 1720; m. 1st Hannah **Andrews;** m. 2nd Sarah **Mosely.**
c. Joseph, b.     1644; d.     1721-22; m.     1st Bethia **Bridges;** m. 2nd Mary **Wheeler.**
d. William, b.     1646; d. Mar. 6, 1699-00; m. 1st Mary **Brown;** m. 2nd Hannah **Hale.**
e. Isaac, b.     1648; d.     1726-7; m. Elizabeth (    ).
f. Sarah, b.     1650; d.     ; m. Abraham **Howe.**
g. 'Hepzibah, b.     1652; d.     ; m. Daniel **Rea.**
h. Mary, b.     1656; d.     ; m. 1st John **Death;** m. 2nd Samuel **Eames.**
i. Ruth, b. May 22, 1658; d. before 1695; m.        .
j. Damaris, b. June 21, 1660; d. Dec. 19, 1660; m. ——.
k. Samuel, b. June 4, 1662; d. Sept. 13, 1667; m. ——.
l. Jacob, b. July 28, 1664; d. Nov. 24, 1689; m. Abigail **Towne.**
m. Hannah, b. May 8, 1666; d.        ; m. Daniel **Andrews.**
n. Nathaniel, b. July 20, 1667; d.     1715; m.        .

IIIc. **Peabody,** William[2] (John[1]), born England 1619 (?); died Little Compton, R. I., Dec. 13, 1707; married Elizabeth **Alden** Dec. 26, 1644, at Plymouth, daughter of John **Alden.** She died May 31, 1717, leaving, it is said, 450 living descendants.

He removed from Plymouth to Duxbury, where he held many offices of trust, being Town Clerk of Duxbury for 18 years, and Deputy to the General Court for many terms.

His will is dated Little Compton of Bristol Co., Mass., May 13, 1707; proved Feb. 27, 1707, wits. John **Woodman,** Peter **Taylor** and Samuel **Wilbore.**

CHILDREN BORN DUXBURY

a. John, b. Oct. 4, 1645; d. Nov. 17, 1669; m.        .
b. Elizabeth, b. Apr. 24, 1647; d. before 1707; m. John **Rogers.**
c. Mary, b. Aug. 7, 1648; d.        ; m. Edward **Southworth.**
d. Mercy, b. Jan. 2, 1649; d.     1728 (?); m. John **Simons.**
e. Martha, b. Feb. 24, 1650; d. Jan. 25, 1712; m. 1st (    ) **Seabury;** m. 2nd William **Fobes.**
f. Pricilla, b. Nov. 16, 1652; d. Mar. 2, 1653; m. ——.
g. Precilla, b. Jan. 15, 1653; d. June 3, 1724; m. Rev. Ichabod **Wiswell.**
h. Sarah, b. Aug. 7, 1656; d. Aug. 27, 1740; m. John **Coe.**
i. Ruth, b. June 27, 1658; d.     ; m. Benjamin **Bartlett.**
j. Rebecca, b. Oct. 16, 1660; d. Dec. 3, 1702; m. William **Southworth.**

k. Hannah, b. Oct. 15, 1662; d. after 1714; m. Samuel **Bartlett.**
l. William, b. Nov. 24, 1664; d. Sept. 17, 1744; m. 1st Judith
(    ); m. 2nd Elizabeth (    ); m. 3rd Mary (**Morgan**)
**Starr.**
  m. Lydia, b. Apr. 3, 1667; d. July 13, 1748; m. (    ) **Grinnell.**

## ROUSE

IVd. **Peabodie,** Annis[2] (John[1]), born England; died 1688 (?);
married John **Rouse** 1639 (?); he died Dec. 16, 1684 and resided
in Marshfield on Careswell Creek. John Rouse was a Quaker,
son of a "gentleman of Barbadoes."

### CHILDREN (ROUSE)

a. Mary, b. Aug. 10, 1640; d.  ; m. (    ) Price.
b. John, b. Sept. 28, 1643; d.  (?); m.  .
c. Simon, b. June 14, 1645; d.  ; m.  .
d. George, b. May 17, 1648; d.  ; m.  .
e. Anna, b.  ; d.  ; m. Isaac **Holmes.**
f. Elizabeth, b.  ; d.  ; m. Thomas **Bourne.**

## ALDEN

IIIb. **Alden,** John[2] (John[1]); born Duxbury 1626 (?); died
Mar. 14, 1701, Boston, Mass.; married 1st Elizabeth (  ?  );
died before 1659; married 2nd Elizabeth (**Phillips**) **Everett** April
1, 1659; daughter of Lt. William **Phillips** of Boston. She died
1695.

### CHILDREN

a. Mary, b. Dec. 17, 1659; d. young.
b. John, b. Nov. 20, 1660; d. young.
c. Elizabeth, b. May 9, 1662; d. May 14, 1662.
d. John, b. Mar. 17, 1663; d.  ; m. 1st Elizabeth **Phelps;**
m. 2nd Sussana **Winslow.**
e. William, b. Mar. 16, 1664; d. June 7, 1664.
f. Elizabeth, b. Apr. 9, 1665; d.  ; m. 1st John **Whalley;**
m. 2nd Simon **Willard.**
g. William, b. Mar. 5, 1666; d. young.
h. Zachary, bp. Mar. 19, 1667; d. young.
i. Capt. William, b. Sept. 10, 1669; d.  ; m. Mary **Drury.**
j. Nathaniel, b.  1670; d.  ; m. Hepzibah **Mountjoy.**
k. Zachariah, b. Feb. 18, 1672; d.  1709; m. Mary **Viall.**
l. Nathan, b. Oct. 17, 1677; d. young.
  m. Sarah, b. Sept. 27, 1681; d. young.

# PHILLIPS

I. **Phillips,** William[1], born England; married 1st Mary ( ); died May 1st, 1646; married 2nd Sussana **Stanley;** she made a will dated Sept. 10, 1650, mentioning children William, Nathaniel, Elizabeth and Phebe; married 3rd Bridget **Sanford,** widow in 1689.

William **Phillips** was admitted to the first church at Charlestown Sept. 23, 1639. He resided in various places, and was in Saco, Maine, 1663 and 1665.

## CHILDREN (PHILLIPS)

a. William, b.    ; d. young.
b. Elizabeth, b.    ; d.    ; m. 1st ( ) **Everett;** m. 2nd John **Alden.**
c. Phebe, b. Apr. 7, 1640; d.    ; m.    .
d. Nathaniel, b. Feb. 5, 1642; d.    ; m.    .
e. Mary, b. Feb. 17, 1644; d.    ; m.    .
f. John, b. Sept. 18, 1656; d.    ; m.    .
g. Samuel, b. Mar. 16, 1658; d.    ; m.    .
h. William, b. Jan. 28, 1660; d.    ; m.    .

## ALDEN

IVc. **Alden,** Joseph[2] (John[1]), born Plymouth 1627 (?); died Bridgewater Feb. 8, 1697; married 1st Mary **Simons (Symonson);** daughter of Moses[1] **Simons;** married 2nd ( ).

### CHILDREN BORN BRIDGEWATER

a. Isaac, b.    ; d. June 24, 1729; m. Mahitable **Allen.**
b. Joseph, b.    1667; d. Dec. 22, 1747; m. Hannah **Dunham.**
c. John, b.    ; d.    1730; m. Hannah **White.**
d. Hopestill, b.    ; d.    ; m. Joseph **Snow.**
e. Elizabeth, b.    ; d.    1705; m. Benjamin **Snow.**
f. Mercy, b.    ; d.    ; m. John **Burrill.**
g. Sarah, b.    ; d.    ; m. Joseph **Crossman.**
h. Mary, b.    ; d.    ; m. Samuel **Allen.**

## SIMONS

I. Simons, **Moses,** born Leyden, Holland, of Dutch parents. His name was apparently written "Symonson."

Moses followed the Mayflower in the "Fortune," 1621, probably bringing his wife. He settled in Duxbury. No doubt he was of the same family that came to New York in 1640, a Samuel Symonson arriving at that time. There was also a Thomas and John.

CHILDREN

a. (?) Moses, b.     ; d.     ; m. Sarah.
d. Thomas, b.     ; d.     ; m.     .
c. Mary, b.     ; d.     ; m. Joseph **Alden**. There may have
   been other children.

Vd. **Alden,** Sarah[2] (John[1]), married Alexander **Standish.**
(See Standish).

## ALDEN

VIe. **Alden,** Jonathan[2] (John[1]), born Plymouth 1627 (?); died
Duxbury Feb. 14, 1697, age 65; married Abigail **Hallett** Dec. 10,
1672; born 1644; died Aug. 17, 1725; daughter of Andrew[1] **Hallett**
and Anne **Berse** of Yarmouth.

### CHILDREN BORN DUXBURY

a. Elizabeth, b.     ; d.     ; m. 1st Edmund **Chandler**; m.
   2nd     .
b. Anna, b.     ; d. June 8, 1705; m. Josiah **Snell.**
c. Sarah, b.     (?) 1682; d.     1739; m. Thomas **South-**
   **worth.**
d. John, b.     1680; d. July 24, 1739; m. Hannah **Briggs.**
e. Jonathan, b. Mar. 1686; d.     ; m. 1st Elizabeth
   (**Arnold**) **Waterman**; m. 2nd Mahitable **Allen.**
f. Andrew, b.     ; d.     ; m. Lydia **Stanford.**

## HALLET

I. **Hallett,** Andrew[2] (Andrew[1]), born England 1615 (?); died
Yarmouth Mar. 16, 1683-4; married Anne **Berse**, daughter of
Anthony **Berse** of Sandwich; she died Apr. 6, 1694.

Andrew probably came to New England with his parents.
He resided in Plymouth before 1639, but in 1642 bought the
Giles **Hopkins** place at Yarmouth and removed there.

### CHILDREN

a. Abigail, b.     1641; d.     ; m. Jonathan **Alden.**
b. Dorcas, b. June 1, 1646; d.     ; m.     .
c. Jonathan, b. Nov. 20, 1647; d.     ; m. Abigail **Dexter.**
d. John, b. Dec. 11, 1650; d.     ; m. Mercy **Howes.**
e. Rahane, b.     ; d.     ; m. Job **Bourne.**
f. Mehitable, b.     ; d.     ; m. John **Dexter.**

Ref. 512.

[ 208 ]

VIIf. **Alden,** Ruth[2] (John[1]); m. John **Bass.**
(See Bass).

## BASS

I. **Bass,** Samuel[1], born England 1601; died Braintree, Mass.,
Dec. 30, 1694, age 94; married Annie (     ); died Sept. 16, 1693,
age 93.

He arrived in Roxbury, 1630, but removed to Braintree, now
Quincy, 1640, and represented the town in the legislature 12
years. He was an outstanding character. The records state
"Deacon Samuel Bass age 94 departed this life upon the 30th
day of Dec 1694, who had bin a Decon at the church of Braintree
for the space of above 50 years, and the first Decon of that church,
and was father and grandfather and great grandfather of a hundred and sixty-two children before he died."

### CHILDREN

a. Samuel, b. Eng.        ; d.        1653; m. Mary **Howard.**

b. Mary, b. Eng.        1631; d. June 29, 1704; m. John **Capen.**

IIc. John, b. Eng.        1632; d. Sept. 12, 1716; m. Ruth **Alden.**

d. Hannah, b. Eng.        1633; d.        ; m. Stephen **Paine.**

e. Ruth, b.        ; d.        ; m. David **Walsbee.**

f. Thomas, b. Roxbury 1635; d. Jan. 8, 1719; m. Sarah
**Wood.**

g. Sarah, bp. Apr. 30, 1643; d.        ; m. 1st John **Stone**; m.
2nd Joe **Penniman.**

h. Joseph, b.        ; d.        ; m. 1st Mary (     ); m. 2nd
Deborah (     ).

Refs. 290, 594, 10, 578, 579.

IIc. **Bass,** John[2] (Samuel[1]), born 1632; died Sept. 12, 1716;
married 1st Ruth **Alden** Feb. 3, 1657; born 1634; died Braintree
Oct. 12, 1674; daughter of John **Alden**; married 2nd Hannah
**Sturtevant,** widow.

John **Bass** was a wheelwright. He made a will dated June
25, 1716.

a. John, b. Nov. 26, 1658; d. Sept. 30, 1724; m. 1st Abigail **Adams**; m. 2nd Rebecca **Savill**.
b. Samuel, b. Mar. 25, 1660; d.     1751; m. 1st Mercy **Marsh**; m. 2nd Mary **Adams**; m. 3rd Bethia **Nightingale**.
c. Ruth, b. Jan. 28, 1662; d. June 1699; m. Peter **Webb**.
d. Joseph, b. Dec. 5, 1665; d.     1733-4; m. 1st Mary **Belcher**; m. 2nd Lois **Rogers**.
IIIe. Hannah, b. June 22, 1667; d. Oct. 24, 1705; m. Joseph **Adams**.
f. Mary, b. Feb. 11, 1669; d.     ; m. 1st Christopher **Webb**, Jr.; m. 2nd William **Copeland**.
g. Sarah, b. Mar. 29, 1672; d. Aug. 19, 1751; m. Ephraim **Thayer**.

IIIe. **Bass**, Hannah³ (John², Samuel¹), married Joseph **Adams**. (See Adams I).

VIIIi. **Alden**, Mary² (John¹), m. Dr. Thomas **Delano**. (See Delano).

# ADAMS

I. **Adams**, Joseph³ (Joseph², Henry¹), born Dec. 24, 1654; died Feb. 12, 1737; married 1st Feb. 20, 1682; Mary **Chapin**; died June 14, 1687; married 2nd Hannah **Bass**; died Oct. 24, 1705; married 3rd Elizabeth **Hobart**.

### CHILDREN BY 1ST WIFE

a. Mary, b. Feb. 6, 1683; d. Jan. 30, 1733; m. Ephraim **Jones**.
b. Abigail, b. Feb. 17 (     ); d.     ; m. Seth **Chapin**.

### CHILDREN BY 2ND WIFE

c. Joseph, b. Jan. 1, 1689; d. May 26, 1783; m. 1st Mrs. Elizabeth **Janvrin**; m. 2nd Elizabeth **Brackett**.
IId. John, b. Feb. 8, 1691; d. May 25, 1761; m. Sussanah **Boyleston**.
e. Samuel, b. Jan. 28, 1694; d. July 17, 1751; m. Sarah **Paine**.
f. Josiah, b. Feb. 8, 1696; d.     ; m. Bethia **Thomson**.
g. Hannah, b. Feb. 21, 1698; d.     ; m. Benjamin **Owen**.
h. Ruth, b. Mar. 21, 1700; d. Aug. 26, 1761; m. Rev. Nathan **Webb**.
i. Bethia, b. June 13, 1702; d.     ; m. Ebenezer **Hunt**.
j. Ebenezer, b. Dec. 30, 1704; d. Aug. 6, 1769; m. Ann **Boylston**.

### CHILDREN BY 3RD WIFE

k. Caleb, b.     ; d.     1710; m.——.

IId. **Adams, John**[4] (Joseph[3], Joseph[2], Henry[1]); born Feb. 8, 1691; died May 25, 1761; married Oct. 31, 1734, Sussanah **Boylston**; born Mar. 5, 1699; died April 17, 1797; daughter of Peter **Boyleston.**

CHILDREN

*a. John, b. Oct. 19, 1735; 2nd President U. S. A.; m. Abigail **Smith.**
b. Peter, b. Oct. 16, 1738; d. June 2, 1823; m. Mary **Crosby.**
c. Elihu, b. May 29, 1741; d.    ; m. Thankful **White.**

Ref. 188.

# DELANO

I. **De La Noye,** Philippe, born Leyden 1602; bapt. 1603; died Bridgewater, Mass. 1681 (?); aged 79 years; married 1st Duxbury, Mass., Dec. 19, 1634; Hester **Dewsbury** of Duxbury; married 2nd Duxbury, 1657, Mary **Pontus,** widow of James **Glass,** and daughter of William **Pontus.**
Philippe was the son of Jean and Marie **de Lanoye,** a French Protestant (Huguenot), who fled to Leyden. Philippe was baptized in the Walloon Church, but grew up under the teaching of Robinson and Brewster of the Separatist Church at Leyden.

CHILDREN BY 1ST WIFE

a. Mary, b.    1635; d.    1656; m. Jonathan **Dunham** (1st wife).
b. Esther, b.    1638; d. Sept. 12, 1733; m. 1st Samuel **Sampson**; m. 2nd John **Soule.**
c. Philip, b.    1640; d.    1708; m. Elizabeth **Clark.**
IId. Dr. Thomas, b. Mar. 21, 1642; d. Apr. 13, 1723; m. 1st Mary **Alden**; m. 2nd Hannah **Bartlett.**
e. John, b.    1644 (?); d.    ; m. Mary **Weston.**
f. Jane, b.    ; d. unmarried.
g. Lt. Jonathan, b.    1647; d. Dec. 22, 1720; m. Mercy **Warren.**
h. Rebecca, b.    1651; d.    ; m. John **Churchill** (1st wife).

CHILD BY 2ND WIFE

i. Samuel, b.    1659; d.    1728; m. Elizabeth **Standish.**

Ref. 572.

[ 211 ]

IId. **Delano,** Dr. Thomas (Philippe[1]), born Duxbury, Mar. 21, 1642; died Apr. 13, 1723; married 1st Mary **Alden** 1667; died before Sept. 12, 1688; married 2nd (     ).

CHILDREN BORN DUXBURY

a. Benoni, b. Oct. 30, 1667; d. Apr. 5, 1738; m.
b. Thomas, b.     1669; d.     1712; m. Hannah **Bartlett.**
c. Jonathan, b.     1676; d.     ; m. Hannah **Doty.**
d. David, b.     1678; d.     ; m. Elizabeth **Eddy.**
e. Mary, b.     ; d.     ; m.     .
f. Sarah, b.     ; d.     ; m. John **Drew.**
g. Ruth, b.     ; d.     ; m. Samuel **Drew.**
h. Joseph, b. Sept. 1, 1685; d.     ; m. Hannah (     ).

## ALDEN

IXj. **Alden,** David[2] (John[1]), born 1646 (?); died Duxbury before Apr. 1, 1719; married Marie[3] **Southworth,** daughter of Constant[2] **Southworth** (Edward[1]).

CHILDREN

a. Henry, b.     1671; d.     ; m. Deborah (     ).
b. Ruth, b.     1674; d.     1758; m. Samuel **Sprague.**
c. Elizabeth, b.     1677; d.     ; m. John **Seabury.**
d. Pricilla, b.     1679; d.     ; m. Samuel **Cheesebrough.**
e. Alice, b.     1685; d.     ; m. Judah **Paddock.**
f. Benjamin, b.     ; d.     ; m. Hannah **Brewster.**
g. Samuel, b.     1689; d. Feb. 24, 1781; m. Sarah **Sprague.**

# MULLINS

I. **Mullins,** William[1], born Surrey County, perhaps Dorking, England; died New England (Cape Cod), or Plymouth, Mar. 3, 1621 (N. S.); married England Alice (    ); died Plymouth early in 1621, after April 2.

He was a wealthy "Merchant Adventurer," and it is understood invested over £500 in the company. Just before his death he sent for Carver, and made a verbal will to witnesses John Carver, Giles Heale, the Surgeon, and Christopher Jones.

The probate record of this will in England is dated July 23, 1621, and carries a date at the top of April 2, 1621, which is probably the date placed there by the clerk in filing.

The will was probably taken on Feb. 21, 1621, the day William Mullins died, and the Mayflower sailed almost immediately thereafter on the return trip to London, with the will and a very ill Captain, who died soon after reaching his home in Rotherhithe (Notes & Queries, 13th Series clii p. 451). Captain Christopher Jones was buried at St. Mary's Rotherhithe, in March, 1622, leaving a wife and four children, Roger, Christopher, Joan and Grace, ranging from ten to four years.

Although there is nothing in Dorking, Surrey, about William Mullins, yet the Parrish Registers do show:

1571  John Mullyn m. Joane Bridger.
1582  Edward Mullyns son of John bp.
1583  (    ) Mullyns died.
1584  (    ) Mullins "son of the widow" died.
1585  Vyncent Benham m. Joane Mullyns.
1610  John Gardyner m. Margaret Mullyns.
1614  Sara dau. of John Mullins died.
1643  John Mullyn "shoomaker" died age 66."

### Will of William Mullins

This will was probably a nuncupative will, possibly written Feb. 21, 1621, old style, the day of his death.

### 2: April 1621

In the name of God, Amen: I comit my soule to God that gave it and my bodie to the earth from whence it came. Alsoe I give my goodes as followeth. That fforty poundes in the hand of goodman Woodes I give my wife tenn poundes, my sonne Joseph tenn poundes, my daughter Precilla tenn poundes, and my eldest sonne tenn poundes. Alsoe I give to my eldest sonne all my debts, bonds, bills (ovely yt forty poundes excepted in the handes of good-

[ 213 ]

man Wood) given as aforesaid w<sup>th</sup> all the stock in his own handes. To my eldest daughter I give ten shillinges to be paied out of my sonnes stock. Furthermore that goodes I have in Virginia as followeth. To my wife Alice halfe my goodes & to Joseph and Precilla the other halfe equallie to be divided betweene them. Alsoe I have xxj dozen of shoes, and thirteene paire of bootes w<sup>ch</sup> I give into the companies handes for forty poundes at seaven years and if thy like them at that rate. If it be thought to deare as my overseers shall thinck good. And if they like them at that rate at the divident I shall have nyne shares whereof I give as followeth twoe to my wife, twoe to my sonne William, twoe to my sonne Joseph, twoe to my daughter Precilla, and one to the Companie. Allsoe if my sonne William will come to Virginia I give him my share of land. furdermore I give to my twoe overseers Mr. John Carver, and Mr. Williamson, twentye shillinges apeece to see this my will performed desiringe them that he would have an eye over my wife and children to be as fathers and freindes to them: also to have a speciall eye to my man Robert w<sup>ch</sup> hathe not so approved himselfe as I would he should have done.

This is a Coppye of Mr. Mullens his Will of all particulars he hathe given. In witness whereof I have sett my hande

> John Carver
> Giles Heale
> Christopher Joanes

In the mouth of July Anno Domini 1621: on the 23d day issued a commission to Sarah Blunden, formerly Mullins, natural and legitimate daughter of William Mullins, late of Dorking in the County of Surrey, but deceased in parts beyond the seas, seized etc. for administering the goodes, rights and credits of the said deceased, according to the tenor and effect of the will of the said deceased because in that will he named no executor. In due form etc. swears.

> Probate Act Book 1621 and 1622.

Note—This last item is a translation from a Latin record.

In the survey of the Dorking Manor of 1622, William Mullins appears holding a tenement, with barn, garden, yard and other features, about one and one-half acres, between West Street and Back Lane. The holder was a man of some position. The property was sold in 1619 to Ephraim Bothell, with a charge unspecified still upon it, for £280. Just which party made the shrewd deal is a question unanswered, but William had apparently sold this holding just before sailing in the Mayflower for the Colonies, with his wife and son Joseph.

CHILDREN (KNOWN)

3262   a. William, b. Eng.        ; d. New England, 1672; m. wid.
          Ann **Bell.**
3261   b. Sarah, b. Eng.         ; d. England.
3263   c. Joseph, b. Eng.       ; d. Plymouth, Mass., early 1621.
3251  IId. Precilla, b. Eng.     ; d.      ; m. John **Alden.**

IId. Precilla Mullins (see Alden I).


## COOKE

44. **Cooke,** Francis[3] (Damaris[2] **Hopkins,** Stephen[1]), born Plymouth Jan. 5, 1663; married Elizabeth[3] **Latham,** daughter of Robert[2] **Latham** (William[1]).

CHILDREN BORN PLYMOUTH

247. Caleb, b.      ; d.      ; m. Hannah **Shurtleff.**
248. Robert, b.     ; d.      ; m. 1st Abigail **Harlow;** m. 2nd
        Lydia **Tilden.**
249. Elizabeth, b.  ; d.      ; m. David **Leach.**
250. Francis, b.    ; d.      ; m. Ruth **Sylvester.**
251. Sussanah, b.   ; d.      ; m. James **Sturtevant.**
252. Sarah, b.      ; d.      ; m. Ephraim **Cole.**

-----

Refs. 177, 133, 134, 145.


## LATHAM

I. **Latham,** William[1], born England; died in the Bahama Islands between Nov. 7, 1645-Mar. 6, 1651.

This William was a "boy" according to Bradford, on the Mayflower, and had been "put" in the Carver family group. He may have been identured for a period to John Carver for the expense of the passage, but there are no records of such an understanding.

The use of the word "servant" in connection with the single men and unattached children on the Mayflower is extremely misleading, especially in modern interpretation.

The heads of family groups prepared their own meals on the Mayflower, and the unattached individuals were "put" into these various groups according to agreement either individually, or through the Virginia Company, Thomas Weston, or, perhaps by Sir Edwin Sandys himself, who took a keen interest in the personnel of his expedition. (See copy agreement Vol. I, p. 31, of this series).

[ 215 ]

William Latham was taxed in Plymouth in 1632, and later resided in Duxbury, but returned to England after 1641, and soon thereafter went to the Bahamas.

Members of his family were financially interested in the Virginia Company and although this particular William, the Mayflower Passenger, left no known issue, yet many of the name were early settlers in New England.

John Carver and his wife, having no children, had "put" to them for transportation, several youthful individuals, including that "lustie younge man" John Howland.

# MARTIN

I. **Martin**, Christopher, born perhaps "Billerike" in Essex County, England, although the Martins were, in a number of instances, merchants, and he may have been born within the shadow of St. Bartholomew the Great. A Christopher Martin and a John Martin of a later generation subscribed to the rebuilding of the tower (or steeple) of the church, and there was a William Martin (Martyn) in 1531, who described himself in a will as "gentleman, dwelling within the close of the monastery of the glorious Apostle Bartholomew."

Numerous merchants had "stalls" in this neighborhood, previous to 1620, among them some of our Mayflower Planters, such as Thomas Rogers, Martin, Hooke and others. In fact, "The Bartholomew Fair" had been famous since the year 1113. Few stories of "Olde Englande" are more thrilling than that of Smithfield, together with St. Bartholomew's Priory, later on the church and parish of St. Bartholomew the Great in West Smithfield.

It was right here in Smithfield, during the short reign of Mary, 1553-8, that beginning with Rev. John Rogers, Feb. 4, 1555, forty-five "heretics" were burnt at the stake "for aronyus opinions, with a grett compene of the gard." During these eventful five years over 288 people were burnt to death throughout England. All of these tragedies were still fresh in the minds of the Mayflower Planters. Their parents and grandparents had been eyewitnesses to some of these infernos.

Christopher Martin was a Merchant Adventurer, actively interested in the Virginia Company of London. He and other members of the Martin family had invested in the colonization idea, apparently with the intention of removing themselves and their own families to the new fields of opportunity in the Colonies. A number of his friends, Rogers, Mullins, Brewster, Hopkins, Allerton, Carver, Robinson and others were evidently of the same mind, for they appear to have purchased shares in the company, either as individuals or through their commercial companies, as early as 1609, in some instances from the very beginning in 1607.

Christopher Martin bought a partnership in Ralph Hamor's settlement on the James River, and, probably was with the fleet that sailed for Virginia in 1609, along with Stephen Hopkins, Capt. Edward Brewster, son of William, and, perhaps, other individuals, later on to become members of that famous group of "Mayflower Planters." Martin also bought of Captain George Percey some interest in land on the James River.

How long Martin remained in the Jamestown Plantation is not known, but he probably was not entirely pleased with the business prospects in that broken tidewater country, and had returned to London before 1619 when Sir Edwin Sandys became Treasurer of the Company, and started a more liberal and progressive policy. He had hopes of establishing a form of self-government in the Colony, of a representative type that would be more encouraging to the Planters.

Naturally Martin, Hopkins, Capt. Edward Brewster and others who had been in Virginia must have been able to enlighten Sandys on real conditions.

In 1620 an expedition was organized and, probably because of his experience, Christopher Martin was made Governor and Treasurer of the Mayflower, representing directly the Virginia Company of London. His duty was to receive and pay out funds in connection with the expedition and the planting of a colony, and to keep a careful account of everything.

Obviously he was the executive, with powers of initiative and decision, and quite possibly was following out tentative instructions in deciding to plant a colony on Cape Cod. Naturally, after the decision, the drawing up of a proper paper to send back to the Company for their records was but a formal matter. Everybody seemed to be unanimous in the decision to settle on the Cape, including Martin. The original of the "compact" has not been found, so it may be somewhere carefully preserved in England.

While the Mayflower was still lying in Cape Cod Harbor, Christopher Martin became ill, and a few days before his death probably made a will, but it has not been found.

Carver was no doubt the oldest passenger, and a brother-in-law of Rev. John Robinson. He was made Governor but died almost immediately thereafter, which must have left the business of the company in much confusion, especially the accounts.

Gov. Christopher Martin died at Cape Cod, Jan. 18, 1621, and his wife died a short time after Jan. 11, 1621.

No descendants have been located; perhaps none ever existed.

## MASTERSON

I. **Masterson** (Margeson), Edmund, born England; died Plymouth Plantation between Jan. 11 to Apr. 10, 1621.

It is probable that the Masterson family were long seated in the parish of Bentley-cum-Arksey, Yorkshire, where Gov. Bradford lived.

He was probably the father of Richard Masterson of Leyden, who came to Plymouth.

Notes on the Masterson Family will appear in future volumes of this series.

# THE VIRGINIA COMPANY
## and the
# MAYFLOWER PLANTERS

Medieval ways of life were being cast aside in England during the 16th century. About the year 1500 individual effort and reward for special ability were bringing a great impetus to economic development. For centuries individual initiative had been discouraged by the stupid selfishness of so-called nobles, and the narrow-mindedness of the clergy. In many instances they had not only been dead weights as "tax-eaters," but had arrogantly refused to give credit where credit was due. During the reign of the Tudors, Henry VII, Henry VIII, Edward VI, Mary and Elizabeth, 1497 to 1603, many shackles to economic development were removed and the "Merchant Adventurers" had been encouraged to proceed with the promotion of trade and commerce throughout the world. Many able men of industry and trade had become interested.

A brief story of the "Merchant Adventurers," with which the Mayflower Planters were so intimately associated, has been attempted under a separate heading in this volume.

The commercial advance under the Tudors had been due to a great extent to private enterprise, encouraged by very liberal royal grants for discovery.

Sir Francis Drake, for instance, had fitted out and prosecuted the naval expeditions into the West Indies against the Spanish, while John and Sebastian Cabot sought a passage to "Cathay" and the East Indies in 1497, inspired only with zeal for exploration and for gold. This same hope for riches probably led Sir Humphrey Gilbert and Sir Walter Raleigh during the later years of the 16th century to seek out the resources of Florida and Newfoundland. No doubt personal gain was likewise the driving force behind John Smith, Henry Spelman and others, in their relations with the Indians.

The ruling classes in Europe were beginning to see the light. They were always short of funds, and the building of a lucrative colonial trade might be to their decided advantage. The nobles, however, were notoriously inefficient, and, in most cases, practically penniless, while the clergy, of course, were not expected to be business men.

Money was needed to arm and pay soldiers, build warships, to bribe diplomats and support the government in general. Gold must be forthcoming. It must be obtained through taxes of the people, or by less laudable means.

If through taxes, the people must be prosperous enough to pay them, and the inhabitants of England during most of the

16th and 17th centuries were far from prosperous. In fact, poverty and distress, together with famine, disease and death prevailed throughout Britain for centuries before 1600. The hard pressed monarch became sold on the idea of building up a colonial empire, in the expectation of bringing gold into an empty treasury by means of a "favorable trade balance." The plan was very simple, although then quite new. Expensive goods, manufactured articles and the like, would be exported, while cheap raw materials would be imported. Naturally, the difficulty with this scheme is to keep the "trade balance" in a "favorable" condition. This becomes more difficult as nations develop self sufficiency. However, England took pains to assure herself a "favorable trade balance" with her colonies for many years, in one way or another familiar to all.

The most popular method for building up a lucrative colonial trade at the beginning of the 17th century was by chartered commercial companies. England in 1600, Holland in 1602, France in 1664, Sweden, Denmark, Scotland, and Prussia, each chartered its own "East India Company" all with the same general purpose in mind.

The English assumed possession and grants on the Atlantic coast of America were shared by the London and Plymouth companies in 1606.

Great activity was engendered in the organization of English companies for trade with Russia, Turkey, Morocco, Guiana, Bermuda, the Canaries and Hudson Bay. Many of these first companies failed to accomplish results satisfactory to the controlling interests. They were disbanded, only to be promptly reorganized. Even in France the commercial companies had become an accepted institution, much to the discomfort of England, who had been considerably behind France and Spain in laying claim to large slices of North America (see Map No. 5).

Our interest in this chapter is not especially concerned with the English East India Company. However, it was the first of the sort organized as a regulated company in 1600, and some of its members became active in the London and Plymouth companies of 1606 and later. No doubt, some of the "Mayflower Planters" such as William Brewster, Christopher Martin, Stephen Hopkins, William Mullins and others were intimately acquainted with every detail of the venture. Surely Carver, Mullins, Allerton, Winslow and the Tillies were deeply interested in these developments, political, social and economic.

The East India Company was reorganized piecemeal for 50 years or more until it acquired the form of a joint-stock enterprise. Most of the chartered colonial companies followed the same general plan. Perhaps, here, was laid the germ of our present-day institution of the "corporation," which the politicians delight in finding so much fault with, especially when running for some elective office. In 1600 the monarchs feared the "corporation" no less, but had to encourage them for tax collecting purposes mainly. Of course, this is all quite modern, happening within the past 350 years. We should remember that in the Middle Ages business had been carried on, for the most part, by individuals or by partnerships, the partners being usually members of the same family.

Naturally, expansion of commerce, trading with another country, forced construction of forts, and building of fleets for protection against savages, pirates or other nations. The time may come in the dim future when there are no more "savages," "pirates" and "vicious" nations. However, it is to be feared selfishness, jealousy and that desire of some one or more nations to maintain a "favorable trade balance" at any cost, will be with us for some time, or until that period when all peoples and nations will have become self sufficient. Then, human nature may have undergone a reformation, and all trading will be "even," there being no more "favorable" trade balance.

Incidentally, the development of the "joint-stock" company (see Vol. I of this series) was accompanied by increased activity in banking. In the Middle Ages lending of money for interest had been forbidden by the Christian Church. It was considered immoral to receive a so-called profit without performing some service or real work. Non-Christians had no such scruples, and found money lending very profitable, although they had some difficulty in collecting from royal and noble debtors. As business had developed in Italy, however, Christians soon adopted the "interest-taking" idea, and the Italian, French and German "money-changers" became outstanding.

To clearly understand this important matter, we must remember that the coins minted by feudal lords and kings were not easy to pass along, except of course, in limited sections of the country. Light weight coins were common. Law and order was loose. Justice was extremely uneven. Therefore "money-lenders," who bought and sold coins of different countries, prospered greatly during the early 16th century in Antwerp, and later in Amsterdam, London, Hamburg and Frankfort.

The bank seems to have originated from this beginning, paying interest on deposits and receiving higher interest on loans. Soon shares of stock were being bought and sold on the "exchange," and complaints were becoming plentiful and loud about the speculation on the rise and fall in prices.

By 1606 the medieval merchant guilds were fundamentally displaced by the great stock companies and powerful banking houses had arisen to operate from. All of this had been brought about in the midst of the most terrible poverty and misery.

The older members of our "Mayflower Planters" were well informed concerning all of these developments, and determined, if possible, to better their economic condition by taking advantage of opportunities as they arose.

King James was selfish and pedantic. He had no patience with dissenters of any sort. His will must be final. However, many of his severest critics were prominent "Merchant Adventurers." Most of them desired a free choice of church affiliation, and also the maximum of free enterprise. It appeared impossible to have one without the other. Therefore, a large number were "Puritans" or "Separatists" at heart, if not in fact.

He hated, for instance, Sir Edwin Sandys, but feared him at the same time. His dislike extended, also, to most of the poets and writers of the period. They were quite apt to be independent in thought and word. This spirit of intolerance on the part of the "Court" under James tended to misrepresent many of our early settlers by unfriendly evidence.

Finally, on the petition of Richard Hakluyt, the geographer, then prebendary of Westminster, James chartered two companies, the London and the Plymouth. The patent, dated April 10, 1606, to Sir Thomas Gates, Sir George Somers, and other "firm and hearty lovers of colonization" involved a vast territory, then little known, lying between the 34th and 45th degrees of north latitude, together with the islands within one hundred miles of the coast stretching from Cape Fear to Halifax. James paid no attention to prior claims of Spain or other countries by right of exploration or settlement.

The code of laws proposed were royal and characteristic of the arrogant James. They provided for "two several colonies and companies," each supplied with a council of thirteen persons directed by the King. Each council to have a seal with the King's arms on one side "and his portraiture on the other."

A resident Council located in England, called the King's Council of Virginia, was to have full control of the settlement, with a seal similar to the other one.

The Church of England must be the established form of worship, and the oath of obedience was obligatory.

Lands were to descend as at common law. A community of labor and property was to continue for five years. Incidentally, this communistic idea was bitterly opposed by the "Mayflower Planters" from the beginning (page 83-84, Vol. I).

The adventurers were permitted to mine for gold, silver, and copper, to coin money, and to collect revenue for twenty-one years from all vessels trading to their ports. There were a few exemptions, such as certain necessities imported for the use of the colonists. These items were exempt from duty for seven years.

James issued his first orders on Nov. 20, 1606, to his Council of Virginia in England, and on Dec. 10, 1606, instructions were issued for the Captains, passengers and mariners to assemble for the first expedition to the Virginia settlement under the patent.

MAP No 5

FRENCH

NEWFOUNDLAND

FRENCH

ENGLISH

SPANISH

ATLANTIC OCEAN

BERMUDA

SPANISH

GULF OF MEXICO

BAHAMAS

CUBA

JAMAICA

SPANISH

SOUTH AMERICA

SPANISH

L.C.H
1941

ENGLISH POSSESSIONS–17th CENTURY
IN AMERICA.

On May 13, 1607, the pioneer colonists landed on a peninsula of Virginia, and promptly named the settlement Jamestown in honor of the King.

The expedition had departed from London on Dec. 20-30, 1606, under command of Capt. Christopher Newport, in three vessels, "Sarah Constant," Capt. Newport, "Goodspeed," Capt. Gosnold, and a pinnace, "Discovery," Capt. Ratcliffe. By a very rough estimate about 120 passengers and 50 sailors made the voyage. Apparently, there is no official list of these first settlers in existence. However, an important group of people in England, including numerous London "Merchant Adventurers," had ventured considerable time and capital in the undertaking. Many of them, in fact, were hoping that the colonization plans would succeed so that they could remove themselves and families to the "New World," and leave the miseries of Europe behind forever. It is suspected that James knew of this rather prevailing sentiment, and greatly feared the loss of so many best tax paying citizens. Anyway, the first charters were not very inviting.

Naturally, the interested parties did everything possible to obtain the right kind of settlers for the first expedition. The most able geographer in England, Richard Hakluyt, was retained to work with Capt. Bartholomew Gosnold in preparing for the settlement. Gosnold spent two years or more in obtaining potential colonizers, and working up a general interest. No abler man could have been found for the job. In 1602, in command of the "Concord," chartered by Sir Walter Raleigh and others, he coasted from what is now Maine to Martha's Vineyard, landing at, and naming Cape Cod and Elizabeth Island (near Cuttyhunk), and giving the name Martha's Vineyard to the island now called No Man's Land. He returned to England with a cargo of furs, sassafras and other commodities obtained in trade with the Indians about Buzzard's Bay.

During the years 1603 to 1606, many of the "Mayflower Planters," and their friends Edwin Sandys, William Davison, Christopher Davison, Robert Nauton, George Cranmer, William Cranmer, Earl of Southampton, Earl of Salisbury, and others were deeply interested in the venture. As a matter of fact the future Governor Christopher Martin of the Mayflower ship itself on the voyage to Cape Cod in 1620, was a partner in Ralph Hamar's plantation near Jamestown, and had purchased certain shares from Capt. George Percy on the James River. It is known also that Stephen Hopkins, William Mullins, William Brewster, his son Capt. Edward Brewster, and others were closely affiliated with the project.

Naturally, the activities of Gosnold and his voyages were probably known personally to many future Mayflower passengers, which would give a rather logical reason for dropping off at Cape Cod in 1620, especially in view of the poor showing at Jamestown.

It is fair to assume, therefore, that Gosnold obtained some good colonizers for the expedition, although, according to Capt. John Smith, there were too many young "gentlemen," and not enough "artisans." The slow and painful progress of the Colony for many years must be laid to the nature of leadership as controlled from England.

Freedom in worship was, of course, desirable. But the real cause for the prevailing discord, bitterness and failure was political and economic.

The "Mayflower Planters," and other first comers to America from England under these first charters, were familiar with the political fight between the "Patriot" or liberal party and the "Court" faction. One advocated a popular form of government in America, the other opposed the idea. There were frequent and bitter words over the matter in Parliament. Sir Edwin Sandys and even Sir Francis Bacon, to some extent, were outspoken for a liberal colonial policy. In truth, this question really remained a burning issue until 1776, when the Americans settled the problem to their own satisfaction.

James was stubborn, and the charter sealed in 1606, was far from "popular" in form. All features were under control of the Crown, very limited plantations being granted the two companies.

His gravest error was in the appointment of the first Council in Virginia. Through his Council in England the following six were appointed:

Edward Maria Wingfield.
Capt. Bartholomew Gosnold.
Capt. John Smith.
Capt. John Ratcliffe.
Capt. John Martin.
Capt. George Kendall.

With the possible exception of Gosnold and Martin this council did not stand very high, either with the merchants or with the planters. However, James had chosen, and matters had to take their course. Being lacking in efficient leaders the colony drifted into a one-commodity, agricultural district, that of tobacco raising, and the importation of negro slaves in 1619 did not improve possibilities.

The story of the First Council in Virginia is tragic if not inspiring.

Wingfield had a questionable record in England, but, nevertheless, was designated President of the Council on landing at Jamestown. He was removed forthwith in Sept., 1607, for cause, and returned to England in 1608. Financial and political trickery may have been the reason.

John Ratcliffe was elected in his place. His real name seems to have been Sicklemore. For some reason he turned the Presidency over to Capt. John Smith in Sept., 1608. Ratcliffe returned to England in July, 1609, but came right back with Sir Thomas Gates, and was slain by the Indians in 1610.

Capt. Gosnold was an able man, and really an important driving force of the expedition. However, he died in 1607.

John Martin was an influential Merchant Adventurer, and prominent member of the Virginia Company until its dissolution. He was an efficient member of the first Council. Other members of the Martin family either came with the first expedition or soon thereafter, including Richard, Thomas and Christopher Martin, later of the Mayflower.

Capt. George Kendall suffered a dramatic finish almost immediately. He was accused of conspiracy, tried and forthwith hung. Whether guilty is a question, but such were the manners of the times.

Capt. John Smith is familiar to everybody as an adventurer. He was really something of a historian and geographer, as his works clearly show. However, he was excessively subserviant and through necessity had to flatter the King continually in order to maintain himself. Between subserviancy and financial need, he developed into a most fascinating liar, and a problem to historians in general. He replaced Ratcliffe as President of the Council on Sept., 1608, but the next year was recalled to England to answer for certain misdemeanors. Through aid of friends he continued to write history.

Perhaps the main reason why the first colony was such a dismal failure under the Crown charter, 1605 to 1609, is substantially disclosed in the following extract of a report forwarded to the Treasurer of the Company in London by Capt. John Smith in 1608. (History by J. Smith, 1624, p. 70-72).

> "When you send again I intreat you rather send but thirty carpenters, husbandmen, gardiners, fishermen, blacksmiths, masons, and diggers up of trees, roots well provided, then a thousand of such as we have, for except we be able both to lodge them and feed them the most will consume with want of necessaries before they can be good for anything."

Apparently, Smith did not feel very confident about England being able or willing to supply the men for in the same report he suggests:

> "Send into Germany for glasse-men and the rest."

During this period the King was having his troubles. Spain was objecting to some of this colonization on her supposed territory. She had captured an English ship, "Richard," on the way to North Virginia. This question was before Parliament, and the King's old stumbling block, Sir Edwin Sandys, was "the chairman of the committee on Spanish wrongs." Then that Hampton Court Conference tended to stir religious hatreds again.

Sandys was the head of the "Patriot" party and considered by James as his "greatest enemy," although Sir Francis Bacon was quite liberal and aided in framing the remonstrance of the Commons to the conduct of James I toward his first Parliament.

The Court party extolled "kingly power," claiming it descended from God. James headed this party and had sent to North and South Virginia the publication called "His Majestie's most prudent and Princelye form of government."

Among the members of the first expedition were a number of "gentlemen," mostly young, and with few opportunities for advancement left in England. They were encouraged to join the colony by relatives and friends.

Among these was William Bruster, Gentleman. It seems quite reasonable to assume this person to have been the young son of William Brewster of the Mayflower, about 20 years of age. At this time his father was having difficulties, of a usual nature, at Scrooby, England, where a "process" had been attempted with the following results:

"Dec 15th 1607 Office V. Richard Jackson & Wm. Bruester of Scrowbie. For Brownisme. An attachment was awarded to W. Blanchard to apprehend them, but he certifieth that he can not finde them, nor understand where they are." (Collections Founders New Plymouth—Hunter).

It is not strange, of course, that the father should have, under the circumstances, used his influence with friends Sir Edwin Sandys, William Davison, Lord John Stanhope, Robert Cecil, Earl of Salisbury and others to send his son to America with the first expedition. As a matter of fact, he was a member of the Virginia Company himself, and his friends were sending their sons also.

When Capt. Newport returned to England late in 1607, to report on "His Majestie's Council for the first Colony to Virginia to His Majestie's Counsel for Virginia in England," he carried with him among many other papers the following letter from William Brewster, gentleman, to the Earl of Salisbury, as follows:

### William Brewster to the Earl of Salisbury

Sir: it had byne my duty to have wroot the whoole jornye unto yoo, & so I would have done had not this our evar renowned Captayne, Captayne Newport, have come himselfe unto you, whoe will so justly and truly declare, better than I cane, all this his discoverye. This is all I will saye to you, that suche a Baye, a Ryvar, and a land, did nevar the eye of man behould, and at the head of the Ryvar, which is 160 myles longe ar Rokes & mountaynes, that prommyseth Infynyt Treasure, but our Forces be yet too weake to make further discovery. Now is the King's Majesty offered the most Statlye, Riche Kingom in the wourld, nevar posseste by any christian prynce, be you one meanes amonge manye to further our secondinge, to conquer this land, as well as you were a meanes, to further the discovery of it, and you, yet may lyve to see Ingland moore Riche & Renowned then anye Kingdom, in all Euroopa x x x x x x

(Copy of letter in "Genesis" of U. S. by A. Brown)

(The rest is torn off, perhaps by Robert Cecil, the Earl of Salisbury himself, son of Sir William Cecil, Lord Burleigh, chief minister to Elizabeth, and well acquainted with William Davison and William Brewster, Sr. Robert Cecil held a high position under King James, but was a powerful backer of the Virginia Company and Sir Edwin Sandy, who was the real driving power behind the company. Certain members of the families of Cecil, Davison, Sandys and Brewster went to Virginia before 1620. Likewise Lord Stanhope, whose father, Sir Michael Stanhope, was beheaded on Tower Hill in Feb. 25, 1553, was the master of posts who had placed William Brewster Jr. in the Post at Scrooby sometime after 1590, and was now deeply interested in the Virginia Company).

The letter is from the "Cecil papers" and indorsed as "a part of a letter of William Brewster, gent, from Virginia."

The career of William Brewster, gent, ended with tragic suddenness in Virginia, according to a report written by the Honorable Gentleman, Master George Percy of the Southern Colony, stating in part:

"Aug 10, 1608 the tenth day died William Bruster, gentleman, of a wound given by the savages, and was buried the 11th day."

The reports of Newport, Wingfield, Smith and Percy were quite discouraging to the Adventurers in England. Finally, Gabriel Archer brought some information from Virginia that even caused James to give up some of his royal prerogatives, and consider a parliament for the colony. Three expeditions had been sent out on Dec. 1606, Oct. 1607 and Aug. 1608, including about 300 settlers, but there was nothing to show for the expense except a few scattered tobacco farms in Southern Virginia. The attempt to plant a colony in Northern Virginia at the mouth of the Kennebec River had failed. The death of the leaders in England, George Popham and John Popham in 1608, discouraged the colonists and they had returned home. This expedition of about 120 persons had sailed from England in

June 1607 in two ships, the Mary & John, and the Gift of God, sent out by the Plymouth Company. No further attempts by the English to settle in this section were made for sometime. The French, however, were more enterprising.

In connection with the first colonies it may be appropriate to mention something of the surroundings the settlers were trying to leave behind in England, especially London. In 1606 most of the citizens of London lived within the old walls on the north side of the Thames. The population was very roughly 300,000. From 1603 to 1611 there was one epidemic or "plague" after another. More than 37,000 died between March and December 1603, and from Thursday December 29, 1605, to Jan. 4, 1607, five days after the sailing of the Newport, 7,920 persons were buried in London. It was thought all this was caused by a large surplus population, and one object of this colonization project was a redistribution of the surplus inhabitants.

James was greatly concerned over the failure of his royal charter to accomplish anything worthwhile. About the best that can be claimed for it is the establishment of England's alleged right to America between 34° and 45° north latitude, although the section was inhabited by Indians, and, in addition, claimed entirely by the Crown of Spain.

The situation was delicate. The Merchant Adventurers held many conferences. Richard Hakluyt mentions some "Solemne meetings at the home of x x x x the Earle of Exeter" about the failures. John Rolfe states "the beginning of this plantation was governed by a president and councell aristocratically x x x and in this government happened all the miserie." Hamor remarks that the years 1606-1610 "were meerely mispent."

Finally, James had to consider a new charter. If he had not done this South Virginia would have been left in the hands of the Spanish and French along with the rest of America.

The crown charter was abandoned and a charter under the company framed. The new charter was drafted by Sir Edwin Sandys, close friend of William Brewster, and many other "Mayflower Planters." Against continual opposition of James, and, possibly aided by Sir Francis Bacon, a charter to a real colonial "body politic" was evolved and signed by the King on June 2, 1609. Of course, this "body politic" had to acquire the land from present owners (Indians, Spanish, French, etc.) by purchase, by diplomacy or by force, and settle it "at the expense of their own blood and treasure, unassisted by the crown." The settlers could "erect a free popular state" and were to have "no government putt upon them but by their own consente."

Naturally, Sandys and his friends were much encouraged, even elated, over this victory. Here was a large portion of real freedom at last. However, they could not foresee the bitter struggle of the powerful court party to overthrow their charter. James controlled vicious political, economic and social forces, all hiding behind the smoke screen of the church, and, for one reason or another, the company charters were changed in 1612, and 1618, until they reverted again to crown charters in 1624.

Meanwhile, in the exhileration of victory, on Feb. 27, 1609, a few months before James signed the new charter, letters were written to certain friends in Plymouth, England, all liberty minded, to join the "body politic," before the signing. Many of them did so. More important still was a nicely worded invitation, sent out on June 9, 1609, only seven days after the charter was signed, by the Earl of Southampton, the Earl of Pembroke, Robert Sidney, Thomas West, Lord de La Warr, Sir Thomas Smythe, Sir Robert Mansfield, Sir Thomas Gates, to

"His majestie's subjects in the Free States the United Provinces,"

offering them in an English colony in America the place of refuge they were seeking in the Netherlands. Now, these people were none other than some of our "Mayflower Planters" in Leyden and elsewhere. The above men sending the invitation were, for the most part, supporters of Sandys in Parliament, and old friends of Philip Sidney and Essex, with whom William Brewster and Davison had served in the Netherlands and other places. They were, to a great extent, the instigators of the "Popular" movement. The execution of Essex in 1601 was probably brought about by the Court party due to his affiliation with the Patriot or Liberal party. Essex was a real friend to Davison and Brewster (see Brewster Family).

Just as soon as James heard of the above invitation he sought Archbishop Bancroft of England, and soon thereafter, the good Bishop finding that certain subjects were preparing to depart "in great numbers, obtained a proclamation from the King forbidding any to go without his Majesty's leave."

However, the organization of the Virginia Company under the new charter progressed in spite of all obstacles.

Sir Thomas Smythe was made Treasurer, chosen probably by his associates because of his assumed loyalty to the Patriot cause. He had been, in fact, imprisoned for his part in the rising of Essex. He was regarded as "a good Patriot."

The new charter of 1609 attracted a long list of adventurers and beneficiaries who affiliated with the company in the undertaking. Many of the surnames are familiar in New England history. Here are a few of the names on the roll. Some came to America, others did not.

Robert Cecil, Earl of Salisbury, friend of William Brewster Sr. and his son William Brewster Jr.

Thomas Cecil, Earle of Exeter.

Robert Sydney, Lord Lisle.

John Stanhope, Lord Stanhope — Postmaster of England. Davison wrote to Stanhope in 1590 regarding the Scrooby Post for William Brewster.

Sir Thomas Smythe
Sir Oliver Cromwell
*Sir Thomas Gates
Sir Robert Kelligrew
Sir Edwin Sandys
Sir Warwicke Heale
Sir Francis Bacon
Sir Samuel Sandys
*Sir George Somers
Sir Baptist Hicks
*Capt. Christopher Newport
Capt. John Martin
Capt. Thomas Button
Esq. John Moore
Esq. Thomas Sandys
Esq. Richard Sandys, son of Sir Edwin Sandys
Esq. William Brewster
   Edward Brewster, son of William Brewster
   John Robinson
   Richard Hakluyt, Minister and Geographer
   John Merrick, Merchant
   John Pory—an old Cambridge friend of William
      Brewster. Visited him at Plymouth in 1622.
   George Sandys, Gentleman
   Nicholas Ferrar
   Ralph Hamor
   George Yeardley, Gentleman
   Peter Latham, Gentleman
   John Fletcher
   Gabriel Archer
   Francis Covell
   Richard Rogers
   Martin Freeman
   William Strachy
   Stephen Hopkins, Clerk to Minister
   Henry Paine
   William Martin
   Christopher Martin

These are only a few of the long list of Englishmen who had become vitally interested in the 1609 charter.

After many meetings, most of them at the spacious home of Sir Thomas Smythe, Treasurer and 'Governor of the Virginia Company, a fleet of ships were obtained and fitted out for the expedition.

Smythe was the shipping magnate of his day. He held many positions in addition to that in the Virginia Company. In 1607 he had been re-elected governor of the East India Company, and held, also, important offices in the Muscovy, Levant, and French companies.

The East India, Virginia and Bermuda offices were in his large house in Philpott Lane. Small courts were held in the upstairs parlor, also festivities on special occasions, such as on that day when the Earl of Southampton, in appreciation of being admitted to the East India Company, sent a couple of bucks "to make merry withall x x x with x x x some dyner x x x for the whole Company x x x Mr. Governour's house."

His house was also popular with colonial administrators and seamen, as well as with merchants. He held open house also for the rough masters of his ships.

Smythe, like most of the London merchants, was really inclined in a quiet way towards the "Patriot" or "Liberal" party in the Commons. However, his position made it impossible to come out in the open, like Sir Edwin Sandys, who accasionally accused Sir Thomas of taking sides with the "Court" party, and eventually forced his retirement from the treasurership of the company.

At last the expedition was ready to depart from Plymouth Sound, England. William Strachy, Esquire, a member of the expedition writing in 1610, states in part

"Know that upon Friday late in the evening, we broke ground out of the Sound of Plymouth, our whole Fleete then consisting of seven good ships and two Pinnaces, all of which from the said second of June unto the twenty-three of July (1609), kept in friendly consort together, not a whole watch at any time looseing the sight of each other."

From available records it appears that the nine vessels were as follows—see letter of Gabriel Archer (Hakluyt series Purchas —Vol. 19, p. 1).

1. Sea Adventure "Admirall"        Sir Thomas Gates
                                    Sir George Somers
                                    Capt. Christopher Newport

2. Diamond "Vice Admirall"         Capt. John Ratcliffe
                                    Capt. King

3. Falcon "Reare Admirall"         Capt. John Martin
                                    Master Nellson

4. Blessing                        Capt. Adams
                                    Gabriel Archer

5. Unitie                          Capt. Wood
                                    Master Pett

| 6. Lion | Capt. Webb |
|---|---|
| 7. Swallow of Sir George Somers | Capt. Moone |
| | Master Somer |
| 8. Catch | Master Mathew Fitch |
| 9. Virginia (Boat of Sir George Somers) | Capt. Davies |
| | Master Davies |

"From Woolwich the fifteenth of May 1609, seven saile weyed anchor, and came to Plimmouth the twentieth day, where Sir George Somers, with two small vessels consorted with us. Here we took into the "Blessing" (being the ship wherein I went) sixe Mares and two Horses; and the fleet layed in some necessaries belonging to the action. In which businesse we spent time till the second of June. And then wee set sayle to Sea, but crost by south-west windes, we put in to Faulemouth, and there staying till the eight of June, we then gate out."

"Now thus it happened; about six dayes after we lost the sight of England, one of Sir George Somers Pinnasses left our company, and (as I take it) bore up for England."

"We ran a Southerly course from the tropicke of Cancer x x x x by the fervent heat and loomes breezes, many of our men fell sick of the Calenture, and out of two ships was throwne over-board thirtie-two persons. The Vice Admirall was said to have the plague in her, but in the Blessing we had not any sicke, albeit we had twenty women and children."

"Upon Saint James day, being about one hundred and fiftie leagues distant from the West Indies x x x x there happened a most terrible and vehement storme, which was a taile of the West Indian Horacano."

The storm lasted five or six days. The fleet became separated so that only four vessels, the Blessing, Lion, Falcon and Unitie, "fell into the King's River haply the eleventh of August (1609)." "The Unitie was sore distressed when she came up x x x of seventy land men, she had not ten sound, and all her Sea men were downe, but onely the Master and his Boy." "In the Unity were borne two children at sea, but both died, being both Boyes."

"When wee came to James Towne, we found a ship which had bin there x x x a month before we came" "her Commander was Captaine Argoll x x x and her Master one Robert Tindall."

In "a few dayes, came in the Vice Admiral, having cut her maine mast overboard," "then three or foure dayes after her, came in the Swallow."

Archer wrote his letter or report at Jamestown the last of August, 1609, at which time no word had been received about the "Admiral" or "Sea Adventure," and all were much concerned over the fate of Sir Thomas Gates and Sir George Somers, in the great storm.

However, although it happened that the Sea Adventure was wrecked in the islands of Bermuda, many of the passengers survived, and one of them, William Strachy, Esquire, was thoughtful enough to write a "true reportory of the wracke," and the "redemption of Sir Thomas Gates Knight" from the predicament. Strachy informs us that

> "the cloudes gathering thicke upon us, and the windes singing x x x x which made us to caste off our Pinnace towing the same."
> "a dreadful storm, and hideous began to blow x x x x at length did beate all light from heaven; which an hell of darkenesse turned blacke upon us."

Strachy evidently had a touch of sea-sickness during this "Horacano," for he states

> "there ariseth commonly no such unmercifull tempest, compound of so many contrary and divers nations, but that it worketh upon the whole frame of the body, and most loathsomely affecteth all the powers thereof, and the manner of the sicknesse it laies upon the body, being so unsufferable, gives not the minde any free and quiet time, to use her judgment and Empire."
> "Howbeit, this was not all x x x x x for in the beginning of the storm we had received a mighty leake x x x x the ship in every joynt almost, having spued out her okam."
> "During all this time, the heavens look'd so blacke upon us, that it was not possible the elevation of the Pole might be observed."
> "We much unrigged our ship, threw overboard x x x many a Trunke and Chest x x x and staved many a Butt of Beere, Hogsheads of Ayle, Syder, Wine and Vinegar."

At last it became necessary to run the ship ashore, and land all of the men, women and children, about one hundred and fifty, on the island.

No complete list of these shipwrecked people has been found, but, no doubt, there were many friends of our Mayflower Planters among the number. Possibly Christopher Martin was one of them, and the story of Stephen Hopkins and his connection with the Sea Adventure is well known (see Vol. I of this series, p. 117).

As a matter of interest it may be noted that the "Tempest" is supposed to have been about the last play of William Shakespeare. The Earl of Southampton, his close friend, used to discuss in 1610 quite frequently the details of the wreck of the "Sea Venture (Adventure)", and the escape of its passengers. Shakespeare became interested and wrote the play, in part, as follows:

### The Tempest

**Prospero**—Hast thou, spirit, Performed to point, the Tempest I bade thee?

**Ariel**—To every article x x x x of sulphurous roaring, the most mighty Neptune seemed to besiege, and make his bold waves tremble. Yea, his dread trident shake.

**Prospero**—My brave spirit! Who was so firm, so constant, that this coil would not infect his reason?

**Ariel**—Not a soul. But felt a fever of the mad, and play'd some tricks of desperation. All but mariners, Plung'd in the foaming brine and quit the vessell.

**Prospero**—But was not this nigh shore?

**Ariel**—Close by, my master.

**Prospero**—But are they, Ariel, safe?

**Ariel**—Not a hair perish'd on their sustaining garments not a blemish. But fresher than before.

**Prospero**—of the King's ship The mariners, say how thou hast dispos'd, and the rest o' th' fleet?

The castaways remained in Bermuda about nine months, during which time two small pinnaces were built, and on May 10, 1610, they sailed away to join their friends at Jamestown, arriving there on May 23rd.

Matters were not progressing favorably in that colony, however, and many of the would-be settlers probably returned with Gates and Newport to England, arriving there in Sept. 1610.

Soon, thereafter "News from Virginia, a ballad by Richard Rich was published, also "A Discovery of the Bermudas" by Silvester Jourdan, both of whom were in the shipwreck with Hopkins and the others.

As a result of some extended consideration a revised company charter was presented to the King sometime in 1611, containing the names of 6 corporations, 325 persons, 25 of the Peerage, 111 Knights, 10 doctors or ministers, 66 Esquires, 30 gentlemen, 83 citizens, and some others not classified. Many of these were on previous lists. The King signed the charter in 1612. It continued to give the company full rights of trade, as well as territorial and governmental rights in Virginia.

MAP No 6

N

POTOMAC RIVER

RAPPAHANOCH RIVER

BAY

YORK RIVER

JAMESTOWN
1607

JAMES RIVER

ATLANTIC OCEAN.

From 1607-1636,
this section, with Jamestown
as the center, consisted mostly
of small tobacco farms located
along the shores of the
tidewater. They did not
prosper. The Company erred
in making a settlement here
and lost heavily from the
start.

JAMESTOWN AND VICINITY

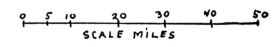

0    5  10      20      30      40      50
SCALE MILES

L·C·H
1941

# MAP No 7

Newbury 1633 •

Ipswich 1634

Beverly 1630  Cape Ann 1623

Danvers 1632

Salem 1625

Lynn 1629

Medford 1630

Charlestown 1629

Cambridge 1631

Concord 1635 •  Boston 1630

Watertown 1630 •

Roxbury 1630 •

Dedham 1636 •  Dorchester 1630

Quincy 1625

Weymouth 1635

Hingham 1635

Scituate 1633

Duxbury 1620 •

Plymouth 1620 •

CAPE ANN

ATLANTIC

OCEAN

CAPE COD
BAY

CAPE COD

N
↑

LCH
1941

○  Early settlements in New England to 1636,
due, primarily, to the enterprise of the
"Merchant Adventurers" in financing the
preliminary explorations, and arranging
for the transportation of "Planters", in order
to promote trade and commerce, especially,
during the liberal rule of Sir Edwin Sandys in
the Virginia Company 1619-1624.

Sir Thomas Smythe was having plenty of difficulty in administering the affairs of the company, and the colony was not growing. It had merely developed into a very weak community of tobacco farmers. In 1613 the adventurers were forced to appeal to the Crown because of complications with France, and a little later Spain became involved. Financial difficulties multiplied, finally, the adventurers appealed unsuccessfully to Parliament for aid. The Privy Council attempted to arouse interest. They passed orders urging the city companies of London to invest sums in the Virginia lottery, and then it addressed similar orders to the "Several Cityes and Townes of the Kingdome," with special letters to the lieutenants of County Surrey.

James, meantime, was waiting for an opportunity to break in and revert the colony back to a Royal Charter. But Sir Edwin Sandys was still fighting the battle for a "Popular" government.

In 1618 Sir Thomas met with reverses. His health was poor, and he lost one of his finest houses by fire. His companies were meeting with hard times, and auditors were pressing.

During the ten years rule of Sir Thomas Smythe over the Virginia Company (1609-1619), a foundation "was laid, whereon a flourishing state might, in process of time by the blessing of Almighty God, be laid." And when it became desirable to "bend their cares to the setting there of a laudable form of government." The good friend of the Mayflower Planters, Sir Edwin Sandys, was called to take his place.

In some directions also the loyalty of Sir Thomas Smythe and Alderman Robert Johnson to the Patriot party had become questioned, also an audit seemed against Smythe.

Therefore at the Virginia Court in London, May 8, 1619, Sir Edwin Sandys succeeded Smyth as Treasurer, and Mr. John Ferrar became deputy in place of Johnson.

Sir Edwin had ventured much money and energy in the undertaking, and, henceforth became the dominant personality in the Virginia Company. He was an idealist, liberal, and eloquent speaker. The Earl of Southampton was his very good friend and backer, while John Ferrar was very able and a hard worker as deputy.

It was decided to thoroughly revise the laws for the company and colony. The goodly sum of £7,000 had been obtained from the recent lottery, and this provided means for some expansion. Sir Edwin was in favor of a representative government in the colony, and the charter was altered accordingly.

Therefore, the first Virginia Assembly was set up in the church at Jamestown during July 1619, with John Pory, the secretary, acting as speaker. The Governor and Council sat in the choir, the speaker was in front of the Governor, and facing the burgesses in the nave.

Pory felt quite elated, and called it the "Great Charter."

The assembly accepted the Company's instructions to promote the cultivation of corn, mulberry trees, flax, hemp and vines. These had been sacrificed to tobacco farming. It limited the "magazine" to 25 per cent profit, and fixed the price of tobacco. It expected to have the initiative in all local affairs.

Sir Edwin, however, was still a thorn in the side of James, especially for his speeches before Parliament in 1614. They were quite plainly opposed to the King's favorite objectives of royal rights, and he was, essentially, under a sort of constant surveillance until 1621, when a new Parliament assembled and he acted again with the "Popular" party.

Plans, nevertheless, were immediately made to organize another expedition under the Sandys-Southampton Company charter. About the last meeting under Smythe was during a "Quarter Court held for Virginia at Sir Thomas Smith's Howse in Philpott Lane Ap 28, 1619." Thereafter the Company meetings were held, either at the house of Mr. John Ferrars in St. Sithes Lane, or at the home of Sir Edwin Sandys near Aldersgate. For instance, there was "a court for Virginia held at Mr. Ferrar's Howse in St. Sithes Lane May 12, 1619," and another one at the same place June 9, 1619, both well attended. No doubt several of the London "Mayflower Planters" attended these meetings, and a special invitation having been extended to the "Netherland" group, it is quite likely some of them were present, including Carver, Cushman, Brewster, Rogers and others.

Probably, the assembly "att a greate and General Quarter Courte Holden for Virginia at Sir Edwin Sandys Howse neere Aldersgate Feb. 2, 1620," included a number of "Mayflower Planters," some of them owning shares in the Company, such as William Brewster (and son Edward Brewster), Christopher Martin, William Mullins, Thomas Rogers, John Carver, Stephen Hopkins, and others. It may be stated that the Aldersgate vicinity was a beehive of "Popular" government adherents, which included most dissenters, separatists and puritans. They were continually on the defensive, as James I would not hesitate to throw them into prison at the least opportunity.

Obviously, changes of residence, if made at all, in some cases, had to be brought about with considerable secrecy. Nevertheless, there appears to be good reason for suspecting that a number of the "Mayflower Planters" had been in Southern Virginia and returned to London with no very high opinion of the tobacco growing country. Among these were Brewster, Hopkins, Martin, and perhaps even John Robinson himself.

It is quite reasonable to suppose that these meetings, and other similar assemblies of the time discussed the possibility of a Cape Cod settlement in Northern Virginia. It is possible that the Mayflower leaders, such as Martin, Brewster, Carver and Hopkins had about decided upon a northern landing before leaving England, the details to be worked out during the voyage. They were, of course, familiar with the voyage of Capt. Gosnold to Cape Cod in 1602, and the very recent, 1614, exploration of that section by Capt. John Smith, who gave it the name New England. However, the Virginia Company itself under Sir Thomas Smythe had failed in the attempt to settle there in 1615 or later, so that Sandys and Southampton, probably, were not seriously displeased at the idea of a colony in New England under the charter of the Company, even if planted somewhat independent of its action. Anyway, Gov. Martin of the Mayflower was qualified to act for the company if a landing in New England should be decided upon.

Furthermore, late in 1620, the Company formed a Council at Plymouth, England, for New England, with territory from Philadelphia to Chaleur Bay 40° N. to 48° N, which was quite inclusive all across the continent. Even James with his old royal charter could not have surpassed this exhibition in the high handed art of claiming.

After numerous negotiations Sir Edwin managed to obtain the use of six ships together with the services of their master owners for transporting the first expedition of about 600 persons overseas under the Sandys-Southampton charter of 1619. Thomas Weston, a Merchant Adventurer of London, aided the Company in. assembling ships, crew, passengers, supplies and equipment for the expedition. Some of the details and names of these six ships are given in a separate article in this volume.

Just before Sir Edwin Sandys became Treasurer of the Virginia Company, his friends John Carver, Robert Cushman, John Robinson and William Brewster sought his aid and advice about transportation to the Colonies. He wrote about the matter to "Mr. John Robinson and Mr. William Brewster" dated London, Nov. 12, 1617, and signed "your very loving friend, Edwin Sandys."

The King, however, had made it difficult for Sandys to send his own friends to the Colonies because most of them were Puritans, Brownists or Separatists, and must obtain leave to go from the Archbishop of Canterbury. He had tried to get the Archbishop to "give leave to the Brownists and Separatists to go to Virginia, and designed to make a free popular state there, and himself and assured friends to be the leaders," but to no avail.

However, from 1618 to the summer of 1622, the Privy Council took no part, directly, in the affairs of the Company, and the Sandys, Southampton influence was quite supreme, in the matter of granting patents under their Company charter, which had substantially been in force since 1609. Therefore, the reframing of a patent grant or "compact" on the high seas if executed by the proper representatives of the Company then present, was probably legal and proper.

It seems clear that Gov. Christopher Martin and his associates on the Mayflower, representing the London Virginia Co., probably with a tacit consent of Sir Edwin Sandys, were within their rights in framing the "Compact" of Nov. 11, 1620. The signers of the document by so doing showed that they were members of the Virginia Company, Merchant Adventurers or, at least, beneficiaries in the matter. The prime change from the original Company grant was merely a shift of location from South to North Virginia. Any other unit of the expedition sent out in 1620, could, probably, have legally done the same thing.

Although Sandys was now being able to transport many of his friends to the colony without obstruction from the King or Court, he had found it necessary for them to take an oath of "supremacie" before sailing. This was done with many mental reservations, and grim determination to worship in their own way on reaching the colony.

During the years 1619, 1620, 1621, the Virginia Co. under Sandys provided and sent to Virginia 42 ships, 3,570 men and women, with provisions, cattle and the like. They also sent out to Bermuda 9 ships and 900 people to settle there.

However, the King harrassed Sandys at every opportunity, especially at any sign of a profit, and the fisheries off the New England shore seemed to be flourishing. In fact, the Virginia Company of London was finding it more difficult to obtain capital from the Merchant Adventurers every day. A large amount of capital had been poured into the attempt to plant a paying colony in America, but no returns had materialized, and none were in sight. About the only source of real income the Company had developed was a modest fishing business. Since 1609 ships from Virginia and Bermuda had stopped at New England for cod before returning to England. Most of these vessels had been hired to transport settlers to America, and without the fish would have returned home practically empty. Now, even this little income was threatened.

Of course, since 1609, the Virginia Company of London had been issuing patents under its charter and making laws for the colony without much royal dictation, and felt that fishing really was a free enterprise. Nevertheless, in May 1621, James brought up the question of the right of the London Company to fish off New England in waters which the old Virginia Company of Plymouth claimed as its own. This was the Popham Company of 1606 under royal charter which failed and was supposed to have become extinct in 1609.

Apparently, with some real income in sight, James was ready to revive the old royal charter. Sir Edwin Sandys immediately introduced a bill in the Commons for free fishing, maintaining that the seas are free, and that the gentlemen interested were merely trying to add another to a long list of royal monopolies. The Commons could not decide. Bitter complications arose, and on June 16, 1621, the Earl of Southampton, Sir Edwin Sandys, and John Selden, counsel for the Company, were arrested. They were kept prisoners until the Virginia Company of Plymouth received its charter. They were released on July 28, 1621. This revival of the old charter did not seriously affect the "Mayflower Planters" at Plymouth, Mass. They were already fixed

Meanwhile, the new leaders selected by the Sandys regime had arrived in Southern Virginia. They were Sir Francis Wyatt as Governor, descendant of several outstanding dissenters. His grandfather was the famous Sir Thomas Wyatt of "Wyatt's Rebellion" in Queen Mary's time. This rebellion had provoked the instant deaths of Lady Jane Grey and her husband on February 12, 1554, of her father, and Wyatt ten days later. (See article on Scrooby Manor).

Under Sir Francis Wyatt as assistants were Master George Sandys, Treasurer, brother of Sir Edwin, and Master Christopher Davison, Secretary, son of William Davison, Secretary to Queen Elizabeth during the hectic days of the wars in the Netherlands, the trial and execution of Mary Queen of Scots, the "Spanish Armada" affair and various other exciting moments in history, during which period William Brewster was a member of Davison's legation, and, in fact, was probably more or less involved with the activities of Davison right up to the time of William Davison's death in 1608. It is doubtful whether Brewster spent much time at Scrooby Manor between 1586 to 1608. That place was, probably, more in the nature of a "living" only. It was a political appointment, the real work being done by others.

In July, 1621, the new government met at Jamestown, Va., and altered the constitution of the colony to include as many "Popular" clauses as possible. It embodied a general assembly. Two Burgesses chosen by each town hundred. The Governor to have veto power. Every enactment of the assembly to require the sanction of the Company. Also, and very important, the assembly could veto the acts of the assembly.

It is apparent that Edwin Sandys was grimly determined to establish in America, if possible, English settlements with a popular form of government, including freedom of worship and enterprise. Many of the Merchant Adventurers and a few of the so-called "nobility" were behind him aiding to the best of their ability and means. He was in thorough accord with William Brewster, Christopher Martin, and other Mayflower Planters in their objectives, even, probably, in the landing at New Plymouth. They must have discussed the shaky condition of the Jamestown Colony quite frequently.

Therefore, Sandys sent into the final fight at Jamestown for a popular government his closest friends and relatives. Tradition and personal preferment impelled him to do this. His own father, Edwin Sandys, had been sent to the Tower by Queen Mary for dissenting views, and on release was forced to leave the country and live in Strasburg until the accession of Queen Elizabeth. As Archbishop of York he had been well acquainted with the Brewster family, and William Brewster was about his own age.

To understand what was really happening behind the scenes in the last dramatic days of the Virginia Company it seems desirable to state the relationship of some of the leading actors, both at London and in Jamestown.

At the meeting in London Feb. 8, 1621, Sir Francis Wyatt had been elected governor to succeed Sir George Yeardley. Now, Sir Francis was a son in-law of Sir Samuel Sandys, brother of Sir Edwin. Master George Sandys, another brother of Sir Edwin, was chosen Treasurer, while Christopher Davison was elected Secretary, probably because both he and his father William Davison, had been steadfast for the "Popular" party. At the meeting also were Sir Richard Bulkeley, father-in-law of Sir Edwin Sandys, and his son Thomas Bulkeley, together with Sir Francis Wenman, another son-in-law of Sir Samuel Sandys. It is also noted that Capt. Edward Brewster, son of William Brewster, passed four shares of his stock to Sir Francis Wyatt.

However, the fishing troubles and arrest of the Company officials in July, 1621, tended to seriously disrupt affairs, and discourage the Adventurers.

In 1622 many petitions were received from Southern Virginia claiming neglect of their interest. At this time there were about 1250 settlers near Jamestown obtaining a bare living from tobacco farming, and the future looked far from bright.

In March, 1622, about 500 settlers were murdered by the Indians in a wholesale slaughter, among them Edward Liester, a Mayflower Passenger, who, somehow, had managed to slip down from New Plymouth. He was killed at Capt. Samuel Maycock's place, Friday morning, Mar. 22-Apl. 1622.

This, of course, was another blow to the Company. Many complications arose. The tobacco business became even less profitable. Spaniards were permitted to undersell the Company in the London market. Sir Edwin tried to get Parliament to stop the importation, but to no avail.

The situation appeared hopeless, so that in Feb., 1623, Sir Edwin offered to surrender his office "with a better will than ever he tooke it."

However, James was not going to permit the Adventurers to take their losses in peace. Had they not promised to make a paying business for King and country? For what purpose had they asked all the privileges?

Therefore, under date of Nov. 4, 1623, to May 24, 1624, Quo Warranto proceedings were started before the Court of King's Bench. In this proceeding most of the Merchant Adventurers, and beneficiaries of the company's charters, were sued by King James for usurpation of the "Liberties, privileges, and franchises over our said lord the King" and that they "be taken to satisfy our said lord the King of their fine for the usurpation of their liberties, privileges and franchises."

The list of defendants is very long and inclusive, and, of course, includes William Brewster and his son Edward. The list places Edward in London in 1623, but William seems to be classed as "other freemen being adventurers" address uncertain. He was probably resting easily in New Plymouth at the time, as his friend John Pory so ably testified, in the midst of his library.

It does not appear whether anyone was "taken to satisfy," but it is of record that on June 16, 1624, a formal proclamation dissolved the Virginia Company, and James I arbitrarily annulled the liberal charter of the London Company, after its members had spent $750,000 estimated above its receipts. They were "broke."

However, under the liberal friendship of Sir Edwin Sandys and his associates, the Mayflower Planters had been established in New England, and the foundation of a representative legislature laid, and with this impetus it is not strange that the New England section prospered to such an extent that many flourishing settlements were established before 1636 (see Map 7), while other portions of the Atlantic coast were decidedly backward.

The Crown now became proprietor over "Virginia." The Privy Council took the place of the Company. They were vested with the powers of disallowance. A large administrative commission was appointed.

The King tried to omit the "assembly," but the colonists put up a fight, and finally won out.

Under the Proprietorship, the Southern Virginia Colony failed to prosper for many years. New England remained more independent.

Sir Edwin Sandys died in 1629. A friend writing to Lady Sandys from the Bermuda Islands regarding this event states in part:

"I have not a little participated in your sorrow at the losse of my noble friend your beloved ptneare woh not these Somers Islands alone, but the State of England have cause to lament x x x x Sir Edwin Sandys having served his time on earth both entered into an eternal inheritance and leaves his memorial with those who bear his name, which. I pray God, that as they be of his blood soe they may inherit his wisdome and vertues."

---

Refs. 476, 475, 47p, 473, 474, 475, 482, 474, 480, 409, 410.

# INDEX

[ 245 ]

AREY
Ruth 83

ARGALL
Gov. Samuel 40, 43, 44, 233

ARIOSTO
Lodovico (1474-1533) 117

ARISTOTLE
(384-322 B. C.) 116

ARNOLD
Elizabeth 144, 154, 208
Oldsworth 158

ATKINS
Bethia 61
Desire 62
Henry 61
Isaac 62
John 62
Joseph 62
Mary 62
Nathaniel 62
Samuel 62
Thomas 62

ATWOOD
Eldad 24
Esther 94
Joanna 94
John 109
Margaret 70, 71
Mary 109

AUCHER
Anthony 76
Hester 77

AUDLEY
Sir Thomas (1488-1544) 41

AUGUSTINE
Saint (354-430) 194

AUGUSTUS
193

BABBINGTON
108, 159

BACON
Sir Francis 116, 117, 225, 227,
229, 231
Nathaniel 85

BAINBRIGG
Reginald 28

BAKER
Daniel 58
Elizabeth 58
Francis 58
Hannah 58

BAKER (Cont.)
John 58
Kenelen 110, 138
Nathaniel 58
Rebecca 153
Robert 158
Samuel 58, 129
Thomas 58, 204
William 58

BALCH
John 189

BALL
Abigail 82

BALSHAM
Bishop 29

BANCROFT
Archbishop 230

BANGS
Apphia 55
Bethia 55
Edward 55, 56, 63, 69, 132
Elizabeth 56
Hannah 51, 55, 56
John 55
Jonathan 55, 56, 85
Joshua 55
Lydia 55, 56
Mary 56, 92
Mercy 55, 56, 66
Rebecca 55, 56, 63
Samuel 56
Sarah 56
Thankful 93
Thomasin 56

BARKER
Elizabeth 173
Isaac 48

BARNABY
James 47

BARNE
William 76

BARNES
Hester 171
Lydia 172
Mary 147

BARO
Peter 28

BARROWS
George 138

BARSTOW
Sarah 152

BARTLETT
Benjamin 47, 205
Elizabeth 47
Hannah 211, 212
Ichabod 154
Joseph 47
Lydia 47
Mary 47
Mercy 47
Rebecca 47, 110
Robert 47. 150, 151
Samuel 206
Sarah 47, 110

BASCOM
Hepzibah 89

BASS
Hannah 209, 210
John 204, 209, 210
Joseph 209, 210
Mary 209, 210
Ruth 209, 210
Samuel 209, 210
Sarah 209, 210
Thomas 209

BASSETT
Hannah 93, 94
Nathaniel 94

BAUGH
Thomas 158

BAXTER
Thomas 164

BAYLY
John 158

BEALE
Winifred 187

BEAMAN
Hester 140

BEARSE (BERSE)
Anne 208
Anthony 208
James 164

BEAUCHAMP
John 48, 49

BELCHER
Mary 210

BELL
Ann 215
Elizabeth 187
Mary 92

BENHAM
Vincent 213

BENNETT
Peter 168

BERKELEY
Richard 157

BERRY
Desire 52

BEVERCOTES
Samuel 36

BICKFORD
Deborah 81
Mary 53, 83

BILLS
Thomas 58

BLACKWELL
John 154

BLAKE
Experience 147

BLANCHARD
W. 227

BLOSSOM
Mercy 164
128

BLUNDEN
Sarah 214

BOCCACCIO
117

BONNEY
John 143

BONUM
George 100, 120

BOSWORTH
David 167
Elizabeth 167
Hannah 167
Ichabod 167
Jabez 167
John 167
Jonathan 163, 167
Mercy 167
Nehemiah 97

BOTHELL
Ephraim 214

BOUND (BOWNS)
Candace 136
Joseph 136
Robert 28

BOURNE
Elizabeth 153
Job 208
Martha 109
Melatiah 166
Richard 165
Thomas 109, 144, 153, 206

BOWERMAN
Experience 97
Thankful 53

BOWLES
Samuel 82

BOYLESTON
Ann 210
Peter 211
Sussanah 210, 211

BRACE
John 76

BRACKETT
Elizabeth 210

BRADFORD
Alice 104, 107, 110
David 110
Elisha 110
Elizabeth 104, 105
Ephraim 110
Hannah 110
Hezekiah 110
Israel 110
John 103, 107, 108, 109, 110, 154
Joseph 107, 109, 110
Margaret 104, 105
Mary 105, 110
Melatiah 110
Mercy 109, 110
Peter 103, 104, 105, 109, 110

BRADFORD
Robert 103, 104, 105, 109, 110
Samuel 110
Sarah 110
Thomas 104, 110
William 25, 26, 31, 35, 36, 38, 40,
41, 42, 99, 103, 104, 105,
106, 107, 108, 109, 110,
122, 123, 126, 128, 130,
139, 148, 150, 151, 156,
175, 181, 215, 218

BRADLEY
Peter 45

BRASSER
Henry 176

BREDMAN
Thomas 180

BREWER
Thomas 38, 39

BREWSTER
Benjamin 45
Edward 36, 38, 39, 40, 43, 44, 45,
217, 218, 224, 231, 239,
243, 244
Elizabeth 45, 78, 110
Fear 43, 46 173
Grace 45, 78
Hannah 45, 212
Henry 26, 74, 77
Humphrey 44, 78
James 77, 78
Jonathan 42, 43, 44, 45, 132, 177
Judith 78
Love 42, 43, 45, 47, 161 177
Mary 45, 79, 144
Nathaniel 46
Patience 43, 46, 47, 48, 49, 86
Prudence 27, 79
Ruth 45
Sarah 45, 46, 47
Sussanah 78
William 23, 25, 26, 27, 28, 29, 30,
31, 32, 33 34, 35, 36, 37,
38, 39, 40, 41, 42, 43, 44,
45, 46, 47, 48. 63, 74, 76,
78, 79, 80, 81, 86, 99,
104, 106, 113, 115, 116,
117, 123, 124, 126, 127,
128, 130, 132, 148, 149,
156, 163, 173, 180, 181,
183, 184, 217, 220, 224,
227, 228, 229, 230. 231,
239, 240, 242, 243, 244
Wrestling 43, 46

BRIDGER
Joane 213

BRIDGES
Bethia 205

BRIGGS
Hannah 102, 208
Robert 104

BRIGHT
Timothy 115

BRODWAY
Alexander 158
Giles 158

BROWNE
Abigail 134
Alexander 228
Anthony 131, 132, 133, 134, 135
Catherine 96

BROWNE (Cont.)
Cornelius 134
Deborah 134
Dorothy 166
George 131
Hannah 134
Hepzibah 134
Hester 134
Isabel 133, 134, 135
Jabez 166
James 33, 163, 166, 167
Jane 131
John 132, 134, 166, 167
Jonathan 134
Katherine 131
Mary 83, 86, 133, 134, 167, 205
Mercy 94
Peter 132, 133, 134, 135
Priscilla 133
Rebecca 133
Robert 131, 132, 133, 134, 135
Samuel 70
Sarah 134
Stephen 131
Thomas 131, 132, 133, 134, 135
William 131

BRUN
Alice Le 131

BRYANT
Lydia 145

BUCK
John 121, 140
Mary 171

BUCKINGHAM
Anne 140

BULKLEY
Katherine 76
Penelope 76
Richard 76, 243
Thomas 243

BUNTER
Joanne 84

BURGE
Samuel 94
Thomas 94

BURR
Mary 137
Simon 95

BURRILL
John 207

BURSELL
Anna 67
James 67

BURSLEY
John 164

BURROUGHS
Elizabeth 134
James 152

BUSBY
Anne 90
Nicholas 90

BUSHROD
Hannah 184, 185
John 185

BUTLER
James 69
Mary 71

BUTTERFIELD
Sarah 147

BUTTON
Capt. Thomas 231

BYSAKER
Faith 158
Robert 158

BYXBEE
Moses 87

CABOT
John 17
Sebastian 18, 219

CAESAR
Julius 117, 193, 196

CAHOON
William 92

CALDERWOOD
David 39

CAMDEN
William (1551-1623), 19

CAMOENS
·Luis Vaz de (1524-1580), 118

CAPEN
John 209
Joseph 204

CARLETON
Sir Dudley 39

CARLISLE
198

CARNE
Nicholas 158

CARPENTER
Agnes 99, 122
Alexander 99, 105, 120, 121
Alice 40, 99, 105, 120, 122
Hannah 72
James 121
John 121
Juliana 120, 122
Mary 122
Priscilla 122
Richard 121
William 121

CARY
Abigail 165
Bathsheba 165
Sarah 135

CARTER
Gyles 158
Robert 214

CARVER
Anna 147
David 147
Eleazer 147
Elizabeth 147
Isaac 147, 148, 149
James 147, 148
John 37, 106, 126, 128, 129, 147,
148, 149, 156, 173, 174, 180,
213, 214, 215, 216, 217, 218,
220, 239, 240
Mary 142
Mehitable 147
Mercy 147
Rebecca 147
Robert 144, 146, 147, 149
William 147

CECIL
Robert Lord Burghley (Bur-
leigh) 30, 32, 33, 34,
35, 81, 112, 114, 124
Robert Jr., Earl of Salisbury 43,
81, 224, 227, 228, 256
Thomas, Earl of Exeter 30, 230
Sir William 228

CERVANTES
Miguel de (1547-1616) 117

CHAMBERS
Winnifred 76

CHAMPNEYS
Catherine 77

CHANDLER
Edmund 128, 208
Mary 110
Roger 101
Sarah 101

CHAPIN
Mary 210
Seth 210

CHAPMAN
22, 115

CHARLES I (1600-1649)
82, 132

CHASE
Elizabeth 58
John 58
Mary 94

CHAUCER
Geoffrey (1340-1400) 116

CHEESEBROUGH
Samuel 212

CHEKE
John 81

CHENEY
144

CHESTER
Joseph L 160
Ruth 59

CHILTON
Christian 101
Elizabeth 101
Isabella 101
Joel 101
John 101
James 101
Mary 101

CHIPMAN
Bethia 166
Desire 166
Elizabeth 166
Hannah 166
Hope 166
John 163, 165, 166
Lydia 166
Mercy 166
Ruth 166
Samuel 166

CHRISTOPHERS
Christopher 45

CHURCH
Abigail 152
Benjamin 100, 145, 152, 165, 168
Caleb 152
Charles 152
Deborah 152
Elizabeth 152
Hannah 152
Joseph 152

CHURCH (Cont.)
Lydia 152
Mary 152
Nathaniel 152
Priscilla 152
Richard 150, 151, 152
Ruth 143
Sarah 152

CHURCHILL
Eleazer 145
Hannah 145
John 145, 211
Joseph 145
Mary 140, 141, 145
William 145

CICERO
Marcus Jullius (106-43 B.C.) 117

CLAGHORN
Elizabeth 97
Experience 97
James 97
Mary 97
Robert 97
Sarah 97
Shubel 97
Thomas 97

CLARKE (CLARK)
Daniel 136, 137
Elizabeth 137, 211
Faithe 138, 139
Hannah 137
Hosea 136
Joel 136
John 136, 137
Josiah 137
Mary 137, 179
Mary Ann 89, 136
Nathaniel 137
Richard 95
Samuel 137
Sarah 137
Solomon 136
Thomas 132, 171
Tristam 138

CLAUDIUS
Marcus Aurelius (d. 270 A.D.)
193

CLEMENT
Anthony 128

CLOUSE
Richard 176

COBB
Elizabeth 57
James 63
Jonathan 166

COBB (Cont.)
Mary 130
Mercy 63, 86, 138
Sarah 63, 166

CODDINGTON
John 49

COE
John 205

COGSWELL
William 182

COLCLOUGH
Elizabeth 177
George 183

COLE
Alice 48
Amias 178
Daniel 46, 57, 59, 87
Elizabeth 171, 181
Ephraim 215
Eunice 178
George 48
Hannah 57, 110
Hepzibah 51, 52, 57, 59
Hugh 171
Israel 51, 59
James 59, 171
Joanna 168
Job 46, 47, 59
John 46, 57, 59
Joseph 57
Martha 168
Mary 57, 59, 87
Rebecca 59
Ruth 57, 58, 59
Sarah 57
Thomas 59
Timothy 59
William 53, 59

COLLIER
Elizabeth 47, 99
Mary 47, 48
Rebecca 47, 59
Sarah 43, 46, 47
William, 46, 48, 59, 99, 132

COLLINS
Hannah 70

COLSON
Ann 162

COLSTON
Charles 186

COLUMBUS
Christopher 17

[ 253 ]

DOTY (DOTEN) (Cont.)
Jacob 138, 142
James 141, 142
John 138, 139, 140, 141, 143
Jonathan 141
Joseph 140, 141, 142, 143
Josiah 138
Margaret 141
Martha 138, 140
Mary 140, 143, 144, 145
Mercy 140, 143
Nathaniel 141
Patience 138, 140
Samuel 138, 140, 141, 142
Sarah 138, 140, 141, 154
Solomon 142
Theophilus 143
Thomas 140, 141, 145

DOUGHTY
Mary 71

DRAKE
Sir Francis 21, 31, 112, 218
Job 137

DRAX
John 78

DREW
John 145, 212
Samuel 212

DRURY
Mary 206

DUDLEY
Robert, Earl of Leicester 30, 31,
81, 114

DUNCOMBE
81

DUNHAM
Abigail 130
Benejah 130
Benjamin 130
Daniel 130
Hannah 130, 207
Israel 170
John 107, 130, 132
Jonathan 130, 211
Micajah 96
Persis 130
Samuel 130
Thomas 130

DUTCH
Samuel 188

DUTTON
Richard 158

DYER
Abigail 84
Ambrose 81, 83, 84
Anthony 82, 83
Benjamin 83
Christopher 82, 83
Ebenezer 83
Edward 82
George 82, 83
Giles 82
Grace 82
Hannah 83, 84, 147
Henry 82, 83
Isabel 83
James 82
Jerusha 84
John 82, 83
Jonathan 82, 83
Joseph 83
Judah 83
Levi 83
Lydia 83
Mary 82, 83, 84
Naphtali 84
Reuben 84
Samuel 83
Sarah 82
Thankful 84
Thomas 82
William 82, 83

DYKE
Anne 84

EARIS
Elizabeth 51

EAMES
Samuel 205

EDDY
Elizabeth 212

EDRIC
The Saxon 78

EDWARD
I (1239-1307) 200
II (1284-1327) 200
III (1312-1377) 14, 200
IV (1442-1483) 200
V (1470-1483) 200
VI (1537-1553) 16, 26, 200, 219

EDWARDS
Hannah 143
Sarah 140, 142

EGBERT
of Wessex (827-836) 196

[ 255 ]

[ 256 ]

FITZ-ALAN (Cont.)
John 131
Richard 131
Thomas 131

FLEMING
Abraham 28

FLETCHER
Henry 105
John 231

FOBES
William 100, 205

FOGG
132

FORD
Bathsheba 141
Hepzibah 89
Martha 132
Michael 153
Millicent 147

FOSTER
Chillingworth 62
Elizabeth 147
Mary 204
Mercy 120
Reginald 204
Richard 47

FOWLER
Samuel 134

FRANCIS I
(1494-1547) 117

FREEMAN
Alice 49, 50, 62
Apphia 48
Bennett 49, 50, 51
Deborah 50
Edmund 48, 49, 50, 66
Eleanor 49
Elizabeth 49, 66
Hannah 50, 86
John 48, 49, 50, 66
Martin 231
Margaret 50
Mary 49
Mercy 50, 67, 81
Nathaniel 49, 50
Patience 50, 51
Prence 50
Priscilla 67
Rachel 50
Rebecca 50
Samuel 48, 63, 100
Sarah 50, 57

FREEMAN (Cont.)
Thomas 50, 63, 86
William 49, 50, 63

FULLER
Abigail 181, 182
John 97
Samuel 41, 99, 122, 173, 174
"Mrs" 132

GABRIELL
Thomas 180

GAMA
Vasco da 17, 118

GARDNER
John 213
Seeth 189
Thomas 189

GASCOIGNE
Grace 79

GATES
Ann 95
Elizabeth 95
Stephen 95
Sir Thomas 222, 226, 230, 231,
233, 234, 235

GAYLORD
John 137

GERARD
Margaret 88
William 88

GIBBS
John 158
Thomas 154

GIFFORD
Isabell 158

GILBERT
Sir Humphrey 218
Judith 67

GILLETTE
Jonathan 134
Mary 132

GILLISON
John 187

GILSON
132

GLAIVE
William 78

GLASS
James 211

GODFREY
Mary 52
Moses 68

GOFFE
Col. 175

GORGES
Sir Ferdinando 23

GORHAM
Desire 164
Elizabeth 164
Hannah 164
Jabez 164
James 164
John 163, 164
Joseph 164
Lydia 164, 170
Mercy 164
Ralph 163
Shubel 164
Temperance 164

GORRAMS, DE
163

GOSNOLD
Bartholomew 21, 22, 23, 224,
225, 226, 240

GOUGE
108

GOULDER
William 176

GOWER
John 88

GRAFTON
Joseph 189
Nathaniel 179

GRAHAM
Sarah 67

GRATWICK
Jane 49

GRAVELEY
Elizabeth 49

GRAY (GREY)
Desire 100
Edward 63, 102
Lady Jane 242
Sarah 151

GREENE (GREEN)
Joane 158
Robert 28
William 154

GREENWOOD
John 127

GRESHAM
Margaret 105

GREVILL
Francis 158

GRIFFITHS
James 92

GRINNELL
206

HAIT
Ephraim 136

HAKLUYT
Richard 20, 21, 222, 224, 229,
231, 232

HALE
George 158
Hannah 205

HALL
Francis 37
Hannah 67
Phebe 170
Priscilla 68
Tabitha 170
Thomas 176

HALLETT
Abigail 203, 208
Andrew 208
Dorcas 208
John 208
Jonathan 208
Joseph 164
Mehitable 208
Rahane 208

HAMBLIN
Bartholomew 87
Benjamin 84
Eleazer 67, 87
Isaac 164
James 87
John 87
Joseph 164, 168
Lydia 24
Mary 87
Sarah 87

HOLMES
Abraham 144
Elizabeth 144
Isaac 144, 206
Israel 140, 141, 142, 144, 145
John 109, 121, 142, 144, 145
Joseph 144
Josiah 144
Mary 109, 144
Nathaniel 121, 171
Rebecca 144
Sarah 144
William 144, 145

HOLMEDEN
John 158

HOOD
Robin 73

HOOKE
John 149, 217

HOOKER
Richard 117
Thomas 89

HOOPER
Sarah 182

HOPKINS
Abigail 62, 66, 87
Benjamin 61
Caleb 81, 83
Constance 24, 50, 52, 53, 54, 56,
57
Damaris 96, 138, 145, 170, 171,
215
Deborah 68, 69, 89, 94, 96, 120
Elisha 87
Elizabeth 61
Giles 60, 61, 62, 68, 81, 83, 87,
208
Hannah 87
John 87
Joseph 61
Joshua 59, 87
Judah 61, 84
Lydia 87
Mary 60, 61, 87
Nathaniel 61, 81, 84
Phebe 87
Richard 158
Ruth 61, 86
Samuel 61
Stephen 24, 41, 43, 54, 56, 57,
60, 61, 62, 66, 68, 81,
83, 87, 89, 94, 96, 120,
138, 145, 156, 170, 171,
184, 215, 217, 218, 220,
224, 231, 234, 239

HOPKINS (Cont.)
Thankful 81, 83
Thomas 81

HOPTON
Sir Owen 34

HOSFORD
John 134

HOSLEMAN
Marion 180

HOSKINS
Alexander 136
Anthony 133, 135, 136
Grace 136
Hannah 136
Isabel 136
Jane 136
John 135, 136
Joseph 136
Rebecca 135, 136
Robert 136
Thomas 135, 136
William 140

HORNBY
Daniel 186

HORNE
Charles 28

HORTON
Hannah 138
Hope 53
Sarah 188

HOWARD
Mary 209

HOWES
Abraham 205
Elizabeth 85
Hannah 60
Hope 67
Jeremiah 48
John 68
Joseph 85
Mary 48
Mercy 67, 208
Sarah 61, 67, 86
Thomas 48

HOWLAND
Abigail 146, 161
Abraham 162
Alice 162
Anne 164
Arthur 48, 160, 161, 162
Benjamin 168

[ 261 ]

[ 263 ]

[ 264 ]

MASON
  Job 162
  Priscilla 110
MASTERS
  George 180
MASTERSON (MARGESON)
  Edmund 218
  Richard 218
MATHER
  Increase 85
MAVERICK
  Abigail 178, 179
  Antipas 178
  Elias 178
  Elizabeth 179
  John 178
  Mary 179
  Moses 177, 178, 179
  Rebecca 179, 182
  Remember 179
  Samuel 178, 179
  Sarah 179
MAY
  Dorothy 99, 105
  Henry 105
MAYCOCK
  Capt. Samuel 157, 243
MAYHUE
  Thomas 176
MAYO
  Alice 51
  Anne 84
  Bathsheba 86
  Bridget 84
  Daniel 86
  Edward 84
  Elisha 86
  Elizabeth 85
  Hannah 61, 63, 84, 85, 86, 89, 90
  James 86
  John 50, 55, 62, 84, 85, 86, 89
  Jonathan 84
  Joseph 85
  Lydia 62
  Mary 55, 84, 85
  Mercy 61, 67, 84, 89
  Nathaniel 48, 52, 84, 85, 86
  Rebecca 84
  Ruth 56
  Samuel 55, 84, 85, 86
  Sarah 50, 84
  Thankful 89

MAYO (Cont.)
  Theophilus 86
  Thomas 84, 86
  William 86, 89, 90
MERRICK
  Agnes 65
  Alice 65
  Benjamin 52, 62, 66
  Edmund 65
  Hannah 62
  Isaac 66
  James 65
  John 62, 65, 66, 67, 231
  Joseph 66
  Joshua 62
  Mary 61, 66
  Maud 65
  Nathaniel 62
  Owain 65
  Rebecca 62, 63, 66
  Reynault 65
  Richard 65
  Roland 65
  Ruth 50, 62, 66
  Sarah 50, 66
  Sionedd 65
  Stephen 55, 57, 62, 66
  Thomas 65
  William 61, 62, 64, 65, 66
MENDFALL
  Mercy 134
MICHELANGELO
  (1475-1564) 118
MIDDLECOTT
  Richard 102
MILLER
  Deborah 170
  Lydia 96, 170
MINTER
  Desire 162
MILTON
  Richard 158
MIRETON
  Thomas 88
MITCHELL
  Experience 132, 204
  Sarah 97
  William 92

[ 266 ]

MOONE
Capt. 223

MOORE
John 231
Joseph 134

MORE
Caleb 188
Christine 188, 189
Ellinora 188
Jasper 188
John 188
Maria 188
Richard 162, 188
Samuel 188
Sussanah 188
Thomas 117, 200
Sir Thomas 200

MORDEN
John 28

MORGAN
Elizabeth 70
Mary 206

MOREY
Jonathan 47

MORSE
Joshua 138

MORTON
Deborah 120
Ebenezer 120
Ephraim 120
George 120, 121, 122
Hannah 120, 146
Joanna 120
John 100, 120
Mary 120
Nathaniel 106, 107, 120, 150
Patience 120, 121
Persis 120
Phebe 120

MORTON
Sarah 120
Thomas 140

MOSELY
Sarah 205

MOUNTJOY
Hepzibah 206

MUDGE
Charity 142

MULLINS
Alice 213, 214
Edward 213
Joanne 213
John 213
Joseph 213, 214, 215
Margaret 213
Priscilla 203, 213, 214, 215
Sara 213
Sarah 215
William 149, 156, 203, 213, 214,
215, 217, 220, 224, 239

MURDOCK
Phebe 154

NASH
Thomas 115

NAUNTON
Sir Robert 39, 224

NELSON
John 47
Master 232
Mehitable 138

NEVINSON
Elizabeth 76

NEWBERRY
Mary 136
Thomas 136

NEWCOMB
Andrew 68, 69
Elizabeth 62
Emlen 62
Grace 69
Sarah 189
Sussanah 69
Thomas 68

NEWLAND
Mary 161
William 161

NEWPORT
Capt. Christopher 24, 227, 228
231, 232 235

NEWTON
184, 185
Allerton 185

NICHOLAS
176

NICHOLS
Abigail 144

RICKARD (Cont.)
John 170
Joseph 170
Lydia 170
Marey 170
Rebecca 170, 181
Samuel 135
Sarah 138, 140

RICKS
Grace 68
William 68

RIDDAN
Hannah 82

RIDER
153
Samuel 47

RIDLEY
Elizabeth 54

RING
Andrew 97
Deborah 95, 97
Eleazer 95, 96, 97
Elizabeth 53, 54, 69, 86, 89, 90,
95, 97
Elkanah 97
Hannah 95
Jonathan 97
Lydia 97
Mary 97, 120
Mercy 69
Phebe 97, 142
Samuel 97
Sussanah 97
William 94, 95, 141

RIPLEY
Josiah 110
Peter 95

RISLEY
Sarah 89

ROBBINS
Thankful 93

ROBERT
of Normandy 101

ROBERTS
Eunice 178, 179
John 179
Thomas 125, 179
Vincent 83

ROBIN HOOD
73

ROBINSON
Anne 123, 127
Bridget 127
Christopher 122, 129
Fear 127, 129
Isaac 121, 127, 129
Israel 130
Jacob 127, 130
John 27, 37, 38, 39, 40, 41, 74, 78,
90, 104, 117, 120, 122, 123,
124, 125, 126, 127, 128, 129,
148, 156, 173, 217, 218, 231,
239, 240
Mary 123
Mercy 127, 129
Peter 130
Sussana 129
Thomas 130
William 123

RODERIGO
113

ROGERS
Eleazer 56
Elizabeth 56
Hannah 56, 70, 110
James 51
John 11, 58, 59, 103, 205, 217
Joseph 53, 54, 56, 58
Lois 210
Mary 59
Nathaniel 56
Richard 231
Sussanah 53
Thomas 40, 56, 58, 149, 156, 217,
239

ROLAND
Margaret 65

ROLFE
John 229

ROUNDS
Sarah 167

ROUNDSVILLE
Phillip 162

ROUSE
Ann 162
Anna 144, 206
Annis 204
Elizabeth 147, 206
George 206
John 140, 142, 204, 206
Mary 206
Simon 206

STANHOPE
Lord John 36, 227, 228, 231
Sir Michael 228

STANLEY
Sussana 207

STAPLES
Joseph 67

STARR
Allerton 184
Benjamin 184
Josias 71
Mary 206
Samuel 45

STEELE
John 110
Samuel 110

STEPHEN
King of England 200

STEVENS
Samuel 110

STONE
John 209

STORRS
Hannah 24

STOURTON
Lord 18

STOW
John (1525-1605) 115

STRACHY
William 231 232, 234

STROUT
Hannah 83

STUART (STUARD)
Catherine 92
Hugh 94
Lydia 93, 94

STURGIS
164
Edward 164
Sarah 164

STURTEVANT
Ann 153
Ephraim 97
Hannah 209
James 215
Josiah 152

STURTEVANT (Cont.)
Mary 151
Mercy 167

STUYVESANT
Gov. 71

SUMNER
Experience 147

SURREY
Earl of 73
Lady 73

SYDNEY
Sir Philip 30, 31, 35, 230
Lord (Robert) Lisle 230

SYLVESTER
Ruth 97, 215

TACITUS
Cornelius (55-120 A. D.) 117

TALBOT
Samuel 100

TALRACE
Adela de 131

TARPLEY
John 186

TASSO
(1544-1595) 117

TAYLOR
Ann 164
Jeremy 117
John 87
Henry 83
Mary 82, 94
Peter 205
Mrs. 93

TERRENCE
Publius Terentius (b. 185 B. C.)
117

TGRILTON
Isabella 101

THATCHER
Anthony 164, 169
Benjamin 169
Bethia 51, 163, 164, 170
Edith 169
Giles 169
John 164, 169, 170
Judah 170
Mary 68, 169

[ 276 ]

# TWENTY MAYFLOWER PLANTERS

## In Volumes I and II

# 26 HEADS OF FAMILY GROUPS—3rd GENERATION
## FROM STEPHEN HOPKINS
### In Volume II

# FAMILY GROUPS OF OTHER NEWCOMERS
## In Volume II

## SYSTEM OF NUMBERING

Many, more or less, unrelated subjects are discussed in this series. Numerous family groups are presented of different names and lineages. It seems desirable to avoid complicated systems of identification numberings, thereby adding chaos to confusion. The author has, therefore, adopted a simple system. Of course, to the many who are unfamiliar with genealogical works, any system would be confusing at first.

Throughout this series numbers such as 43, 111, 252, etc., will be given to lineal descendants of Stephen Hopkins; sometimes these may be noted as Fam. No. 43, or Fam. No. 252.

All other family records will be identified in the simplest manner possible, usually starting with I, followed by children a, b, c, d, etc., the children may be carried down by IIa, IIIb, etc., or sometimes, when a number of generations is involved, by Gen. 8, 15 or the like. Once in a while, this routine may be changed slightly for special purposes.

However, no matter what system is used, the searcher should always trace the line from the beginning for possible errors.

~PSIA information can be obtained at www.ICGtesting.com
'nted in the USA
ⁿW011605190612

'20BV00005B/14/P

9  780806 307756